ADVANCED

DATABASE

MACHINE

ARCHITECTURE

ADVANCED DATABASE MACHINE ARCHITECTURE

DAVID K. HSIAO, *Editor*
Department of Computer Science
Naval Postgraduate School

PRENTICE-HALL, INC.
Englewood Cliffs, New Jersey 07632

Library of Congress Cataloging in Publication Data
Main entry under title:

Advanced database machine architecture.

   Bibliography: p.
   Includes index.
   1. Data base management. 2. Computer architecture.
I. Hsiao, David K. (date)
QA76.9.D3A343 1983   001.64   83-11032
ISBN 0-13-011262-3

Editorial/production supervision: Nancy Milnamow
Cover design: Jeannette Jacobs
Manufacturing buyer: Gordon Osbourne

Printed in the United States of America

10   9   8   7   6   5   4   3   2   1

ISBN   0-13-011262-3

/

Prentice-Hall International, Inc., *London*
Prentice-Hall of Australia Pty. Limited, *Sydney*
Editora Prentice-Hall do Brasil, Ltda., *Rio de Janeiro*
Prentice-Hall of Canada Inc., *Toronto*
Prentice-Hall of India Private Limited, *New Delhi*
Prentice-Hall of Japan, Inc., *Tokyo*
Prentice-Hall of Southeast Asia Pte. Ltd., *Singapore*
Whitehall Books Limited, *Wellington, New Zealand*

CONTRIBUTING AUTHORS

F. Bancilon, INRIA, BP. 105, 78150 Le Chesnay, France and Universite d'Orsay, LRI, Bat. 490, Universite d'Orsay Cedex, France.

Philippe Bernadat, University of Paris VI and INRIA, BP. 105, 78150 Le Chesnay, France.

D. De Luca Cardillo, Istituto Mathematico "U. Dini," V. Morgagni 67/a, Florence, Italy.

F. Cesarini, Istituto di Informatica e Sistemistica, Facolta di Ingegneria, V.S. Marta 3, Florence, Italy.

Wing Hong Chow, Department of Computer Science, University of Utah, Salt Lake City, Utah 84112, U.S.A.

Tsugunori Doi, Nippon Electric Co., 10, 1-chome, Nisshin-cho, Fuchu, Tokyo 183, Japan.

Perry A. Emrath, Department of Computer Science, University of Illinois, Urbana, Illinois 61801, U.S.A.

D. Fortin, INRIA, BP. 105, 78150 Le Chesnay, France.

S. Gamerman, INRIA, BP. 105, 78150 Le Chesnay, France.

Georges Gardarin, University of Paris VI and INRIA, BP. 105, 78150 Le Chesnay, France.

Tatsuo Goto, Nippon Electric Co., 10, 1-chome, Nisshin-cho, Fuchu, Tokyo 183, Japan.

Katsuya Hakozaki, Nippon Electric Co., 10, 1-chome, Nisshin-cho, Fuchu, Tokyo 183, Japan.

Roger L. Haskin, IBM San Jose Research Laboratory, 5600 Cottle Road, San Jose, California 95193, U.S.A.

Xin-Gui He, Laboratory for Database Systems Research, The Ohio State University, Columbus, Ohio 43210, U.S.A.

W. Hell, Institut für Datenverarbeitungsanlagen, Technische Universität Braunschweig, Postfach 3329, D-3300 Braunschweig, West Germany.

Masanobu Higashida, Laboratory for Database Systems Research, The Ohio State University, Columbus, Ohio 43210, U.S.A.

Lee A. Hollaar, Department of Computer Science, University of Utah, Salt Lake City, Utah 84112, U.S.A.

David K. Hsiao, Department of Computer Science, Naval Postgraduate School, Monterey, California 93940, U.S.A.

Douglas S. Kerr, Laboratory for Database Systems Research, The Ohio State University, Columbus, Ohio 43210, U.S.A.

J. M. Laubin, INRIA, BP. 105, 78150 Le Chesnay, France.

H.-O. Leilich, Institut für Datenverarbeitungsanlagen, Technische Universität Braunschweig, Postfach 3329, D-3300 Braunschweig, West Germany.

Takenori Makino, Nippon Electric Co., 10, 1-chome, Nisshin-cho, Fuchu, Tokyo 183, Japan.

M. J. Menon, IBM San Jose Research Laboratory, 5600 Cottle Road, San Jose, California 95193, U.S.A.

M. Missikoff, I.A.S.I.-C.N.R., Via Buonarroti 12, Roma, Italy.

Ali Orooji, Laboratory for Database Systems Research, The Ohio State University, Columbus, Ohio 43210, U.S.A.

P. Richard, INRIA, BP. 105, 78150 Le Chesnay, France.

M. Scholl, INRIA, BP. 105, 78150 Le Chesnay, France.

H. Schweppe, Lehrstuhl D für Informatik, Technische Universität Braunschweig, Postfach 3329, D-3300 Braunschweig, West Germany.

Akira Sekino, Nippon Electric Co., 10, 1-chome, Nisshin-cho, Fuchu, Tokyo 183, Japan.

Zhong-Zhi Shi, Laboratory for Database Systems Research, The Ohio State University, Columbus, Ohio 43210, U.S.A.

Kent F. Smith, Department of Computer Science, University of Utah, Salt Lake City, Utah 84112, U.S.A.

G. Soda, Istituto di Informatica e Sistemistica, Facolta di Ingegneria, V.S. Marta 3, Florence, Italy.

G. Stiege, Lehrstuhl D für Informatik, Technische Universität Braunschweig, Postfach 3329, D-3300 Braunschweig, West Germany.

Paula R. Strawser, Laboratory for Database Systems Research, The Ohio State University, Columbus, Ohio 43210, U.S.A.

Ken Takeuchi, Nippon Electric Co., 10, 1-chome, Nisshin-cho, Fuchu, Tokyo 183, Japan.

Yuzuru Tanaka, Department of Electrical Engineering, Faculty of Engineering, Hokkaido University, Sapporo 060, Japan.

W. Teich, Institut für Datenverarbeitungsanlagen, Technische Universität Braunschweig, Postfach 3329, D-3300 Braunschweig, West Germany.

Nicole Temmerman, University of Paris VI and INRIA, BP. 105, 78150 Le Chesnay, France.

M. Terranova, I.A.S.I.-C.N.R., Via Buonarroti 12, Roma, Italy.

D. Tusera, INRIA, BP. 105, 78150 Le Chesnay, France.

Patrick Valduriez, University of Paris VI and INRIA, BP. 105, 78150 Le Chesnay, France.

A. Verroust, INRIA, BP. 105, 78150 Le Chesnay, France and Universite d'Orsay, LRI, Bat. 490, Universite d'Orsay Cedex, France.

Yann Viemont, University of Paris VI and INRIA, BP. 105, 78150 Le Chesnay, France.

H. Ch. Zeidler, Institut für Datenverarbeitungsanlagen, Technische Universität Braunschweig, Postfach 3329, D-3300 Braunschweig, West Germany.

Contents

Foreword

This collected work marks an important turning point in the annals of computing—the departure of traditional emphasis on nonnumeric processing of data by general-purpose mainframes and the arrival of innovative solutions to nonnumeric processing of data by special-purpose backends. One of the most important backends is the database computer. This machine is intended to cost-effectively replace the conventional database management software, on-line I/O routines, and on-line secondary storage (currently supported by the general-purpose mainframes) while offering better performance.

The arrival of database machines is prompted by a number of factors: the user's application requirement for very large databases and for a wide range of database activities, the enhancement of existing and advancement of new technologies, the poor performance of today's software-laden mainframe-oriented database management systems, the lack of reliable and secure software solutions to database management, and better research and understanding of hardware and software approaches to database machine architecture. The Office of Naval Research is proudly playing a major role in database machine research in the United States. The Office has supported some of the important work cited, referenced, and reported herein.

The work reported herein also represents a broad effort in database machine research on an international scale. Not only the United States but also the rest of the world is forging ahead in database machine research. Thus we have, in addition to four American papers on three different database machine research efforts, two French papers on two separate French database machines, one German paper on a "second-generation" German database machine, two Italian papers on an Italian database machine, and two Japanese papers on two different database machines. All the papers are well written in English.

All the database machine activities reported herein are in prototype stage. Furthermore, these prototyped efforts are new and on-going, representing the most current thinking and understanding. Their progress and outcome will be carefully watched. I believe that this work will profoundly impact the community of database machine researchers, developers, and users for years to come.

Marvin Denicoff
Information Sciences Division
The Office of Naval Research

Preface

In this book are eleven chapters on nine database machines. How does one go about reading them? This question is related to the organization of the chapters and the classification of the database machines.

As far as the organization of the chapters is concerned, we have sequenced them in the alphabetical order of their nationality: French, German, Italian, Japanese, and United States.

Database machines may be classified by their applications. Two broad application classes are those for text search and retrieval and those for formatted database management. Machines for text search and retrieval are characterized by the use of stored texts, character strings, and captioned facsimiles. To search the stored information, the machine is given a logical combination of terms words, or captions and pattern-matches them against the database. However, the database is usually with limited formats and the database administrator does not have a priori knowledge of the database usage. The stored information tends to be archival in nature, requires no alteration and update, and grows large in capacity.

Machines for formatted database management are characterized by the presence of some data models and formats. The machine is required to search stored information via predicates, which may involve both inter- and intrarecord processing. However, some a priori knowledge of the database usage is available to the database administrator and user. Formatted databases such as personal records and financial statements require update and back-up. Furthermore, owing to the personal and proprietary nature of the databases, some form of access control and data security is necessary.

The impact of text search and retrieval on the machine architecture may be manifold. It requires the machine architecture to come up with a very large on-line store for the database, to form matching patterns quickly, to perform loading of both the patterns and the database readily, and to match the patterns against the database with exceedingly high speed. Chapter 9, by Lee Hollaar and his colleagues, is aimed primarily at addressing the architecture issues of the text search and retrieval database machines.

Formatted database management also affects machine architecture in many ways. For formatted databases, on-line storage does not have to be as large as for text search and retrieval machines, since archival information is always purged and placed in back-up storage; however, the database machine must be provided with fast access to the on-line store. The application also requires the machine to address the database by content via predicates. Owing to the peculiarity of a data model, the machine architecture tends to be configured in terms of its primitives (or basic operations). The requirements of update and recovery, access control and data security, and auxiliary information for fast access further complicate the architecture of the database machine for formatted databases. Thus, we have a large variety of such architectures. Chapters 1 through 8 and Chapters 10 and 11 are on machine architectures for formatted databases.

We may view the database machines in terms not only of their applications but also of the technologies that they have utilized. In terms of technologies we may classify the machines into three categories:

"Now" machines, whose software and hardware are available commercially.

Emerging machines, which are forthcoming as soon as the required software and hardware technologies have matured.

Future machines, which depend on certain technologies that are not yet in sight.

Britton-Lee's IDM 500 and Intel's iDBP are the now machines. We have no paper here that deals with future machines. A future machine has been described elsewhere that utilizes gigabyte associative memories (or arrays). Such high-capacity and high-performance associative memories are a distinctly distant technology. The eleven chapters in this book deal with the architectures of emerging machines—"emerging" because either the software technology or the hardware technology, or both, utilized in the machine are not commerically available, but are within reach. These technologies include the VLSI realization of various components, design of highly parallel or concurrent modules or components for comparators and scanners, parallel-transfer and on-the-fly-processing disks and disk controllers, communication lines with broadcast capability, and modules for software replication and distributed control.

Finally, we may also classify our machines in terms of their architectural configuration. In contrast to the conventional solution to database management (or text retrieval), where the database management system and its on-line I/O routines are run in the same mainframe computer (see Figure Pref. 1), database machines are backends that off-load the database management (or text retrieval) functions and I/O routines from the mainframe computer (known as the host) and perform the intended functions and routines with specialized software and hardware. Thus, there are software backends and hardware backends.

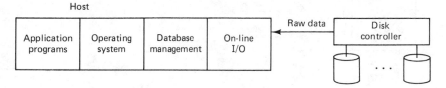

Figure Pref. 1.   The Conventional Approach to Database Management

The software single-backend approach utilized only one database machine to support one or more hosts. The first published result on this approach to database management was due to Bell Lab's work in 1974, which is frequently cited in the papers of this book (see Figure Pref. 2). No hardware modification or enhancement was done on the database machine. The major contribution was in the innovative architecture for the software database management system.

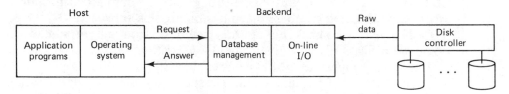

Figure Pref. 2.   The Software Single-Backend Approach

The software multiple-backend approach attempts to improve the performance of the single backend by utilizing a number of identical backends and by replicating the same software on them (see Figure Pref. 3). Like the single-backend approach, the multiple-backend approach does not modify the hardware and relies only on innovative software architecture. The work reported herein by David K. Hsiao and his colleagues in Chapters 10 and 11 is on the multiple-backend database machine.

The intelligent-controller approach is typical of commercial database machines such as Britton-Lee's IDM 500 and Intel's iDBP, where the controller itself is specially built with microprocessors, memory boxes, and communication lines. However, the high-level data manipulation language

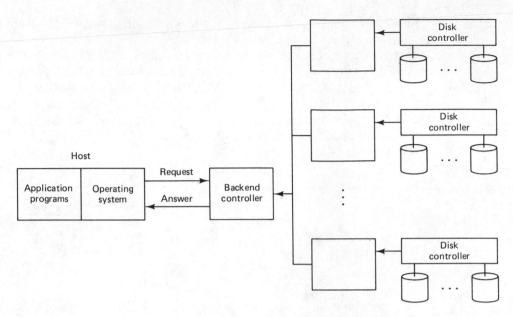

Figure Pref. 3. The Software Multiple-Backend Approach

of the machine is usually implemented in a host and run in the host. Since only the controller is specially made with off-the-shelf hardware, no modification of the disks and backend-to-host communication lines has attempted (see Figure Pref. 4). The Japanese IQC database machine by Akira Sekino and his colleagues in Chapter 6, although not a commercial product, is one of the sophisticated database machines taking this approach.

The hardware-backend approach differs from all others in entailing some modification and enhancement of existing hardware technology. For example, developers of both the French VERSO and German RDBM database machines in Chapters 1 and 3 respectively are considering a hardware filter for parallel scanning and processing of incoming data. Another example is their use of parallel transfer disks with parallel processing capability in their controller. Both the Italian DBMAC and Japanese Data-Stream database machine in Chapters 4 and 7 respectively use such on-line database storage. On the very large-scale integration (VLSI) for implementing memory-intensive-and-processor-intensive components for performance gains, we have

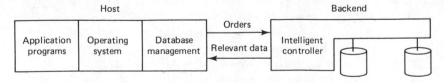

Figure Pref. 4. The Intelligent-Controller Approach

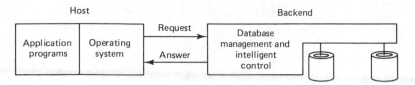

Figure Pref. 5. The Hardware-Backend Approach

the American full-text information retrieval system in Chapter 9, which utilizes VLSI chips for realizing the finite-state-automaton comparators, and the American DBC in Chapter 8, which employs VLSI designs for relational join operations.

Some database machines do not lend themselves easily to such classification. The French SABRE database machine may be viewed on the basis of its software as a software single backend and on the basis of its hardware as an intelligent controller. Nevertheless, these categories and classifications should give the reader some perspective in approaching the machines. Good reading!

ACKNOWLEDGEMENTS

The first workshop on database machines was held in Florence, Italy, in 1981. It was decided to hold a second workshop in Mexico City in 1982 (to coincide with the International Conference on Very Large Data Bases), so that researchers might brief one another on their progress. However, instead of Mexico City, we found a workshop site in San Diego, thanks to the diligent work of Ms. Nancy Anderson.

The projects involved on-going prototype work on database machines. We emphasized long presentations for them in the second workshop, at least 90 minutes each.

The original proceedings consisted of papers by nine database machine projects: two French, one Italian, one German, two Japanese, and three American. Consequently, there were nine sets of papers. Mr. Karl Karlstrom, Assistant Vice President of Prentice-Hall, encouraged us to polish up and develop the papers for their publication here as a hardcover volume with the writers of the papers as co-authors.

We would like to take this opportunity to thank the participants of the Second Workshop. Others might have joined us but for our lateness in getting out program announcements and registration forms and in seeking out other database machine projects such as those in Canada and elsewhere.

We would like to thank also the French Research Institute (Institut National De Recherche En Informatique Et En Automatique), the Italian Research Council (Consiglio Nazionale Delle Richerche), and the Japanese Society (Information Processing Society of Japan) for sponsoring the Second

Workshop. Last, but not least, we would like to thank the Naval Postgraduate School for sponsoring the Second Workshop, Dean Max Wood for his encouragement, Mrs. Ruby Kapsalis for her diligence, Ms. Rosalie Johnson for her work in putting the proceedings and program announcement together, and the office staff of the Computer Science Department of the Naval Postgraduate School for helping out on the final preparation of the manuscript.

David K. Hsiao

1

VERSO: A Relational Backend Database Machine

*F. Bancilhon, D. Fortin, S. Gamerman, J. M. Laubin, P. Richard, M. Scholl,
D. Tusera, and A. Verroust*

1.0. ABSTRACT

VERSO is a backend relational database machine being developed at INRIA.
Its main feature is a hardware filter that can process data at the speed of 2
million characters per second. This filter can perform the unary operations
from relational algebra (insert, delete, select, and project) and the binary
operations on sorted relations (union, intersection, difference, join, and division). The main objective of the VERSO machine is to show that a complete
database management system with good performance can be built around
such a filter.

We give a complete description of the software design of VERSO—
external interface, query and update processing, and transaction management—and then a detailed presentation of the hardware structure.

1.1. MOTIVATIONS AND OBJECTIVES

The VERSO project was started at INRIA in early 1980. Its first objective
was to specify and realize a database machine (DBM) offering a complete
relational interface. As in other DBM designs [1 to 10], most data management tasks are relegated to a backend machine which interfaces with a terminal concentrator, a frontend general-purpose computer, or a (local)

network. The major motivation behind such an architectural approach is to increase the performance of the database management system (DBMS). In order to satisfy this performance objective, most proposed or prototyped DBMs to some extent speed up data access by scanning and processing data while they are being transferred from the mass memory to the main memory. This "on-the-fly" filtering capability allows saving CPU time as well as channel traffic. For filtering data, some DBMs use a special hardware device called a filter [1, 2, 5, 8], while others use standard microprocessors [4, 6, 7, 10].

Furthermore, in order to meet the objective of fast access, many DBM designs take advantage of the parallelism provided by a multiprocessor organization such as ICL [8] and IDM [9], where a single query runs against an entire block of data at a time. In RDBM [5], the same query is run in parallel on different blocks of data. Finally, several queries may be processed in parallel on different data in MIMD fashion, as done by DIRECT [4], DBMAC [6], and SABRE [7].

Current DBM designs also differ in the set of the DBMS primitives implemented by specific microprocessors. While most DBMs emphasize the efficient implementation of the selection/projection operator (by means of the filter), some designs have implemented other functions by means of a dedicated hardware—e.g., in the ICL machine, there is a JOIN processor; in RDBM, SORTING and JOIN are run by dedicated hardware; and in DBC [3] index processing is to be implemented by a specialized processor.

A uniprocessor architecture has been chosen for the VERSO machine, emphasizing design simplicity for overall performance. Again hardware filter capable of executing any unary relational operation (selection/projection, insertion, deletion) as well as binary operations (union, intersection, division, JOIN) is used as long as the data are sorted. An automatonlike device performs these operations in a linear time with respect to the size of the scanned data (independently of the query's complexity) [11].

Although the usefulness of hardware filtering has been widely accepted and several experimental filters have existed for some time [1, 2, 12, 13, 16], none of these has been included in a complete DBMS design. Thus the second objective of the VERSO project was to validate the approach of on-the-fly filtering in a complete and fast DBMS and to compare the advantage of such an approach with conventional ones.

The last but not least objective was to augment the classical relational interface with new functionalities. The VERSO data languages are based on the concept of *V*-relations. A *V*-relation, a generalization of Codd's relations [14], allows us to include decomposition, null values, and inclusion dependencies and to easily process unnormalized relations.

The external interface of VERSO, i.e., the description of *V*-relations, is presented in Section 1.2. In Section 1.3 we give an overall description of the VERSO DBMS. The hardware structure of the machine is presented in Section 1.4.

1.2. THE RELATIONAL INTERFACE

1.2.1. Motivation

Consider the following relation:

$$R(\text{course, student, grade, hour, room, teacher}).$$

The semantics of the relation is that $(CSGHRT) \in R$ if the student S had the grade G in the course C, where the course C is being taught in the room R at the hour H by teacher T. This relation has some well-known properties:

1. It can be decomposed into three relations $R_1(CSG)$, $R_2(CHR)$, and $R_3(CT)$.
2. Equivalently, we might want to update "subtuples" in the relation—for instance, insert (C, T) or delete (C, S, G).
3. It would be nice to accept some null values in the relation. For instance, a student might have no grade in a course, or a course could be created having no schedule, student, or teacher.

These properties correspond to well-known concepts of the relational theory, namely, join dependencies and null-value representation. To manage such a relation two different approaches can be considered:

1. The normalization approach.
2. The universal relation approach.

In the first approach the relation could be represented by a set of normalized relations:

$$R_1(C), \quad R_2(CS), \quad R_3(CSG), \quad R_4(CHR), \quad \text{and} \quad R_5(CT)$$

In this case the user manages these relations by himself. For instance, if he creates a course having no student, schedule, or teacher, he merely inserts that course into R_1. This might, however, cause problems: when inserting a tuple, say (CSG), in R_3, one must check that CS is in R_2 and C in R_1; otherwise, one has to insert the tuple in them. Similarly, deleting a course from the relation requires its deletion from R_1, R_2, R_3, R_4, and R_5. Finally, one of the major drawbacks of the approach is the performance degradation due to frequent joins. When the database is completely normalized, most queries require joins to "denormalize" it [22].

The universal relation approach allows the user to see only one relation [23]. The main advantage is query simplicity. There are no joins but many selections. Updates become problematic, however, owing to the numerous anomalies of nonnormal forms [24]. Finally, the sample relation, including null values, requires a new formalism.

To avoid the shortcomings of these approaches, we have introduced the notion of V-relation.

1.2.2. Informal Description

The above example would be represented as a V-relation R that has an *attribute set* {C, S, G, H, R, T} and a set of *update units* (or atoms) consisting of

$$\{C, CS, CSG, CHR, CT\}$$

This means that the user can insert or delete subtuples defined on these subsets of attributes, namely, update units. The value of the V-relation R consists of ordinary relations $R_1(C)$, $R_2(CS)$, $R_3(CSG)$, $R_4(CHR)$, and $R_5(CT)$. These five relations satisfy the following *implicit inclusion dependencies:*

$$R_2(C) \subseteq R_1(C), \quad R_3(CS) \subseteq R_2(CS), \quad \text{and} \quad R_4(C) \subseteq R_1(C)$$

1.2.3. Formal Definition

A V-relation is described by a schema

$$R\langle U, A \rangle$$

where R is the name of the V-relation, U the attribute set, and $A \subseteq \mathcal{P}(U)$ is the set of update units or atoms that covers U, such that the hypergraph associated with A is a tree.

The definition A, being a tree hypergraph, can be restated as follows:

1. $\forall\, X \subseteq U$, {X} is a tree with root X and leaf $\emptyset$
2. if A_1 is a tree with root R_1 and leaf L_1, if A_2 is a tree with root R_2 and leaf L_2, and if $L_1 \cap L_2 = \emptyset$, then $A_1 \cup A_2$ is a tree with root $R_1 \cap R_2$ and leaves $L_1 \cup L_2 - R_1 - R_2$

The value of a V-relation is a function V that associates with each atom X_i a relation $R_i(X_i)$ defined on its attribute set X_i, and such that

$$X_i \subseteq X_j \Rightarrow R_j(X_i) \subseteq R_i(X_i)$$

For instance, the value of the sample V-relation consists of five relations

$$R_1(C), \quad R_2(CE), \quad R_3(CEN), \quad R_4(CHS), \quad R_5(CP)$$

such that

$$R_3(CE) \subseteq R_2(CE), \; R_2(C) \subseteq R_1(C), \; R_4(C) \subseteq R_1(C), \; \text{and} \; R_5(C) \subseteq R_1(C)$$

Update operations are defined on V-relations that allow the insertion, deletion, and replacement of subtuples, thus freeing the user from the anomalies due to unnormalized relations. For a complete treatment, see [20].

The main advantages of the V-relations interface are that (1) it allows the user to deal with unnormalized relations, thus saving a number of joins, and (2) it provides a practical tool for dealing with some types of null values (namely the nonapplicable type). However, we accept the possibility that some users will reject the new approach. We shall provide them an ordinary relational interface, nevertheless.

1.3. SOFTWARE DESCRIPTION

1.3.1. Query and Update Processing

The System-V consists of four layers. This classical design method should allow the implementation and test of the system in successive steps.

Each layer is defined by a set of *objects* and a set of *operations* that can be performed on them. Objects are specified by *descriptors* and take *values,* while operators are defined by their input, their output, and their semantics (which can be the modification of our object value).

Objects of level i can be either self-defined or defined in terms of objects of level $(i - 1)$. Similarly, operations at level i can be defined intrinsically or as algorithms using level$-(i - 1)$ operations.

The four levels of System-V are shown below:

	System-V interface
4	Logical relations
3	Formatted relations
2	Physical relations
1	Relation blocks
0	Hardware

At level 4, only logical relations are seen. The operations performed on these relations are the standard relation updates and the assignment of a value to a relation. The value is computed from the other relations' values by an expression from the relational algebra. At level 3 relations are seen as having a physical representation (their format). The operators are also updates and value assignments, but values are computed through the use of elementary algebra operators and format changes. At level 2 relations are seen as sets of blocks having a physical locality. Finally, level 1 deals with blocks of data on which one performs binary and unary operations.

1.3.2. Logical Relations

There are three types of logical relations: base relations (which are stored on the disk) and input and output relations (that are placed in the front end). A relation is described by its name, its attribute set, and its set of update units. Relations can be created and destroyed. They can be updated through insertion, deletion, or replacement of subtuples corresponding to update units. Finally, a value can be assigned to a relation, computed from a relational algebra expression. Therefore, queries are processed by creating output relations and assigning them a query expression.

For instance, we can consider the following two base relations:

$$R_1 \text{ (Course, Student, Grade, Hour, Room, Teacher)}$$

with update units ($CSG; CHR; CT$), and

$$R_2 \text{(Teacher Address Income)}$$

with update unit (TAI). We also consider them in terms of the two output relations

$$Q_1 \text{(Student, Grade)} \quad \text{and} \quad Q_2 \text{(Income)}$$

Typical operations of the logical relations level could be

> **insert** (C = Math, Hour = 1500, Room = 108) **into** R_1
>
> **delete** (C = Maths, T = Bourbaki) **from** R_1
>
> $Q_1 \leftarrow (R_1 \mid C = \text{Maths})(S\ G)$
>
> (query: students and their grades from the maths course)
>
> $Q_2 \leftarrow (R_1 \mid C = \text{MATHS}[T = T]R_2)(I)$
>
> (query: income of the math teacher)

1.3.3. Formatted Relations

At the formatted relations level, we find input, output, and base relations that correspond to logical relations. We also find temporary relations and a special relation, the schema. The *schema* contains the description of all other relations. At this level each relation has a name and a format. The *format* is a regular expression describing the compact structure of the file that implements the relation. For instance, the format of R_1 could be

$$R_1((C(SG)^*(HR)^*T^*)^*)$$

expressing that the file R_1 consists of a sequence of records, each record beginning with a course followed by a sequence of (student, grade) couples, followed by a sequence of (hour, room) couples, and followed by a sequence of teachers. The format of R_2 could be

$$R_2((I(AT^*)^*)^*).$$

For an in-depth study of compact formats, see [21]. Formats are either specified by the database administrator at the creation of the relation or automatically generated by the system from the logical description.

The operations at this level are

1. Update operations identical to those of the upper level.
2. Selection and projection operations.
3. Binary operations between relations having compatible formats, such as

$$R_3((AB^*)^*) \leftarrow R_1((AB^*)^*) \cup R_2((AB^*)^*)$$

or

$$R_3(AB^*C^*)^* \leftarrow R_1((AB^*)^*) * R_2((AC^*)^*)$$

4. Format change of a relation such as $R_2((BA^*)^*) \leftarrow R_1((AB^*)^*)$.

All operations of types 1, 2, and 3 can be done in linear time at a speed compatible with that of the disk transfer rate (1.2 million characters per second). Thus a logical operation of level 4 will be translated into the creation of a (possibly empty) set of temporary relations and a sequence of operations on formatted relations.

For instance, let $R_1(AB)$ and $R_2(AC)$ be two logical relations with formats $R_1((AB^*)^*)$ and $R_2((CA^*)^*)$. The level-4 operation

$$R_3 \leftarrow R_1 * R_2$$

will be translated into the following sequence:

create $R_4((AC^*)^*)$

$R_4((AC^*)^*) \leftarrow R_2((CA^*)^*)$

$R_3((AB^*C^*)^*) \leftarrow R_1((AB^*)^*) * R_4((AC^*)^*)$

1.3.4. Physical Relations

The physical representation of the formatted relations is as follows: all files are completely sorted in lexicographic order. For instance, in the file $R((C(SG)*(HR)*T*)*)$ all "records" are sorted by course name; inside a course record (student, grade) couples are sorted by student name, (hour, room) couples by hour, and so on. Files are then partitioned into blocks. Each block corresponds to a disk track of 16 Kbytes, which is the smallest addressable unit of the system.

Thus a physical relation is represented by a name and a list of block addresses. The translation from formatted into physical is accomplished by a master index. The master index indicates for each base for each relation and for each value of the first attribute the corresponding block address. This nondense index is unique for the machine and has the following format:

$$MI(Base(Relation(Value(Address)*)*)*)*$$

1.3.5. Filtering and the Finite-State Automaton

The main hardware feature of the VERSO machine is a special-purpose processor that filters data sequentially at the rate of 2 million characters per second. This filter (see Section 1.4) performs the operation of types (1), (2), and (3) of level three; therefore, it handles all the update and unary operations (select and project) on any relation and the binary operations (union, intersection, difference, join and division) on relations with compatible format. To perform these operations the filter must be loaded with the description of the corresponding finite-state automaton (FSA). This FSA is produced by a compiler from the format and operation description; it is then loaded in the filter that can process relations sequentially. The filter operates

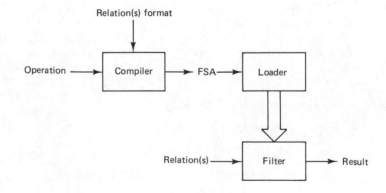

on blocks, filtering one track into a target buffer (see Section 1.4). It sends interrupts to request a new block or a new target buffer.

Finally, format change operations are done by first restructuring each block of the relation (this is done by software, using a treelike structure to store intermediate results), then merging all the resulting blocks by the filter through an $(n \log n)$ process.

1.3.6. Dynamic Aspects

A user of the machine sees a *set of databases*. A database includes a set of relations, *R*, a set of indexes, *I*, a set of transactions, *T*, a transaction log, *J*, and a back-up copy, *C*.

A database is in one among the three states {open, closed, active}. The "create base" command sets the state to open, and the base has the value for *R, I, T, J*, and *C*.

The base becomes active as soon as there is a transaction operating on it $(T \neq \emptyset)$. When there is no more transaction in progress on this base, the base becomes open. One may then close the base, in which case no transaction is allowed on that database. The accompanying diagram summarizes the base's state transitions.

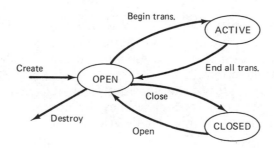

A *transaction* is created by a command: "begin transaction." A transaction is a sequence of some of the following operations: creation/destruction of a relation or an index, relation update, relation affectation. The effect of a transaction on the database is postponed until its *validation*. If the transaction is aborted, it has no effect on the database. The transaction is *archived*; i.e., a sequential journal will record the operations and input data for a transaction.

The user may create a safety copy of the database with a "copy base." The command "restore base" will give to the database the value contained in the copy. Finally, the transactions recorded in the journal may be rerun with the command "restart base," which will empty the journal.

1.4. CONCURRENCY CONTROL IN VERSO

As usual we take the transaction as the consistency unit; i.e., we assume the database is consistent at the beginning of a transaction and will be consistent at the end of the transaction.

We are currently studying two concurrency algorithms. One has been implemented; the other one is under evaluation. Both use the physical block as the granularity unit. Recall that in VERSO a block (page) is 16-Kbytes long, corresponds to a disk track, and is also the update unit.

1. *A concurrency control algorithm with a shadow system.* The first algorithm is based on the shadow system [17]. Each transaction processes its work in a shadow area without actually modifying the database. If no conflict occurs—i.e., if no other transaction tries to read or write on a page to be modified by the transaction—then, upon its validation, the set of blocks accessed by the transaction is updated. This updating is done through an address translation mechanism and thus does not necessitate any actual rewriting on the disk.

This algorithm is a good candidate because of its simplicity and its efficiency (no time overhead upon validation or abortion). However, its main drawback is due to its refusal of some transaction schedulings that are indeed correct. This is why we are studying the following algorithm. It is based on the sufficient condition of transactions' serialization and does not use any locking.

2. *A concurrency control algorithm without locking.* This algorithm allows a larger number of transactions to be interleaved. The counterpart is that the abortion of a transaction may trigger the abortion of a large number of other transactions.

The basic idea of the algorithm is to let as many transactions as possible share the resources, as long as they are processed in the right sequence. In presenting the algorithm, let us also give a few definitions, notations and explanations:

1. *The precedence graph.* In this graph the nodes, T_i, are the transactions. A branch goes from T_1 to T_2 when for the first time T_2 accesses a page already accessed by T_1. We denote this branch with $T_1 < T_2$. T_2 is said to be the destination of the branch. A cycle is formed at T if one or more branches go from T to T. The nodes of these branches are termed the successors of T. As soon as a cycle is detected upon trying to insert a branch whose destination is T (i.e., T accesses a page), then T and its successors are aborted.

2. *There is no locking.* We note that T_2 can access (read or write) a page already accessed by another transaction, say T_1, as long as there is no cycle in the precedence graph.

3. *State of a page p.* A page is either valid (V), read (R), or modified (W).

4. *The set of transactions T(p).* This is the set of all transactions currently accessing p.

5. *The algorithm.* It works as follows: Transaction T wants to access page p. We define "CONFLICT" by

$$\exists\, T' \in T(p) \quad \text{such that} \quad T' > T \;.$$

(a) T wants to read (write) p in the valid state:

$$\textbf{state } (p) := \text{Read(Write)}$$

$$T(p) := \{T\}$$

(b) T wants to read p in the read state:

$$\textbf{insert } T \textbf{ into } T(p)$$

(c) T wants to write p in the read state:

if "CONFLICT" **abort** T *and its successors* **else**

set $T > T'$ **for all** $T' \in T(p)$

set *state of p* **to** *write.*

(d) T wants to read (write) p in the write state:

if "CONFLICT" **abort** T *and its successors* **else**

set $T > T'$ **for all** T' *belonging to* $T(p)$

(e) When T is finished, T is validated only if all T' such that $T' > T$ are finished. Otherwise, wait.

(f) When T is validated (aborted), T is deleted from the graph and from $T(p)$ for all p accessed by T. If $T(p)$ is empty, set state of p to valid.

This algorithm is under evaluation. It presents some similarities with algorithms used in distributed database systems [18, 19]. The fact that it allows more transactions to enter into the system is an advantage, especially if conflicts among transactions are infrequent. However, one may have to abort a large number of transactions each time a cycle is detected. Furthermore, its implementation seems not as simple as the one with a shadow system mentioned earlier.

1.5. HARDWARE ARCHITECTURE

1.5.1. General Description

The current prototype realization is based on the use of standard Motorola 68000 components together with special-purpose hardware processors designed and realized at INRIA.

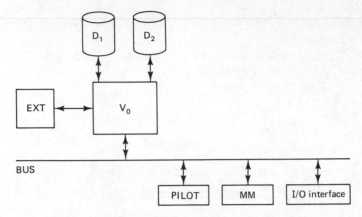

Figure 1.1. The Overall Architecture of VERSO Machine

As shown in Figure 1.1, the VERSO machine includes the following components, which share a VERSABUS bus: a general-purpose processor (PILOT) and its main memory (MM), a specialized processor (V_0), two disks D_1 and D_2, a disk extension (EXT), and an I/O interface.

PILOT is in charge of the dialogue with the frontend—i.e., a network or a host computer. The interface with external hardware has not yet been specified. It also handles intermediate DBMS functions such as query decomposition and optimization, access path and physical space management of memories (EXT) and disks (D_1 and D_2), and concurrency control and recovery. Finally, it controls V_0 by sending elementary operations to it for execution. These operations are in the following two categories:

1. Processing one or two blocks of data (filtering, sorting, and data transfers).
2. Handling the automata (compiling, loading, and archiving them).

The V_0 processor is to be rather independent of both the main memory and the microcomputer PILOT. It is described in some detail in the next section.

1.5.2. The V_0 Processor

V_0 includes components sharing another VERSABUS. It performs filtering, sorting, automation generation, archiving, and loading. It exchanges data with PILOT (output results, input data). It receives from PILOT the addresses of blocks to be filtered and commands about the operation to be performed (see Figure 1.2). V_0 includes another Motorola 68000 processor, the RAM memory (M-Versabus), a controller (C), a filter (F) and its memory (TM), a source buffer (SB), and a target buffer (TB).

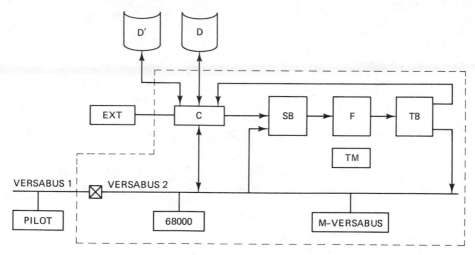

Figure 1.2. The Organization of the V_0 Processor

1. The 68000 processor is in charge of the dialogue with PILOT, the I/O commands (dialogue with C), filtering control (dialogue with F), internal sort of a block, and automaton generation.
2. The controller is realized from AMD microprocessors and is in charge of disk I/O, transferring data between D, EXT, SB, TB, and M-Versabus, and automaton loading into TM.
3. The filter, F, is also realized from AMD processors. It scans data in SB and places the result (filtered data) into TB. SB is loaded from EXT, D, or M-Versabus. This loading (writing into SB) may be performed in parallel with filtering ("on-the-fly" filtering). TB is unloaded into EXT, D, or M-Versabus. SB is a 32-Kbyte RAM memory and can be decomposed into two logical 16K source buffers, one for each input in the case of binary filtering operations (e.g., JOIN). TB also has a 32-Kbyte capacity. The filter's architecture is described in the next section.

In the current state of realization, we use a single VERSABUS and a single 68000 processor for implementing both PILOT and the above functions (sorting, automaton generation, controller, and filter control). If the load on the 68000 processor is too heavy, we will choose to implement PILOT on one 68000 and the above functions on a separate 68000.

1.5.3. Filter Design

It was shown in [11, 15] that an automatonlike device is sufficient to perform on the fly the relational algebra operations (the relations being sorted in the case of binary operations). Filtering is based on data recognition by a

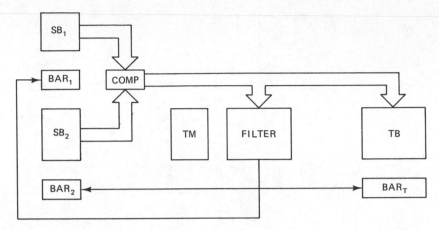

Figure 1.3. The Filtering Mechanism

finite-state automaton. The time to perform any algebraic operation is then linear with respect to the size of the data and is independent of query complexity.

Given a request for an algebraic operation and the description of the format of the relation(s), a compiler generates an automaton to be loaded into the filter's memory (TM). Once the automaton is loaded, the filter scans the relation(s) in the source buffer (SB) one byte at a time. Consequently, one or more blocks of data are successively loaded into SB. If the algebraic operation to be performed is binary, SB is decomposed into two logical source buffers, SB_1 and SB_2, one for each input relation (see Figure 1.3). The filter analyzes a character read in SB_1 or SB_2 and eventually writes one character into the target buffer, TB.

A comparator allows the filter to read the smallest (largest) of the two characters in SB_1 and SB_2. Before reading a character, the automaton is in a given state. To the (state, character) couple corresponds a next state and an output function. The latter consists basically of the updating of the registers BAR_1 and BAR_2 (where to read the next source character) and register BAR_T (where to write the character).

Filtering may be performed on the fly; i.e., the filter does not have to wait for SB to be loaded with one (or two) block(s) of data before starting its scan of characters. In other words, while the controller is writing into SB, the filter reads data. A hardware mechanism blocks the filter, if it gets ahead of the source loading. Once SB has been scanned, an interrupt causes another block of data to be loaded.

If TB is full before filtering, a block is allocated to TB. This block may be in D, Ext, or M-Versabus. The filter's memory, the transition matrix (TM), is a 256-line (256 states) by 256-column (256 bytes) matrix. Each (state, character) couple addresses a 32-bit word in TM, which contains the next

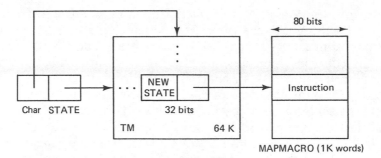

Figure 1.4.   The Filter

state and the address in the MAPMACRO memory of the output function to be interpreted and run before going to the next state (see Figure 1.4).

A cycle of the filter starts when, in a given state, a character is read. The output function generally is composed in one microinstruction that is loaded into MAPMACRO. The cycle for such a microinstruction does not last more than 550 ns. It may happen, however, that some complex output functions require a program of several MAPMACRO instructions to be run. Nevertheless, the filter's cycle time is on the average 400 ns long. Each microinstruction is divided into four fields, each being interpreted and run in parallel. An AMD 2910 processor is used for sequencing instructions.

1.5.4. The Controller System

As shown in Figure 1.5, the controller system C consists of two DMAs (one for the extension, one for the disk), a formatter, and the controller itself (not shown in the figure).

The controller itself includes a microprogrammed controller (AMD 2910), an ALU (AMD 25116), and an interrupt controller with eight levels

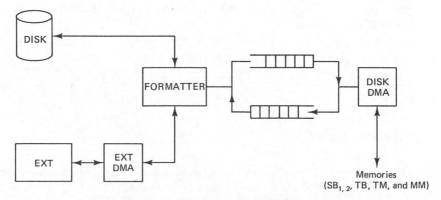

Figure 1.5.   The Controller

of interruptions (AMD 2514). Its basic tasks are transferring data and loading the FSA into the filter. The possible data transfers are between disk and extension and between disk (or extension) and SB (or TB, or M-Versabus). The controller prepares these transfers by initializing the EXT and/or DMAs, controlling the disk, or controlling the formatter.

Owing to the size of the FSA, it is important to have a very fast loader. A special-purpose processor, PAGE-MODE, uses the technological characteristics for dynamic RAM to load a sequence of states of the automaton (150 ns per 32 bit word). PAGE MODE is controlled by the controller.

The disk DMA is programmed, initialized, and triggered by the controller. It facilitates data transfer between the disk (or Ext) and another memory. It generates the address and control signals for the memory during the transfer. Since the disk is slow, the formatter works continuously during the data transfer. Disk DMA is faster. By means of two FIFO buffers, it may send bursts of data, thereby minimizing the memory buses utilization.

The extension DMA is initialized by the controller, which specifies the beginning address in EXT and the number of bytes to be transferred. During the transfer between EXT and the formatter, the EXT DMA generates the address into EXT. Thus the extension is seen as a sequential access memory similar to the disk.

The formatter is the interface between the FIFO memory and the disk (or EXT). The formatter is in charge of converting bit parallel into byte serial (when reading from the disk), and byte serial into bit parallel (when writing onto the disk). It also synchronizes the FIFO memory with the disk. Finally, it performs SRC computation and checking and disk formatting.

1.6. CURRENT STATE OF DEVELOPMENT

Hardware has been completely designed and is currently being put together. It will consist of eight wrapped cards (four for the filter and four for the controller) and four standard Motorola cards. Testing should start at the time of this writing.

The software is under design. The lower level (e.g., compiler, loader) has been implemented and is operational on an emulation of the filter. This emulation is written in Pascal on a computer with MULTICS operating system.

REFERENCES

[1] Copeland, G. P., Lipovski, G. J., and Su, S. Y. W., "The Architecture of CASSM: A Cellular System for Non-Numeric Processing," *Proc. 1st Annual Symposium on Computer Architecture,* December 1973, pp. 121–128.

[2] Oskarahan, C. A., Schuster, S. A., and Smith, K. C., "RAP—An Associative Processor for Data Base Management," *Proc. 1975 NCC,* Vol. 45, AFIPS Press, Montvale, N.J., pp. 379–387.

[3] Banerjee, J., Baum, R., and Hsiao, D. K., "Concepts and Capabilities of a Database Computer," *ACM Trans. Database Systems,* Vol. 3, No. 4 (December 1978), pp. 347–384.

[4] Dewitt, D. J., "DIRECT—A Multiprocessor Organization for Supporting a Relational Database Management System," *IEEE Trans. on Comp.,* Vol. C28, No. 6 (June 1979), pp. 395–406.

[5] Auer, H., et al., "RDBM—A Relational Database Machine," *Information Systems,* Vol. 6, No. 2 (1981), pp. 91–100. (See also Chapter 3 of this book.)

[6] Missikoff, M., and Terranova, M., "An Overview of the Project DBMAC for a Relational Database Machine," *Proceedings of the 6th Workshop on Computer Architecture for Non-Numeric Processing,* Hyères, France, June 1981. (See also Chapter 4 of this book.)

[7] Gardarin, G., et al., "Objectifs Principes et Architecture d'une Machine Bases de Données Réparties," *Actes des Journées Machines Bases de Données,* Sophia-Antiopolis, 10–12 Septembre 1980. (See also Chapter 2 of this book.)

[8] Babb, E., "Implementing a Relational Database by Means of Specialized Hardware," *ACM Trans. Database Systems,* Vol. 4, No. 1 (March 1979), pp. 1–29.

[9] Epstein, R., and Hawthorn, P., "Design Decisions for the Intelligent Database Machine," *Proc. 1980 NCC,* AFIPS Press, Montvale, N.J., pp. 237–241.

[10] Michel, F., et al., "La Machine de Gestion de Base de Données: l'Unité Centrale des Nouveaux Systèmes Informatiques," *Actes des Journées Machines Bases de Données,* Sophia-Antiopolis, France, Sept. 10–12, 1980, pp. 105–116.

[11] Bancilhon, F., and Scholl, M., "Design of a Back End Processor for a Data Base Machine," *Proceedings SIGMOD,* 1980, Los Angeles, pp. 93–93g.

[12] Leilich, H. O., Stiege, G., and Zeidler, H. Ch., "A Search Processor for Database Management Systems," *Proceedings VLDB,* 1978, pp. 280–287.

[13] Mastri, El, Rohmer, J., and Tusera, D., "A Machine for Information Retrieval," *Proc. Fourth Non-Numeric Workshop,* Syracuse, N.Y., August 1978, pp. 117–120.

[14] Codd, E. F., "A Database Sublanguage Founded on the Relational Calculus," *Proc. 1971 ACM SIGFIDET Workshop on Data Descr., Access and Control,* 1971, pp. 35–68.

[15] Bancilhon, F., Richard, P., and Scholl, M., "The Database Machine VERSO: Binary Operators," *Proceedings of the 6th Workshop on Computer Architecture for Non-Numeric Processing,* Hyères, France, June 1981.

[16] Rohmer, J., "Applications du Filtrage Séquentiel," Thèse d'Etat, Grenoble, France, 1981.

[17] Lorie, R., "Physical Integrity in a Large Segmented Database," *ACM Trans. on Database Systems,* Vol. 2, No. 1 (1977).

[18] Rothnie, J., and Goodman, N., "An Overview of the Preliminary Design of SDD-1: A system for Distributed Database," *Proc. II Berkeley Workshop on Distributed Data Management and Computer Networks,* May 1977.

[19] Thomas, R. H., "A Solution to the Concurrency Control Problem for Multiple Copy Databases," *Proc. COMPCON '78 Spring,* March 1978.

[20] "Les V-Relations," *Note technique VERSO No. 1,* Mai 1982.

[21] Bancilhon, F., Richard, P., and Scholl, M., "On-Line Processing of Compacted Relations," *Proc. the 8-th International Conference on Very Large Data Bases,* Sept. 1982, Mexico City, Mexico.

[22] Schkolnick, M., and Sorenson, P., "The Effects of Denormalization on Database Performance," *IBM Research Report* RJ 3082 (38128), 3.12.81.

[23] Korth, H. F., and Ullman, J. D., "System/U: A Database System Based on the Universal Relation Assumption," *Proc. XP1 Conference,* Stonybrook, N.Y., June 1980.

[24] Codd, E. F., "Further Normalization of the Database Relational Model," in *Database Systems, Current Computer Science Symposia 6* (R. Rustin, ed.), Prentice-Hall, Englewood Cliffs, N.J., No. 5, 1971, pp. 33–64.

2

SABRE: A Relational Database System for a Multimicroprocessor Machine

Georges Gardarin, Philippe Bernadat, Nicole Temmerman, Patrick Valduriez,
and Yann Viemont

2.0. ABSTRACT

SABRE (Système d'Accès a des Bases Relationneles) is a portable data management system, mainly designed for a multimicroprocessor configuration. This system, of which version 0 is actually operational at INRIA on MULTICS, presents several original ideas in the areas such as clustering of data, multiple views of a database, join algorithms for relations, concurrency control, integrity control, query evaluation. This paper summarizes the objectives, the basic concepts, and the functional and operational architectures of the SABRE system.

2.1. INTRODUCTION

A new class of database management system characterized by high-level manipulation languages and based on the relational model is actually being commercialized [1, 2]. More functionality is provided to the user but with three main drawbacks: high response times, no integration of such systems into a computer network, and lack of data management of nonalphanumerical data.

To avoid the first drawback of conventional systems, proposals have been made to relieve the main computer of the data management functions and to entrust them to database machines. We distinguish such database machines in terms of hardware-oriented and software-oriented systems. *Hardware-oriented systems* use special-purpose hardware to perform almost all the database management functions. CAFS [3] and VERSO [4] are examples of such systems. In *software-oriented systems* most of the database management functions are implemented by software, although a small amount of special-purpose hardware may be used. Thus, for example, DIRECT [5] and MDBS [6] are considered to be such systems. The rapid growth in the development of low-cost and powerful general-purpose processors encourages us to believe that this second approach holds much more promise for avoiding the drawbacks of conventional systems.

The SABRE system [7] reported in this chapter is a software-oriented system. Its first aim is to avoid the drawbacks of high response times and the impossibility of integrating such a system into a computer network. To improve the performance of the database management functions, we investigate several approaches, such as the utilization of parallelism, data filtering on the fly, new access (path) methods, efficient clustering of data, and disks with large memory caches. To avoid the second drawback, we develop SABRE as a system portable on different computers—big computers such as HB.68 MULTICS as well as autonomous multimicroprocessor machines. Therefore, the system is written in Pascal, easily portable. The project would lead to an autonomous system implemented on a multimicroprocessor machine and connectable to a local or general network. This system will be a basic tool for investigating the management of integrated databases, where different data types have to be handled, thereby overcoming the third drawback.

This chapter is organized as follows. First, the objectives of the project are stated (as presented in [7]). Then, the basic concepts sustaining the project are described: associative partition, filtering on the fly, multidimensional clustering, parallel operations, query optimization, deferred update, view mechanism, and data manipulation protocol. Then the functional architecture and the different operational architectures of the successive versions of the system are presented. Finally, the multiple stages of the project are described.

2.2. OBJECTIVES

The main objectives of the SABRE project are the following:

1. To develop an extensible and portable relational database manager. This manager should serve as a basic tool to build integrated and distributed database systems.
2. To achieve a response time better than those of the conventional relational database systems. To do so, we investigate the possibilities of intrarequest parallelism; i.e., a request is divided into a set of functional units which are executed in parallel.
3. To reduce the number and time necessary to perform I/O. For that, we investigate two devices: a large cache memory where intermediate and final results of data are stored, and a filtering processor which operates partly in parallel the selection of data on the fly and the transfer of data from disk to cache.
4. To allow various views of the database to be defined and queried by different groups of users. Each view can contain virtual relations derived from other views and actual data known only at the view level.
5. To determine efficient access paths to relations. For this we use indices. However, we believe that B-trees are not well suited for relational, multiattribute queries, so we propose not to balance multiattribute trees in order to accelerate query evaluation and access-path determination.
6. To guarantee the database integrity when data are updated simultaneously by concurrent transactions or when erroneous updates may occur.
7. To obtain a slow degradation of the system performance without any loss of functionality when a component fails.

More specifically, we try to fulfill these seven objectives by developing a software system and by using off-the-shelf hardware. Even if some of them will be only partially reached at the end of the project effort, we hope to give coherent partial solutions to all of them.

2.3. BASIC CONCEPTS

The SABRE system is built from a set of basic concepts, more or less currently developed in the project. These we present here.

2.3.1. The Data Manipulation Protocol

The system is designed to be connected to host processors, which send commands to the system and receive answers from the system. The set of commands and the corresponding answers composes an application protocol of

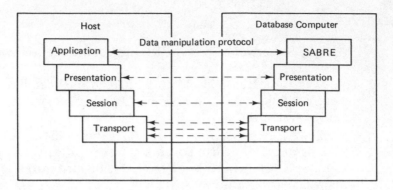

Figure 2.1. Levels of Protocols

the ISO architecture [8]. We call the set the *data manipulation protocol* (see Figure 2.1). The protocol is composed of two types of commands: transaction control commands and formatted data manipulation commands. In the future, we wish to extend the protocol with unformatted data manipulations, such as long text or bit strings.

The *transaction control commands* are very simple. The command

BEGIN (TRANSACTION-ID, MODE, USER-ID, VIEW-ID)

allows a user to start a new transaction on the identified view in the given mode. The mode specifies whether the user wants to perform a real transaction with update commitment or to simulate a transaction for debugging.

The following commands enable us to implement a two-step-commitment protocol [9] to support distributed transaction atomicity. PRECOMMIT (TRANSACTION-ID) performs the preparation of the identified transaction for commitment. If the transaction has been well executed up to this point, its updates are recorded in a stable memory and are ready to be either integrated into the database or canceled according to the host decision. COMMIT (TRANSACTION-ID) integrates the precommitted updates into the database and signals an end of the commitment unit. ABORT (TRANSACTION-ID) aborts the identified transaction and invalidates its noncommitted updates. END (TRANSACTION-ID) terminates a transaction.

The *data manipulation commands* allow a transaction to retrieve and update data in an existing database.

SUPPRESS (RELATION, QUALIFICATION) removes tuples that satisfy the qualification from the relation to which they belong.

MODIFY (ATTRIBUTES = VALUES or EXPRESSION, RELATION, QUALIFICATION) changes the value of the attributes specified for all the tuples of the relation that satisfy the qualification.

RETRIEVE (ATTRIBUTES or EXPRESSION, QUALIFICATION) put

the attributes or expression of attributes of tuples that satisfy the qualification in a result relation, which can then be sent to the host when requested.

Two commands that allow the user to create specific access paths to a relation are CREATE (RELATION-ID, ACCELERATOR-DEFINITION) and DESTROY (RELATION-ID, ACCELERATOR-DEFINITION).

2.3.2. A Hierarchy of Views

We define a database by describing a hierarchy of views. In the first view, the root of the hierarchy, we describe all the database relations and attributes. In this case, it is a classical relational schema of the database. A derived view is defined by a database administrator of a source view from which the derived view is composed. Database administrators may then be appointed for the new derived view. Consequently, the derived view may in turn be used as a source view. Thus, a hierarchy of views may be defined.

Among the relations of a view, certain relations are virtual relations derived from the source view. Other relations contain real data. These data may be the same data defined in a hierarchically superior view, or they may be new data defined for the first time at the view level. Thus, the database definition control may be very distributed among the various database administrators, and private data may be associated to a given view. These possibilities are illustrated in Figure 2.2.

To specify the composition rules of a virtual relation, a set of queries is used to associate them with a view. When a query is submitted through a

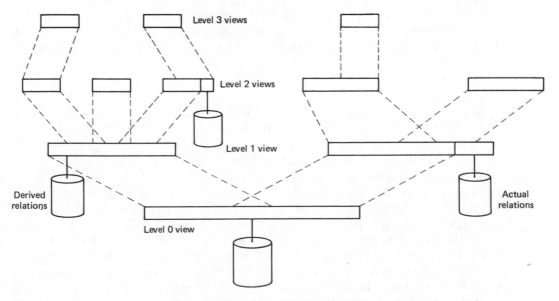

Figure 2.2. A Hierarchy of Views

view, it is enriched with the queries that define the virtual relations. This process is similar to the query modification process of INGRES [2]. For the time being, updates through views are not possible, but we envision such possibilities by including update mapping rules in the view definition.

2.3.3. The Metabase

The schema of the views (and therefore of the database) is defined by inserting tuples in the metabase. At present, this metabase is composed of the following conceptual relations. The VIEW relation contains the name and basic properties of the views. The RELATION relation contains the name and basic properties of the relations of the views. The ATTRIBUTE relation specifies the domains and the various characteristics of each attribute. The RIGHT relation defines the user access rights to the views.

The metabase is manipulated as a normal database, because it contains its own schema. However, the metabase schema is known only to the system and thus cannot be easily changed.

2.3.4. Request Decomposition and Optimization

Request decomposition is the process that decomposes a host request into a tree of relational algebra operations. The operations implemented in SABRE are select (restriction and projection), join, sort, duplicate elimination, union, difference, aggregation, and arithmetic functions (sum, average, count, minimum, and maximum). An optimization algorithm gives an optimized decomposition for each request. The algorithm first optimizes on the I/O and CPU costs. It then tries to optimize on operations for parallelism. The optimization is based on a statistical evaluation of the size of intermediate results.

2.3.5. Intrarequest Parallelism

To increase the throughput of the system, each request is decomposed in a set of functional steps. Each step is executed by a virtual processor, which can be either a real processor or a process, according to the configuration of the machine supporting the system. Thus, SABRE is decomposed in virtual processors. Each of them performs some specific functions. Moreover, a distributed execution kernel carries out efficiently synchronizations and communications among processors. Figure 2.3 gives an overview of the steps isolated for request processing. Each box corresponds to a virtual processor.

Several virtual processors may collaborate to perform a request in parallel. This intrarequest parallelism may be obtained in two ways: (a) by running in parallel independent operations of the same request (such operations are identified by the query decomposition algorithm; for example, several selections can be performed in parallel for the same host request), and (b) by

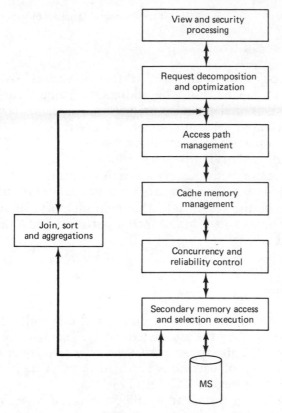

Figure 2.3. Request Processing Steps

using several functionally identical processors to perform a unique operation (for example, several virtual processors can collaborate to perform a join [10] or a semijoin [11]).

Finally, to achieve a high degree of parallelism, it is necessary to build an architecture where several virtual processors are associated to each functional step, as sketched in Figure 2.4.

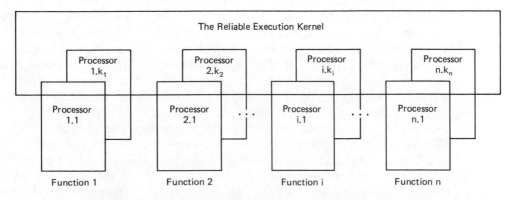

Figure 2.4. The Principle of the SABRE Virtual Processor Architecture

25

2.3.6. Associative Partitions

Tuples are stored in associative partitions. The size of such a partition is generally a disk track but can be less. The addressing inside a partition is done by Boolean expressions of elementary predicates. An elementary predicate is of the form (Attribute-Id.Θ.Value) where Attribute-Id is an attribute number, Θ a comparison operator is selected among $\{=, <, >, \neq, \leqslant, \geqslant\}$, and Value is a numerical, or alphabetical, or textual value.

A virtual filter processor is associated to each disk unit. Such a filter can retrieve all tuples inside a partition satisfying a Boolean expression and bring selected attributes of the tuples into the main memory. In addition, the filter performs insertion of new tuples into a partition and deletion of selected tuples if requested.

2.3.7. The Reduced Cover Tree

A database is divided into partitions located on a set of disk units. The disk units can be accessed in parallel by the associated filters. The SABRE clustering strategy should assure that the tuples answering to a given query can be retrieved in a minimal number of partitions accessed in parallel. To do so, a multiclustering strategy is proposed in SABRE [12].

This strategy is based on a formal tool called a *reduced cover tree*. For each relation, an ordered subset of the attributes $(A_1, A_2, \ldots, A_p)$ is given by the database administrator. For each attribute of the subset, say A_i, the set of values in which A_i takes a value is "covered" by a list of domains D_{i_1}, $D_{i_2}, \ldots, D_{i_n}$. A domain can be defined in one of three ways: by enumeration (of the exact list of values), by intervals, and by hashing. Each attribute A is associated with a level of clustering. For a level i, all tuples whose attribute A_i takes values in the same domain D_{ij} are clustered in parallel partitions, as much as possible. If a partition is full and contains tuples having the same value for attribute A_i, but different values for attribute A_{i+1}, it is split into new partitions when a new tuple is inserted. In this case, the attribute A_{i+1} is used to cluster the tuples in the resulting partitions. Finally, successive splits of partitions at different levels using different attributes lead to the construction of a multidimensional tree. For example, the relation WINE(V, WINEYARD, YEAR, DRINKER) can be clustered by the attribute sequence (WINEYARD, YEAR, V) as portrayed in Figure 2.5.

Moreover, besides multiattribute clustering the reduced cover trees allow us to implement primary or secondary indices. An index for a unique key can be built in using, for level i of the tree, the character i of the key, in which case we get a trie [13]. For example, we use the two digits of the attribute V as levels 3 and 4 of the reduced cover tree represented in Figure 2.5.

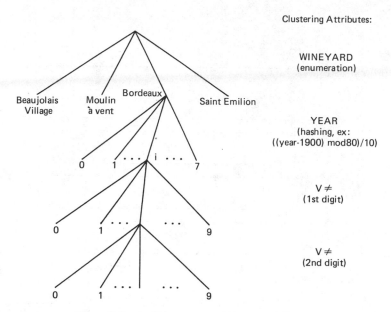

Clustering Attributes:

WINEYARD
(enumeration)

YEAR
(hashing, ex:
((year-1900) mod80)/10)

$V \neq$
(1st digit)

$V \neq$
(2nd digit)

Figure 2.5. An Example of a Reduced Cover Tree

2.4. FUNCTIONAL AND OPERATIONAL ARCHITECTURES OF SABRE

2.4.1. Basic Principles

We distinguish SABRE's unique functional architecture from the operational architectures of its various implemented versions. The functional architecture is composed of a set of virtual processors organized in classes of parallel processors. Each operational architecture is composed of a set of real processors supporting one or more virtual processors. These real processors are interconnected by buses. There is one operational architecture for each version of SABRE.

2.4.2. The Functional Architecture

We shall give here a top-down presentation of the various classes of virtual processors of which the functional architecture is composed. Each processor type is associated with a functional step. The functional steps have been introduced in Figure 2.3, and the global functional architecture is portrayed in Figure 2.6.

View and Integrity Processor (VIP). This processor is the most external of the machine and works on a database view. Its roles are (1) to control

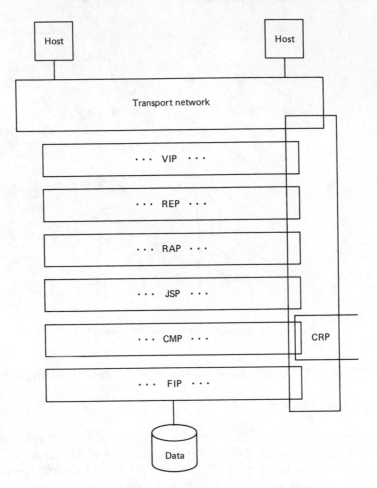

Figure 2.6. The Functional Architecture of SABRE

the user rights on the view, (2) to translate the request expressed on virtual relations described in the view into a request expressed on real relations stored on disks, and (3) to perform some integrity control at each update.

Request Evaluation Processor (REP). This processor works on a set of real relations and performs the request decomposition and optimization. It breaks queries into relational algebra operations and decomposes an update into a query followed by a deletion and an insertion.

Relation Access Processor (RAP). This processor works on a real relation and manages access paths. More precisely, when an insertion of tuples is performed, it determines the partitions at which to insert the tuples, and it updates a bit map that defines the reduced cover-tree extension [12]. When a restriction is performed, it determines which partitions should be scanned.

Join, Sort, and Aggregate Processors (JSP).   These processors perform join, sort, and compute aggregate functions on partitions. Several join processors generally work in cooperation to carry out efficiently joins and sortings [10].

Concurrency Control and Recovery Processor (CRP).   This processor performs concurrency control by way of an algorithm based on two time-stamps. This algorithm ensures a unique update order, the transaction commit order [14]. It also performs update logs and manages the two step-commitment protocol [9].

Cache Memory Processor (CMP).   This processor is responsible for allocating secondary and cache memories. It also performs the replacement of cache memory pages into partitions when the cache memory is saturated.

Filtering Processor (FIP).   These processors perform selection, insertion, and deletion of tuples in a partition. They work as much as possible on the fly, during the transfer of data from disk to cache.

2.4.3. The Operational Architectures

An operational architecture is associated with each implemented version of SABRE. It is composed of one or more real processors supporting a set of virtual processors. It is possible to describe an operational architecture by a relation of schema: SABRE.Vi (virtual processor, number, real processor). This relation defines for each virtual processor implemented in the version how many occurrences appear and on which real processor they are executed. Three versions of SABRE are currently under implementation: V0, V1, V2.

The relation defining SABRE.V0 is given in Figure 2.7 and the operational architecture of this version in Figure 2.8. This version is running on MULTICS at INRIA and can be demonstrated. It is a single-user, uniprocessor version that has been implemented mainly to validate the first design.

Virtual proc.	Number	Real proc.
Host	1	HB.68
REP	1	HB.68
JSP	1	HB.68
CMP	1	HB.68
FIP	1	HB.68

Figure 2.7.   The Relation Defining SABRE.V0

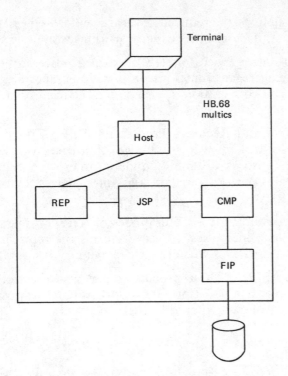

Figure 2.8. The Operational Architecture of SABRE.V0

The relation defining SABRE.V1 is given in Figure 2.9 and the operational architecture in Figure 2.10. This multiuser, multiprocess, uniprocessor version of SABRE is currently under implementation at INRIA and was due for completion in December of 1982. All the virtual processors are written in Pascal, for compatability with other systems. In the next section we present in some detail SABRE.V2, which will be a true multiprocessor database computer.

Virtual proc.	Number	Real proc.
Host	q (q $\geqslant$ 1)	HB.68
VIP	1	HB.68
REP	1	HB.68
RAP	1	HB.68
JSP	1	HB.68
CMP	1	HB.68
FIP	1	HB.68
CRP	1	HB.68

Figure 2.9. The Relation Defining SABRE.V1

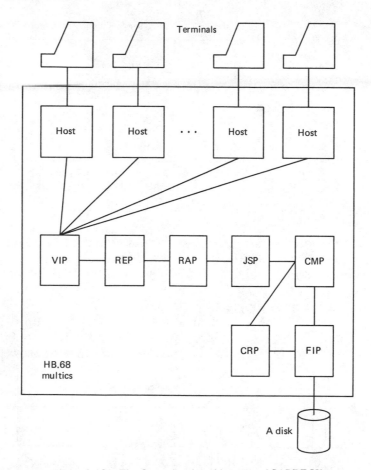

Figure 2.10. The Operational Architecture of SABRE.V1

2.5. SABRE VERSION 2—A TRUE MULTIPROCESSOR DATABASE COMPUTER

2.5.1. The Operational Architecture

The relation defining SABRE.V2 is given in Figure 2.11 and the operational architecture in Figure 2.12. This is a true multimicroprocessor database computer. It should include three parallel processors and be usable by two users simultaneously in the beginning. The software should be the same for SABRE Version 1. The hardware has been ordered, and the implementation of this version is scheduled to begin in 1983.

Virtual proc.	Number	Real proc.
Host	2	A
VIP	1	A
REP	1	B
RAP	1	B
CRP	1	C
JSP	2	C
FIP	1	C
CMP	1	C

Figure 2.11. The Relation Defining SABRE.V2

2.5.2. A Hardware Overview

The hardware we are receiving was developed by the French PTT (CNET) and is called the SM90. An overview of our architecture in terms of SM90 is given in Figure 2.13. Each 68000 should run the UNIX system. It can address its private memory, its local memory, and the common memory through mapping facilities supplied by the MMU.

We would like to implement the user interface (with the host processor) and the view and integrity processor (VIP) on the first 68000 (P1). Then, the second 68000 (P2) will run the query evaluation processor (PEQ) and the re-

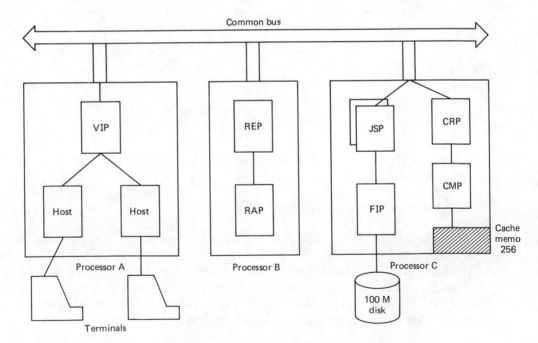

Figure 2.12. The Operational Architecture of SABRE.V2

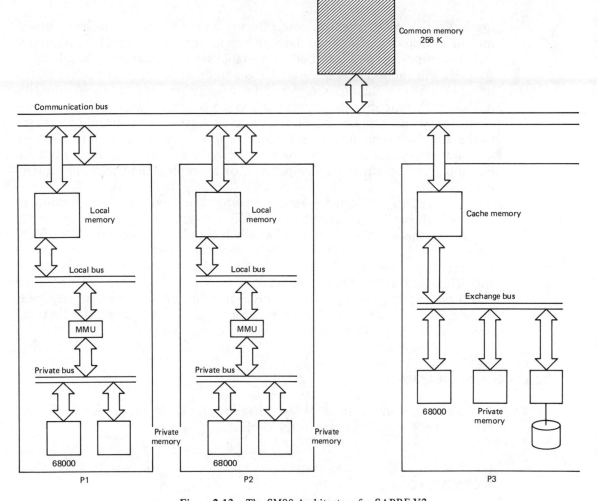

Figure 2.13. The SM90 Architecture for SABRE.V2

lation access processor (RAP). Finally, the third processor (P3) will support the join-and-sort processor (JSP), the cache memory processor (CMP), the concurrency and reliability control processor (RCP), and the filter processor (FIP). We hope to convert virtual processors into real ones in order to compare performances. We will have more to say next year about this experience.

2.6. THE CONCLUSION

This chapter has presented the SABRE system. The first aim of the project is to improve the performance and functionality of the system for managing large relational databases. The main basic concepts have been defined, including utilization of parallelism, data filtering on the fly, use of cache memory, multidimensional clustering of data, and concurrency control of transactions. Another important aim is to build a portable system, written in Pascal.

The distinction between functional and operational architectures allows us to distinguish functions required from software needed. Thus, concepts dealing with functions have emerged and led to the definition of virtual processors supporting these functions. We can map the set of virtual processors, called the functional architecture, into various operational architectures by assigning real processors to one or more virtual processors. So the system can be embedded on different computers (for example, HB68 and multimicroprocessor).

The realization of the system is accomplished in steps corresponding to successive operational versions of SABRE. This gradual approach began with testing of the working version 0, which is a uniuser system on MULTICS. This version has permitted the validation of the interfaces and algorithms in a uniprocessor context. Version 1 is a complete relational DBMS based on the original ideas and was to be working by the end of 1982. Version 2 is a relational database system implemented on a multimicroprocessor machine. A future and more sophisticated version would allow integrating text and image types of data to reach a new class of integrated DBMS.

2.7. ACKNOWLEDGMENTS

The authors wish to thank M. Bouzhegoub, K. Karlsson, J. Madelaine, and M. Thonnet for participating in the project.

REFERENCES

[1] Chamberlin, D. D., Gilbert, A. M., and Yost, R. A., "A History of System R and SQL/Data System," *7th Int. Conf. on Very Large Data Bases,* Cannes, September 1981.

[2] Stonebraker, M., Wong, E., and Kreps, P., "The Design and Implementation of INGRES," *ACM Trans. Data Base Systems,* Vol. 1, No. 3 (September 1976).

[3] Babb, E., "Implementing a Relational Data Base by Means of Specialized Hardware," *ACM Trans. Database Systems,* Vol. 4, No. 1 (March 1979), pp. 1–29.

[4] In this book. See Chapter 1.

[5] Dewitt, D. J., "Query Execution in DIRECT," *Proceedings of the ACM-SIGMOD 1979 International Conference on Management of Data,* May 1979, pp. 13–22.

[6] Hsiao, D. K., and Menon, M. J., "Design and Analysis of a Multi-Backend Database System for Performance Improvement, Functionality Expansion and Capacity

Growth," Technical Report OSU-CISRC-TR-81-7, Ohio State University, Columbus, July 1981. (See also Chapters 10 and 11 of this book.)

[7] Gardarin, G., "An Introduction to SABRE: A Multi-Microprocessor Database Machine," *6th Workshop on Computer Architecture for Non-Numeric Processing,* Hyères, France, June 1981.

[8] ISO/TC97/SC16 N227, "Reference Model of Open System Interconnection," June 1979.

[9] Baer, J. L., Gardarin, G., Girault, C., and Roucairol, G., "The Two-Step Commitment Protocol: Modeling Specification and Proof Methodology," *5th International Conference on Software Engineering,* San Diego, 1981.

[10] Valduriez, P., and Gardarin, G., "Multiprocessor Join Algorithms of Relations," *2d Int. Conf. on Data Bases: Improving Usability and Responsiveness,* Jerusalem, June 1982.

[11] Valduriez, P., "Semi-Join Algorithms for Multiprocessor Systems," *ACM-SIGMOD Int. Conf. on Management of Data,* Orlando, Fla., June 1982.

[12] Karlsson, K., "Reduced Cover-Trees and Their Application in the SABRE Access Path Model," *Proc. the 7th Int. Conf. on Very Large Data Bases,* Cannes, September 1981.

[13] Litwin, W., "Trie Hashing," *ACM-SIGMOD Int. Conf. on Management of Data,* Ann Arbor, Mich., September 1981.

[14] Viemont, Y., and Gardarin, G., "A Distributed Concurrency Control Based on Transaction Commit Ordering," *12th Int. Conf. on FTCS,* Los Angeles, June 1982.

3

RDBM—A Dedicated Multiprocessor System for Database Management

H. Schweppe, H.Ch. Zeidler, W. Hell,
H.-O. Leilich, G. Stiege, and W. Teich

3.0. ABSTRACT

The Relational Database Machine (RDBM) is a special-purpose computer system currently under development at the Technical University of Braunschweig, West Germany. This chapter outlines the architecture, the system design, and current research of RDBM.

Research activity in the field of database machines started at the T.U. Braunschweig with the design and implementation of the search processor (SURE) and an associative disk storage system. The experience gained during that period provided the basis for the development of RDBM.

The overall architecture of the RDBM as a centrally controlled multiprocessor system with dedicated processors and a commonly shared main memory is presented. Details of the RDBM system are given in the main part of the chapter. The common main memory, together with its built-in data management facility providing tuple-oriented access, offers a solution to the problem of coordinating the operation of independent processors working on different parts of a common task.

The secondary memory system, which employs a logical data-access interface and data-filtering processors, is discussed. The advantages of tuple buffering in filter processors are also outlined, as opposed to on-the-fly data filtering. The various processor structures for interrecord operations, sorting, and data conversion are presented, together with their interfaces to the other system components. Algorithms for execution of high-level database operations on RDBM are also discussed—in particular, transaction processing. This includes the implementation of the multiuser facility in the control processor. Finally the current state of the system is given.

3.1. INTRODUCTION

3.1.1. Objectives and Background

The user of a database system should not be concerned with the implementation of a task once it has been expressed in the database query language. He expects the system to provide a high degree of availability and fast response, together with data security and high reliability.

The construction of such a system must not merely translate the high-level query language expression into a bit-level control language that can ultimately be interpreted by hardware consisting of microprocessors, special processing and control units, RAMs, disks, and communication circuitry. It must also recognize the class of problems to be solved and break them down into subtasks (e.g., relational operations) using intermediate languages and control structures performable on a set of microprocessors, which are specialized for certain processes and capable of working in parallel.

The primary goal is efficiency, an old-fashioned word hailing from the early days in electronic computing, when hardware was very expensive. The concept of efficiency is by no means outdated, even in the age of VLSI. It refers here, apart from component minimization, to higher speed, fewer pins, lower power requirements, better documentation, less storage space, lower failure rate, and other factors in order to provide a desired standard of user service.

In the Braunschweig RDBM a system of dedicated microprocessors supports the main subtasks, namely mass data operations (e.g., searching and sorting) and memory management operations, while the user communication, compilation, and the overall process control are centrally performed by a general-purpose computer [1].

Although the investigations into the individual subtasks themselves represent substantial contributions, their actual merits, features, and problems can really be gauged only in the context of their cooperation within the entire system. The research group in Braunschweig, as a forerunner of the RDBM project, has worked, for example, on a processor tailored to the associative searching of a file (SURE; see Section 3.1.2), with little emphasis on the other necessary subtasks (e.g., memory management). Similar research results on search processors have been reported elsewhere [2, 3, 4].

The objective of the present project is to design a complete database machine (DBS) that supports the frequently used and time-consuming software database management functions with appropriate hardware components. We have also attempted to implement the most significant aspects of a relational DBS with emphasis on cooperation between the individual components, and we are convinced that an experimental machine has to be built in order to demonstrate that the concept as a whole is feasible.

Experimental projects are all very well as a means of convincing onlookers that a serious attempt is being made to transform a theoretical concept into a real system, provided that the final research vehicle works and can be used for further investigations. Before this stage is achieved, a great deal of work is necessary in the implementation of the hardware and software components. It is the cumulative sum of all the ensuing minor problems of a conventional nature that consume most of the time and money. Since many design specifications have to be frozen a long time before completion, it is not always possible to include new design ideas in the actual implementation. On the other hand, the actual construction of any complex system provides insight into many problems—some major—that can easily be overlooked in a theoretical investigation. Furthermore, the essential structural design decisions can be realistically assessed only by actually constructing and measuring an experimental pilot machine.

In what follows, some of the basic design ideas of our project are given, together with a report on the current state of our implementation.

3.1.2. The Search Computer (SURE) System

The predecessor of the RDBM is a search computer, known as SURE (Such-Rechner), an experimental project completed in 1978 [5] (see Figure 3.1).

The basic idea, not altogether novel, involved was to scan data completely and sequentially while they were being read from a disk, using special comparison units. The data do not have to be stored in a predetermined order but can be accessed on a content-addressed basis from a large associative disk store of 72 Mbytes.

The features of content-addressable storage have often enough been praised: no directories, no predetermined access paths, no sophisticated navigational access systems, and simple updating. The disadvantages of such sequential search machines are also well known: all data, for the greater part irrelevant to a specific query, have to be read and scanned. The search time is thus proportional to the file size divided by the data rate.

The maximum data rate for scanning by modern electronic circuitry (even at the point of design conception in 1974) was in the range of 10 Mbyte/sec. The standard data rate from disks was then 0.8 Mbyte/sec. We

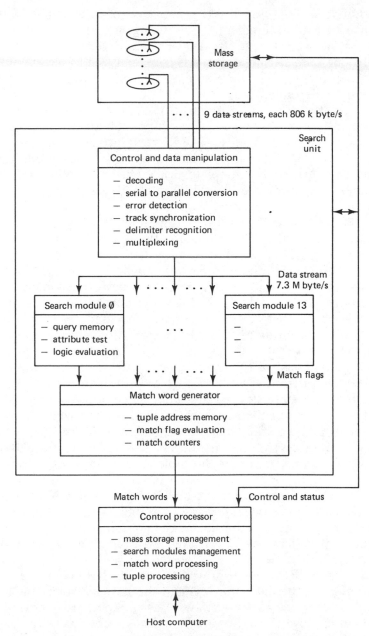

Figure 3.1. Structure of the Search Processor (SURE)

modified a 72-Mbyte disk by Siemens so that all nine information tracks could be read simultaneously, searching an entire disk cylinder in one revolution. These track-data streams were multiplexed at a rate of 7.3 Mbyte/sec into one data stream which was then analyzed by search modules using byte interleaving, so that the nine data streams (one from each track) were each treated independently.

At the time of planning SURE, integrated semiconductor memories were rather expensive and it was impossible to envisage transferring the contents of an entire cylinder (144 Kbytes) into a RAM. The data therefore had to be scanned "on the fly." This means that during one time slot (137 ns) one byte had to be completely processed and only a minimum amount of cumulative information could be retained, essentially constituting a "match bit."

Despite the sophisticated three-stage pipelining technique applied, the result of this on-the-fly approach is that one search module can perform only one comparison on each attribute value during a search scan. Queries of the type, "Is the data item in between two given limits?" or "Is the data item equal to A_1 or A_2 or . . ?" cannot be performed solely by one module in one scan. In order to keep down the number of scans with such different queries, a number of search modules was used, each of which scans the entire multiplexed data stream in parallel for the same query. Fourteen modules were installed in the prototype.

A fairly powerful set of query instructions (including comparison between two attributes within a tuple) was implemented and a two-level logical evaluation system devised and built to combine the logical results for each attribute to form the final match result for the whole tuple. The syntax of the logical expression is, as already mentioned, restricted by the sequential on-the-fly access to the attributes. The main practical disadvantage of the on-the-fly concept is that the tuple itself is already lost by the time a match is signaled by one of the search modules. The hardware addresses of the tuples under investigation are held in registers and, in the case of a "hit," are delivered to the control processor together with the "match vector" (14 bits, one for each search module). If the contents of the matching tuples are required, they have to be retrieved by a separate access following the search process itself.

The SURE control processor (an HP 2100 computer) also handles the selection of the disk cylinders and the user interface (including the translation of the queries) at a software level. Apart from testing and demonstration runs, several large evaluation trials were run with tasks derived from actual fields of application [6]. The experience of the search processor project gave us confidence that a special-purpose machine could be built that would satisfy the speed requirements for a class of existing search problems.

A valuable, but negative, result is that such a machine was rather costly in terms of both hardware and software, and the scope of suitable applications did not appear broad enough to justify the mass production of a search machine of this type. The conclusion drawn was that it was necessary to revise the technique employed in the search operation, exploiting advances in microprocessor and memory technology, while at the same time tackling other database problems (sorting and memory management) using hardware assistance. This led to the RDBM concept, which will hopefully represent a step toward a new generation of database machines with a broad field of application and a favorable cost/performance ratio.

3.2. AN OVERVIEW OF THE RDBM ARCHITECTURE

3.2.1. Design Goals

The primary goal was to implement a complete DBS that supports frequently used and time-consuming software database management functions using appropriate hardware components. It is not obvious that the system design has to comprise all the essential DBS components, such as a multiuser environment, checkpointing and recovery, and a functionally powerful user interface.

Although there are, for example, several well-known recovery techniques, it is by no means obvious that they can be utilized without any modification in a database machine environment. Therefore, our design concentrates on certain key points in the actual implementation:

Support of heavily used functions such as data retrieval.

Interrecord operations such as the relational join and data aggregation.

Consistent processing of concurrent transactions.

The user interface is based on the relational data model. This decision has some influence on the internal data structure and on the selection of functions requiring hardware support. The design of the machine is oriented toward set processing as opposed to single-record manipulation.

One of our primary goals is the exploitation of parallelism in database processing. This includes multitasking facilities as well as cooperative execution of an operation on the database (e.g., qualification of tuples) by several hardware components in parallel.

In general, a system design will be influenced heavily by technological evolution (it might otherwise become obsolete). Insofar as possible, we have tried to limit this effect. In particular, the system should be capable of being interfaced with any host computer by way of a channel as well as via a networking facility. Advanced mass storage devices should also be applicable.

3.2.2. Data Structure and User Interface

As already mentioned, the basic decision was to employ the relational model as the conceptual basis of the database machine. This decision influenced three levels of the system design: the user interface, the operations on data supported by specialized hardware, and the structuring of data.

Normalization of relations is a valuable tool for defining the conceptual schema of a database. Normalized relations on the physical level can, however, have a heavy impact on performance. For example, data that are strongly related may be scattered across the secondary memory. Therefore, internally structured tuples are not normalized. A *tuple* is a set of attributes, each of which may be simple, multivalued, or composed. Whereas a simple attribute may take at most one value in a particular tuple, a multivalued one may have an arbitrary number of individual values. A composed attribute is a sequence of different simple attributes. There may be arbitrarily many value sequences for a particular composed attribute in each tuple. Composed attributes are also sometimes called *repeating groups.*

In order to avoid semantic difficulties, certain relational operations, such as the join, are performed only on simple attributes.

The join is the most typical relational operation that is supported by RDBM. Specialized devices for operations such as sorting or qualifying tuples are of particular interest in a relational environment. They are, however, useful for different data management systems as well.

A subset of SQL has been chosen as the user interface. The subset comprises the data definition and manipulation facilities, but not integrity constraints. It should be emphasized that different descriptive user languages can be translated into an intermediate language of RDBM. Thus the system can be supplied with different "personalities." The interface between the database machine and host's application programs is similar to the program/ DBS interface between a conventional database system and its application programs.

3.2.3. Overall Architecture

Interpretation of the design goals led to a configuration consisting of three major components:

A mass storage device with its own storage manager and quasi-associative data-access facility.

A multiprocessor system consisting of special-function processors with common access to a large main memory.

A general-purpose minicomputer to control the different hardware components and to perform the database operations not supported by specialized hardware, such as query analysis.

The RDBM system (see Figure 3.2) may be used in a stand-alone mode by a local user, as a specialized node in a computer network by means of a networking interface, or as a backend processor when locally connected to a host computer via a high-speed channel.

After its reception, a query is decomposed by the RDBM software system into the elementary operations, which are then performed—partially in parallel—by the RDBM hardware. This includes query preprocessing, such as syntax analysis, code optimization taking into account data statistics, and the generation of code executable by the hardware components. (Note that

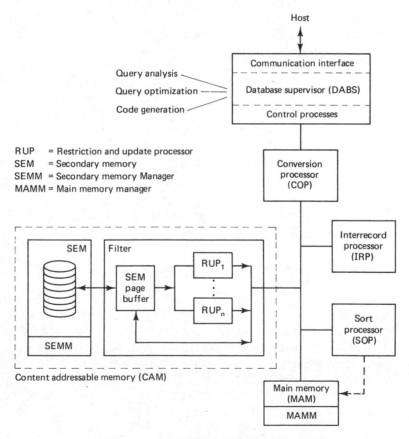

Figure 3.2. The RDBM System Configuration

"query" means all types of user tasks provided by the user interface and not just retrieval operations.) The sequence of executable elementary statements is sent to control processes, which are responsible for activating the specialized processors as far as possible in parallel during task execution.

The multiprocessor system consists of various special-function processors with common access to a large main memory. Information is exchanged between the different components via a bus system offering separate paths for data, instruction, and status transfers. Details are given in Section 3.3.

3.2.4. Basic Processor Hardware

The individual specialized processors of the RDBM are built around a standardized 8-bit microprocessor unit [7]. The processor kernel (AMD 2900 series) consists of an ALU, a sequencer program control unit, an interrupt controller, and a DMA controller. The program memory comprises 8 Kbytes and can be expanded up to 32 Kbytes using a special add-on board. The microprogramable memory has a capacity of 4K 128-bit words.

The bus interface also constitutes a standard hardware component of the processors, over which they are connected to the bus system. The hardware of this interface ensures compliance with the various bus protocols and in this way allows considerable simplification of programming and a relaxation of processor timing requirements. It also isolates the processor hardware from the bus system. A fault in one processor will therefore not lead to a failure of the bus system, lessening the sensitivity of the RDBM to failures in individual processors.

3.3. DETAILED DISCUSSION OF RDBM

3.3.1. Synchronization of Processor Actions

3.3.1.1. Characterization of the problem. It was shown above that the RDBM contains a heterogeneous multiprocessor system, composed of a number of dedicated processors. Owing to the functional specialization adopted, an individual processor can provide only a limited set of data manipulation operations; nevertheless, it can perform them very efficiently. The data manipulation operations provided are considerably more powerful than those available at the storage interface of a conventional DBS, enabling the execution of database functions (e.g., data search, update, and join), which are grouped together to form a user task. These functions require the cooperation of several individual RDBM processors. Thus, the processors must be synchronized by suitable constructs. In addition, execution of the database functions requires the provision of an adequate communication capability between the processors.

3.3.1.2.   Message transfer solutions.   We saw in Section 3.2. that the RDBM processors make use of a shared main memory to exchange data, so that this memory must contain shared address spaces. To guarantee a correct data flow between the processors, an appropriate mechanism must ensure that a shared address space may be accessed only by a reading processor after this space has been released by any currently writing processor. This requirement can be met by synchronizing the processors with the use of the control software running on the processor responsible for the overall control of the multiprocessor system, in that a writing processor sends a completion message via its individual section of control software (driver, control process) to the common centralized execution control (Figure 3.3). This execution control module responsible for resource sharing and scheduling can then activate the next processor via its corresponding driver, and so on. It is clear that this can lead to considerable delays in the processor's running the control software, owing to messages' having to pass through several layers of software.

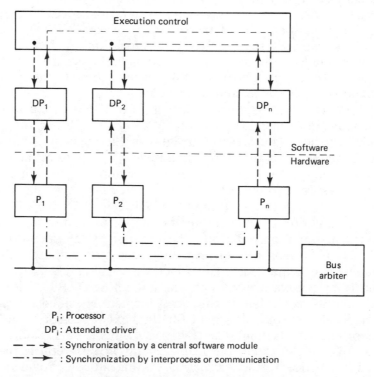

P$_i$: Processor
DP$_i$: Attendant driver
— — — ➤ : Synchronization by a central software module
— · — ➤ : Synchronization by interprocess or communication

Figure 3.3. Synchronization by Message Transfer

The synchronization can also be transferred to the individual processors themselves, if a suitable communication path is provided in the hardware (refer again to Figure 3.3). When a processor has concluded a series of write operations, it sends a completion message to its driver as well as an initiation command to the next consecutive processor. Complete interconnectivity between the processors is offered only by a crossbar. In a real implementation, however, alternative interconnection networks (e.g., a bus) have to be chosen in order to reduce costs and to ensure flexibility of the machine configuration. As the interconnectivity is now limited, the access to the bus has to be controlled, e.g., by a bus arbiter implemented in hardware.

After a processor has completed its operations, the function to be performed determines which processor has next to be initiated. This way of processor synchronization thus requires more complex addressing facilities on the part of the processor hardware.

3.3.1.3. Synchronization by logical addressing of the common main memory.

The message-passing synchronization techniques considered up to now restrict the attainable degree of parallelism, because the data flow can be controlled only on the level of shared address spaces and thus in possibly very large data packets. These data packets are processed purely sequentially by the processors. The attainable degree of parallelism is further reduced by the fact that, with the adopted static allocation of address spaces, these have to be made large to avoid as far as possible the occurrence of overflows. For a given size of main memory, this causes a drop in the number of possible concurrently available address spaces and thus in the potential degree of parallelism. To eliminate this bottleneck, the RDBM was provided with its own attendant main memory manager (MAMM), which permits the processor to address logical data areas (segments) in the memory. The address space of such a data area is thereby not limited by the physical address space of the main memory, since a replacement algorithm was implemented. In addition, the tuples within a segment are not accessed via physical addresses but rather by the use of operations such as GET.NEXT or PUT.NEXT.

In addition to the considerably better utilization of the main memory (avoidance of fragmentation), the concept of logical addressing also offers an elegant means of synchronizing processor activity. All processors required to execute a database function (e.g., search, join) can be activated jointly by the control software running in the DABS. At least one processor deposits its result data in the target segment specified for it, which then in turn forms the source segment for the next processor, from which this processor extracts its input data (Figure 3.4). If the data required by a processor are not available, then the management process returns the corresponding read instruction to the instruction waiting queue. Provided that the various segment names have been correctly allocated, the memory manager auto-

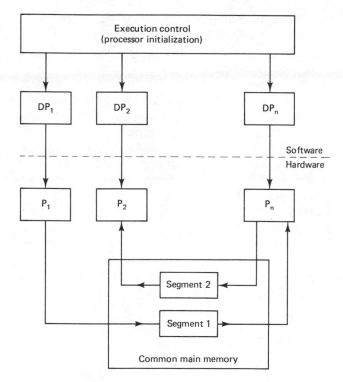

Figure 3.4. Synchronization by Logical Addressing

matically ensures that the desired flow of data occurs between the processors. The synchronization can be made optionally at segment level (a segment can only then be read after the writing processor has released it) or at tuple level (as soon as a tuple has been written, it can then be read). The second technique allows a further enhancement of throughput.

Synchronization by means of logical addressing automatically guarantees optimal data flow between the processors, as the main memory data segments employed for data exchange act as FIFO buffers and thus enable good processor utilization and a correspondingly high throughput.

3.3.1.4. The main memory: hardware structure and interface. The core of the main memory (MAM) system is formed by a large data memory with a net capacity of 1 Mbyte. To keep costs low, relatively slow dynamic memory chips are employed. Word-oriented operation (4 bytes in parallel) enables the required interface data rate of 8 Mbyte/s to be achieved. The large word width also reduces the proportion of memory capacity used to provide error-correction redundancy.

The main memory manager processor employs the same board assemblies as the other RDBM processors, whereby the internal instruction set is, of course, matched to the specific task by special microcode.

A command directed to the main memory manager initially arrives via the instruction bus (IB) in a command waiting queue (Figure 3.5), which is realized as a buffer memory having FIFO characteristics. If the current command is not executable at that moment, because for example the required data are not yet available, the command is again attached to the waiting queue by the processor. As the logical address space is not to be limited by physical memory size, a page-swapping technique must be implemented that exchanges pages between the main and secondary memories. Instructions that are concerned with page swapping are routed straight to the processor, bypassing the waiting queue. This is necessary to prevent deadlocks that would occur if the waiting queue contained also commands that were executable after pages had been swapped.

If the processor encounters an executable data transfer command, then the logical address must be transformed into the physical address. To achieve this, the memory manager stores the appropriate information, including the segment tables which contain all information pertaining to segments, and the frame description tables which contain the necessary information on the pages currently occupying the individual frames, e.g., the start addresses of

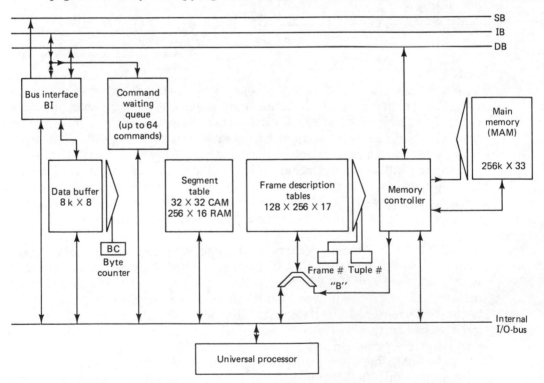

Figure 3.5. Structure of the Main Memory Manager Hardware (MAMM).

the tuples within a page. To prevent a deterioration of the throughput due to address transformation, the time required here must not exceed the average time needed for data transfer. To achieve this, the segment and frame description tables consist of not only RAMs but also processing units, which, after receiving corresponding operation codes and the accompanying parameters, are able to perform autonomously the required read, write, and search operations.

Figure 3.6 shows in some detail how the address transformation is performed. For the sake of clarity only the details important for the following example are outlined. Assuming that the command extracted from the command waiting queue by the processor is "GET NEXT TUPLE OF SEGMENT 'SUPPLIER' ", the processor will address the segment table and load the segment name into the comparand register of the associative segment name table. Assuming that the current segment was previously declared, its name is stored in the segment name table. Thus, as a result of the compare operation, a match vector is generated in the response register, in which the bit corresponding to the loaded segment name is set. In the actual implementation the associative segment name table is not a content-addressable semiconductor memory, but a hardware-implemented mapping device employing a hash function.

The address for accessing the segment description table is gained by concatenating the encoded match vector and a displacement that depends on the operation to be performed by the memory manager. In case of a "GET" operation the displacement is set such that the so-called read pointer of the relevant segment is read. This pointer consists of the number of the frame holding the current page of the relevant segment and a tuple number. The latter designates the tuple to be read within the current page. After the reception of the read pointer from the segment table, the processor is able to find out the physical address of the tuple to be read. By means of the frame number the relevant frame description table is selected, whereby the tuple number forms the address within the table. As already mentioned, the frame description table, in addition to other information, also contains the tuple start addresses. These tables are set up automatically by decoding on the fly the delimiter characters used to separate the different data partitions, such as tuples and attributes (see Section 3.3.6.1). Whenever the delimiter "B" (= beginning of the tuple) is detected on the data bus during write operations—i.e., whenever a new tuple is written to main memory—the 13 least significant bits of the current main memory address are stored in the frame description table selected by the 7 most significant address bits (128 page frames, each of 8 Kbytes).

The processor now forms the physical tuple start address by concatenating the frame number and the start address read from the frame description table. The address transformation is completed by reading the succeed-

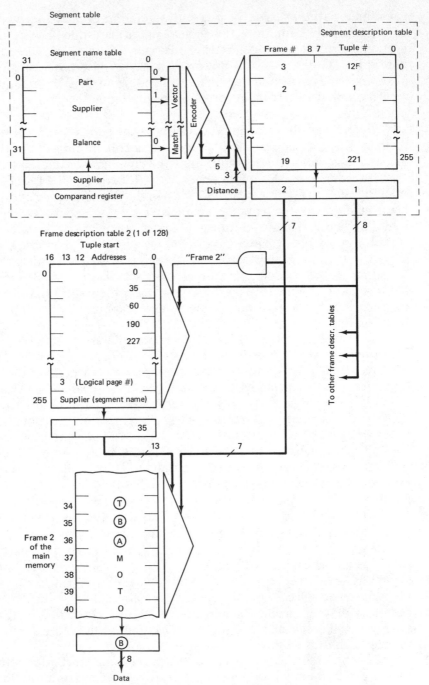

Figure 3.6. Address Transformation

ing start address in order to compute the tuple length key. The processor then directs the read or write command to the memory control, giving the physical address and length key, and increments the tuple number within the read pointer stored in the segment description table. The memory control synchronizes with the memory the processor that sent the current command to the main memory manager in accordance with the protocol of the data bus, over which it then autonomously performs the data transfer. Any necessary error correction is carried out during read operations. By virtue of the data paths specially adapted to the respective operations and the use of special hardware components (e.g., fast comparators, quasi-associative access using hardware-implemented hash coding), the operations can be performed considerably faster than would be possible for the processor solely under program or microprogram control via the general-purpose processor I/O ports.

We now return to Figure 3.5. The bus interface enables the loading of the processor's program store, whereby this function is actually unnecessary, as the manager is a permanently interpretative processor. The program code is nonetheless held in a RAM so as to allow other algorithms to be tested or time measurement functions to be incorporated, without having to make alterations to the hardware (e.g., replacement of a set of ROMs). The program code of the main memory manager has therefore to be loaded once in the context of the RDBM starting-up procedure. Furthermore, the bus interface allows the processor to output commands (in this case directed at the secondary memory manager during the handling of page swapping) and status reports (to the DABS). The DABS also has the facility via the bus interface of interrupting and aborting the processing of current programs by means of privileged commands. Finally, all data to and from the data bus pass through the bus interface.

The data buffer allows the manager processor to perform operations on the data itself. Thus the manager is treated by the main memory control as being the same as the other processors. An example of an operation on the data themselves is the generation of the physical sorting of the tuples within a segment. To this effect, the sort processor (SOP) supplies the tuples' start addresses in the correct order. Tuples with duplicate keys are also marked.

The main memory manager provides the DABS with an interface with which it can create and delete segments, unload particular data, or influence the page-replacement strategy at the segment level. In addition, statistics operations are available. The processors are offered a logical interface with automatic synchronization. Tuple-by-tuple accesses are supported. The page-swapping process with look-ahead techniques ensures short access times. Specific processor requirements are also catered to, such as data access in loops with the interrecord processor (IRP) during join, and the processor (RUP) during update.

3.3.2. The Secondary Storage System

3.3.2.1. Physical and logical addressing.   The storage of mass data requires the use of external devices, as amounts of data realistic in a database environment cannot be held in a RAM. Only disks offer low cost per bit and nonvolatility, combined with tolerable access time. However, data cannot be manipulated directly on the disk, as the relevant part of the database first must be loaded into a RAM, e.g., the main memory of RDBM. Thus, the logical designation (e.g., name of a relation) of the relevant part of the database that is given within a user task has to be mapped to the corresponding physical (page) addresses of the secondary memory in order to be able to perform the load operation. Moreover, the secondary memory space is to be allocated automatically and dynamically, as the contents of the secondary memory are not constant.

These requirements are fulfilled by conventional file management systems, but an investigation of these systems revealed that the space required for administrative information was considerable in relation to the total space available. In view of the continual reduction in the prices for secondary storage capacity, this is not so much a decisive disadvantage from a cost standpoint. To be able to carry out an address conversion, the processor performing it must be provided with the relevant tables in its main memory. The greater the extent of these tables, the more often the required portions first have to be fetched from the secondary memory. The number of secondary memory accesses is, however, the decisive factor in the access time for the required data. Some conventional file management systems have the additional characteristic of scattering the pages of an intensively updated file over the secondary memory, leading to a rise in access time due to the greater number of seek movements. If "clustering" is to be achieved, then the support of the database administrator and an occasional data reorganization is necessary.

For these reasons alone, a different technique had to be developed for the management of the secondary memory. Thus from the beginning a DBS can take into consideration the design of the secondary memory manager. These requirements are, for example, the support of transaction-oriented user task processing, the provision of statistics operations to enable the optimal choice of algorithm to be made on the basis of data statistics for the task preparation, and, specific to RDBM, the support of page swapping necessary in the main memory.

A consideration of the range of tasks shows that secondary memory accesses and the consequent address conversions and other services are used with great frequency. The placement of the secondary memory manager in the DABS raises problems, as the DABS processor is a general-purpose computer which has been burdened by software modules for communication with the host, user task analysis, parsing, and optimization, control of the specialized processors, and so on. In fact, just the workload produced by the secondary memory manager in directing heavy message traffic between DABS and the calling components will form bottlenecks.

An obvious way of solving this problem would be to place the management function on an autonomous processor, as is the case with the main memory. The secondary memory therefore also receives its own logical interface, whereby the communication between DABS and the secondary memory is considerably reduced. As DABS no longer has to handle each individual page swap, it can address larger logical data units with a single command.

3.3.2.2. Structure of the secondary memory manager.

The structure of the secondary memory manager (SEMM in Figure 3.7) shows the concept underlying this element. It is strongly similar to that of the main memory manager. The processor unit is also connected via the bus interface with the RDBM bus system. Commands arriving from DABS or MAMM are deposited

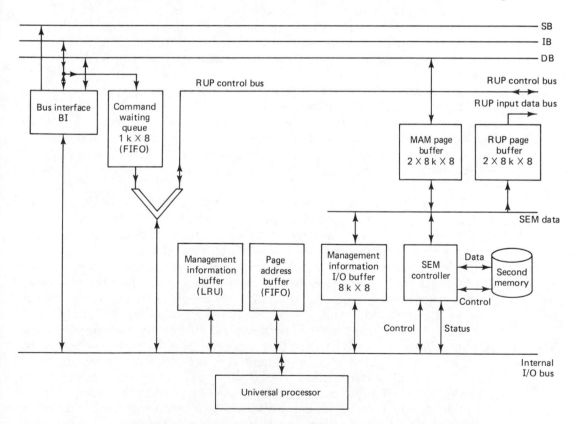

Figure 3.7. Structure of the Secondary Memory Manager Hardware (SEMM).

in a FIFO buffer, the command waiting queue. If the processor is in a position to process a command, then it is extracted from the waiting queue and any necessary address conversion is carried out, using the information stored in the management information buffer. If the required information is not present, it is read using the secondary memory controller and is then available in the management information I/O buffer. It is then loaded into the buffer store itself, where a least-recently-used replacement strategy is employed.

If the command embodies the task of making data available to RUPs, then, as a rule, a series of physical page addresses have to be derived, which are deposited in the page address buffer. Whenever the RUP data buffer is free to take more data and the secondary memory controller is available, a page address is removed from the buffer and transferred in an appropriate read command to the controller, whereupon the next page is loaded into the RUP data buffer. However, should a command from the main memory manager arrive, this can refer only to a particular page. Such a command always has priority over the processing of the page address buffer and is carried out as soon at the MAM data buffer, which contains a page buffer for each transfer direction, is free and the secondary memory controller is available. Commands from MAMM must be processed with high priority, as they are frequently connected with page replacement in MAM due to insufficient main storage capacity and are therefore necessary to release deadlock situations blocking MAM.

Commands sent by RUPs via the RUP control bus are processed with even higher priority. These deal with, for example, locking requests in the context of update operations. The secondary memory manager transmits information over the same bus as to whether the locking request was granted. Fast response to these commands is important, as the data flow to the RUP data buffer is blocked during this processing interval.

3.3.2.3. Functions of the secondary memory manager.

The most important function of the secondary memory manager is the conversion of the logical designation of quantities of data into their physical addresses and assembly of the data in the corresponding buffers. Relations, segments, and pages can be referred to at a logical level, i.e., by using their names without caring about their physical addresses. A relation can be distributed over an arbitrary number of segments, where the values of particular attributes can serve as a distribution criterion. A possible algorithm for performing such clustering, termed *segmentation,* is described in [8]. In this way, if these attributes form a search criterion in a request, the data to be scanned by RUPs can be restricted to one segment. The segmentation therefore represents a very rudimentary access path. The pages of a segment are numbered consecutively, but these numbers serve only to provide the linkage among the pages of one segment. It can no longer be guaranteed that a tuple occupies a definite position within a particular segment. The logical interface not only supports the search function, but also simplifies the exchange of pages within MAM.

The secondary memory manager is a processor executing a constant program code, which is interpreting the commands and accompanying parameters received from the other RDBM components. It was, however, designed with such flexibility that it can be adapted to the current application during system generation by the specification of a few parameters (e.g., mean segment size, available secondary memory capacity). The memory management algorithm ensures that the pages of a segment that are frequently accessed in connection with one another are stored in physical proximity on the secondary memory, thereby avoiding large seek movements. This also applies to shadow segments, which are stored in the neighborhood of the original data to be updated.

The shadow segments are required as part of the transaction-oriented processing of user tasks, the support of which can be seen as the second important function of the secondary memory manager. To be able to perform update operations, including system-enforced data consistency, the manager allows the setting of locks at page level. It deletes all the shadows generated by a transaction if the transaction is reset. If a transaction is successfully completed, then the manager propagates the shadows of this transaction to the database in a pseudoatomic operation. Propagating the shadows only requires updates in tables held in the management information buffer, which is supported by batteries so that the tables will also survive a power failure. The sequence of updates within the tables is such that after a system crash a repetition of the commitment command that was not yet completed at crash time within the recovery procedure will result in the desired state of the database. Besides this, the secondary memory manager provides statistics operations for the investigation of the current state of the data and time measurement functions.

Initially, certain hardware components will only be simulated by a program package. This package runs on a small general-purpose computer, which also functions as a disk controller.

3.3.3. Data Filtering

One of the basic database operations is that of searching for data items among quantities of data held in a mass storage device. In such cases there are large amounts of data, which have to be filtered to give the relevant information. In addition to various possible access-path strategies, this can also be achieved directly by quasi-associative access, using linear search based on simple comparison operations. This search process can be performed in two possible ways: either synchronized with the data stream read from a sequential memory device (such as a disk), i.e., on the fly, or fully decoupled via intermediate data buffers.

3.3.3.1. Comparison of search on the fly and search via data buffers.
In the search processor (SURE) the on-the-fly scan was employed for reasons of cost, as stores were comparatively expensive in the mid 1970s. Data comparisons in the RDBM are made asynchronously via a buffer store. The advantages and disadvantages of both principles can be summarized as follows.

For the on-the-fly procedure of the search processor:

1. All data must be completely searched in an order determined by that in which they have been deposited in the mass storage device. The search time is equal to the read time, given by the ratio of data quantity to data rate.
2. A search match provides only the address for the subsequent access of the actual data.
3. Constraints are imposed on the instruction set by the "fly-past" of the data. Neither jumps over irrelevant data nor repeated processing of data read are possible.
4. Parallel processing can be achieved only by performing separate search tasks in units operating in parallel.
5. The exploitation of the potential degree of parallelism depends on the number and complexity of the concurrently available queries.
6. The allocation of data to the processor units is implicit in the structure (all of them see the same data). The hardware is thus reduced by the savings in intermediate data storage and data request mechanism.

The following aspects apply to the application of buffering and asynchronous data processing:

1. The data, buffered in a RAM, can be searched at random according to an optimized sequence.
2. The relevant data themselves are directly available for further processing.
3. Asynchronous processing enables complex instructions (e.g., arithmetic operations) to be realized, whereby repeated access to individual attribute values is possible.
4. Several processors can be employed in parallel to perform the identical search task concurrently on different tuples. Each processor may execute more then one query on the stored tuple.
5. The potential degree of parallelism is determined by the number of search processors.
6. The data are distributed on demand to the individual processors; i.e., the allocation process must be catered to explicitly. Additional hardware is therefore necessary, in the form of supplementary buffer stores and request mechanisms.

3.3.3.2. Restriction-and-update operations in RDBM.   In RDBM, relevant tuples are selected by applying qualifying conditions. The tuple qualifications on a relation are directly interpreted by the restriction-and-update processors in the form of qualifications on attributes, these being the smallest addressable components of a tuple.

A search operation requires the cooperation of three independent hardware components: the secondary memory manager, the restriction-and-update processors, and the main memory manager. The atomic software and hardware operations performed and the control flow are illustrated in Figure 3.8. Searching is one of the elementary database functions (see Figure 3.15) implemented in RDBM. There is thus an individual software subroutine responsible for supervising restrictions—the search execution module—which forms part of the database supervisor's control software. On activation, it has to notify the abovementioned hardware components via the corresponding

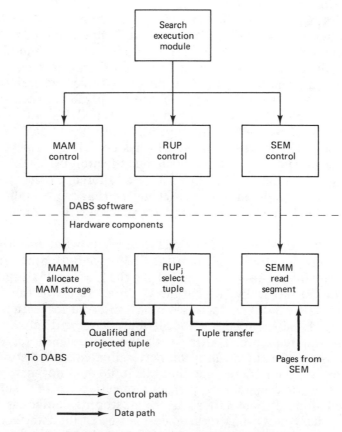

Figure 3.8. Control of Restriction Execution

control processes, which also form part of the operating system, being adjacent to the software/hardware interface.

Initially, the main memory manager is activated. A name for the relation forming the results of the restriction operation is inserted into the main memory directory (segment table), and free storage may be allocated if necessary. This allocation may also be performed automatically, when the results are ready for transfer to the main memory. The main memory manager is now ready to receive tuples from the restriction-and-update processors.

In a next step the secondary memory manager, which handles allocation and management of the secondary memory, is activated. This activation involves the reading of the segments relevant to a query and thus of the corresponding pages. After determining the addresses of the physical pages in the secondary memory, these are read page by page into the RUP page buffer using a double-buffering technique (Figure 3.7).

Finally, the restriction-and-update processors must be supplied with the qualification expression itself. A set of standard elementary qualification predicates has been implemented, including tests on attributes involving arithmetic computations. When all RUPs have finished execution, successful completion is in turn notified to the search execution module.

All restriction and update processors execute the same program on different data, more precisely on different tuples, whereby one program may contain several queries. Thus, if the workload on each individual RUP becomes small, the total throughput of the RUPs will become large, being limited only by the rate at which data can be extracted from the secondary memory. The system will thus always be able to achieve the best response time attainable with the installed hardware. By changing the number of RUPs, the database machine can be tailored to the desired performance ratio. It is the intention of the concept that the overall throughput should reach the speed of the secondary memory (the prototype is geared to 8 Mbyte/s).

After the initial loading of the query program into the RUP, the data is extracted tuple by tuple from the SEM page buffer into an input store using the principle of task quoting. During the loading of a tuple a pointer table is set up automatically, which allows direct access to the different attributes of the current tuple. In this way, as observed in Section 3.3.3.1, a RUP is not restricted to processing the attributes consecutively but can rather use an optimized sequence, starting with the most significant qualifications. The processing of a tuple can often be terminated after testing only a few bytes, if these suffice to determine that this tuple does not match the query.

If a tuple matches a query, its specified attribute subset is selected and stored in an output buffer. As a final step its content is transmitted to the main memory. Owing to the logical nature of the interface, merely the specified name of the target relation is needed in order to allocate the storage space in the main memory. This allocation is dealt with by the main memory manager (see Section 3.3.1.4). Thus another form of parallel processing is possible in the RUP: during data transfer to the main memory the next tuple can be loaded from the page buffer and scanned.

3.3.3.3. Hardware structure.

These considerations lead to the overall structure of the restriction-and-update processor shown in Figure 3.9.

The structure of a RUP consists of two major parts: the microprogrammed universal processor and individual hardware dedicated to the particular function of the processor. This individual hardware essentially comprises a memory to store unqualified data input from the secondary memory (tuple buffer), enhanced by a pointer table for attribute addresses, an output buffer for collecting selected attributes of qualified tuples ready for transfer to the main memory, and additional logic that interfaces the RUP to the secondary memory.

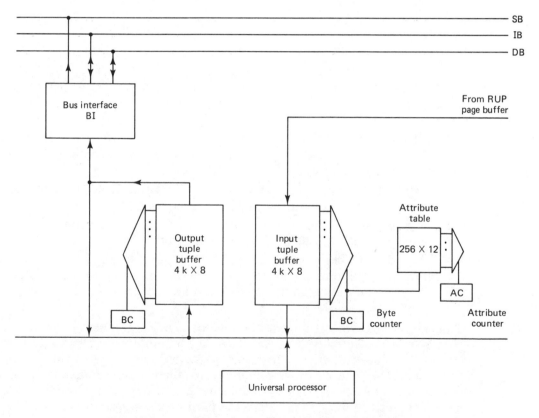

Figure 3.9. Structure of the Restriction-and-Update Processor (RUP)

3.3.4. Sorting in RDBM

The implementation of all relational interrecord operations can be effectively based on sorting. A sort processor SOP has therefore been designed that is able to support both the internal and external sort operations. It essentially consists of special-purpose hardware, controlled by its own internal microprogram unit, which autonomously carries out the various phases of the sort. Overall control of the sort process is provided by macro commands issued by the built-in universal bit-slice microprocessor unit responsible for overall control of a sort task.

3.3.4.1. The sorting algorithm.

A general consideration of the various sort algorithms showed that an address table list sort using a merge procedure appeared to be most compatible with the RDBM environment.

A four-way merge reduces the total number of comparison accesses on a set of n tuples to

$$\left(\frac{n}{2}\right) \log_2 (n)$$

Each merge operation involves an elementary sorting loop consisting of the following steps:

1. Selecting the largest/smallest of four sort keys at the head of the four already sorted input strings in a single operation using a built-in four-way merge selection unit.
2. Chaining the address of the corresponding tuple so selected to the address of its predecessor via the link address table.
3. Fetching the successor of the largest/smallest in the corresponding input string with the aid of the link address table.
4. Should there be no successor (i.e., the input string is exhausted), then the corresponding input to the four-way merge comparison unit is blocked and only the remaining strings are merged.

This process is repeated until the end of the merge pass, when the four strings have been merged to produce one complete string. Starting with strings of one element, the first sort pass produces sorted strings, each of four elements. These strings are input to further sort passes to produce strings of 16, 64, 256, . . . presorted elements. A maximum of 4096 sort keys can be completely processed within the hardware configuration.

3.3.4.2. Hardware structure and interface to the common main memory. The tuples to be sorted are held in the common main memory. The sort processor merely contains a table of main memory address pointers to these tuples. This address table is initially built up automatically by the main memory manager while the main memory is being loaded with the tuples from the secondary memory; it is then transferred to the sort processor in the sort initialization phase. As the elements of this pointer address table refer to the begin marker of a tuple, it is only necessary to stipulate that the sort key starts at the beginning of the tuples. This requirement can be achieved by a standard routine inside the RUP, which performs the appropriate exchange of attributes within the tuple. This operation does not entail any additional overheads because the tuple normally passes from secondary to main memory via the RUPs (Figure 3.2).

Clearly, it has to be ensured that the address table remains consistent during the whole of the sort procedure. In other words, the pages reserved in main memory for the tuples to be sorted have to be resident for the entire period during which they are subject to random accesses. This type of access differs from the page swapping that is normally performed by the main memory manager.

The maximum number of allocated pages that can be resident in the main memory at one point in time constitutes an upper limit to the size of the internal sort operation. The maximum number of tuple pointers that can be accommodated in the sort processor hardware forms another limit.

The interface to the main memory needs both address and data paths. In the initialization phase of the sort procedure, the main memory address table has to be transferred to the sort processor address and link table. After this operation, carried out as a fast block transfer, the sort can start. Whenever the sort algorithm needs to read part of a tuple, the relevant address is passed to the main memory via the address path. The corresponding tuple data bytes are then received by the sort processor via the RDBM data bus (DB). To take account of the high random-access activity caused by the sort processor, these addresses are multiplexed directly into the main memory control with the aid of a special address path, in the form of a parallel address bus (AB). The priority for this direct access is to be set at a fairly high level.

After the sort procedure is completed, the content of the sort processor internal link table is used to return the main memory addresses of the tuples in the sorted order. This is also performed via the special address bus. As the main memory manager generates the physical sort order while receiving this address sequence (involving data manipulation within the main memory), this transfer is performed by a handshake mechanism, rather than in block form. An additional part of each address is a single bit of information as to whether a tuple represents a duplicate of its predecessor. If the sort task specifies "duplicate elimination," then the sort processor automatically ignores duplicates when outputting the sequence of addresses.

The main hardware components are shown in Figure 3.10:

The address table containing the tuple main memory addresses, the internal table link addresses between tuples during the sort, and an additional bit indicating whether successive tuples have duplicate keys.

A cache memory of 4 × 16 bytes to store the current portions of each of the four keys being compared to determine the largest/smallest (comparison is thus from left to right on a "slice-by-slice" basis).

A fast, parallel four-way merge selection unit with a comparison window of two bytes, implemented in Schottky TTL technology, which in turn receives two-byte slices from the cache memory.

An anchor address table to store anchor link addresses pointing to the top of the sorted strings generated during a sort pass, which are then used to access the strings in the subsequent sort pass.

Microprogrammed sort control logic, whose microprogram consists of 256 words, each of 128 bits.

An internal bus to/from the appropriate universal bit-slice microprocessor (see Section 3.2.4).

3.3.4.3. Timing considerations.

The overall control of the most elementary cycles is performed by a microprogram, which activates the operations within an elementary sorting loop, such as read/write access to the address tables, loading the merge comparison unit, and updating the link addresses. By using fairly fast circuitry where possible, the networks, memories, and registers can be clocked at 8 MHz. The merge selection unit is constructed with parallel comparator devices in Schottky TTL technology. The time needed for the sort operation depends to a large extent on the characteristics of the sort keys (e.g., length, value distribution, and the number of attributes). For a maximum number of tuples (4K) the minimum sort time can be estimated as follows:

The elementary sorting loop within the sort processor (see Section 3.3.4.2) requires a processing time of 3.5 μs. In addition, data access and transfer time takes 1.5 μs. Thus the total sort procedure requires

$$\left(\frac{4096}{2}\right) \times 12 \times 5 \ \mu s = 123 \ ms$$

3.3.4.4. External sorting.

The external sort situation is similar to the situation immediately before the last sort pass of an internal sort is about to commence. Given that a number of (internally) presorted strings of tuples

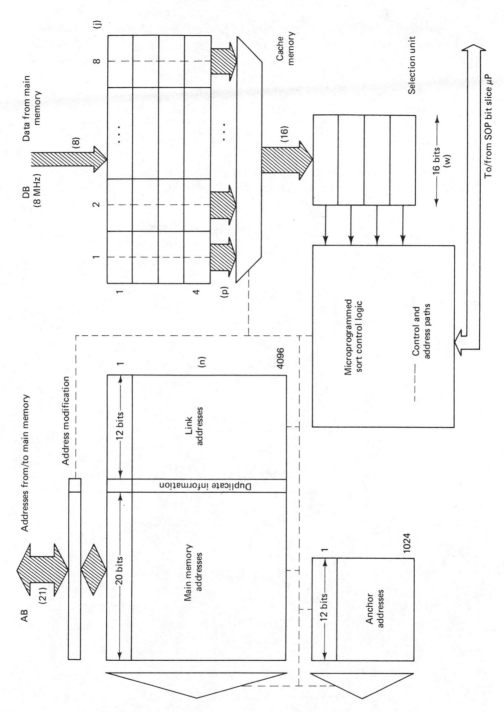

Figure 3.10. The Main Components of the Sort Processor

are situated on segments within the secondary memory, it is then possible to store portions of them consecutively in the main memory, for instance in groups of 1024 tuples, each equal in length to one-fourth of the internal address table (Figure 3.11).

These presorted strings are to be merged by the SOP. For a merge pass in an external sort, the exhaustion of the portion of an address chain in the address table does not lead to a blocking of the corresponding merge string, but rather to a request to provide the next portion of the segment containing the string.

Before this portion can be loaded in the address table, the linked addresses currently occupying the segment must be output and appended to

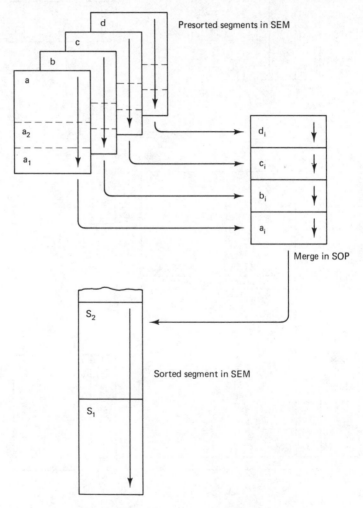

Figure 3.11. The External Sort Procedure

the end of the string already produced by the current merge. This is achieved by outputting the whole of the linked address sequence in the address table, starting with the current anchor address for that string, up to the end of the exhausted portion. The main memory then rearranges the corresponding tuples physically in the correct order and appends them to a target segment in secondary memory. After this, the main memory fetches the next portion of the exhausted string and transfers the corresponding addresses to the appropriate portion of the sort processor address table. By using a suitable sort strategy comprising many merge passes, an external sort can be performed without any limitations on the size or number of the presorted sequences. The database supervisor system (DABS) retains overall responsibility for the management of the entire external sort procedure.

3.3.5. Interrecord Operations

One of the basic design decisions of the RDBM was to employ specialized and thus distinct processors for different classes of operations. All intra-record operations, such as the comparison of attribute values or the calculation of arithmetic expressions involving the attributes within one tuple, are performed in the RUPs—that is, in conjunction with I/O to the secondary memory. If more than one tuple simultaneously form the arguments of an operation, this is performed in a separate processor. Two processing units in the RDBM handle multiargument operations: the sorter subsystem as described in Section 3.4 and the interrecord processor (IRP), which performs all interrecord operations other than sorting.

The main functions offered by the IRP are the joining of relations, the evaluation of aggregate functions (e.g., the calculating of the average of an attribute, maximum, minimum, sum), and the evaluation of the set-comparison operations of SQL (which are used to perform the relational division and evaluate universally quantified expressions). In contrast to the RUPs, the main assumption concerning the data to be processed by the IRP is as follows: all data have to be accessible via the main memory manager. This implies that before an interrecord operation may be commenced, an intermediate relation has to be created in the main memory. This is, however, the typical manner in which interrecord operations are scheduled; e.g. a restriction of relations will in general precede the join. The IRP reads tuples from relations via the logical main memory interface [in particular: GET.TUPLE(rel), SET.CURSOR(rel), READ.CURSOR(rel), PUT.TUPLE(rel)]. As already discussed, this kind of object-oriented addressing allows for a data-flow implementation of several sequences of operations. A simple example is given below:

Let R_1 be an "order entry" relation:

$$R_1 = \text{orders (cust\#, part\#, quantity, } \ldots)$$

We are looking for a list of all orders of a particular part ("*xyz*") and the total quantity ordered. While the RUPs are evaluating R_2 according to the qualification part# = "*xyz*", the IRP already begins calculating the total of the "quantity" attribute. As soon as an intermediate tuple (cust#, part#) has passed the qualification and been stored in the main memory, a get-tuple request from the IRP will be performed. Since the secondary memory I/O is slower than access to the main memory and the activity of the IRP CPU, the result relation and the aggregated attribute value will be available shortly after the scan of R_1 by the RUPs is complete. This example is very simple but nonetheless serves to demonstrate the principle. Most interrecord operations may be executed by employing this kind of concurrency. The join and the relational division are discussed in more detail in subsequent subsections.

3.3.5.1. The join operation.

Since the relational join is of great importance, particularly in the context of the relational data model, the join algorithms designed for the RDBM architecture are presented in more detail.

The relational join tends to be a very time-consuming operation in conventional database systems. Thus—if the join operation is implemented at all—specific access paths are often provided to speed up the operation. However, this implies that only predefined joins can be processed with adequate efficiency. A hardware device for supporting joins has been described by [10]. However, only semijoins are supported; i.e., the resulting tuples may consist only of attributes belonging to one of the relations involved in the join.

Our main assumption is that sorting relations on the join components (sort-merge join) will guarantee efficient execution in most cases.

Analytical studies show that this assumption is justified [11]. Using the sorting device described in Section 3.3.4, the sorting process itself can be speeded up considerably.

Since data statistics (such as the number of tuples to be joined or the number of values in one column of a relation) heavily influence the performance, it is of great advantage to be able to provide different execution strategies. Each of these strategies is oriented toward a particular situation characterized by the data statistics.

The relational join is not usually an isolated operation but rather forms part of a more complex user task. In general, the relations to be joined are the results of previous restrictions on certain permanent relations. The execution of such a user task is illustrated in Figure 3.12. The particular strategy exploits the potential parallelism of the RDBM processors. The figure also shows the decomposition of a complex task into the elementary operations to be performed by the appropriate processors. Using an abstract notation, the original query may be stated as $R(Q)(A = B)R'(P)$. This means that an equijoin is to be performed on the columns A and B of relations R and R',

Result ← R(Q) [A = B] R'(P)

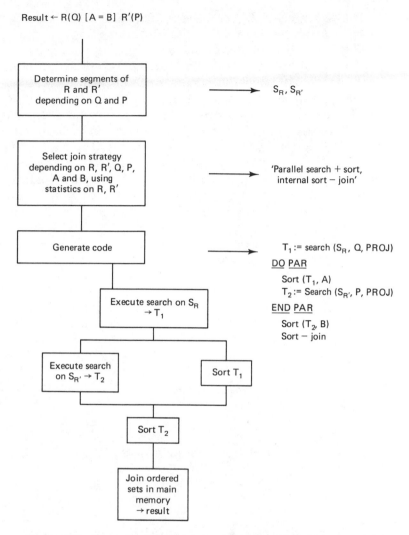

Figure 3.12. Example of the Execution of Relational Join (Sort-merge join)

respectively, after R has been restricted by the qualification expression Q and R' by P.

As already discussed, certain processing and optimization steps are performed before the code to be executed is generated. In the example depicted in Figure 3.12, it is assumed that the restricted sets $R(Q)$ and $R'(P)$ are small enough to fit into main memory. Thus an internal sort can be performed on each set. The execution is now scheduled in the following way: after $T_1 := R(Q)$ has been determined by searching the relevant segments of R, T_1 is sorted on the join component A.

The searching of R' can be executed parallel to the sorting of T_1. After sorting on B the result set of the second restriction T_2, the join can be performed by linearly scanning T_1 and T_2.

This algorithm also works for the case where T_1 and T_2 do not fit into main memory, although the performance in this case will suffer considerably. The application of an alternative strategy is therefore worthwhile.

We are not going to discuss these algorithms in detail but instead refer to [1]. Two strategies are of particular interest in the context of the RDBM: query modification and the partial sort-merge. The qualification expression P of R' will be modified by the values of the join attribute of $R(Q)$. Thus only those tuples of R' will be qualified that will participate in the join. This strategy is particularly useful if the cardinality of $R(Q)$ is small. The situation is completely different if $R(Q)$ and $R'(P)$ are very large. If they even do not fit into main memory, a partial sort-merge join algorithm can be applied. Subsets of $R(Q)$ and $R'(Q)$ are each sorted, and the IRP has to keep track of the interleaving of joining and merging. (See [1] again.)

3.3.5.2. The relational division.

The implementation of the division is now illustrated by means of an example. Furthermore, this example gives some insight into the structure of the IRP algorithm.

In addition to the relation R_1: orders (cust#, part#, quantity, . . . ,) already used above, the relation R_2: parts (part#, price, . . . ,) is also employed. A query that involves a relational division (in SQL notation) has the following structure:

> good customers := *SELECT* (cust#) *FROM* orders
>   *WHERE* quantity *GT* '50'
>   *GROUP BY* cust#
>   *HAVING SET* (part#) *CONTAINS*
>   *SELECT*   (part#)
>   *FROM*   parts
>   *WHERE*   price *GI* '1000'

or in words, those customers are searched who ordered all the parts that cost more then '1000' in quantities greater than '50'.

The usual way of evaluating such an expression is as follows: determine the temporary relation $R'_1 :=$ (cust#, part#), which comprises all the tuples of R_1 with quantity greater than '50'; sort R'_1 on cust# and eliminate duplicates; determine $R'_2 :=$ (part#), where the price of each part represented in R'_2 is greater than '1000', and finally make a set comparison between R'_2 and the subsets of R'_1 that contain part# for each of the cust#. These steps of the algorithm may be performed partially in parallel:

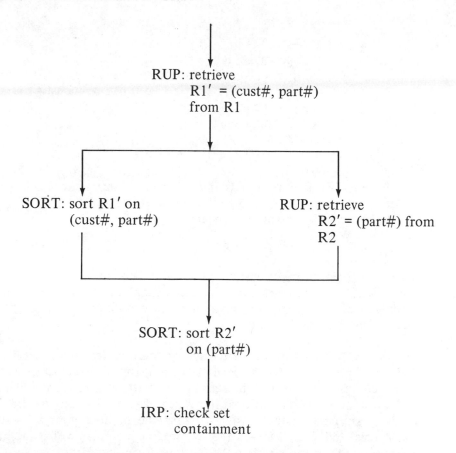

The final step is performed by the IRP according to the following algorithm, which requires R'_1 and R'_2 to be sorted and to be accessible by the main memory manager.

```
BEGIN
GET_TUPLE (R1');
WHILE tuples in R1'
    next_cust: current_cust := cust#;  /*store current cust#
                                     in a temporary variable */

    GET_TUPLE (R2')
    WHILE tuples in R2'
        WHILE R2'.part# GT R1'.part#
        GET_TUPLE(R1');
        IF R1'.cust# ≠ current_cust THEN
            cursor(R2') := 1;
            GOTO next_cust;
```

```
            FI;
         END_WHILE;
         IF R2' .part# LT R1 .part# THEN
            Skip_rest_of_this_customer;  /* read tuple from R1'
                                             until new cust# found */
            cursor(R2') := 1;
            GOTO next_cust;
         FI;
      GET_TUPLE (R2');
      END_WHILE;
      OUTPUT (current_cust);  /* the set containment check has been
                                 successfully passed */
      Skip_rest_of_this_customer;
   END_WHILE;
   END; .
```

Some overlapping of operations is provided for in the above algorithm. As the IRP has several separate input/output tuple buffers (see the next section), reading and writing to/from main memory can be performed in parallel with internal processing.

3.3.5.3. Structure and interface of the main memory.

Like the other dedicated processors in the RDBM system, the interrecord processor (IRP) also includes the universal microprocessor with its attendant CPU, I/O ports, and so on as well as additional hardware. The additional IRP hardware particularly supports data transfer to/from the main memory. Its structure is less specialized than that of the sorter, for example, which facilitates later enhancements to the number of functions it can perform.

The specialized hardware (Figure 3.13) contains two 8-Kbyte data input buffers and a 4-Kbyte data output buffer. To accelerate logical random access to the individual tuples, an internal attribute pointer address table is also provided for each input buffer, which is filled during reading into the buffer.

In this way it is possible, particularly in the context of the join operation, to employ double-buffered access to each relation involved. After processing, the result tuples are assembled in the output buffer for sequential transfer to the main memory.

3.3.6. Data Input/Output

Another dedicated processor, also forming part of the RDBM multiprocessor system, provides the data input/output conversion to the system (Figure 3.2). This conversion processor (COP) interfaces the system data bus with the controller (DABS). The processor is controlled by its own internal program, initially loaded via the system instruction bus (IB) and by short commands also

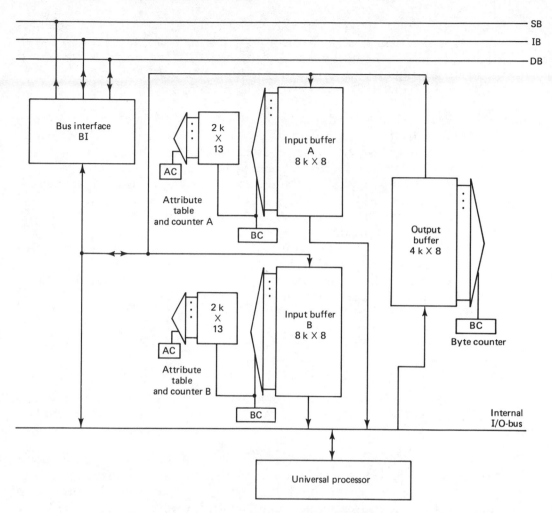

Figure 3.13.   Structure of the Interrecord Processor (IRP)

received via this bus. Feedback reports to the DABS in the form of status information are sent over the status bus (SB).

In addition to its originally conceived task of buffering to provide an interface between the different data rates of the DB and DABS, the conversion processor fulfils other functions at a logically higher level:

Conversion of data from external to internal system data format and vice versa.

Data conversion into predefined codes.

Elimination and alteration of attribute ordering within a tuple for output generation.

Segments of data are transferred between the MAM and the COP either as tuples or as pages of the main memory, while data are transferred between the COP and DABS in tuples. The internal COP processing is performed sequentially tuple by tuple. The instructions at a task level each encompass one attribute, the smallest processing unit being one byte.

3.3.6.1. External and internal data format.

All data partitions are of variable length. Data length keys are provided external to the RDBM system. These keys, which refer to tuples, attributes, values, and subvalues, are inserted in front of the respective data as a pair of additional bytes.

The individual tuples, attributes, and other partitions are separated internally by special delimiters, whose bit combinations do not occur as normal byte coding. Internal nonnumeric data are represented in ASCII code. On the other hand, numeric data are represented as floating-point numbers (BCD-encoded) in compact form, two symbols per byte. A maximum of seven bytes is allowed for the mantissa.

External to the system, nonnumeric data can be represented in either ASCII or EBCDIC code, which must be specified for each task. The following data representations are possible for numeric data:

Binary integers in two's-complement form with a fixed length of 16 or 32 bits (including sign bit).

Floating-point numbers with a fixed length of 32 or 48 bits.

Decimal numbers in packed or unpacked form. Packed form indicates two BCD numbers per byte, unpacked one number per byte (right half byte).

3.3.6.2. The hardware structure.

Like the other dedicated processors in the RDBM system, the COP comprises the universal microcomputer CPU, I/O ports, and so on plus additional hardware to support the individual operations (Figure 3.14). It essentially contains two 8-Kbyte buffers (RDBM and DMA buffer) for data transferred between the system main memory and the DABS, together with firmwired tables to support the conversion of data. To speed up logical random access to the tuple stored in the RDBM buffer an attribute address table is provided to store on-line generated attribute pointers.

3.3.7. Control of the RDBM Multiprocessor System

3.3.7.1. Structure of the control software.

The RDBM software system performs several functions and is organized in different layers. Starting from the host interface, the outermost layer is the communication subsystem. The next is the job control process, which keeps track of a user task by means of appropriate control blocks. The query translator generates code

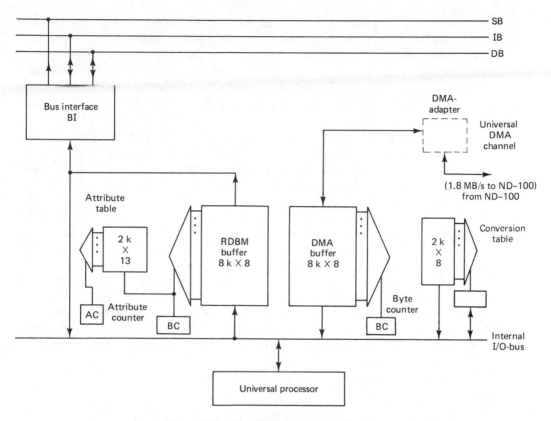

Figure 3.14.   Structure of the Conversion Processor (COP)

executable by the RDBM processors. Query translation is omitted if the precompile option is used. The principal parts of the system concern the control of tasks executed in parallel. The execution control module schedules the parallel processing of independent user tasks. Subtasking (i.e., concurrent execution of operations within one task) is performed on the next level, which consists of various database functions. Finally, one control process is provided for each processor. A control process sends commands (or executable code) to the corresponding processor on demand of a database function and handles completion and error interrupts from the processor. Operation of the RDBM system—including manual activation of hardware and software tests—is performed by an operator console process.

In the sections that follow, the components of the software system are discussed in more detail. The operating system and even the language adopted are of considerable importance in many design decisions—a fact often experienced in the implementation of complex software systems. An impression is given in the following section of the basic software and the process communication system implemented in the RDBM-used control software.

3.3.7.2. The basic software system. The RDBM system is centrally controlled by the database supervisor (DABS), which also runs the communication subsystem. In order to be flexible, a minicomputer, incorporating a standard combined realtime/timesharing operating system, was chosen for a prototype implementation. However, another microprocessor should prove to be adequate to the task. This question will be investigated in the context of performance measurements as soon as the system is running.

The 16-bit architecture unfortunately limits the address space of each process, an obstacle observed by different system implementors [12]. Message and data transfer between processors is consequently a critical factor. Process scheduling is done by the operating system realtime monitor on the basis of dynamically alterable priorities.

Considerable parts of the software can be executed in parallel. Fast response to external events—i.e., events occurring in the RDBM hardware— is mandatory. A programming language (PEARL) was therefore chosen that embodies the process concept and provides synchronization tools [13], although it unfortunately does not offer message transfer primitives such as SEND(mess) and RECEIVE(mess). Three alternatives for message communication are available through the utilization of the operating system and the PEARL run-time system: file transfer, internal devices, and shared memory. The third alternative proved to be the most efficient and therefore has been implemented.

The main loop of each process is as follows:

$$\text{DO FOREVER}$$
$$\text{AWAIT message;}$$
$$\text{process message;}$$
$$\text{END;}$$

That means that a process performs actions on demand from some other process that has sent a message. The actions may be quite different, e.g., activating a processor, cancelling an action, recovering from an error, or processing a ready message.

A mailbox system has been implemented for message transfer. Each process has its private box, organized as a queue (at present FIFO) that is accessible by all processes; i.e., it is located in a global common area. Access is synchronized by semaphores. A message box and its access routines are implemented as monitors [14]. Pointers to messages are transferred and not the data themselves. A common free-space administration—implemented as a buddy system—is used to store the variable-length messages.

A semaphore technique keeps track of the pending messages. If a message queue assigned to a semaphore is empty, the process P_1 executing the "AWAIT message" statement will be put into a waiting queue of the realtime monitor. It is then scheduled into the ready queue when some other process P_2 sends a message to P_1.

Messages from the RDBM operator console are handled in exactly the same way.

3.3.7.3. Process communication and query translation.

Since these system components are standard, we will not deal with them in detail but rather give an impression of the main design decisions.

Although most prototype systems ignore operator control, such a system component was regarded as particularly useful in a research and development environment. This is because it allows for dynamic intervention and monitoring of the system behavior, which is an invaluable help in testing and performance evaluation. A simple but expandable set of commands has been implemented. In addition to starting, stopping, and terminating RDBM, the detailed status of each process and even each processor can be requested. Tests can be dynamically activated, and the system may be reconfigured to a limited extent (e.g., changing the number of active RUPs).

The communication subsystem manages the message transfer to and from host computers, local application programs, and local terminals. Up to now, no investigations have been made into the necessary enhancements to the host computer operating system software. A study is currently being carried out into system performance at the host/backend interface. Although this communication problem is of decisive importance, no definite investigations have yet been made.

The query translator has been designed but not yet implemented. Parsing and schema operations will be realized conventionally. However, code generation and optimization differ from common software DBS implementation because of the functionally specialized hardware system employed. The code has to reflect the potential parallelism of the multiprocessor system as well as the specific structure of each processing unit.

Some preliminary investigations concerning optimization have already been made. The overall goal of the optimization procedures is to minimize the amount of data that must be transferred between secondary storage and the processors.

3.3.7.4. Two levels of executable code.

The code generated from a high-level user query (or passed directly from an application program) has two levels: the top level is interpreted by the execution control process, the bottom level is executed (or interpreted) by one of the RDBM processors.

A user task is a sequence of commands having the form:

(op code, user-ident, parameters)

Up to 20 parameters are allowed in the present implementation. Parameters may be direct or indirect—i.e., references to control or code blocks. The opcode is interpreted by the execution control process (actually three independent servers concurrently process user tasks; see the next section).

A major design decision was the selection of the opcode. One user task consists of several primitive operations that can be partially processed in parallel. In the initial design, each primitive operation—e.g., selection, sort, join—has its opcode (for explanatory reasons, this approach was used in Figure 3.12). Execution control transfers the arguments to the control processes and to the processors. Parallelism is achieved through additional control statements, in particular DO PAR and END PAR. In this initial design of the intermediate code, a user task normally has the following logical structure:

```
BEGIN
      DO PAR
            op 1, argument vector;
            .
            .
            .
            op n, argument vector;
      END PAR;
      AWAIT return codes;
      process return codes;
END;
```

There are, however, good reasons for using more sophisticated operations with inherent parallelism at this level in order to avoid having to schedule parallel operational steps completely at the level of execution control. In the following design, a complex operation that is visible on the execution control level is formed by a program (termed a database function). The scheduling of primitive operations in the RDBM hardware is performed completely within the program. Execution control now becomes extremely simple:

The sequence of commands making up the user task is elaborated by simple subroutine calls, and the subroutines perform the complex functions.

It might be argued that this conceals the problem of scheduling parallel primitive operations but does not simplify it. This is true. The main advantages are, however, that (a) the implementation chosen allows for completely transparent modifications of execution strategies and (b) the system sophistication can be increased in steps, purely by supplying more complex database functions. The following example illustrates these points.

A typical user task, which can be performed partially in parallel, is the selection of data with a directly following output of the results. Using control structures on the execution control level, the code generated would be (in drastically simplified form):

```
BEGIN
      DO PAR
            RESTRICT, arguments for RUPs;
            OUPTUT, arguments for COP;
```

```
            END PAR
            AWAIT    ready messages;
            SEND     ready to user;
            END;
```

The effect is to produce overlapping operation of the RUPs and the COP. This is a typical producer-consumer situation.

To investigate the performance gains of this kind of parallelism, it can be compared with strictly sequential processing:

```
            BEGIN
                RESTRICT,    arguments for RUPs;
                AWAIT        ready message;
                OUTPUT,      arguments for COP;
                AWAIT        ready message;
                SEND         ready to user;
            END;
```

This implies, however, changes in the code generation procedure. Using the more sophisticated database functions explained above, the code is identical in both cases. Its structural appearance is as follows:

```
            BEGIN
                RESTRICT-AND-OUTPUT,    arguments for RUPs;
                                        arguments for COP;
                    SEND                ready to user;
            END;
```

What has been changed is the coding of the database function. Different schedules can now be programmed. The subroutine has to be replaced, but the interfaces to the context remain invariant. This kind of flexibility is particularly useful in a research environment, since experiments concerning the system behavior and different scheduling strategies can then be easily conducted.

Another advantage is the increase in efficiency, as time-consuming interpretation on the part of execution control is avoided.

As yet, only the code level of execution control has been discussed. The next level applies to the processors of the RDBM system itself. Since the processors have already been discussed above, only a brief description of the general philosophy of this code level is given.

There are two types of processors: those which perform parameterized functions and those which execute different programs for different user tasks. A typical example of the latter are the RUPs. Since qualifications usually differ markedly from one user task to another, a program is generated for each restriction/update operation. This program, written in high-level code adapted to the typical RUP operations, is transferred via the instruction bus to the processor and executed. Most processes (memory management, sorting, data conversion) have a fixed program that interprets a set of arguments supplied by execution control.

3.3.7.5. Overall structure of the control software.   We have discussed individual components of the system and the general concept of communication between them; now we shall investigate their interaction.

The system is designed as a set of processes connected by queues. The upper levels are organized in a pipeline fashion (see Figure 3.15). Parallel execution of user tasks on the execution control level is achieved by three independent server processes, which have a common queue of compiled user tasks.

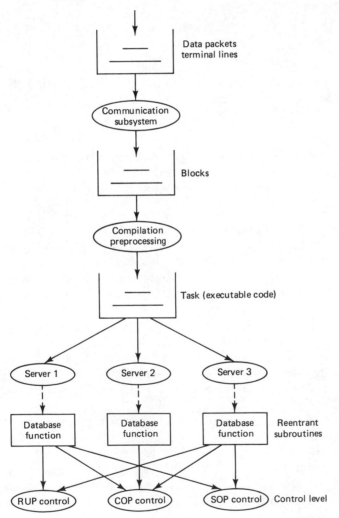

Figure 3.15. Control Software: Overall Structure

A server takes a task from the queue and executes the code described in the previous section. Multiuser service of the RDBM is realized by the independent servers. As mentioned above, scheduling of primitive operations is done within the database functions, which are reentrant subroutines activated by a server. We now ask how to achieve synchronization of the different processes, as different servers may need the same resources. Semaphores are employed for this purpose, if the processor works in exclusive mode. Otherwise (e.g., during secondary memory management), no synchronization is necessary. Deadlocks are prevented, since each processor may finish its task independently of all the others. The only critical resource is the main memory. It is, however, guaranteed that at least one page frame exists for each active processor. Furthermore, a time-out facility was implemented, so that no processor may be active longer than its scheduled time period.

Suppose a server has taken a task from the entrance queue. A command by the server is executed as described below. Figure 3.16 illustrates the technical procedure.

The server calls the database function corresponding to the opcode of the command. These reentrant subroutines may be concurrently called by independent servers. Thus the requests for a processor must be protected from one another. This is achieved by semaphores. A processor request, if granted, updates control blocks and calls the instruction bus adapter in order to transmit the program or parameter set, incorporated in the command, to the processor. Immediately after the transmission has been successfully completed, control returns to the database function. Depending on the particular logic of the function, it will now request another processor—i.e., if a parallel schedule is employed—or it will wait for a message in the message box belonging to the server. Status messages from the processors are received via the status bus adapter. The corresponding control process resets the control block entries, handles low-level errors, and returns the status to the server that executed the particular command.

3.3.7.6. Execution of a particular database function.

In the preceding section we discussed primarily the technical side of command execution. Now we describe the logical structure of query execution by means of an example, namely the database update function.

One of the major difficulties in updates (as well as insertions and deletions) is the necessity to perform all changes of data in a consistent manner. This means that the database must reflect a valid state, even after machine failures. Single updates could be implemented in a consistent manner by simple techniques. However, consistency must also be guaranteed for user transactions. A transaction can be a sequence of several elementary updates, but either all are performed correctly or none.

Furthermore, different users must be prevented from changing the same tuple simultaneously, so that appropriate locking mechanisms have to be

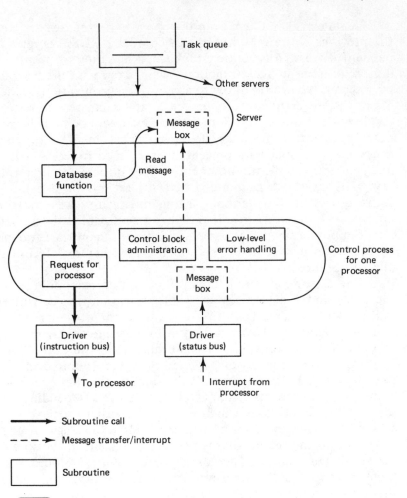

Figure 3.16. Execution of Commands: Technical View

provided. For these reasons, a more sophisticated updating scheme has been developed, which is supported by hardware functions.

Recovery from failures is ensured by using shadow pages. When a transaction is finished, the shadow pages—those pages containing the changed data—replace the original pages. The replacement is implemented as an atomic operation and it is performed when the transaction has been committed.

Physical page locks and relation locks are used to prevent update collisions by different users. Since deadlocks may occur, a deadlock detection and resolution mechanism is implemented in the update control module.

The flow of control and data during an update operation is shown in Figure 3.17. Three processors are involved in performing updates. The synchronization of their actions and their individual control flow is depicted in the figure. MAM, SEM, and the RUPs are supplied with their commands by the control system. The RUP program, for example, specifies which and how tuples are to be changed. Either tuple keys for single-tuple updates are supplied, or qualifications for updates of tuple sets are used in restrictions. Furthermore, the manner in which the attributes are to be changed is specified in the command.

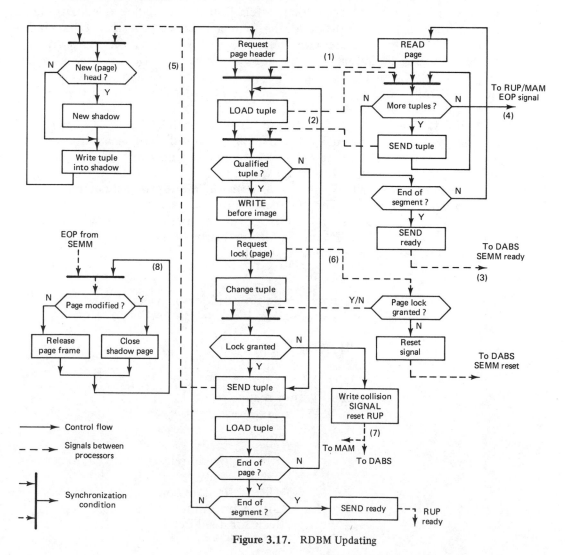

Figure 3.17. RDBM Updating

The secondary memory manager now reads the pages of the segment that might be affected by the update. For each page, the header is supplied to each RUP (1). Tuples of the current page are transferred into the input buffer of a RUP that has signaled a tuple request (2). The SEMM will give a ready message to the DABS if the end of a segment has been noticed (3). However, if only a page boundary was recognized, the RUPs are notified and the next page is read from the disk (4).

Each RUP that is given a tuple checks it for qualification. If it is not qualified, it is transferred to the MAM and stored in the shadow page (5), otherwise it is updated prior to transfer. Before the update is performed, a lock request is given to the SEMM, which manages a page lock table. If no other user has updated the page in use, the lock is granted and the particular tuple belonging to the page is changed (6). Otherwise a collision is signaled to the DABS, which makes an entry in the wait-for graph (and checks for deadlocks). Furthermore, the RUPs are reset and the shadow of the current page is released by the MAMM (7).

A different tuple will be requested from the SEMM if end of page (EOP) has not yet been signaled by the SEMM. EOP will also cause the MAMM either to release the current shadow page because no tuple of this page has been changed or else the close shadow will (8).

Until now we have described how the different processors cooperate in performing the update. The database function (see Sections 3.3.7.4 and 3.3.7.5), which initiates and controls this execution, is fairly simple. It merely activates the RUPs and SEMM and processes the returned messages according to the following control structure:

```
BEGIN
        SIGNAL update intention to lock-manager
        IF        relation in exclusive mode WAIT
        ELSE
            WRITE log record
            SEND   read-request  → SEM
            SEND   update-prog  → RUPs
            REPEAT until ready
                WAIT for message from processors
                CASE
                    = RUP      'ready'
                    write      logrec, release intention lock
                    SIGNAL ready
                    = RUP      'update collision on a page'
                    make entry in lock-table
                    check for deadlock
```

```
                        IF deadlock THEN reset transaction
                        ELSE WAIT
                     = SEM/RUP/MAM error
                        IF unrecoverable THEN reset transaction
              END CASE
            END REPEAT
       FI
     END
```

The lock manager is a process that runs on the DABS, as does the database function.

3.4. THE CURRENT STATE OF THE PROJECT

3.4.1. System Components

In addition to the actual RDBM multiprocessor system with its common main memory, further system components are employed, namely the secondary memory for the mass data, and a minicomputer controlling the RDBM (DABS), which at the same time also represents the interface to the host computer (Figure 3.2).

To save costs, the existing disk from the SURE project was employed as a mass data store. Its capacity of 72 Mbyte and its 0.8 Mbyte/s data rate do not represent the latest state of the art, but they can be viewed as sufficient for the implementation and evaluation of a prototype system. The HP 2100 minicomputer from the SURE project also serves as the disk controller, which provides the data connection to the FIFO buffer serving the RUPs. In addition to the disk control program, this minicomputer also contains the emulation of those parts of the secondary memory manager that currently are not implemented in hardware.

A NORSK DATA NORD-100 minicomputer with a 512-Kbyte store is employed to provide overall control of the RDBM system. The NORD-100 is equipped with extensive peripherals to support its additional functions of testing and development. During the development phase, extensive software is being coded at various levels, from the RDBM user interface down to the microprogram code, for the individual special processors. In addition, it runs programs for the simulation and testing of the various hardware components. As system integration proceeds, an increasing proportion of RDBM control tasks is to be assigned to the NORD-100. The programs necessary for this then run under the existing realtime operating system.

3.4.2. The State of Implementation

3.4.2.1. The hardware.   Various hardware components of the RDBM have already been developed, implemented, and tested to a certain degree using semistatic functional tests. Full-fledged tests under realistic dynamic conditions will have to await the construction of complete subsystems.

With regard to the bus system, the controllers for the instruction and status buses have been fully implemented, these representing separate board-mounted hardware components, in contrast to the data bus controller, which is embedded in the main memory manager system. The central clock generator unit together with the bus cabling and buffering have also been implemented. Two of the bus interfaces to the DABS, the instruction and status bus adapters, also exist in tested hardware form.

The basic bit-slice processor (see Section 3.2.3), exists in prototype form with its full instruction set.

The specialized hardware of the restriction-and-update processor, conversion processor, and sort processor has been implemented and tested. Although the functions required of the interrecord processor have already been fixed, the logical circuitry has yet to achieve maturity.

Some boards belonging to the main memory and its attendant manager have also been developed and implemented in prototype form, but it will be some time before all the constituent elements are complete. The algorithms inherent in the main memory manager have been simulated with a view to achieving an optimization of its special-purpose instruction set.

On the other hand, the secondary memory manager will be supported by special hardware only to a certain extent. Most of its functional components will be implemented in the software running on the minicomputer controlling the mass storage device. The relevant programs are under development.

3.4.2.2. The software operating system.   At the outermost system level, the first version of the communication interface has been implemented. In addition to control of the locally connected terminals, it supplies standardized procedures for transmission of data blocks from local application programs and remote host computers. The data link protocols for nonlocal access have not yet been put into effect. The next system layer—query translation, authorization checks, and optimization—has been designed but not yet implemented. Only the generation of appropriate control blocks for a user and his queries has been realized. Executable code that is to be interpreted at the execution control level is at present entered directly into the system.

The execution control level with three servers and a simple database function is implemented as well as the drivers of the instruction and status bus. A simplified control process—mainly used for test purposes—has also been completed. Detailed control processes for the RDBM processors as well as more sophisticated database functions are being designed. The message communication system as well as the operator process are completed. This is a key component of the RDBM operating system and constitutes the information flow inside the RDBM software system. The system is now being expanded in stages using the semantic procedures—i.e., database functions and control processes.

3.4.3. Further Project Activities

Apart from the work on the interrecord processor and on the two memory managers, the hardware component development is largely complete. The production of the commonly used boards is under preparation; some samples of multiwire board technology are already available. The individual hardware components were expected to be available by early 1983, so that the system integration could then be started on a broad front.

Parallel to this, the programs for the individual processors are being developed and realized, as a first step, exclusively at the macro level. The further step can then be taken of implementing individual program sections at a microprogram level.

We foresee extensive work in performance evaluation, in conjunction with hardware and software optimization of both the individual functions and the whole system.

3.5. ACKNOWLEDGEMENTS

The authors gratefully acknowledge the substantial contributions by the other members of the project, in particular by Hagen Auer and Silke Seehusen and by many students. Thanks are due to John Thornton, the only member of the group whose native tongue is English, for his invaluable help in the preparation of the paper.

This research project, initially supported by the Fraunhofer Society, is now funded by the Federal German Ministry for Research and Technology.

REFERENCES

[1] Auer, H., Hell, W., Leilich, H.-O; Schweppe, H., Stiege, G., Seehusen, S, Lie, J. S., Zeidler, H. Ch., Teich, W., "RDBM—A Relational Database Machine," *Information Systems*, Vol. 6, No. 2 (1981).

[2] "CAFS 800" (a short overview of the CAFS system), ICL World Headquarters, Putney, London.

[3] Copeland, G. P., Lipovski, G. J., Su, S. Y., "The Architecture of CASSM: A Cellular System for Non-Numeric Processing," *Proc. 1st Ann. Symp. Comp. Arch.,* 1973.

[4] Ozkarahan, E. A., Schuster, S. A., Smith, K. C., "RAP—An Associative Processor for Database Management," *AFIPS Conf. Proc.,* Vol. 44 (1975).

[5] Leilich, H.-O., Stiege, G., Zeidler, H. Ch., "A Search Processor for Database Management Systems," *Proc. of the 4th International Conference on Very Large Data Bases,* West Berlin, 1978.

[6] Hartwig, W., "Hardware vs. Software Retrieval—A Comparative Example," *Proc. 6th Workshop on Comp. Arch. for Non-Numerical Processing,* Hyères, France, June 1981.

[7] Hell, W., "RDBM—A Relational Database Machine Architecture and Hardware Design," *Proc. 6th Workshop on Comp. Arch. for Non-Numerical Processing,* Hyères, France, June 1981.

[8] Aho, A. V., Ullman, J. D., "Optimal Partial-Match Retrieval When Fields Are Independently Specified," *ACM Trans. Database Systems,* Vol. 4, No. 2 (June 1979).

[9] Teich, W., "The Sort Processor of the RDBM," *6th Workshop on Comp. Arch. for Non-Numerical Processing,* Hyères, France, June 1981.

[10] Babb, E., "Implementing a Relational Database by Means of Specialized Hardware," *ACM Trans. Database Systems,* Vol. 4, No. 1 (March 1979).

[11] Blasgen, M., Eswaran, K., "Storage and Access in Relational Databases," *IBM System Journal,* Vol. 4 (1977).

[12] Stonebraker, M., "Retrospection on a Database System," *ACM Trans. Database Systems,* Vol. 5, No. 2 (1980).

[13] Werum, W., Windauer, H., "PEARL—Language Reference Manual," Vieweg, 1978.

[14] Brinch-Hansen, P., *The Architecture of Concurrent Programs,* Prentice-Hall, Englewood Cliffs, N.J. 1977.

4

The Architecture of a Relational Database Computer Known as DBMAC

M. Missikoff and M. Terranova

4.0. ABSTRACT

In this paper we present the major issues of the design of a multiprocessor system for relational database management, known as DBMAC. DBMAC is designed to be connected as a backend to a host computer or as a node in a distributed database system. In the design phase, particular attention has been paid to the organization of the database for enhancing the parallelism in data processing. This is achieved by means of an attribute partitioning of the database, leading to a domain-based internal structure. DBMAC implements all the functions of a relational database management system. As a logical architecture (independent of the hardware), all the functions required in a complete system have been defined for the DBMAC. The physical architecture, consisting of a multiprocessor system capable of parallel disk accesses, is based mostly on standard commercial hardware. Special devices are few. One is included for a class of simple functions for processing data streams coming from the disks.

4.1. INTRODUCTION

DBMAC is a relational database machine with a multiprocessor architecture. The project started in 1979 in the context of the Italian "Progetto Finalizzato Informatica" (the Italian Applied Program for Informatics).

The design of DBMAC proceeded in three main areas: (1) to define a physical data storage organization suitable to be processed in parallel, (2) to design the logical architecture, including the interfaces, functions, and data structures of DBMAC, (3) to design the physical architecture, consisting of processing units, memory devices, and their interconnections with a view toward a high degree of parallelism.

The parallel execution of the transactions (characteristic of a MIMD machine) is the main goal of the system. To this end, great attention has been paid to the organization of the physical storage (known as the internal schema), in order to obtain a good response time even under heavy workload conditions.

In this introductory section we describe the data structures employed to implement the internal schema of DBMAC. We also introduce our design of the physical architecture, which will be presented more extensively in Section 4.3. The introduction illustrates the functional characteristics of DBMAC, whose logical architecture is presented in Section 4.2.

4.1.1. A Domain-Based Internal Schema

The internal schema of DBMAC has been devised to overcome two main problems generally encountered in the database machines (DBM):

> The processing power of many DBMs is related to the degree of parallel processing that they can carry out. However, parallel processing is not fully exploited because of the conflicts that occur among different transactions in accessing large data sets of relations of the database (DB).

> The join operation, even when a parallel architecture is used, remains the most complex and time-consuming relational operation.

To overcome these limitations DBMAC has adopted a physical data organization (i.e., internal schema) that includes:

1. A total attribute partitioning of the relations (thus increasing the overall system capacity of parallel processing of the database).
2. A prejoined structure that implements the domains of the DB; it contains (embedded in the structure) information regarding common values of different relations on join domains.

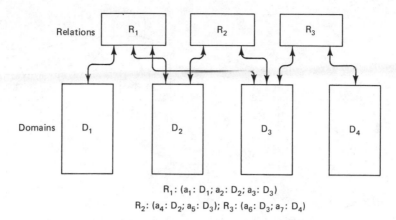

$$R_1: (a_1: D_1; a_2: D_2; a_3: D_3)$$
$$R_2: (a_4: D_2; a_5: D_3); R_3: (a_6: D_3; a_7: D_4)$$

Figure 4.1. A Sample Structure of a DP-Based Database

In the proposed internal schema, the basic data aggregate is a domain. The database is represented by the set of domains on which all the attributes are defined. The relations are represented by means of control information. The data sets, each of which contains the values of a domain and the control information, constitute the *data pool* (DP).

In Figure 4.1 we sketch a DP-based database having three relations on four domains. The control information indicates, for each domain value, the relation(s) and the tuple(s) to which the value belongs. Since the DP contains only atomic and unique values, it is likely that a value belongs to more than one relation (in the case of shared domains) and to more than one tuple (in the most general case).

It has been shown [1] that a DP-based database always takes less storage space than database in a flat-file organization (i.e., an internal schema implements the relations by means of flat files).

Values and control information are maintained in the DP using a hierarchical structure called *domain tree* (DT). The domain tree has a constant height of 4. The root (i.e., level 0) contains the name of the domain, *d*. At the other levels we have different nodal information as follows:

> level 1: node v—contains a value of the domain
> level 2: node r—contains a relation identifier (RID)
> level 3: node t—contains a tuple identifier (TID)

Each path from the root to the leaf

$$(d, v, r, t)$$

identifies an instance of an attribute. In Figure 4.2 we depict a domain tree.

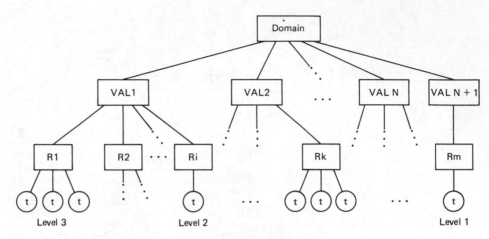

Figure 4.2. A Domain Tree

There have been different proposals for the implementation of the DP [2, 3, 4]. In any case a search on a DP produces an intermediate result (temporary relation called TIDAR) formed by an array of TIDs. In Section 4.2 we introduce some operations characteristic of DP.

4.1.2. Database Machine Modularity

Another major goal of the design of DBMAC is the machine's modularity and its flexibility with regard to system configuration on the basis of the application. To gain a perspective to our approach to modularity, let us first review database machine modularity.

Available database machines can be divided into two groups with regard to their flexibility of configuration and possibility of modular upgrade. The

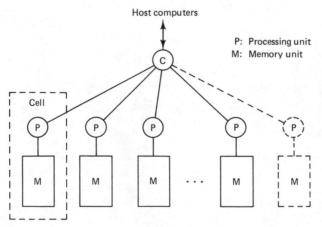

Figure 4.3. The Cellular System Architecture

first group takes the *cellular approach*. The basic architecture of this group is sketched in Figure 4.3. These architectures, as in RARES [5,6] CASSM [7, 8], RAP [9,10], and DIRECT [11], are characterized by the "functional replication" philosophy. This means that memory-processor pairs (cells) are basically similar to each other and able to perform in parallel the same set of functions. The addition of a new unit (dashed in the figure) leads to an upgrade of the system in terms of processing and storage capabilities, while the class of functions it can perform remains the same. We refer to this characteristic as *horizontal modularity*.

The second group specializes the different units for different classes of functions (*functional specialization approach*). This idea can be represented using the configuration of the DBC [12, 13] (see Figure 4.4). Other architectures of this group are RDBM [14] and SABRE [15]. In this case when we add a new element we introduce a new class of functions in the capabilities of the system, thus raising the level of the functional capability while the throughput remains basically the same. We call this *vertical modularity*.

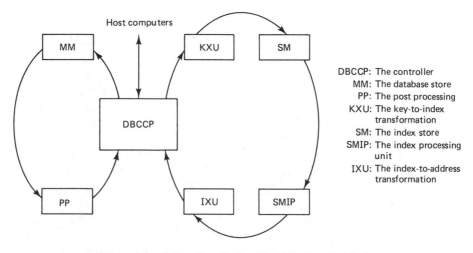

Figure 4.4. A Functionally Specialized System Architecture

The architecture of DBMAC has been designed to obtain a bidimensional modularity. Figure 4.5 shows that DBMAC allows both vertical upgrade (to expand functional capabilities) and horizontal upgrade (to expand processing power and storage capacity). This goal is achievable if in the first steps of design we keep the functional or logical architecture (LARC) separate from the physical or hardware architecture (PARC). Their independence allows us to approach their design with different philosophies. For LARC we use the functional specialization approach to define functional modules (dedicated to perform well-defined classes of tasks) and their connections. For PARC we adopt the functional replication approach to define the multi-

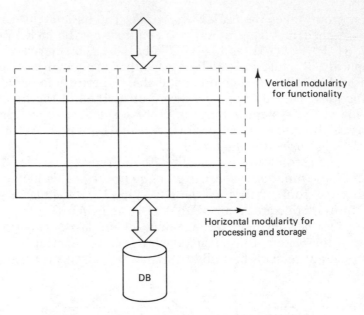

Figure 4.5. The DBMAC Bidimensional Modularity

processor structure. Using these approaches, we can design the different aspects of the system with the most desirable results. The functional specialization approach applies naturally to the logical architecture and allows us to define a modular architecture whose structure is determined by its intrinsic characteristics and functionalities. For the physical architecture, the cellular approach brings the advantage of the use of the same processing units (PU) and storage devices (SD) with replications. Moreover, the busing technique adopted permits us to bind the cells (i.e., PU-SD pairs) dynamically at run time, aiming to optimize the resource utilization.

The problem of mapping the logical architecture on the physical one is resolved by means of a distributed operating system [3, 16]. It implements functions of communication and synchronization between system processes of the logical architecture installed on different PUs. Such a distributed control avoids the necessity of a backend controller, which, in the cellular architectures, represents a critical element for the reliability and the throughput of the entire system.

4.1.3. Functional Characteristics of DBMAC

The DBMAC system can be considered as a database utility [17], in the sense that it is able to perform a complete set of database management functions. It can be connected as a backend system to a host computer or as a specialized node in a computer network. In the first case it offloads the host from all tasks inherent to the database transaction processing. In the second case it represents a sophisticated resource at the disposal of any host computer on the network.

The main characteristics of DBMAC are as follows:

Functional completeness. The system can manage transactions of the following types: data definition, data manipulation, data retrieval, and the administration of the database.

Security. DBMAC maintains a list of users of the system and their access rights in terms of the types of transactions allowable and their data-access capabilities. Moreover, in the context of a network, it maintains a list of nodes that are eligible to connect with and use DBMAC.

Concurrency control. The system can manage concurrently different transactions for different users. It provides the concurrency control necessary in such parallel activities.

Precompiled transactions. To ease repetitive interactions required by some categories of users, DBMAC maintains a library of precompiled transactions (PCTs). The user can activate a PCT by simply specifying the identifier of the PCT and its parameters.

Multilevel parallel processing. The multiprocessor/multibus architecture allows a high degree of parallelism at different levels of operation granularity:

1. *intertransaction,* i.e., concurrency control,
2. *intratransaction,* allowing different database primitives of the same transaction to be executed in parallel, and
3. *intraprimitive,* allowing different processors to cooperate for the parallel execution of a single database primitive.

The features introduced are implemented in the software of the system, as described in the next section.

4.2. THE LOGICAL ARCHITECTURE

During the design of the functional architecture, we identify functional areas that are highly independent of each other (i.e., with clear interfaces). At first we distinguish two basic sections of the system: *high system* (HS) and *low system* (LS). HS is basically devoted to the management of the transactions; i.e., it receives, validates, and prepares the transactions for execution. LS is devoted to the actual execution of the transactions; in particular, it executes the DB primitives against the physical database without being concerned with the transactions to which the primitives belong. It is the task of HS to keep track of the progress of each active transaction during the execution of the primitives.

At the first refinement, we can structure the system in four functional layers (see Figure 4.6). The first three layers (i.e., the components of HS) manage the transactions. They do not refer to the extent of the database that is being managed by the fourth layer.

The COMM layer manages the communication with the outside world, sending and receiving messages. It can be reconfigured for different protocols for both local and remote links.

The TRANS layer receives the transactions in an external format and encodes them in internal format. It verifies the validity of operands and operators. It fills a transaction skeleton with the actual parameters when a PCT is submitted. It provides a first level of scheduling, deciding which transaction will be the next to be activated—i.e., sent to the next layer.

The RELMAC layer receives the transactions in an internal format. Since the transactions refer to their data in relational operations and entities, its task is to transform them into a set of operations and entities defined on the internal schema of the database. In doing so it builds a graph that represents the best way of executing the given transaction on the DBMAC internal data structures, i.e., the data pools. The execution graph (EG) represents explicitly all the parallel computation achievable in a given transaction. The

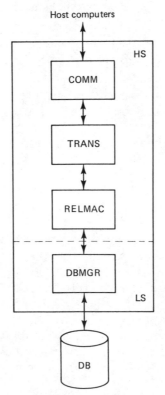

Figure 4.6. Overall LARC Structure

nodes of EG are the primitives defined on the internal schema. The second major task of RELMAC is, for each active EG, to follow through all the independent paths. For each node of the path, it activates the corresponding primitive.

In the above three layers, we have an increase of semantics, concerning the objects that are manipulated. The first layer deals with messages without being concerned with their content. The second deals with the syntax of the transactions—i.e., transforms the transaction into operations and operands. The third layer arranges the operations and operands of the transaction into its execution graph. This is the only level of HS that is concerned with the internal schema. This layered organization of HS allows a highly modular design of the logical architecture and, consequently, of the software that implements it.

The fourth layer, DBMGR, consists of all the procedures necessary to manage the physical data structures of permanent and temporary relations. The primitives of DBMGR are the only ones that access DP for search or update. The service primitives allow us to restructure DP, acting on the new schema of database.

Next we present in greater detail the logical architecture of DBMAC with its processes and system data structures (SDS). We also discuss a first evaluation of HS.

4.2.1. The Logical High System

The high system of the logical architecture will be described as a graph, where the nodes represent processes and system data structures, and the arcs represent the access rights of the former on the latter. To store the transactions entered in the system and to keep track of their progress, HS utilizes the control information in the system data structures.

SDS are of two types: The first type consists of general information (e.g., on users, sites, and schema) and is consulted mostly by the processes. The second type consists of specific information on the states of the transactions and is used mainly for communication between processes. SDSs are organized as tables in the first type and as queues in the second. The choice of queueing is aimed to render more asynchronous operations of the logical architecture, since queueing is more suitable for asynchronous operations.

The processing elements, at this level of representation, are the system process families (SPF). Each SPF belongs to a given layer and is devoted to a class of well-specified functions. It communicates with other SPFs always through one or more SDSs. In a further step of refinement, the SPFs are decomposed into the final processes.

The logical architecture HS is presented in Figure 4.7. Table 4.1 lists the SDSs with a brief description of each. Table 4.2 specifies the SPFs.

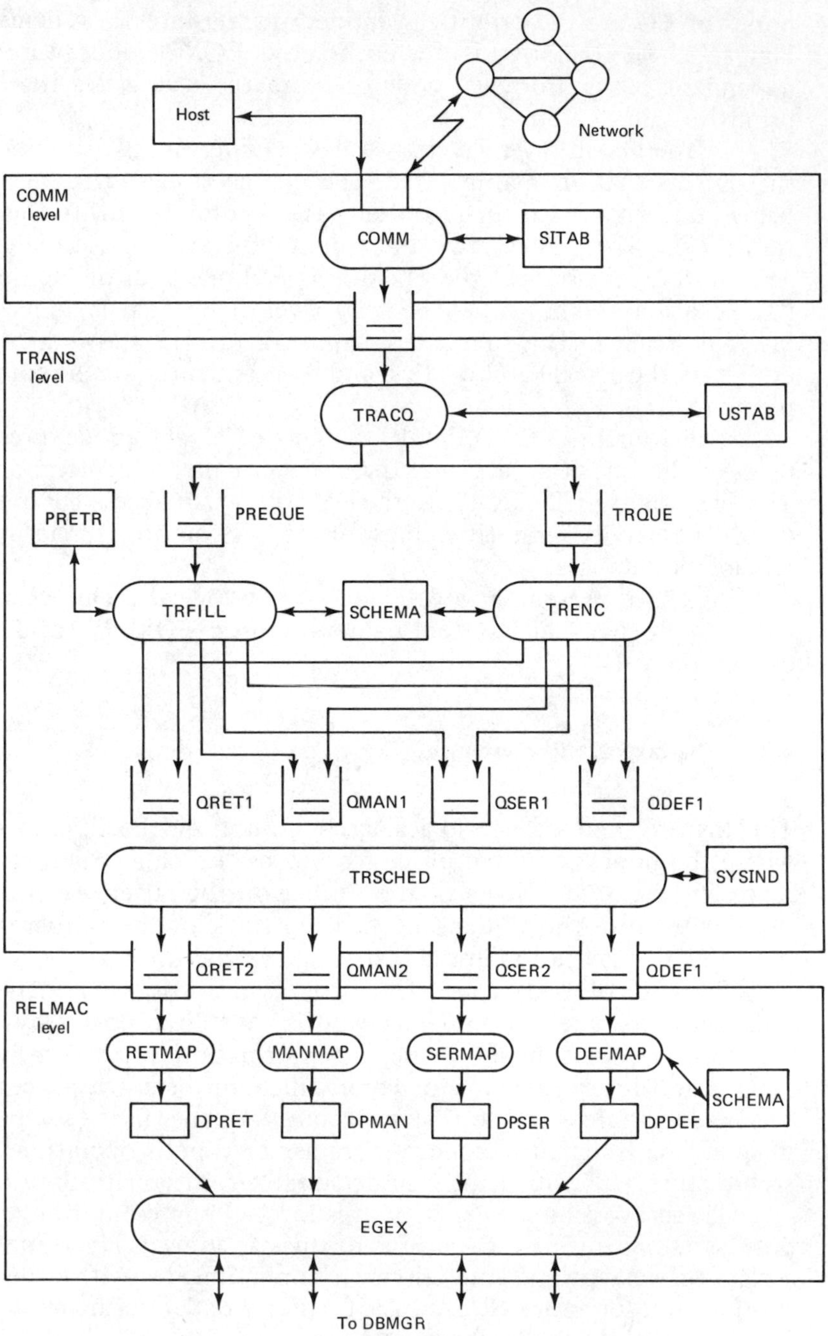

Figure 4.7. The High System of the Logical Architecture

TABLE 4.1. SYSTEM DATA STRUCTURES

PRETR	Library of precompiled transactions
SCHEMA	Schema of the actual database
SITAB	Table of the sites from where a user can connect to DBMAC
SYSIND	Table of system workload indicators
MSGQUE	Queue of arriving messages
PREQUE	Queue of precompiled transactions
QDEF1, QMAN1, QRET1, QSER1	Queues of internally formatted transactions waiting to be activated (separated by types: data definition, manipulation, retrieval, and service, respectively).
QDEF2, QMAN2, QRET2, QSER2	Queues of transactions ready to be mapped onto the data pool format for execution
DPDEF, DPMAN, DPRET, DPSER	Sets of active transactions presently executing in the system

TABLE 4.2. SYSTEM PROCESS FAMILIES

TRACQ	Transaction acquisition, user validation, transaction type selection
TRENC	Transaction validation and encoding into internal format
TRFILL	Precompiled transaction validation and parameters substitution
TRSCHED	Transaction scheduling; first level of concurrency control
DEFMAP, MANMAP, RETMAP, SERMAP	Mapping of ready transactions from an internal format to the DP format (i.e., in the form of an execution graph)
EGEX	Execution of active transactions visiting the corresponding EGs

4.2.2. Performance Evaluation of the High System

At this point we seek some quantitative evaluation of the behavior of the logical architecture just presented. In particular, we attempt to determine the time spent by HS in processing a transaction.

The main objectives of this evaluation are:

1. Identification of bottlenecks in SPF or SDS.
2. Analysis of the system-performance bounds imposed by the logical architecture.
3. Preliminary indication of allocation strategies for SPFs and SDSs on the processing units. This is essential at system configuration time in order to find for the SDS-SPF pairs the allocation that reduces the communication volume among the processing units.

To reach these objectives we developed a model in which we assign a weight to each SPF and SDS and their interactions. We assign the weight to each process on the basis of the time that it needs, when activated, for execution. In addition we evaluate, for each SDS, how much time a process spends in accessing it; the sum of all the accesses for a given SDS gives the weight of the SDS in terms of system accesses supported.

To assign the weight to each entity we have introduced two basic concepts:

1. *Transaction type* refers to a classification of the transactions depending on the operation required.
2. *Transaction intensity* measures the workload generated by the transaction and is related to the number of attributes that it involves.

We have classified the transaction types depending on the operation performed (retrieval, definition, manipulation, and service) and whether they are precompiled or not. In this manner we obtained eight transaction types, each one following a different path in HS.

To express the weights independently of the hardware characteristics, we have introduced a time measurement unit called "processing grain." The processing grain is the time required to perform an elementary action such as access to a scalar datum within a data structure. This measurement unit makes the model independent of both the hardware speed (i.e., the speed of the processors, memories, and buses) and the processor power (i.e., instruction set, addressing modes, and operation characteristics).

The logical architecture has been modeled using the following three arrays, where:

p = the number of SPFs,
d = the number of SDSs,
t = the number of transaction types.

Activation matrix (A) is defined as

$$A_{h,k} = \begin{cases} 1, & \text{if the transactions of type } i \text{ activate the process } j, \\ 0, & \text{otherwise,} \end{cases}$$

$$\text{where } h = 1, \ldots, t, \ k = 1, \ldots, p$$

Process/system data structure matrix (PSD) is defined as

$$PSD_{h,k} = f_{h,k}(I), \qquad \text{where } h = 1, \ldots, p, \ k = 1, \ldots, d$$

The function f is the number of processing grains spent by the hth SPF accessing the kth SDS when activated within a transaction of intensity I.

Process vector (*PV*) is defined as

$$PV_h = g_h(I) + F_h(I), \qquad \text{where } h = 1, \ldots, p$$

The hth vector element gives the weight of the process h, represented by its two components g and F: g is the number of processing grains spent in its internal operations; F represents the grains spent in accessing SDSs and is given by

$$F_h(I) = \sum_{k=1}^{d} f_{h,k}(I)$$

The functions f and g, assumed linear on the intensity (I), can be expressed in the form

$$a \times I + b$$

where the parameters a and b depend on the particular SPF and SDS involved. The a value refers to the cost (measured in processing grains) of the operations that must be iterated for each attribute; b is generated by the remaining operations.

The expression given for f and g is justified by the nature of the operations performed by HS: transaction recognition, analysis, and encoding. These functions are performed accessing tables and comparing elements. Their cost is independent of the transaction type and the database content; it depends essentially on the transaction expressions. The transaction type determines only the path through HS—i.e., the processes that have to be activated (see the activation matrix A).

Having quantified HS, we can then calculate some parameters as the lower bounds for the HS time (time taken by the transactions to pass through the HS). They can be obtained from the product of the two matrices A and PV defined above:

$$THS = A \times PV$$

where *THS* indicates the vector in which the kth element ($k = 1, \ldots, t$) is the HS time of the transactions of type k. The expression above assumes that the HS operates in a pipeline fashion. If we introduce some parallelism, the *THS* values can be reduced. For data-retrieval transactions (precompiled and on-line) we have obtained the result shown in Figure 4.8.

To obtain the values of *THS* when more than one transaction is in the system, we must take into account the delay introduced by the concurrent accesses to SDSs. To this end a queueing network model has been realized, which considers each process as a customer and the SDS as a server.

The proposed model for a single SDS appears to be very simple. Assuming a single-cycle mutual-exclusion arbitration strategy, we can apply the

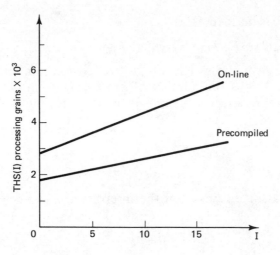

Figure 4.8. The High-System Time for Data-Retrieval Transactions

processor-sharing results to evaluate the delay in SDS access due to the congestion. Figure 4.9 shows the normalized access delay for a typical SDS, varying the congestion level with two different types of transactions.

Notice that the results obtained took into account only the logical architecture, without considering the constraints introduced by the physical one. To get more general indications of the performance of the system, we need to model both the logical and physical architectures. Nevertheless, this model appears to be useful, since it gives some preliminary indications of the behavior of the system. Besides, it can be included in the more general one.

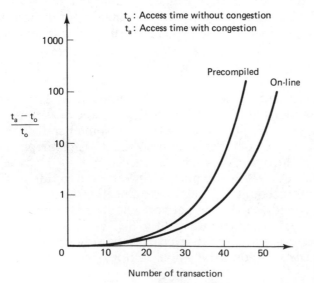

Figure 4.9. SDS Access Delay for Retrieval Transactions

4.2.3. The Logical Low System

The low system is characterized by a parallel structure and a multiple inter-connection with the upper layer. Figure 4.10 represents, at a first level of detail, the four process families that are in charge of physical database management. The two queue sets show that each activation of a process of LS is followed by an answer that allows EGEX to trace continuously the progress of the transactions.

The DP primitives operate on the basis of a complete scan of the DPs. The result produced by a primitive is represented by an array of TIDs (called TIDAR). There are three types of DP primitives:

1. Primitives that operate on a given DP.
2. Primitives that receive a TIDAR and use it to access a DP.
3. Primitives that receive two TIDARs and operate on both jointly.

These primitives are implemented using two elementary actions: selective scan to check a condition on a value and/or RID and intersection of two sets of TID.

The selective scan is performed "on the fly" during a read operation on DP. The intersection can be performed differently, depending on the size of

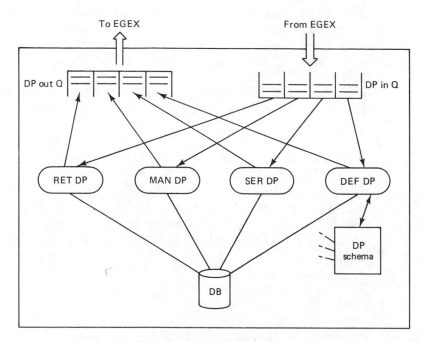

Figure 4.10. The Low-System Structure

the operands and the degree of parallelism the system can carry out at a given moment (generally this depends on the number of PUs that can be dedicated to an operation). Another operation that DBMGR is in charge of is the sort. It can be required as a preliminary step before an intersection. In general the answer to a query is represented by means of a TIDAR. A final step to associate values to TID is necessary in order to send the result back to the user in the form of a flat file.

The evaluation of the LS is heavily dependent on the database content, schema, and size and the algorithms adopted to execute each DP primitive. A first evaluation of the behavior of the DP primitives is given in [1]. A more complete analysis, which considers different alternatives for the architecture and the algorithms, is on-going at the present time.

4.3. THE PHYSICAL ARCHITECTURE

In the previous section we presented the logical architecture in terms of its tasks (SPF), data structure (SDS), and overall topology. Now we describe the physical architecture with its processing units, mass storage devices, and interconnections. The physical architecture (PARC) will be divided into HS and LS, because the computations and hardware devices of each section have different characteristics. The two sections of the system are characterized essentially by the type of data involved in the processing: exchange of small packets (transactions descriptions) and access to large tables in HS, processing and exchange of large amounts of data and disk accesses in LS. We shall introduce separately the principal aspects of HS/PARC and LS/PARC and then the complete system.

From the characteristics of the logical architecture we derive the following observations concerning the processing requirements of the physical HS:

1. The processing power required by a given SPF can vary greatly from one type of application (i.e., mix of transactions) to another and, for a given application, from one moment to another.
2. The SDS usage, which represents almost the entire volume of interprocess communication, presents a certain degree of locality; i.e., for a given SDS a limited number of SPFs are responsible for the majority of accesses.

To meet these computational requirements the following facilities must be available:

(a) Process replication on different processing units (PU) in order to reduce the bottleneck caused by multiprocessing of the same task.

(b) SDS-SPF clustering on the same PU in order to obtain a general reduction of the inter-PUs communication.

(c) Autonomous allocation of nonclustered SDSs to have them symmetrically accessed by any PU.

Moreover, it is highly desirable to be able to define the number of PUs in the system without affecting the functional performance. This means that from the users' requirements it should be possible to derive the processing power required and the configuration in terms of hardware devices (number of PUs and disks) and allocation of logical system components (SDS and SPF on PUs, DP on disks).

4.3.1. The Physical High System

From the above considerations we can derive the following characteristics for HS/PARC:

1. Modular multiprocessor architecture, fully interconnected with multi-master capabilities.
2. Two levels of buses to allow both local (intra-PU) and global (inter-PU) communications, reducing the interferences among PUs.
3. Three levels of memory:
   (a) private: in each PU, to store the programs.
   (b) public: in each PU, to store clustered SDSs.
   (c) global: connected at the global bus to hold unclustered SDSs.

Notice that the increase of memory accessibility implies the raising of access conflicts, which in turn implies the reduction of the parallelism of the system. A good allocation strategy must take into account this potential bottleneck. The HS/PARC can be sketched as in the Figure 4.11. The global bus

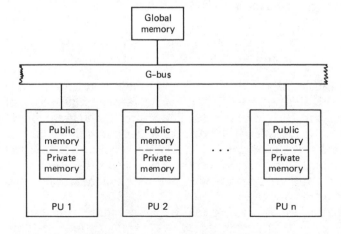

Figure 4.11. The Physical High System

(G-BUS) can be multiplexed among PUs, since the optimization of SDS-SPF clustered allocation on the PUs reduces the need for inter-PU communications. Most of the time the processing can proceed in parallel on each PU. The HS section of PARC is actually implemented with elements of the MULTIBUS (TM Intel Corp.) standard family.

4.3.2. The Physical Low System

In Section 4.2.3 we saw that the primitives of LS are based essentially on three kinds of computation acting on a large amount of data: selection, integer intersection, and sorting. Simple operations on fairly large amounts of data allow the introduction of special-purpose devices. In some cases parallel processing of the same data stream is required; in other cases parallel processing of different data streams for different instructions (MIMD operating mode) is also required. To meet these different requirements we must allow any group of processors to connect to a desired disk device (DD). We call this connection the *mass-memory bus* (MM-BUS).

A sketch of the PARC LS is presented in Figure 4.12, where the crossed boxes are special-purpose devices for on-the-fly filtering (in particular, selection and integer intersection). The communications between PUs and DDs are performed in a serial fashion. The data are transferred by means of a connection dedicated to a single DD and bused among PUs. Control information (commands and handshake packets) is carried by a control bus to which all the PUs and DDs are connected. The MM-BUS architecture and operation result from the following considerations:

1. Database applications are characterized by high data block traffic, and a unique bus can easily be saturated.
2. Serial connections can be replicated at a small cost if arbitration problems can be avoided.
3. Control information generates a very small fraction (0.1%–0.01%) of the PUs-DDs traffic.
4. The disk throughput (500–1000 Kbyte/s) can be supported at a rate of 10 MHz and handled with standard ICs.

A communication link in the MM-BUS is established as follows. A PU wishing to link with a DD delivers to the control bus a command message containing the command and the disk address. The addressed DD recognizes the command, and its local controller (IMI) queues the command. When it is ready to perform the data transfer, it sends the command-acknowledge message to the PU via the control bus. As soon as the PU receives the command-acknowledge, it establishes the connection with the data bus of the selected DD and performs the data transfer.

The proposed architecture allows as many parallel data transfers as

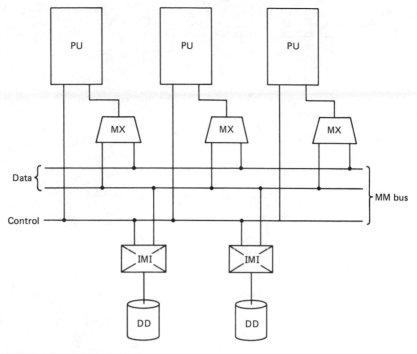

MX: Data bus multiplexing logic
IMI: Intelligent mass-memory interface

Figure 4.12. The Physical Low System

there are DDs in the system, thus reaching the highest degree of parallelism on disk data streams. Every PU can be connected to every DD with a single-bit multiplexing logic. These connections allow data broadcasting so that a given data stream can be received by multiple PUs.

In the proposed architecture the arbitration is required only for the control connection, which is unique and can be realized using well-known techniques proposed for multimaster buses [18]. Dedication of each data connection to a unique DD avoids line contention, thus allowing a low-cost single-wire bus. This justifies the proposed replication for each DD. IMI manages both the communication protocol for DD and basic functions for data stream filtering. Moreover, the IMI processing capabilities and the presence of an independent control bus (which allows command handling during disk operations) permit us to queue disk commands and to implement strategies for disk-access optimization.

4.3.3. The Physical Architecture: A Complete View

The complete architecture is composed of HS and LS. In Figure 4.13 we illustrate their relationship. Note that the most critical interface, between HL and LS, is not implemented with a connecting hardware device (i.e., a bus),

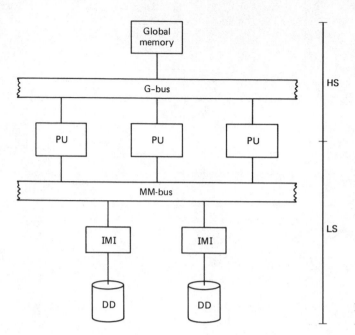

Figure 4.13. The DBMAC Physical Architecture

but instead by means of message passing among processes. This choice guarantees that the hardware does not introduce a bottleneck or problems of reliability at the most critical point of the architecture.

4.4. CONCLUSIONS

In this chapter we have presented the major features of project DBMAC. First, the parallelism can be carried out within the system at different levels of granularity—i.e., at the levels of hardware architecture and of functional architecture. The physical organization of data has been designed for this purpose.

Second, the cost reduction of the machine has been achieved. This goal is attained in two ways. The decision to use mostly standard hardware leads to a general reduction of production cost. The only "special device" adopted is the filter. Owing to its utility, the filter will soon be widely available at reasonable prices. The modularity of the architecture permits us to find, for each application, the appropriate hardware configuration, leading to a reduction of acquisition cost for the user as well as of costs related to the successive upgrades.

Functional completeness is another major feature of DBMAC. It allows the use of the system in different applications. Despite its diversity, the internal schema organization appears to be extremely effective when the majority of the queries are rather complex with a high selectivity factor (i.e., high ratio between source data and answer sizes). DBMAC appears therefore more suitable for sophisticated applications, where complex queries and low response times are required, than for applications with high rate of update or mass retrieval operations (such as airline or payroll applications).

At present the design of the system has been completed and a validation phase is taking place along two lines: (1) modeling and evaluation of the system performance with particular attention to the critical parts, (2) implementation of specific key algorithms to study their feasibility and possible alternatives. As a result, certain modifications to the design may prove necessary. After completion of this phase we plan a first version of a DBMAC prototype.

REFERENCES

[1] Missikoff, M., "A Domain-Based Internal Schema for Relational Database Machines," *1982 ACM-SIGMOD Conference.*

[2] Missikoff, M., "RELOB: A Relational Storage System," *1978 ACM SIGMOD Conference.*

[3] Missikoff, M., and Terranova, M., "An Overview of the Project DBMAC for a Relational Database Machine," *Proc. 6th Workshop on Computer Architecture for Non-Numerical Processing,* Hyères, France, June 1981.

[4] Pinzani, R., and Pipplini, F., "Organizzazione fisica dei dati su una macchina per basi di data," *1980 AICA Annual Conference.*

[5] Lin, C. S., Smith, D. C. P., and Smith, J. M., "The Design of a Rotating Associative Memory for Relational Database Application," *ACM Trans. Database Systems,* Vol. 1, No. 1, March 1976.

[6] Smith, D. C. P., and Smith, J. M., "Relational Data Base Machines," *Computer,* March 1979.

[7] Healy, L. D., Lipowski, G. J., and Doty, K. L., "The Architecture of a Context Addressed Segment Sequential Storage," *1972 NCC AFIPS Conf. Proc.,* Vol. 41.

[8] Su, S. Y. W., and Lipowski, G. J., "CASSM: A Cellular System for Very Large Data Bases," *Proc. First International Conference on Very Large Data Bases,* Mass., 1975.

[9] Ozkarahan, E. A., Schuster, S. A., and Smith, K. C., "RAP: An Associative Processor for Database Management," *1975 NCC, AFIPS Conf. Proc.,* Vol. 44.

[10] Schuster, S. A., Nguygen, H. B., Ozkarahan, D. A., and Smith, K. C., "RAP.2: An Associative Processor for Databases and Its Applications," *IEEE Trans. Computers,* Vol. C28, No. 6, June 1979.

[11] DeWitt, D. J., "DIRECT—A Multiprocessor Organization for Supporting Relational Database Management System," *IEEE Trans. Computers,* Vol. C28, No. 6, June 1979.

[12] Hsiao, D. K., and Madnik, S. E., "Database Machine Architecture in the Context of Information Technology Evolution," *Proc. Third International Conference on Verag Laige Data Bases,* Tokyo, Japan, 1977.

[13] Banerjee, J., Baum, R. I., and Hsiao, D. K., "Concepts and Capabilities of a Database Computer," *ACM Trans. Database Systems,* Vol. 3, No. 4 (December 1978).

[14] Auer, H., et al., "RDBM—A Relational Data Base Machine," *Information Systems,* Vol. 6, No. 2.

[15] Gardarin, G., et al., "Objectifs, Principes et Architecture d'une Machine Bases de Données Réparties," *Actes des Journées Machines Bases de Données,* Sophia-Antiopolis, September 1980.

[16] Missikoff, M., and Terranova, M., "EXEMAC: un Sistema Esecutivo per Data Base Machines," *1980 AICA Annual Congress.*

[17] Baum, R. I., and Hsiao, D. K., "Database Computers—A Step Towards Data Utilities," *IEEE Trans. Computers,* Vol. C-25, No. 12 (1976), pp. 1256–1259.

[18] Barthmaier, J., "Intel MULTIBUS Interfacing," *Intel Corp. Application Note* 28A.

5

An Assessment of the Query-Processing Capability of DBMAC

F. Cesarini, D. De Luca Cardillo, G. Soda

5.0. ABSTRACT

This chapter concerns the simulation of query processing in the database machine DBMAC. Owing to this machine's multiprocessor architecture and the particular scheme used to store the data (i.e., the data pool), two main query schemes are introduced to represent the machine workload. These schemes are characterized by their parallel and pipeline structure. The model of the physical architecture and of the basic operations is also introduced. The results of certain simulation experiments are obtained for the purpose of evaluating the behavior of different machine configurations.

5.1. INTRODUCTION

This paper concerns the simulation of query-processing capability of a relational database machine known as DBMAC [1]. DBMAC is a multiprocessor system based mostly on commercially available components. The disks are, however, supplied with specially designed filters to perform on-the-fly selections and intersections. A distributed executive system [2] allows various processing units to activate different procedures operating on different data, thereby supporting MIMD activity. The relations are stored on the disk devices by way of attribute partitioning. The stored database is referred to as *data pools* (DPs) [3, 4].

Performance of database machines has been evaluated by both analytical models [5, 6] and simulation techniques [7, 8, 9, 10] of DBMAC. Some evaluation of performance and the cost of the individual DP primitives in terms of bytes scanned, tested, or produced in output has appeared in [3]. A more general evaluation of data retrieval has been conducted by means of a simulation model. In fact, simulation can model much of the details of actual operations and give performance measures of the DBMAC system on global throughput and mean response time as well as individual device utilization. As a first simulation, we focus on the query execution instead of the update operation.

The simulation of query execution is designed in parallel to the development of the DP implementation and the related algorithms. An earlier version, corresponding to an inverted DP implementation and without the filtering capability (i.e., using only the standard disk devices), is described in [11, 12]. The simulator, written in GPSS V language, was then modified in order to reflect the current DP implementation, as outlined in Section 5.2.

The aim of the simulation is to validate the basic architectural choices with respect to data retrieval (involving the data pools, filters, and multiprocessor) and to give some measure of their global performance. It is also possible to analyze the performance of query processing with respect to different configurations of the hardware devices. From a software point of view, different query-execution algorithms have been tested in order to investigate the performance of the machine with respect to a pipeline or a parallel execution of a query. The influence of the submitted workload—i.e., the number of active queries and their type—is also analyzed.

The query schemes considered in the characterization of the system workload are described in Section 5.2. The simulation model of the physical architecture, the execution of the data primitives, and the execution of the queries is described in Section 5.3. The system parameters are listed in Section 5.4. In Section 5.5 we show the results of the simulation experiments. Further results referring to a larger database and a more powerful disk device are reported in Section 5.6. Finally, some remarks are made in Section 5.7 about the hardware and software features modeled in the simulation and their role with respect to the performance of the system.

5.2. THE WORKLOAD MODEL

5.2.1. Queries

We consider only queries consisting of selections of four attributes followed by a projection on a single attribute. Although simple, they are interesting to investigate from a user point of view. There are four main reasons for such

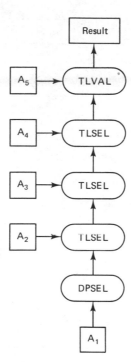

Figure 5.1. Pipeline Execution of a Selection on Four Attributes

an investigation:

1. Since we use the DP approach for storing the data, different DPs have to be searched independently, and the resulting TID lists have to be intersected together. Thus, selections may involve several DPs, whereas a join operation, which in other machines usually requires the most complex execution, can easily be done here with a single data pool.

2. There are different implementation schemes for the same query. Look at Figures 5.1 and 5.2, where the A's identify the attributes involved and where the primitives operating on the data are circled. The scheme in Figure 5.1 consists of fewer primitives and follows a pipeline approach, while that in Figure 5.2 shows an intrinsic parallelism, even if it requires more DP primitives.

3. A join operation is executed by the DPJOIN primitive, which has the same execution model as the DPSEL primitive. By substituting DPSEL for DPJOIN in some nodes, more complex relational queries involving joins can be represented.

4. The queries in Figures 5.1 and 5.2 can be viewed as the basic skeletons of all the queries. Owing to their distinct structures in pipelining and parallelism, they can be considered as the basic schemes by which every query is executed. We call the queries in Figure 5.1 the Q_1 type, those in Figure 5.2 the Q_2 type.

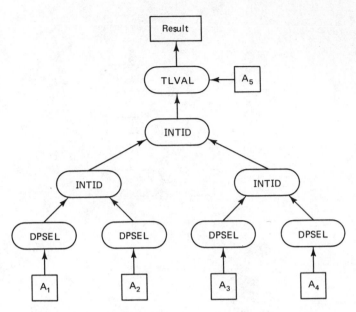

Figure 5.2. Parallel Execution of a Selection on Four Attributes

5.2.2. Data-Pool Primitives

The DP implementation for these query-execution schemes is depicted in Figure 5.3, where VAL is a value belonging to the domain under consideration, the RIDs are the identifiers of the relations sharing that domain, and the TID_i are the corresponding tuple identifiers.

The primitives operating on the DPs are described in [3]. The operational characteristics of some of them are reported below in order to show the intent of the two implementations.

DPSEL searches the data pool associated with the intended attribute for the TIDs of tuples satisfying the select condition. Moreover, such TIDs are intersected with a TID list that belongs to the input of the primitive itself. Its output is a list of TIDs.

INTID performs the intersection of two lists of TIDs.

TLVAL searches the data pool associated with the intended attribute for the values corresponding to the TIDs of a list. Its output is a list of couples in the form of (TID, val).

DPJOIN, not appearing in these queries and performing joins, searches the data pool associated with the intended attribute to test whether each value belongs to both of the relations involved. In case of implicit joins, its output is a list of TIDs.

VAL	RID_1	TID_1^1 TID_2^1	RID_2	TID_1^2 TID_2^2 ....

Figure 5.3. Data-Pool Representation on the Disk Track

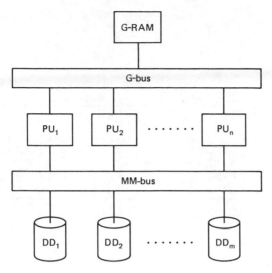

Figure 5.4. The Physical Architecture of DBMAC

5.3. THE SIMULATION MODEL

5.3.1. The Physical Architecture

The hardware structure of DBMAC is based on the multiprocessor architecture sketched in Figure 5.4 [1]. The processing units (PUs) are single-board computers, each with its own memory, connected to one another by a multibus (G-BUS). The same multibus provides for the access to a global memory (G-RAM). A mass-memory bus (MM-BUS) connects the processing units to the disk devices (DDs). The disk devices are supplied with special-purpose devices (filters) to perform selections and intersections on the fly. Thus, this architecture combines on-the-fly selecting capability with a multiprocessor system.

The proposed model of the hardware architecture does not take the global memory and the global bus into consideration because they are devoted mainly to message management, while the aim of the present simulation is to study the performance of the data access during a query execution. So the physical resources considered in the model are the processing units, the disk devices, and the mass-memory bus. See Figure 5.5, where three PUs and two DDs are indicated.

The processing units are identical and do not specialize; i.e., every process can be run on any of them. Moreover, several instances of the same process can be activated on any PU when necessary. We assume the existence of a suitable executive system providing for the required interprocess communication mechanisms [2].

Considered as a board, the CPU is allocated in a time-slicing way to the processes being multiprogrammed. The round-robin scheduling algorithm is

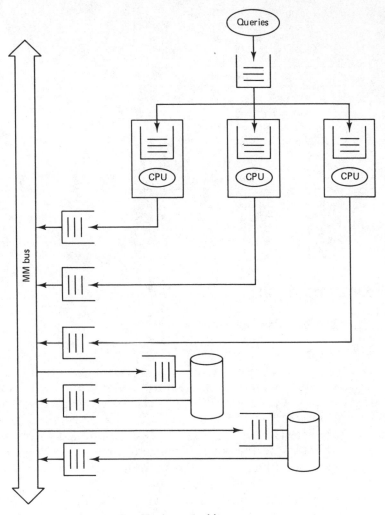

Figure 5.5. The Hardware Architecture

followed, giving each process the same level of priority. The requests to a disk device are placed in the first-in-first-out queue local to it. The requests for the bus arrive from the processing units and from the disk devices. Each PU also uses a FIFO queue to hold its own requests. The top elements of such queues are served in a random way.

We will introduce additional primitives together with the aforementioned ones in order to relate to the various parts of the modeling. Each primitive is represented by a process running in the simulation model in correspondence with its execution in the real system.

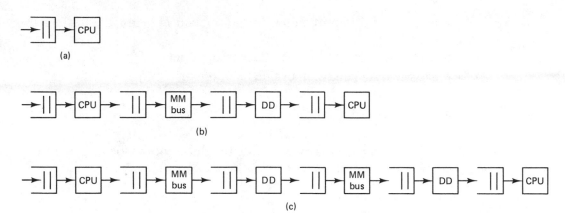

Figure 5.6. Schemes of the Processes Running Through the System

The processes running in the system can be classified according to schemes (a), (b), and (c) depicted in Figure 5.6, where they are shown to request, occupy, and leave the various resources.

(a) Processes requiring only CPU service.
(b) Processes requiring a disk operation. The bus service is limited to the transfer of the command specifying the operation and the subsequent disk service of the requested operation.
(c) Processes performing a data transfer between disk devices. The first bus service is due to the command transfer. The second bus service is for data transfer.

Note that the services provided by the bus and a disk device are in sequence. In fact the existence of a buffer, local to the disk device, is assumed. Such a buffer holds information received from the bus before the information is decoded by the disk device. Similarly, it holds data read from the disk before placing the data on the bus. Each process begins and ends with a CPU service to simulate the activation and completion of the process.

5.3.2. Data Allocation

We introduce the following notation.

s = share degree of the domain D

N_i = cardinality of the relation R sharing D $(1 \leqslant i \leqslant s)$

n_i = number of different values in the domain D belonging to the relation R

n_0 = total number of different values in the domain D

v = average byte length of a value in a domain

b = byte length of a RID

a = byte length of a TID

The number of bytes necessary to store the data pool associated with domain D is given by the following formula [3]:

$$ZD = n_0 \times v + b \times \sum_{i=1}^{s} n_i + a \times \sum_{i=1}^{s} N_i$$

A DP is assumed to be entirely stored on a single disk device (possibly occupying a set of adjacent tracks). Furthermore, the DPs are uniformly distributed on the disk devices.

The temporary data are generated by primitives appearing in the execution of a query in order to be used by successive primitives belonging to the same query. Each DD is assumed to have room for temporary data. The data produced by a primitive operating on data stored on a certain DD are stored on the same DD.

5.3.3. Primitive Execution

A processor-per-disk architecture has been assumed for the filters. A detailed simulation of a filter has not been performed, since the aim was to have global information about the hardware and software design of DBMAC. A processor (with a RAM buffer) capable of performing simple tests on the bytes coming from the disk has been assumed. A certain time has been assigned to each operation, without specifying the details of the algorithms or the buffer management.

The time necessary to execute a primitive operating on a DP has been assumed to depend on the qualifying conditions associated with the primitive. In a case of a "simple" condition, as for example in the DPSEL primitive, the execution is performed during a DP scan. Let DTR be the time (in μs) that the processor has to examine each incoming byte. Assuming that three instructions are necessary for such processing [5], the processor must be approximately a (3/DTR) MIP processor. In case of conditions involving TID lists, as for example in the TLVAL or TLSEL primitives, the execution time is greater (a factor of 1.3 has been assumed). In any case the execution flow of a DP primitive follows scheme (b) in Figure 5.6, and the time necessary to perform the disk operation includes also the writing of the results on the same disk.

When a DP primitive operates on two data streams, as for example INTID or TLVAL does, one of the data streams is assumed to be stored on the disk while the other is held in the buffer local to the disk. In this case, a process must be executed ahead of these primitives. Such a process facilitates data transfer of a disk (or among disks) on the basis of the allocation of the data streams on the same DD (or on different ones). In the first case, one of the data streams is transferred to the local buffer and the process follows scheme (b) in Figure 5.6; otherwise, a data transfer between the two disks involved is performed, following scheme (c).

Scheme (a) in Figure 5.6 refers to the execution of processes for the beginning and end of the query processing.

The time necessary to read or write Z bytes on the disk has been modeled as the sum of the average seek time, the time to seek the tracks occupied by the data, and the time to transfer Z bytes:

$$\text{READ}(Z) = \text{WRITE}(Z) = \text{SEEK} + \text{TKTK} \times \left[\frac{Z}{\text{TRACK}}\right] + \text{DTR} \times Z$$

where TRACK is the byte size of a disk track, SEEK is the average seek time, TKTK is the track-to-track seek time, and DTR is the byte-transfer time.

5.3.4. Query-Execution Graphs

The schemes of the queries in Figures 5.1 and 5.2 have been transformed into graphs (known as query-execution graphs) whose management in the simulation program is detailed in [12]. Figures 5.7 and 5.8 show their corresponding execution graphs.

The execution graphs are directed graphs with one source and one sink. The nodes represent the processes whose execution has to be simulated, and the directed arcs represent the precedence relationships between the processes. The TR processes indicate disk transfer operations, depending on the data storage. In fact the disk where a certain DP is stored is randomly chosen among the available disks. The type of transfer operation is determined by the allocation scheme used for the chosen disk (see Section 5.3.5). A complete characterization of the execution of the processes belonging to the graphs can be derived from the DP characteristics and from the execution flow of the primitives themselves [13].

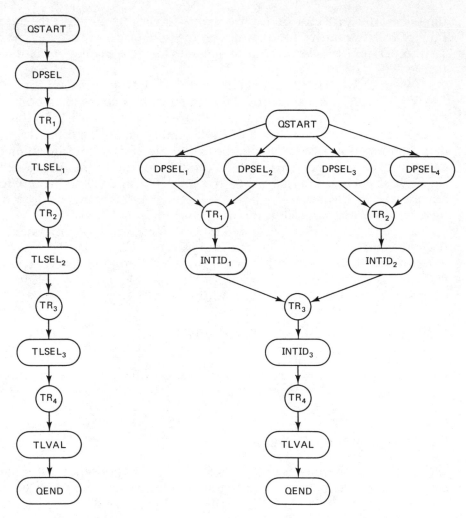

Figure 5.7. The Query-Execution Graph of Q_1 Type

Figure 5.8. The Query-Execution Graph of Q_2 Type

5.3.5. Query Activation and Execution

The system is characterized by the number of active queries (i.e., the activity level, AL). Thus, we must generate new queries. A new query is generated whenever an existing query has completed its execution. The generation of a query involves also the generation of the parameters that characterize the database and the selectivity of the operations (see the next section). The size of DPs and the temporary data is also calculated to allow determination of the service times required by the system facilities for each process. Furthermore, DDs where relevant DPs are stored are randomly chosen. With these calculations and preparations, we can now define the type of TR processes and characterize their execution flows.

A query execution consists of the activating and running of the processes belonging to the query (more specifically, the query-execution graph of the query). The maximum number of processes that can be activated is ($n \times m$), where n is the number of processing units and m their multiprogramming degree. Each PU can run any process. The allocation of PUs is based on the choice of a PU whose multiprogramming level is minimum.

When a query requires the execution of a new process but all PUs have already reached their maximum multiprogramming level, the process waits in a FIFO queue. In this way, no priority between queries or processes is considered.

5.4. SYSTEM PARAMETERS

The following assumptions are used for the results to be presented in Section 5.5. The queries in Figures 5.1 and 5.2 are processed to obtain those results.

1. Hardware assumptions:
   (a) Disk device:

TRACK = 8000 bytes	(track size)
SEEK = 50 msec	(average seek time)
TKTK = 10 msec	(track-to-track seek time)
DTR = 2 μsec	

   (b) Mass-memory bus:
       byte transfer time = 1 μsec
   (c) Processing unit:
       instruction execution time = 2 μsec
   (d) Hardware configuration:
       number of processing units = 2
       number of disk devices = 2 to 8
2. Database assumptions:

   s = uniform distribution between 1 and 3 (share degree of a domain D)

N_i $(1 \leqslant i \leqslant s)$ = exponential distribution with mean 7000, min 300, max 30,000 (relation cardinality)

n_i $(1 \leqslant i \leqslant s)$ = wN, where w (data integration factor) is generated by an exponential distribution with means 0.05 to 0.7 and max 1 (number of attribute original values)

v = 20 bytes (size of the attribute values)

a = 2 bytes (TID size)

b = 1 byte (RID size)

3. Selectivity assumptions:

σ = exponential distribution with mean 0.125 (σN is the number of tuples satisfying a condition on a single attribute)

4. Software assumptions:

Time quantum for the PUs = 12 msec

PU multiprogramming degree = 3 (maximum number of active processes in a PU)

Activity level = 2 to 12 (number of active queries in the system)

The parameters for disk device take typical values of disks such as DEC RL01. The value 2 msec for the byte transfer time assumes the presence of a 1.5-MIP processor for the filter. The hardware configurations considered in our simulation correspond to feasibility criteria at low cost. Furthermore, a minimum number of PUs has been considered, since the data primitives in utilizing the filter involve a PU only briefly.

The database is a small relation of 10 tuples. This is because we use small disks in the simulation. The formula in Section 5.3.2 shows the important role of the data integration factor for the purpose of determining the byte size of DPs, which are the basic physical structures to be operated. Setting w equal to 1 means that the values of the attributes are all different and the DP gets its maximum size. The mean value for w mostly used in the experiments is 0.5 (each attribute value appears on the average twice). Finally, by varying the size of the database, unfavorable situations are attempted in order to test the performance of DPs in a less suitable environment.

5.5. SOME RESULTS

The simulation results are presented in three categories: the query execution, data integration, and device utilization.

TABLE 5.1. THROUGHPUT OF QUERIES OF TYPE Q_1

Number of DDs	Throughput (Number of queries of type Q_1 processed per minute)				
	AL = 2	4	6	8	12
2	19.4	23.3	25.6	25.5	25.2
4	24.4	34.4	39.3	38	34.7
6	25.1	40.4	48.3	48.7	44.8
8	26.2	41.5	53.4	56.2	49.1

5.5.1. Query Execution

The performance of the queries in Figures 5.1 and 5.2 has been investigated from two points of view. The first is concerned with the comparison of these two types of queries at certain system activity level. The second is concerned with the performance analysis of a mix of such queries. This set of experiments refers to a w value of 0.5. The system throughput (number of queries executed in a minute) is reported in Tables 5.1 and 5.2 as a function of the activity level and of the number of disk devices present in the hardware configuration (the number of processing units is always equal to 2).

The throughput increases as the number of DDs increases, as was expected because of the allocation model of DPs. In fact, each DP involved in the queries is stored on a DD chosen in a random way. Thus, the more DDs are used, the fewer the access conflicts.

As far as the influence of the activity level is concerned, its increase causes the throughput to gain. However, after reaching a maximum value, the throughput decreases. This behavior, shown in the rows of the tables, depends on the load condition of the system. After the system is fully loaded, the throughput degenerates. In particular, we note that in most cases

TABLE 5.2. THROUGHPUT OF QUERIES OF TYPE Q_2

Number of DDs	Throughput (Number of queries of type Q_2 processed per minute)				
	AL = 2	4	6	8	12
2	22.5	24.5	24.6	24.8	24.2
4	29.5	36	38.9	36.8	37.4
6	35.5	45.6	45.6	46	43.2
8	37.1	49.8	54	50.9	51.4

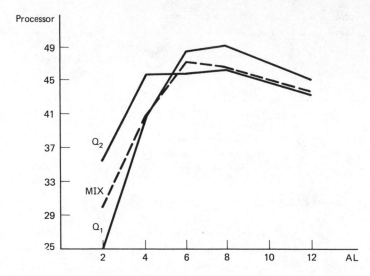

Figure 5.9. Throughput (q per min) in Case of 6 DDs and with Mean Value 0.5

the Q_2 type of queries gets its maximum throughput before Q_1 because of its intrinsic intraquery parallelism. In fact, the parallel execution of the processes tends to saturate the system at a lower activity level.

Comparison of the two tables points out the different performance achievable by the two implementation schemes. They are characterized on the one hand by pipeline structure and low number of processes (see Figure 5.8). In case of low values for *AL* (up to from 4 to 6), the parallel structure of Q_2 allows the system to activate more processes than does the pipeline structure of Q_1. It also exploits better multidevice architecture. When the number of active queries is higher, the throughput of Q_1 shows that the interquery parallelism balances its lack of intraquery parallelism. Furthermore, Q_1 takes advantage of its low number of processes and has a higher throughput. Thus if we consider Q_1 and Q_2 as different implementations of a relational operation on several DPs, the performance of one with respect to the other depends on the activity level.

On the other hand, Q_1 and Q_2 can be considered as the basic models of a wide class of queries—pipeline and parallel queries. For this reason the behavior of a mix of such queries has been analyzed. The experiment used a medium configuration with 2 PUs, 6 DDs, and a 50-50 mix of Q_1 and Q_2 types of queries. The resulting values for the throughput are shown in Figure 5.9 as a dotted line. The solid lines corresponding to Q_1 and Q_2 are also shown to point out that the behavior of the mix is between the two other workloads.

As far as the mean response is concerned, we report in Table 5.3 the times (in seconds) relative to the configuration with 2 PUs and 6 DDs. The comparison between the times corresponding to Q_1 and Q_2 shows a behavior analogous to the throughput, in the sense that Q_2 is characterized by a lower response time until AL reaches 6 and by a higher response time for values of AL higher than 6.

TABLE 5.3.   MEAN RESPONSE TIME OF A MEDIUM CONFIGURATION

Query type	Mean response time in seconds				
	AL = 2	4	6	8	12
Q_1	4.8	5.95	7.46	9.85	16.09
Q_2	3.38	5.24	7.88	10.41	16.71

5.5.2. Data Integration

The influence of data integration on system throughput has been tested by means of a set of experiments involving different values of the parameter w, which determines the number of original attribute values; the mean value for w has been varied from 0.05 to 0.7. The DP size is obtained analytically by the formula in Section 5.3.2. We set the values $N = 7000$ and $w =$ from 0.05 to 0.7. Thus, the DP size ranges from 39,200 to 184,800 bytes. These experiments are related to the physical configuration with 2 PUs and 6 DDs, and to an activity level equal to 6, which on average gives the best performance. The values for the throughput and the average disk operations time are reported in Table 5.4.

TABLE 5.4.   THROUGHPUT AND AVERAGE TIME REQUIRED BY THE DISK
OPERATIONS FOR 6 DDs and AL = 6

		Data Integration Factor				
		w mean val = 0.05	0.1	0.2	0.5	0.7
Q_1	throughput (q per min)	110.4	96.7	72.5	48.3	42.1
	av. disk oper. (in msec)	136	157	207	307	352
Q_2	throughput (q per min)	98.9	86.6	67.3	45.6	38.9
	av. disk oper. (in msec)	123	137	173	246	285

The throughput decreases very quickly as the DP size increases. In particular, the throughput for w with mean value 0.7 is on average 0.4 times the throughput for w with mean value 0.05. Thus, the DP size is one of the most important parameters affecting throughput.

5.5.3. Device Utilization

5.5.3.1. CPU utilization. In all the experiments illustrated above, CPU utilization ranged between 1.5% and 6%. In fact, the processes we have simulated work almost always on disk devices. Such processes are related only to data retrieval, whereas other processes related to, for example, transactions management and query optimization utilize the CPU more intensively.

In order to check the influence of the CPU-bound processes, we have performed an experiment involving mixes formed by Q_1, Q_2, and a query type using only CPU. The mix composition considers one CPU-bound query for each other query—i.e., 25% Q_1, 25% Q_2, and 50% CPU-bound query type. The total CPU time required by the new query has been varied from 0 (the query is absent) to 6000 msec. As an example, the query compilation modeled in [5] corresponds to 104 msec. In these experiments we have considered 2 PUs, 6 DDs, w with mean 0.5, and AL equal to 12 (twice the AL considered above).

The results we obtained are reported in Table 5.5, where the throughput considers only the number of Q_1 and Q_2 queries executed in a minute. For the limit value of 6 seconds, there is a drastic reduction of throughput and of DD utilization corresponding to a strong increase of CPU utilization. We note that for the other values the throughput remains stable with the increased presence of the CPU-bound. This is an important property, because it is possible to provide for a certain elasticity in the design of the transactions management mentioned above.

5.5.3.2. Disk-device utilization. As always, DDs are utilized extensively. Some sample utilizations are reported in terms of the execution of Q_1

TABLE 5.5. INFLUENCE OF CPU-BOUND QUERIES ON THE MIX OF 50% Q_1–50% Q_2 FOR 6 DDs, AL = 12, AND w WITH MEAN VALUE 0.5

CPU-bound query time in msec	Throughput Q_1, Q_2 per min	Average CPU utilization	Average DD utilization
0	43.6	0.024	0.476
120	43	0.066	0.479
240	43.6	0.109	0.494
360	43.5	0.151	0.471
600	43.1	0.233	0.478
6000	18.8	0.921	0.205

TABLE 5.6. AVERAGE DD UTILIZATION AND AVERAGE QUEUE LENGTH FOR AL = 8 AND w WITH MEAN VALUE 0.5

	Q_1		Q_2	
Number of DDs	Average DD utilization	Average queue length	Average DD utilization	Average queue length
2	0.835	2.147	0.807	2.173
4	0.655	0.831	0.614	0.870
6	0.534	0.454	0.493	0.494
8	0.450	0.290	0.421	0.318

and Q_2 (see Table 5.6). The average disk utilization and the corresponding average queue length are reported in the table as functions of the number of DDs for an activity level of 6 and w with mean value 0.5.

5.5.3.3. Mass-memory-bus utilization.   The bus utilization is 0.1% of its capacity and the average queue length is zero. This low utilization is due to the filter, which in our modeling performs basic data management without involving the processing units. The bus is heavily used only to transfer data from one DD to another when the data primitive operates on data streams coming from different disk devices.

5.6. FURTHER EXPERIMENTS

The disk drives referred to in Sections 5.4 and 5.5 are low-cost devices. For this reason, another set of experiments involving a more powerful DD has been performed. This new DD has been modeled on the basis of the IBM 3330 disk, which has also served as a basis for other reported performance evaluations [5, 7, 8]. Its parameter values are:

TRACK	= 13000 bytes	(track size)
CYL	= 19 tracks	(number of tracks in a cylinder)
SEEK	= 38.6 msec	(average seek time)
TKTK	= 10.1 msec	(track-to-track seek time)
DTR	= 1.284 μsec	(byte-transfer time)

This disk can be considered about twice as powerful as the disk previously modeled, in that it requires about half the time to read the same amount of data. Some throughput values obtained by the simulation with this DD are reported in Table 5.7. These results, compared with those in

TABLE 5.7. THROUGHPUT FOR AL = 8 AND w WITH MEAN VALUE 0.5

Query type	Throughput (q per min) with 3330-like DD			
	DDs = 2	4	6	8
Q_1	50.8	80.3	96.6	109.1
Q_2	49.4	72.8	88.7	100.3

Tables 5.1 and 5.2, confirm the two-to-one power ratio; in fact, the throughput is twice that of the former DD. Furthermore, the qualitative considerations about the performance of Q_1 and Q_2 are still valid.

The experiments performed reported in Sections 5.4 and 5.5 are concerned with a relation size of 10 tuples. Experiments with this same relation size have also been performed for IBM 3330-like DDs. In particular, the relation size has been generated by an exponential function with mean 70,000, min 300, and max 100,000. Some results, depending on the data integration factor, are reported in Table 5.8 at an activity level equal to 8 and a configuration with 2 PUs and 8 DDs. Only the results for type Q_2 queries are reported, because the behavior of type Q_1 queries shows similar characteristics, as discussed earlier.

TABLE 5.8. THROUGHPUT FOR RELATION SIZE OF 10 5-TUPLES FOR AL = 8 AND 8 DDs

Query type	Throughput (q per min) with 3330-like DD				
	w mean val = 0.05	0.1	0.2	0.5	0.7
Q_2	49.2	42.5	30.9	19.4	16.9

Data integration becomes one of the most important characteristics of the database that affect the performance of the data-pool mode. Comparing, for example, Table 5.4 with Table 5.8, we conclude that, with appropriate w values (0.7 and 0.05, respectively), the same performance can be achieved for a relation size 10 times greater than the original one and disk devices only twice as powerful as the original.

5.7. SOME REMARKS

The DP structure decreases space requirement for the data and allows attribute partitioning in such a way that parallel operations can be achieved.

Consider, for example, relations with cardinalities 7000 and 70,000, where the average tuple is of 100 bytes, the attribute value is of 20 bytes,

TABLE 5.9. BYTE SIZE AND CORRESPONDING READ TIME
IN CASE OF FLAT FILE AND DATA POOL

Relation cardinality	Flat file		Data pool	
	Rel. size	Read time	DP size	Read time
7,000	700,000 bytes	0.967 sec	140,000 bytes	0.228 sec
70,000	7,000,000 bytes	9.319 sec	1,540,000 bytes	2.086 sec

the share degree for the domains is equal to 2, and the data integration factor w is equal to 0.5. The byte sizes of the stored physical structures, for flat file and data pool, are reported in Table 5.9, together with the time needed for their reading in a processor-per-disk scheme, using an IBM 3330-like DD.

A processor-per-disk architecture has been supposed for the pseudoassociative disks. The time needed to read a DP is low, as we have seen. For a selection on one attribute followed by a projection on another attribute, the scanning of two DPs is sufficient, which requires less time than a relation scanning does. If more DPs are involved, the total work necessary to operate on the data increases, but the multiprocessor structure allows us to exploit the DP partitions by parallel execution.

Analogous considerations apply to a join operation followed by a projection on attributes belonging to one relation. An explicit Cartesian product is not necessary, and the operation is performed by scanning the DP related to the joined attributes and the other DPs involved in the projection. The total work required by such an operation is about the same as the select requires. We note that the total work necessary to perform a join operation in case of flat file is much larger. For example, using the formula given in [5] for the processor-per-disk scheme, in case of relations of 7000 tuples and a 3330 disk, we arrive at 8000 sec. The value obtained by the formula for the multiprocessor-cache scheme with 19 processors is much lower. Nevertheless, this scheme requires more work than our scheme. The multiprocessor architecture allows us to activate in parallel different data primitives operating on different DPs. For this reason it can sustain a high workload with complex queries operating on several DPs. For our sample queries of a selection on four attributes depicted in Figures 5.1 and 5.2, the total work involved is higher than for flat file. Nonetheless, the throughput obtained by the simulation experiments, where parallel executions are activated whenever possible, seems to indicate good performance.

A detailed analysis of our modeled operations and the derived implications can be found in [13]. We note that the simulation models each data primitive in a standard way, independent of its context. The data are operated in one or more data scans (depending on the particular primitive); the results are always stored on the disk, independent of their successive usage.

Thus, some data may be read immediately after they have been written. In this case, some optimization could be employed to improve the performance.

5.8. CONCLUSIONS

In this chapter we have described a simulation model for query execution in DBMAC and the results obtained by various sets of experiments. In particular we have studied two types of sample queries, with pipeline and parallel structures, respectively. They represent different implementations of the selection operation. Because of their generality, they can be also considered representative of wide classes of queries.

Their performance has been analyzed with respect to different system configurations. A measure of the influence of the number of active queries on the throughput is thus obtained. The parallel structure gives better results until certain values of the activity level are reached; for higher values the pipeline structure shows better throughput. Since the simulation model takes only data processing into account, without considering transaction management, CPU-bound query has been introduced to simulate the presence of other activities in the system. The activity of the CPU-bound query has been varied. However, various values of the activity level for an almost constant throughput are possible. The dependence of the system throughput on the data integration of the DPs has also been pointed out.

The results obtained by the simulation and the execution analysis pertain to overall behavior in query execution. They confirm our belief that good performance is achieved by the basic choices made in the DBMAC project—i.e., the attribute partitioning used for DPs, query execution by means of data primitives implemented on processor-per-disk devices, and the activation of processes on the processing units following a MIMD strategy. Furthermore, since the performance depends entirely on the amount of data to be filtered, the maintenance of suitable indices is under investigation in order to reduce the data space to be examined. In fact, indexing, as shown in [8], can improve the performance of a processor-per-disk scheme to a point approaching that of a processor-per-read one with a lower hardware cost. Future work will be devoted to detailed analysis of the implementation of the data primitives and the transformation of relational queries into optimized execution graphs based on such data primitives.

REFERENCES

[1] Missikoff, M., and Terranova, M., "The Architecture of a Relational Database Computer, Known as DBMAC," in this book.

[2] Missikoff, M., and Terranova, M., "EXEMAC—un sistema esecutivo per database machine," *Proc. AICA '80,* Bologna, 1980.

[3] Missikoff, M., "A Domain Based Internal Schema for Relational Database Machines," *Proc. ACM-SIGMOD Conf.,* Santa Monica, 1982.

[4] Missikoff, M., and Terranova, M., "An Overview of the Project DBMAC for a Relational Database Machine," *Proc. 6th Workshop on Computer Architecture for Non-Numerical Processing,* Hyères, France, 1981.

[5] DeWitt, D. J., and Hawthorn, P. B., "A Performance Evaluation of Database Machine Architectures," *Proc. 7th Int. Conf. on Very Large Data Bases,* Cannes, 1981.

[6] Su, S. Y. W., Lupkiewicz, S., Lee, C., Lo, D. H., and Doty, K. L., "MICRONET—A Microcomputer Network System for Managing Distributed Relational Databases," *Proc. 4th Int. Conf. on VLDB,* Berlin, September 1978.

[7] Boral, H., and DeWitt D. J., "Processor Allocation Strategies for Multiprocessor Database Machines," *ACM Trans. Database Systems,* Vol. 6, No. 2 (1981).

[8] Boral, H., DeWitt D. J., and Wilkinson, W. K., "Performance Evaluation of Four Associative Disk Designs," *Information Systems,* Vol. 7, No. 1. (1982).

[9] Brownsmith, J. D., "A Simulation Model of the MICRONET Computer System during Join processing," *Annual Simulation Symposium,* 1980.

[10] Schuster, S. A., Ozkarahan, E. A., and Smith, K. C., "A Virtual Memory System for a Relational Associative Processor," *Proc. National Computer Conference,* Vol. 45 (1976).

[11] Cesarini, F., De Luca, D., and Soda, G., "An Approach to DBMAC Query Processing Simulation," *Workshop on Database Machines,* Florence, September 1981.

[12] Cesarini, F., De Luca, D., and Soda, G., "Transactions Management through Dynamically Expanded Graphs," *Proc. 2d Int. Symp. Applied Modelling and Simulation,* Paris, 1982.

[13] Cesarini, F., and Soda, G., "Analysis and Simulation of Query Execution in DBMAC," *ISIS Tech. Rep.* 1/1983.

6

Design Considerations for an Information Query Computer

Akira Sekino, Ken Takeuchi, Takenori Makino, Katsuya Hakozaki,
Tsugunori Doi, and Tatsuo Goto

6.0. ABSTRACT

This chapter describes design considerations and implementation efforts of an information query computer (IQC), a database machine which offloads database management functions from a host computer at the data query level. A database machine of this kind is believed to provide a high degree of database independence from hosts and significant cost-effectiveness improvement of database management. It is therefore possible to envision a common database resource, i.e., a common database machine, shared by a wide variety of host computers with different architectures, in a distributed processing environment. The chapter also discusses design considerations of the host-IQC interface, of software, implementation tradeoffs of software, firmware, and hardware, and aspects of machine reliability, availability, serviceability, integrity, and security.

6.1. INTRODUCTION

Database management systems have gained wide acceptance among computer users. A huge number of data-intensive applications today depend heavily on database retrievals. Flexible access to databases, new type of services, ease of use, database protection, and overall system performance, among other factors, become the major concerns of many database users. On the other hand, remarkable advances in semiconductor technology have strikingly reduced the hardware cost of computers. It is widely expected that the computer performance as well as functionality could be greatly improved by introducing some additional application-oriented hardware, provided that it is suitable for VLSI implementation. This expectation naturally leads to growing interest in database machines from a practical viewpoint. At present, the results of past research on database machines are being reviewed in the light of their usefulness in developing commercial database machines.

Many research projects were formed in the 1970s to study various kinds of database machines. To mention only a few of them, logic-cell machines such as RAP and CASSM, processor-complex machines such as DBC and DIRECT, associative-memory machines such as STARAN, and backend-computer machines such as XDMS are well-known results of these research projects [1, 2, 3]. Research on database machines has been active also in Japan during the last several years. An experimental machine, known as EDC, which uses bubble memory as the database store [4], a backend computer, GDS [5], to be reviewed here, and a system based on sort/search engines [6] are examples of Japanese activities.

Considered from a practical or cost-effectiveness viewpoint, however, several problems apparently remain unsolved. One is a choice of storage devices other than ordinary moving-head disks for storing databases, although it does not seem that these devices will be commercially available. It is important to note that the industry foresees only a few new devices for the near future. Other machines seek relief from this problem by counting on the advances of LSI memory devices. However, their accommodation of large databases solely on the LSI memory is far from realistic.

Another critical problem is lack of consideration for database accessibility from a wide range of computers. Today's database users desire access, for example, to common databases by multiple and heterogeneous mainframe computers within a small area such as a computer room; they also want database accessibility by a wide range of geographically distributed computers, small and large, with different architectures. More research is needed on the database machine's independence from host computers.

Based on the above observations, research on a database machine is underway at NEC Corporation, Tokyo, as described in this chapter. This machine is intended for use not only in a computer room, but also in a distributed processing environment. Its role is shown in Figure 6.1. This machine is called an *information query computer* (IQC). The present chapter describes major motivations of this research, various design considerations on host-IQC interface, architectural choices, requirements for reliability, accessibility, serviceability, and security, and some details of an implementation of the prototype IQC as it exists at NEC.

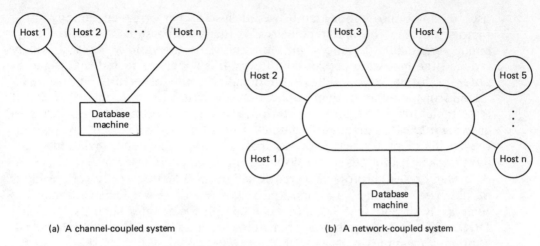

(a) A channel-coupled system   (b) A network-coupled system

Figure 6.1. The Role of the Information Query Computer Among Host Computers: (a) A Channel-coupled System, (b) A Network-coupled System

6.1.1. Database Machines Research at NEC

NEC Corporation manufactures a wide range of computer products: small to large general-purpose ACOS series computers, MS series minicomputers, small business computers, ASTRA and personal computers. Database management systems are provided for most of these computers. Both CODASYL (ADBS) and relational (INQ and RIQS) database management systems have been supported for the customers [7]. In this environment, it was felt important to develop database machines that have sufficient expandability and excellent cost/performance characteristics.

NEC started basic research on database machines in 1976, with the GDS project [5]. Diverse approaches to such research can be taken, depending upon its purpose. The following issues were chosen as the research targets:

1. Pursuit of a machine that effectively supports both CODASYL and relational databases, and establishment of a general host-database machine interface suitable for the multiple data model environment.
2. Verification of performance improvement brought about by tradeoffs among software, firmware, and hardware.
3. Establishment of a storage hierarchy system that accommodates a large-capacity LSI memory.
4. Evaluation of system performance for the effect of offloading from a host.

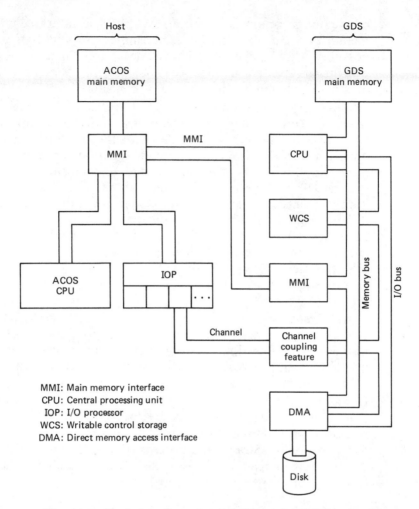

Figure 6.2.   Physical Configuration of the Experimental System (GDS)

An experimental system called the Generalized Database Subsystem (GDS), shown in Figure 6.2, was developed to evaluate the above issues quantitatively. A CODASYL database management system (ADBS) and a relational model query system were built on the machine. For experiment details, the readers are advised to read [5, 8, 9]. Major conclusions are summarized as follows.

1. A high-level and general database interface (GDI) was established [5]. As long as the communication overhead between a host and the database machine is kept low, GDI can efficiently support multiple data models. GDI utilizes shared memories and required a rather high fre-

quency of communication. If a slow physical interface without shared memories were chosen, the establishment of the GDI would not be possible. This implies that if a loose couple such as via communication line is desired, a single data model environment with a low frequency of communication should be considered.

2. Three-to-five execution-speed ratios between a software routine and a firmware (microprogram) routine for equivalent database functions were observed [9]. This coincides with the result of other experiments on other functions. As the database functions are few by nature and, moreover, highly used functions tend to concentrate on even fewer, software-firmware tradeoff brings about a significant performance improvement. For example, microcoded database management routines (amounting to 1000 microsteps) were found to take about 40% of the execution time of their software counterparts in GDS, thereby shortening the total execution time by a factor of more than two. It was also felt that a few primitives were suitable for hardware implementation, such as address translation, character-string comparison, and bit manipulation.

3. It was found that database references do not show obvious locality like that of program references [8]. The least-recently-used (LRU) storage management algorithm commonly used for virtual storage systems is not always satisfactory for database buffer management. More studies are needed on this problem.

4. It was observed that about 70% of ADBS functions can be offloaded from a host to GDS. It was also observed that 40% of the total host workload in a data-intensive application (assuming that ADBS accounts for a little over 50% of the host workload) can be offloaded to GDS. Throughput increase is therefore significantly high for the host, unless GDS becomes a performance bottleneck.

6.1.2. The Information Query Computer (IQC)

Applied research on database machines has been in progress in several directions at NEC on the basis of the above results of GDS. Research on an information query computer (IQC) described in this chapter represents one of these directions. Briefly, an IQC is a database machine that offloads database management functions from the central processor (the host) at the data query level. Major motivations for initiating research on this type of database machine include the study of (1) database independence from one or more hosts, and (2) cost-effectiveness improvement of database management by a database machine.

The requirements on user environment are becoming more and more diversified, as database management systems (DBMS) reach various sectors of users. The first study is to provide a high degree of system configuration flexibility in meeting these requirements. It is hoped that by moving most of the host DBMS functions to IQC, multiple hosts with mutually different architectures may then share the IQC DBMS functions. Each heterogeneous host communicates with the IQC at the data query level, usually without knowing either the IQC machine configuration or physical data organizations. Such a high-level data independence permits independent system expansions (e.g., hardware additions and upgrading, database expansion, new DBMS services) by the hosts and by the database machine. The second study mentioned above will potentially be achieved by managing commonly shared databases under the direct control of IQCs specialized in database functions, avoiding the well-known complexity of general-purpose operating systems. It also becomes easier, in this configuration, to adopt various performance improvement techniques suitable for database processing and to apply a uniform integrity and security mechanism. Furthermore, maintenance of existing DBMS functions and addition of new ones will become easier. All these factors significantly contribute to the cost-effectiveness improvement of database management.

On the other hand, the IQC must support a full set of DBMS functions such as those associated with logical and physical database, file storage and file space, command execution, security control, concurrency control, and error recovery. It is also desirable that the IQC have some provision for managing various forms of information, e.g., alphanumeric data, textual data, images, and voices. High-speed connection is generally required between a host and the IQC for transmission of host commands and IQC responses. The choice of high-level data query as the host-IQC interface is expected to allow high-level independence between hosts and the IQC. Thus, it becomes realistic to envision an IQC that manages common multi-purpose information for a wide range of independent host computers, as shown in Figure 6.1.

In designing database machines of this kind, however, many serious questions arise. Major questions are listed below.

1. What kind of performance changes will result from choosing the data query level, rather than other levels, as the logical interface between hosts and the database machine? What proportion of DBMS and host processing will be offloaded to the database machine? How much communication traffic will there be on the host-database machine interface?

2. How can this interface be implemented physically? How much overhead will there be in communication between hosts and the database machine, depending on the choice of physical interface?

3. How much performance gain can be expected by employing firmware and hardware implementation of critical DBMS functions? Which DBMS functions are critical?

4. To what extent can the specialized machine architecture be expected to contribute toward lowering machine cost?

5. What kind of reliability, availability, serviceability, integrity, and security (RASIS) considerations are important in database machines like IQCs?

6. How much cost-performance improvement can be expected from the database machine environment?

7. Won't the development cost of database machines become too high? What considerations are important in reducing the cost?

Most of these questions are appropriate not only to IQCs but also to database machines in general. For this reason, this chapter presents results obtained concerning these problems in a general manner, wherever possible. Finally, it should be added that the most essential questions concerning IQCs are:

8. To what extent can database independence from hosts be achieved? How much merit will it bring to users?

9. How much improvement can be expected in terms of cost-effectiveness by designing database machines like IQCs?

6.2. LOGICAL AND PHYSICAL INTERFACES

It is important to exercise great care in deciding a specification of the interface between host systems and a database machine. This decision includes a physical interface level and a logical interface level. Major concerns here are communication overhead through the interface and offloading rate of the database processing load.

6.2.1. The Logical Interface

The logical interface between a host system and the database machine is a breakpoint, through which a host system invokes the functions of the data-

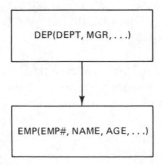

DEP(DEPT, MGR, . . .)

EMP(EMP#, NAME, AGE, . . .)

Figure 6.3. Logical Structure of a Sample Database

base machine [10]. There are several candidates for this breakpoint; we term them the (1) end-user query language (EUL) level, (2) data manipulation language (DML) level, (3) logical input/output (LIO) level, and (4) physical input/output (PIO) level. For each level, the frequency of database machine invocations and the offloading rate of database processing load are examined quantitatively in this section.

For the purpose of discussion, we assume that the following simple query is issued against the database shown in Figure 6.3 and that three qualified records (tuples) are to be obtained:

"Select names of employees who work in Department A and are 29 years old."

It is assumed that an EMP relation with 50 employee records is sequentially stored in the order of DEPT attribute values in database pages 200 through 204, as shown in Figure 6.4. Then the retrieval request is expressed at each of these four interface levels, as follows.

1. At the EUL level, we have

   .SELECT NAME WHERE DEPT='A' AND AGE='29',

2. At the DML level, we have

   .FIND ANY DEPT-REC /* find department 'A' */
   .FIND NEXT DEPT-EMP-SET /* find the next employee record
                    in DEPT-EMP-SET */
   .GET EMP-REC /* get the current employee record in the depart-
                    ment and examine whether the age is 29 */

3. At the LIO level, we have

   .GET PAGE#=200,LINE#=1,
   .GET PAGE#=200,LINE#=2,
   .GET PAGE#=200,LINE#=3,

   .

   .

   .

   .GET PAGE#=204,LINE#=6.

4. At the PIO level, we have

   .READ PAGE#=200,
   .READ PAGE#=201,

   .

   .

   .READ PAGE#=204.

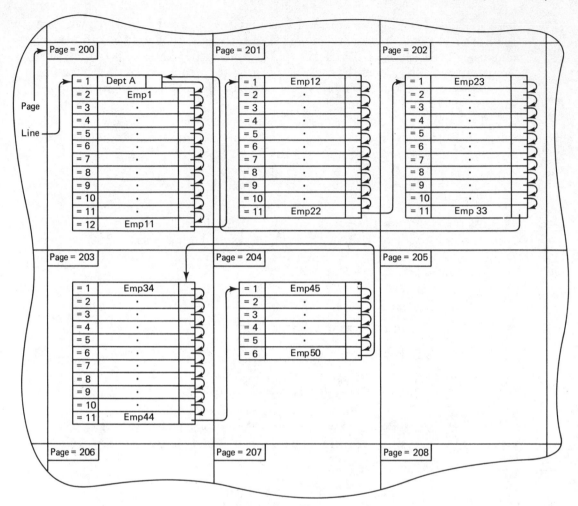

Figure 6.4.   Physical Structure of the Sample Database

In this example, the frequency of communication between the host system and the database machine for each interface level is obtained: one at the EUL level, 101 at the DML level, 51 at the LIO level, and five at the PIO level. It should be noted that if the relation is stored randomly, the frequency of communication at the PIO level may increase to the same number as at the LIO level.

Execution time for each level can be obtained on the basis of the estimated execution times of major components of a conventional database management system. Figure 6.5 shows the result of execution time and the database processing offloading rate, when the sample query is carried out on

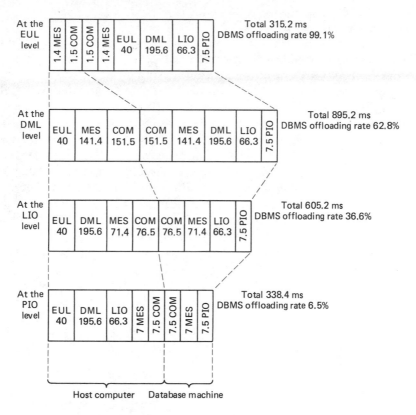

COM: Communication processing
MES: Message processing
EUL: End user language processing
DML: Data manipulation lanugage processing
LIO: Logical I/O processing
PIO: Physical I/O processing

Figure 6.5. Breakdown of Execution Times and Offloading Rates

a medium-scale conventional computer capable of executing about one million instructions per second. It is assumed in deriving this figure that the message processing time required to send or receive a message is 1.4 milliseconds and that the associated physical communication overhead is 1.5 milliseconds, temporarily disregarding the differences resulting from a choice of physical interface. The terminal communication processing required on a host computer, which typically accounts for about 30% of the total processing, is not included in this figure. It should be noticed that the breakdown of DBMS execution times and their associated DBMS offloading rates changes markedly, depending on the choice of logical interface of the database machine.

6.2.2. The Physical Interface

A selection of physical interface between a host system and the database machine is also important from the viewpoint of system organization and system performance. The physical interfaces are generally classified into communication interface, channel interface, and shared memory interface.

The interface between the database machine and a host system is desired to be versatile, so that various host systems can be connected with the database machine. Communication interfaces have been rigorously standardized. The resulting network architecture therefore allows connection of a wide variety of computer systems. On the other hand, channel interfaces have not been standardized among various computer systems. The database machine that is connected to host systems through the channel interface limits the desired system to a specific system architecture. Shared memory interfaces fully depend on host processor architecture, because a processor memory interface may be different from system to system.

Communication overhead of these interfaces can be estimated by the following formulas.

1. For communication network interfaces, we have

$$T_{\text{com}} = t_{\text{pn}} + \frac{D}{B_{\text{com}}}$$

where T_{com} denotes the communication delay time, t_{pn} the polling and network control processing time, D the data transfer size, and B_{com} the data transfer speed of a communication line (bytes/sec). For a typical communication network, the communication delay time is expressed as

$$T_{\text{com}} = 36.0 + 0.15D \quad \text{(milliseconds)}$$

2. For channel interfaces, we have

$$T_{\text{ch}} = t_{\text{it}} + \frac{D}{B_{\text{ch}}}$$

where T_{ch} denotes the channel delay time, t_{it} the channel initiation and termination time, and B_{ch} the data transfer rate of a channel (bytes/sec). For a typical channel interface, the channel delay time is expressed as

$$T_{\text{ch}} = 1.5 + 0.005D \quad \text{(milliseconds)}$$

3. For shared memory interfaces, we have

$$T_{\text{sm}} = t_{\text{ps}} + \frac{D}{B_{\text{sm}}}$$

where T_{sm} denotes the shared memory delay time, t_{ps} the process switching time, and B_{sm} the memory cycle time per byte. For a medium-scale computer system, the delay time is expressed as

$$T_{sm} = 0.03 + 0.001\,D \quad \text{(milliseconds)}$$

6.2.3. Host-Database Machine Interface Problems

In previous sections the logical and physical interfaces between a host system and the database machine were discussed separately. In designing a database system, however, we must consider the interfaces from a total system viewpoint.

For simplicity, let us take the same query example. From the communication frequency and the communication overhead derived in the previous section, we obtain the total communication overhead, as shown in Table 6.1, for various combinations of a physical interface and a logical interface. In this table the data transfer sizes D are realistically assumed to be 120, 80, 90, and 2000 for the EUL, DML, LIO, and PIO levels, respectively.

Based on Table 6.1, the following conclusion may reasonably be drawn:

1. If a database machine should become a part of a host system—i.e., the database machine is a processing unit in the host system—the combinations of the shared memory interface at one of the PIO, LIO, and DML level are useful. In this case, the database interface mechanism depends on the host system.
2. If a database machine should become a shared resource among several computer systems with an identical architecture, the combinations of the channel interface at either the PIO or the EUL level are useful.
3. If a database machine should become a shared resource among various computer systems, the physical interface should be a communication network and the logical interface should be at the EUL level. The associated communication overhead is larger than that of the channel

TABLE 6.1. EXPECTED COMMUNICATION OVERHEAD

Logical interface level	Frequency	Data transfer size (bytes)	Communication overhead (milliseconds)		
			Communication interface	Channel interface	Shared memory interface
EUL	1	120	54	2	0.2
DML	101	80	4850	192	11.1
LIO	51	90	2520	99	6.1
PIO	5	2000	1680	58	10.2

interface, but it seems tolerable in various situations. Further details of this kind of environment will be discussed later.

6.3. ARCHITECTURAL CONSIDERATIONS

A database machine architectural design depends not only on the system requirements on a database machine, but also on the existing implementation technology. In particular, it must be recognized that a good-performance database machine is widely sought at a cost reasonable to ordinary users. This section discusses various performance improvement techniques applicable to database processors and their storage management, within the framework of traditional von Neumann computers. It will be shown that if proper techniques are used, various implementation tradeoffs greatly improve the cost-performance characteristics of an IQC.

6.3.1. Considerations of Basic Database Operations

One of the important implementation objectives is to achieve a high performance level by using a processor specialized in database processing. In this approach, high-performance database processing is sought by deriving an optimum mixture of software, firmware, and hardware implementations [11].

For later discussion of these tradeoffs, execution times by software, firmware, and hardware implementations are first evaluated for the following five basic database operations:

1. Index search and scan operations.
2. Bit-map operations.
3. Sorting operations.
4. Address translation.
5. Tuple fetch.

These are very general basic operations in database systems, so that an examination of them is useful for overall evaluation of various database machine architectures. In the next section, higher-level database performance will be discussed using these results.

The specification of a database machine processor under consideration is shown in Table 6.2. This specification represents roughly that of a processor capable of executing one million instructions per second—i.e., a MIPS processor.

6.3.1.1. Index search and scan operations.

Index search is a basic operation of database systems. B-trees are used on many systems, because

TABLE 6.2. SPECIFICATION OF PROCESSOR UNDER CONSIDERATION

Database buffer:	
Word length	32 bits
Cycle time	$T = 450$ ns
Instructions:	
Load/store	900 ns ($2T$)
Register instructions	450 ns (T)
Microinstructions:	
Micro cycle time	150 ns (t)
Microcode length	64 bits
Hardware logic	Transistor-transistor logic (TTL)

the worst-case search time does not become intolerably long. The B-tree provides an index structure in which each node is a fixed-size page. Entries in a page are sorted binarily in the order of key values of those entries. Therefore, searching in each page is carried out in a binary search manner. Thus, the index search execution time for N index entries is expressed as

$$A(\log_2 N + 1) + B$$

where A and B are, respectively, the search time for an entry and the binary search housekeeping overhead. The actual execution time may be evaluated by their programs coded in software and firmware (see the appendix to this chapter). The constants A and B are obtained as follows:

$$A = 14T \qquad \text{and} \quad B = 56T \qquad \text{for software implementation}$$

$$A = 3T + 4t \quad \text{and} \quad B = 3T + 23t \qquad \text{for firmware implementation}$$

where T and t denote, respectively, the memory cycle time and the microprogram cycle time. The execution of index search via firmware is heavily memory-cycle bound, since the memory cycle time contributes $1.35 (= 3T)$ microseconds whereas the microcycle time contributes only $0.6 (= 4t)$ microseconds. It is therefore clear that hardware implementation will not bring about further performance gains.

When multiple tuples may exist for a given key value or key-value range, successive entry readings by way of the index will be needed. That is, the first tuple is located by an index searching and then the following tuples are located by reading the successive index entries sequentially. The operation of finding the next entry in the index is called an *index scan*. The execution time of an index scan is evaluated as follows:

$$140T \text{ for software implementation}$$

$$30T + 20t \text{ for firmware implementation}$$

The comment about the index search execution time given earlier applies also to this case.

6.3.1.2. Bit-map operations.   Bit-map operations are used not only for set operations in relational databases, but also for storage-space management. These operations are not well executed on conventional processors, which are byte- or word-oriented. Typical bit-map operations include finding the location of the first "1" in a bit stream, setting "1" at a given location in a bit stream, and logical operations (AND,OR) between bit streams.

As a simple example, consider finding the bit location of the first "1" in a bit stream whose length is 64 bits. In software and firmware implementations, the operation is carried out in a manner similar to binary searching. That is, first a check is made to determine whether the first half of the bit stream is zero or not. Next, if this check is a failure, the first one-fourth of the same bit stream is checked, and so on. Therefore, the execution time is expressed as

$$A(\log_2 N + 1) + B$$

where N is the bit-stream length. Coding the above algorithm for software and firmware implementations in a manner similar to those in the appendix, we have the values of A and B as follows:

$$A = 6T, \quad B = 4T \qquad \text{for software implementation}$$

$$A = 4t, \quad B = 2T \qquad \text{for firmware implementation}$$

Firmware implementation is more than four times faster than the corresponding software implementation.

On the other hand, this operation can be implemented using a tree of priority encoders, which are available as trivial MSI logic devices [12]. For a 64-bit stream, the tree height becomes two if 8-bit priority encoders are used, so that the delay time becomes less than 100 nanoseconds, assuming the delay time of 30 nanoseconds per TTL priority encoder. This, in turn, makes it possible to execute this operation in 1.2 microseconds, including the bit-stream loading time. The hardware implementation gives a remarkable performance improvement over the corresponding firmware implementation, which gives an execution time of about 5.1 microseconds.

Setting "1" at a given location in a bit stream is similarly carried out in a binary search manner. The execution time is therefore expressed as $A(\log_2 N + 1) + B,$ and the values of A and B are almost the same as above. A logical operation (AND,OR) between two bit streams is, however, simply carried out by a processor's logical instruction, giving the execution times of $2T$ and $T + t,$ respectively, for software and firmware implementations.

6.3.1.3. Sorting operations.   Sorting is an important operation in database systems. It is useful for supporting a data sorting command and a join operation in relational databases. Many sorting algorithms are proposed [13]. A B-tree index, described in the previous section, can maintain a sorted object, but it takes a long time because dynamic data-page creation is involved. Quick sort, heap sort, and Batcher's bitonic sort, among others, are widely known as high-speed sorting algorithms. These algorithms are used selectively according to the objectives and system environments.

Quick sort is about two times faster than heap sort on the average, but the worst-case execution time becomes proportional to N^2, where N is the number of elements to be sorted. On the other hand, the worst-case execution time of heap sort is proportional to $N \log_2 N$. Batcher's bitonic sort is by nature oriented to parallel processing.

The heap-sort algorithm is discussed here because it is suitable to sequential operation. For details of this algorithm, readers are referred to [13]. Letting N be the number of entries, the expected execution time of heap sort is expressed as

$$AN \log_2 N - BN - C$$

where A, B, and C are constants. Coding the algorithm for software and firmware implementations in a manner similar to those in the appendix, the values of constants are evaluated as

$$A = 19T, \qquad B = 19.6T, \qquad C = 46T$$
for software implementation

$$A = (5.5T + 4t), \quad B = (6.6T + 1.8t), \quad C = (5T + 5t)$$
for firmware implementation

In the case of firmware implementation, the memory cycle time occupies most of the execution time, and therefore this heap-sort algorithm is not effectively implementable by hardware logic, owing to the memory cycle bottleneck. We note that $T = 3t$, for large N; firmware implementation is therefore about three times faster than software implementation.

6.3.1.4. Address translation.

A database buffer is physically managed by a paging mechanism for swapping and dynamic space allocation. A logical-to-physical-address translation facility is essential, because all database pages are referenced by the database management system in logical addresses. Even though the database buffer may not be large, a database machine must efficiently handle it. Therefore, a facility suitable for large database buffer address translation is needed.

One of the most useful methods of address translation in this environment is provided by a hashing technique. This technique makes it possible to translate a given logical address to the corresponding physical address much faster than a simple table look-up technique based on linear searches. The address translation facility based on hashing may be implemented in software, firmware, or hardware. If it is implemented in hardware, the facility becomes a look-aside table, often used for cache memory control of large-scale computers, as shown in Figure 6.6. The execution time of address translation based on hashing is evaluated as follows:

$$60T \qquad \text{for software implementation}$$

$$5T + 30t \qquad \text{for firmware implementation}$$

$$2T + 0.3 \qquad \text{for hardware implementation}$$

It is clear from this result that the hardware implementation remarkably shortens the execution time.

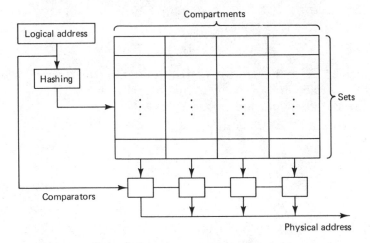

Figure 6.6. Hardware Logic for Address Translation

6.3.1.5. Tuple fetch. Tuple fetch time is the time required to fetch a tuple located by its physical address after an address translation. It is expressed as

$$AN + B$$

where N is the number of bytes to be fetched, and A and B are constants. The values of these constants are evaluated as follows:

$$A = 1.5T, \quad B = 10T \qquad \text{for software implementation}$$

$$A = 0.5T, \quad B = 4T + 5t \qquad \text{for firmware implementation}$$

We see that the execution time for firmware implementation is heavily memory-cycle bound. Therefore, the tuple fetch operation is not suitable for hardware implementation.

6.3.1.6.   Tradeoffs of software, firmware, and hardware.   In previous sections we examined software, firmware, and hardware implementations for several basic database operations. These results are summarized in Table 6.3. The following observations may be made about the tradeoffs:

1. *Firmware effect.* A module implemented by firmware is about four times faster than one by software. The reasons are that the control storage microcycle is three times faster than the memory cycle, that many instruction fetches as well as some operand fetches are avoided, and that concurrent operations, say, between an arithmetic unit and a memory unit, are possible. Moreover, a microprogram is coded more carefully in comparison with a conventional program.

2. *Hardware effect.* The performance of an operation with any memory-cycle bottleneck cannot be effectively improved by hardware implementation. There are, however, several operations that are suitable for hardware implementation. For example, the bit-map operations and address translation facility implemented by hardware would be very valuable, because these operations are quite basic and frequently used in database systems.·

TABLE 6.3. COMPARISON OF BASIC OPERATION EXECUTION TIMES (IN MICROSECONDS)

Basic operation	Software implementation	Firmware implementation	Hardware implementation
Index search (256 entries)	81.9	22.4	–
Index scan	63.0	13.8	–
Bit-map operation (64 bits)	20.7	5.1	1.2
Sorting (1024 entries)	78,500.0	28,200.0	–
Address translation	27.0	6.8	1.2
Tuple fetch (64 bytes)	47.7	17.0	–

It should be cautioned that there are disadvantages peculiar to these implementations. Firmware memory devices are rather expensive and the firmware coding productivity is relatively low. Hardware implementation generally requires a more careful and quantitative evaluation early in the design stage. Therefore, it usually follows that firmware and hardware implementations are rather limited to those critical operations that produce especially large improvements.

6.3.2. Expected Database Machine Performance

This section evaluates the expected higher-level database machine performance for various implementations, based on the basic database operation execution times obtained in the previous section. In particular, the following three operations are considered:

1. Single tuple retrieval through an index.
2. Set operation (AND,OR) on two restrictions.
3. Join operation on two relations.

It is assumed that an index for each database attribute is provided and no page fault occurs during the operation execution. Figure 6.7 outlines the steps of execution for these three operations.

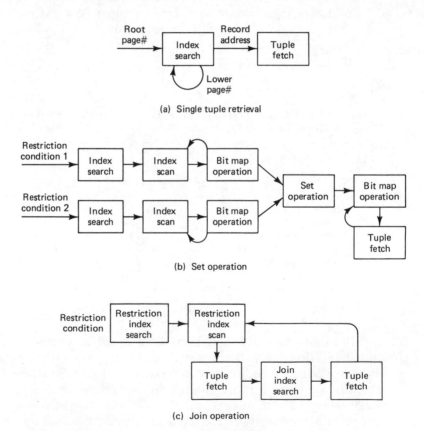

(a) Single tuple retrieval

(b) Set operation

(c) Join operation

Figure 6.7. Outline of the Execution Steps: (a) Single Tuple Retrieval, (b) Set Operation, (c) Join Operation

6.3.2.1. Tuple retrieval by way of indices.   Assuming that the index level is three in height [Figure 6.7(a)] the execution time is obtained as

3[index access time] + [data access time]

$$= 3[\{(\text{address translation time}) + (\text{index search time})\}]$$

$$+ [(\text{address translation time}) + (\text{tuple fetch time})]$$

The execution time of this operation is then evaluated as follows:

1. If all constituent basic operations are implemented by software, the execution time is 401 microseconds.
2. If the address translation is implemented by hardware and other operations are implemented by firmware, the execution time is 89.0 microseconds.

Case 2 represents an ideal implementation, giving a 4.5 times performance improvement over a software implementation represented by case 1.

6.3.2.2. Set operations.   Set operations are carried out using bit maps made by two restriction conditions for a relation. Following the execution steps of Figure 6.7(b), a bit map is created by index searching for the restriction condition. Let N be the number of tuples in the relation and let α and β be the selectivities [14] for the restriction conditions such that $\alpha \geqslant \beta$. Then the execution time is obtained as

$$2\{(\text{address translation time}) + (\text{index search time})\}$$

$$+ (\alpha + \beta)N\{(\text{address translation time}) + (\text{index scan time})$$

$$+ (\text{bit-map operation time})\} + \alpha N(\text{set operation time})$$

$$+ \alpha\beta N\{(\text{bit-map operation time}) + (\text{address translation time})$$

$$+ (\text{tuple-fetch time})\}$$

When $N = 10^5$, $\alpha = 0.01$, and $\beta = 0.01$, the execution time for each implementation becomes as follows:

1. If all basic operations are implemented by software, the execution time is 223 milliseconds.
2. If the address translation and bit-map operations are implemented by hardware and other operations are implemented by firmware, the execution time is 33.2 milliseconds.

This comparison indicates that the effect of hardware implementation of the address translation and bit-map operations is large.

6.3.2.3. Join operations. There are many ways to carry out a join operation. Assume, as a typical case, that two relations are joined by recurrent operations, as shown in Figure 6.7(c) [14]. Let N_1 be the number of tuples in the first relation and α and γ, respectively, be the restriction selectivity and the average number of tuples in the second relation to be joined with a restricted tuple. Then the execution time is obtained as

[restriction index access time] + [join index access time]

$$= [(\text{address translation time}) + (\text{index search time})$$

$$+ \alpha N_1 \{3(\text{address translation time}) + (\text{index scan time})$$

$$+ (\text{tuple fetch time}) + (\text{index search time})\}]$$

$$+ [\alpha \gamma N_1 \{2(\text{address translation time}) + (\text{index scan time})$$

$$+ (\text{data fetch time})\}]$$

When $N_1 = 10^5$, $\alpha = 0.01$, and $\gamma = 1.2$, the execution time becomes as follows:

1. If all basic operations are implemented by software, the execution time is 471 milliseconds.
2. If the address translation is implemented by hardware and other operations are implemented by firmware, the execution time is 97 milliseconds

An ideal implementation of case 2 gives a 4.9 time performance improvement over a software implementation of case 1.

6.3.2.4. Implementation considerations. In previous sections we have examined in detail the performance of several typical database operations implemented in software, firmware, or hardware. We observed that a firmware implementation is useful for almost all operations, improving performance about fourfold over an equivalent software implementation. A hardware implementation, on the other hand, is effective only when the operation is not memory-cycle bound. Bit-map operations and address translation are good candidates for hardware implementation, which improves performance more than tenfold over an equivalent software implementation. These results indicate that the performance of a given software DBMS can be greatly improved by implementation changes, potentially by a factor of up to five. It is therefore very important to consider to what extent hardware and firmware implementations should be introduced into the real design of a database machine. It is felt that microcoding of critical DBMS functions, amounting to several thousand microsteps, together with some hardware-assisted functions, would improve the system performance remarkably.

A realistic way to achieve still higher performance is by the introduction of multiple database processors, which share the database buffer. Problems associated with a multiple-processor configuration are already well understood through years of experience with conventional general-purpose computers. The multiple-processor configuration is also useful for improving system reliability, as discussed later. To go beyond this, the use of a faster basic processor or the use of many processors as a processor complex is necessary. A recent paper reports that, for complex queries, database machines with parallel processing capabilities such as RAP, DBC, and DIRECT are much faster than traditional von Neumann computers [15].

6.3.3. The Storage Hierarchy

A central consideration of a DBMS is how to achieve fast access to desired data in the large stored databases. This problem may be solved if all the databases can be stored on fast devices such as MOS random-access memory. This straightforward solution is technically feasible, but economically infeasible.

Accordingly, a DBMS uses a storage hierarchy, consisting of fast devices for storing a relatively small amount of frequently accessed data and slow but inexpensive devices for storing a large amount of infrequently accessed data. Inexpensive devices that are suitable include magnetic disks, mass storage systems [16], and new optical disks. The more successful the storage hierarchy management is in keeping frequently accessed data in the fast MOS-memory database buffer, the more effective the storage hierarchy will become. For this purpose the storage hierarchy management usually uses the well-known LRU algorithm, but it has been found relatively effective because of the low locality of database references [8].

It is now becoming easier to include a larger MOS-memory database buffer in this storage hierarchy. A reasonable storage hierarchy of a near-future database machine would be a 50-Mbyte MOS-memory database buffer and a tens-of-gigabytes magnetic disk storage with disk cache, and so on. This environment apparently necessitates a new strategy for a more effective storage hierarchy management.

One of the most effective uses of the large database buffer is to store a large amount of database indices. By keeping higher-level components of hierarchically organized indices in the database buffer, fast access to desired data will be greatly facilitated. These index pages sometimes must be resident in the database buffer, rather than being paged with the LRU algorithm. Some prior knowledge of the content of database pages greatly improves the paging effectiveness, as demonstrated by the file adaptive control of the NEC disk cache [17]. Many more new ideas to improve the current simple-minded paging control mechanism are needed. It should be borne in mind that, in a database machine environment, the storage hierarchy management is entirely left to the ingenuity of a database machine.

6.4. RASIS CONSIDERATIONS

The database machine manages a wide variety of shared information for many mutually independent users. It is essential, in this environment, that the information be fully immune from various accidents. The database machine must have high enough availability to assure that users can always access desired information. The information should not be lost or corrupted, even partially. Unauthorized access to the information must be detected, while intended sharing of the information is freely allowed. Thus, reliability, availability, serviceability, integrity, and security (RASIS) considerations are crucial to the satisfactory operation of a database machine. This section describes major RASIS considerations for the IQC.

6.4.1. Reliability, Availability, and Serviceability

The requirement for reliability, availability, and serviceability (RAS) may not be absolute if a database machine is just for an individual's personal use. However, if the machine is shared by many users on multiple hosts, it plays the role of a common information center, and the RAS requirement accordingly becomes paramount. System service losses due to machine component failures or arbitrary data losses in the database could cause immeasurable damage to many users.

In particular, it seems very important to design a database machine in such a way that each host need not know details concerning various internal failures that occur in the machine (see Figure 6.8). First, the design must make the machine's hardware/software complex as reliable as possible. Inclusion of redundancy at major machine components and support of a graceful degradation capability are useful for this purpose [18]. It is often possible to achieve high system availability by using a dynamic reconfiguration capability concerning redundant access interfaces, data transfer paths, processors and memory units, and various control tables.

Second, quick repair and return of the failed components are important

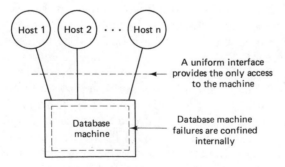

Figure 6.8. Basic RASIS Requirements

to avoid occurrence of multiple failures. For this purpose, various serviceability considerations, such as error-checking mechanisms, on-line diagnosis for suspected components, and good operator interfaces, are definitely useful.

Third, the database machine must support various data-recovery techniques to avoid losses of information due to unexpected hardware/software failures. Though keeping two copies of data is very effective, it is not realistic to rely totally on this expensive technique. Other cost-effective techniques, such as those based on back-up copies and journals, are also needed. Owing to possible data failures, all existing transactions related to the data may have to be backed up. Similarly, for possible host crashes, all transactions on the failed host may have to be backed up. It is important that transactions be backed up quickly whenever a failure is detected.

In the event of host crashes, it is no longer realistic to expect the failed host to back out its transactions after it recovers from the crash. Instead, the database machine should detect a host crash and back out the affected transactions, keeping the usability of common information on the database machine as high as possible for the benefit of many other healthy hosts.

6.4.2. Data Integrity

In a multihost environment, it is important that the database machine have a good data-integrity strategy. In particular, a uniform integrity control, equally applicable to all host accesses, seems very attractive (Figure 6.8). Various integrity control mechanisms at various levels are desired [19]:

1. *User-view consistency checks.* User view is employed not only to provide convenient data models for users, but also to specify user access rights to the logical databases.
2. *Assertions.* Assertions, such as "Salary is less than $50,000," are useful in detecting malicious updates.
3. *Triggers.* Triggers provide a mechanism to cause a selective execution of prescribed action routines when certain unexpected events are detected.
4. *Locks.* Locks are used to preserve logical consistency of data, while maximizing dynamic data availability, by controlling concurrent database accesses.

Host transactions making access to the database machine can no longer bypass these integrity checks at their convenience, since these checks are centralized in the database machine environment. It is therefore reasonable to expect that data integrity will be substantially improved. Finally, it should be noted that, if a host uses multiple database machines, some provision may be required to resolve deadlocks involving lock controls of multiple database machines.

6.4.3. Data Security

When its database must be shared by many users on multiple hosts, a strict yet flexible security control scheme should be incorporated into the database machine. A uniform application of security checks by the machine, which does not permit bypassing of these checks by host transactions, is very important in a multihost environment.

The security control technology ranges from ciphering confidential data using a capability protection mechanism based on authentication of transactions to confining the database machine to a safe compound. In any event, a database machine without appropriate security measures cannot be operated in a satisfactory manner.

6.5. THE IMPLEMENTATION OF AN INFORMATION QUERY COMPUTER

Previous sections have described various design considerations that are believed important in the development of an IQC. Most of these arguments also seem more or less applicable to the design of database machines in general. This section describes a prototype implementation of an IQC at NEC, including a system overview, the system architecture, design highlights, and so on.

6.5.1. A System Overview

A prototype IQC was constructed, after study of various design considerations, to explore the extent to which system objectives described in Section 6.1.2 could be achieved: (1) database independence from the hosts, and (2) cost-effective improvement of database management by a database machine. The major design decisions made in constructing the prototype IQC (denoted hereafter simply as IQC) were as follows:

1. IQC serves as a backend computer for existing host computers.
2. Host computers range from very small to very large ones with various architectures.
3. The logical interface for communication between host application programs and IQC is chosen at the data query level. Physically, various interfaces are provided for the convenience of a wide variety of host computers.
4. The DBMS of IQC supports a relational data model suitable for casual diversified queries.

5. IQC is capable of managing large-scale databases with various purposes.
6. IQC takes full advantage of today's mass-production computer technology, such as VLSI components and large-capacity disks. The IQC architecture allows gradual improvements in performance and RASIS.

Figure 6.9 shows a typical environment where an IQC is shared by various host computers, such as small to large general-purpose computers, personal computers, and local and remote terminals. IQC is physically connected to these hosts, depending on their circumstances, by a variety of interfaces. However, the logical interface between a host computer and the IQC is always the same (except for data transmission performance), regardless of the choice of physical interface. The IQC environment allows direct connection of such small hosts as personal computers and terminals, provided that they have a certain limited amount of intelligence. Thus, IQC is expected to serve not only as a backend computer for many host computers, but also as a database node for a distributed processing network.

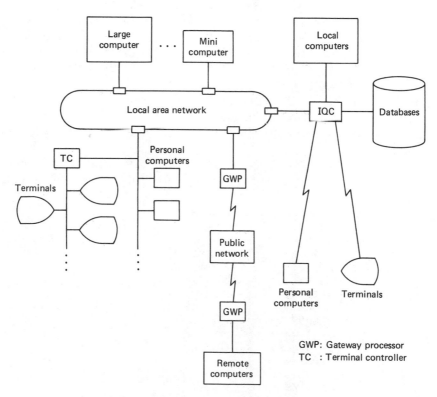

Figure 6.9. An IQC Environment

6.5.2. The IQC System Architecture

We now give some details on important aspects of the IQC system architecture—specifically, the IQC data model, its data structure, logical and physical interfaces, and the overall system structure.

6.5.2.1. Its data model and data structure.

The IQC supports relational DBMS functions, and its data is logically represented in terms of tables. One feature, however, is to allow multivalued domains by ignoring the normalization rule, as in NEC's DBMS called INQ [20]. This is equivalent to allowing hierarchical structures in a relation. Such hierarchical structures can be very natural in modeling real-world information structures of business data processing; some examples are found in employee data, bibliography data, statistical data, and the like. Thus, inclusion of this feature provides the IQC applications with more flexibility, at the expense of normality. Figure 6.10 shows an example of a typical IQC relation described in IQC's data definition language, where fields with "(N)", e.g., FAMILY(N) and SKILL(N), are repeating groups.

The user of IQC sees data organized into one or more independent databases. Each database is a collection of relations for which user views can be provided by user-view definitions. The end user sees data only through these user views without knowing individual relations. Thus, a user view of relations is a static form of join operations on the relations, providing users with a capability similar to that of subschema of CODASYL database. Since it is often possible to predict beforehand how relations are used in database accesses, the user view becomes an effective means for IQC to access data efficiently, avoiding run-time access-path selections for on-line queries from users.

The IQC relation contains an arbitrary number of domains, each of which may be a key field for data retrievals. To assure reasonable response

FDL	EMP-F.
DATABASE	EMPLOY.
PASSWORD	ABC,XYZ.
02 EMP#	PIC 9(6) PKY.*
02 NAME	PIC X(20).
02 AGE	PIC 9(2).
02 ADDR	PIC X(40) DSP.†
02 FAMILY (N).	
03 F-NAME	PIC X(40).
03 F-AGE	PIC 9(2).
02 SKILL (N).	
03 S-NAME	PIC X(10).
03 S-YEAR	PIC 9(2).

*Primary key   †2 Display only

Figure 6.10. An IQC Relation Described in Data Definition Language

time to data-retrieval requests, the inverted index is used. Creation and successive maintenance of this index is automatically performed with a B-tree structure by IQC. However, for those domains that are not used as keys—i.e., the display-only domains—the index will not be created (Figure 6.10).

6.5.2.2. Logical interface.   The logical interface between host computers' application programs and IQC is at the data query level—i.e., the level where queries are given in predicate expressions. The reasons for adopting this level as the logical interface are as follows:

1. At the data query level, the interface is mostly in natural language between independent application programs and the relational DBMS on IQC.
2. As analyzed earlier, the frequency of host/IQC communication is minimized at the data query level, offering more choices of physical host/IQC interfaces.
3. Software required on a host computer is minimized at the data query level. Thus, small computers, such as personal computers and intelligent terminals, can serve as the hosts of IQC.

The host/IQC communication takes place in the form of host commands and IQC responses, using the IQC protocol which defines communication procedures and data formats. Figure 6.11 shows an example of host/IQC communication, where a host requests IQC to send the names, sorted by employee number, of those employees who work in department A and are 29 years old. Host commands and IQC responses are organized into a specific format, which begins with the message identifier followed by a command name and its parameters (or responses). IQC is supposed to interpret the host commands, execute them, and return the results as the IQC responses to multiple hosts.

A host's tasks are the creation and transmission of simple host commands with the above formats, and the receipt of IQC responses in accordance with the IQC protocol. The responsibilities of a host concerning IQC database processing are so limited that the scale of related software required on the host is accordingly small. Thus, even a small computer can serve as an IQC host.

6.5.2.3. Physical interface.   Three kinds of physical interfaces are being considered for connection of host computers and the prototype IQC: a direct channel connection interface by block multiplexer channels, a high-speed loop connection interface, and a general communication interface. Regardless of the choice of physical interface, the logical interface between the host and IQC remains the same, as discussed in the previous section.

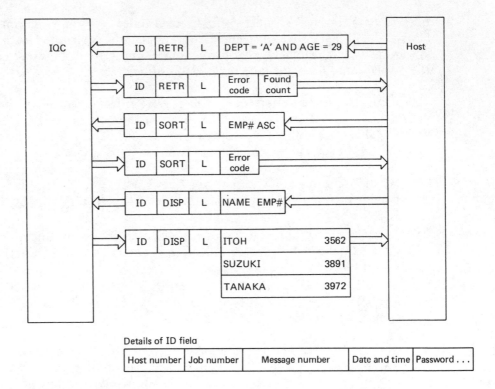

Details of ID field

Host number	Job number	Message number	Date and time	Password . . .

ID: Identification
Commands RETR: Retrieve
        SORT: Sort
        DISP: Display
L : Message length

Figure 6.11. An Example of Host/IQC Communication

In general, the choice of physical interface should be based on the following factors:

1. Physical distance between a host and IQC.
2. Frequency of access made to IQC.
3. Provision on a host for the connection of IQC.

6.5.2.4. The overall system structure.   Figure 6.12 illustrates the conceptual organization of the IQC environment, depicting its major components and interfaces. Though this figure is almost self-explanatory, some comments may be in order. The IQC hardware includes IQC processors with main memory, on-line disks as database storage, magnetic tapes for database back-up, physical interfaces for IQC/host connection, and so on.

On the other hand, the IQC software includes the IQC control program

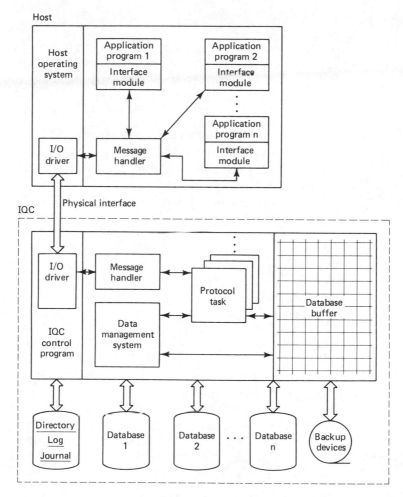

Figure 6.12.   The Conceptual Organization of IQC

and various programs that run under its supervision, such as the message handler, protocol tasks, and the data management system. The message handler is responsible for maintaining smooth communication with its counterpart on a host in accordance with the IQC protocol. It receives a host command as a message from a host and passes it over to a waiting protocol task. The protocol task then executes the host command with the help of the data management system and returns the result to the message handler, which in turn sends the result to the original host as a message from IQC.

Input/output requests for database access by the protocol tasks are all handled by the data management system. It performs efficient input/output operations, using a large common database buffer under its hierarchical storage control.

6.5.3. Design Highlights

We now describe some of the IQC design highlights—in particular, considerations pertinent to facilitation of IQC database sharing among a wide variety of hosts, practical storage management based on the traditional index technique, and RASIS in the IQC environment.

6.5.3.1. Facilities for database sharing among various hosts.
In meeting the increasing need for processing power and database services to a user institution in a distributed computer environment, it is desirable that the installation can satisfy this requirement by adding a new cost-effective computer to the existing system, rather than by upgrading the entire system totally. It is becoming more and more common that a user installation has computers of different makes or often different architectures. This tendency brings them various benefits on the one hand, but causes some serious interconnection problems on the other hand. One interconnection problem is that of database sharing among computers with different architectures. At present, it is rather difficult to solve this problem; today's commonly used method of exchanging data by manual transfer of magnetic tapes or by file transfer on a network gives only a partial solution. IQC aims to provide a more efficient and more complete solution to this problem by allowing direct connection of various computer systems to IQC.

We noted earlier that the choice of a data query level as the logical interface between a host application program and IQC facilitates the connection of various heterogeneous hosts. Major functions required on a host are communication with IQC using the physical interface, and preparation and interpretation of messages in accordance with IQC data format. The former is performed by a program called the message handler and the latter by an interface module linked with an application program.

The Message Handler. The responsibilities of the message handler on a host including sending and receiving messages interacting with the IQC, and passing and receiving the same messages interacting with the interface modules of application programs. Thus, the message handler renders IQC access services to application programs on the host. Communication between the message handler and an individual interface module is accomplished using an intertask communication facility of the host operating system. The message handler requires about one thousand steps of coding, including exception handlers, table initialization routines, and so on, with a core of about two hundred steps.

Interface Modules. An interface module provides its associated application program with access entries corresponding to individual commands, for ease of programming. It receives an IQC access request from the application program, prepares a message in the prescribed data format, and passes it to the message handler. An interface module may be called using a CALL statement with appropriate parameters from an application program written in COBOL, FORTRAN, PL/I, and so on.

An example, shown in Figure 6.13, indicates that an application program requests the names and employee numbers of employees who work in department A and are 29 years old and that the IQC finds three employees with this qualification. It should be noted that, though communication in terms of command and response between the message handler and the interface module occurs twice (retrieve and display messages), communication between the interface module and the application program occurs four times (one retrieve message and three display messages). The interface module returns the result message containing information regarding three employees actually as three submessages to lighten the burden on the application program.

An interface module requires about two thousand steps of coding, including service routines for all commands, with a core of about one to two hundred steps. The program sizes mentioned above represent those of the NEC ACOS environment, but those figures are believed not to change too much on other mainframe computers. However, for small host computers that do not require multiprogramming, the host software size can be significantly reduced by combining the interface module and the message handler into a single program.

6.5.3.2. Storage management techniques.

The storage management techniques used on IQC are based on traditional indexing with a B-tree organization. This traditional method has the following practical advantages:

1. It has high flexibility in making full use of rapidly advancing large-capacity database-buffer and low-cost disk-storage technologies.
2. It is capable of handling up to large-scale databases, without incurring significant performance degradation.

Prearrangement of indices used on IQC has an immense effect on reducing the number of data access incurred, though it may somewhat decrease the flexibility of processing of actual retrieval requests. The indexing method is most useful when the database is large, whether it is stored on moving-head disks, disk cache, bubble memory, or other storage devices.

The IQC manages a large database buffer in the main memory according to the least recently used (LRU) algorithm. Pages that store a higher-level index tend to be referenced frequently by retrieval transactions and therefore tend to remain in the database buffer under the LRU algorithm, assuring a relatively short response time. This indicates that the LRU storage manage-

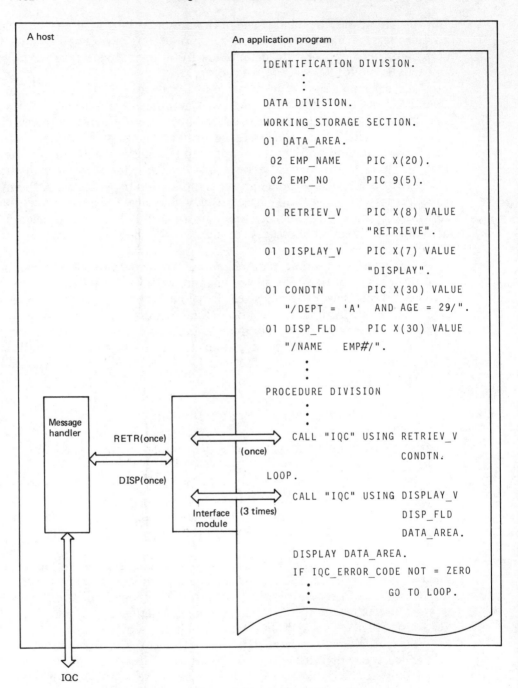

Figure 6.13. Sample of an Application Program Interface

ment and indexing are largely compatible. However, references to database pages do not necessarily show high locality. JOIN operations (equijoin) on two relations are also performed by indexing on IQC.

The foregoing arguments suggest that wide and proper use of indices on IQC provide a very practical means to maintain reasonable system performance without significantly increasing the system's overall cost. The large database buffer is also useful in moderating the difficulties of handling heavy update requests.

6.5.3.3. RASIS considerations of IQC. When IQC databases are shared by a variety of application programs on multiple host computers, the RASIS considerations are essential to the usefulness of IQC, as discussed in Section 6.5. The IQC software/hardware complex specifically has the following considerations:

1. The dynamic reconfiguration capability of IQC allows on-line removal of a faulty IQC component, such as an IQC processor, a main memory unit, or a disk unit, without stopping its service. The system performance will be gracefully degraded in such a case.

2. IQC allows creation of back-up copies of disk databases on magnetic tapes as needed.

3. IQC performs journaling of before and after images in terms of logical data images each time the database is updated.

4. If IQC detects a host crash, it will automatically back up all the transactions that were running on the host to their previous states at the last checkpoint.

5. If IQC detects an internal failure that damages a portion of the database, it will similarly back up just the affected transactions to their previous states at the last checkpoint.

6. IQC does not allow any host access that does not observe the IQC protocol. The message identifier of a host message has a field to carry a password to IQC. The DBMS on IQC has various security measures.

6.5.4. Future extensions. The prototype IQC described above is not a completed system. As a matter of fact, there are still plans to experiment on this prototype to gain more practical experience with this kind of database machine. Major extensions of this prototype that are now envisioned include performance improvement and its adaptation to office automation applications.

In two areas a large performance improvement can be expected. The first area is database buffer expansion. The continuing progress of VLSI technology leaves no doubt that future computer systems can afford extremely large MOS main memory. For example, a 50-Mbyte database buffer would make storage management based on traditional indexing very efficient, even for very large databases stored on many volumes of ordinary large-capacity disks. The second area for improvement is that of processing speed. The adoption of a high-speed processor as an IQC processor is one way. Tuning the existing IQC processor, using additional firmware and hardware, is another way. As discussed in detail in Section 6.3, a firmware implementation of index access operations, set operations, sort operations, and the like, together with a hardware implementation of address translation, bit-map operations, and so on, for example, would surely improve the processing speed to a great extent.

It is widely believed that database machines will play an important role in the office of the future. IQC has several provisions for managing various kinds of information, in addition to those needed simply for supporting a relational DBMS. However, full-scale provisions for managing various variable-length information, such as texts, documents, images, and voices, will become essential in the office environment. It is also very important that a wide variety of small office machines of different makes can receive the benefit of information services by a database machine. The host/IQC independence described in this chapter will provide a starting point in the study of such environments.

6.6. CONCLUSIONS

The database machine concept first emerged in the mid 1970s, but it has been only two or three years since the first commercial database machine became available. Database machines that are useful to diversified database users seem to be still in their infancy. Much more effort is needed to develop mature database machines for the future database environment. This chapter has introduced one of these efforts underway at NEC by describing IQC design considerations and its prototype implementation.

After a short review of NEC's basic research on database machines, major motivations for initiating research on IQC were stated. One of them is the study of database independence from hosts. This property is crucial in the realization of a common database machine, which is a backend of multiple host computers, small and large, with different architectures. Furthermore, liberation of a database from all sorts of host constraints in software and hardware permits the database to grow independently without being a part of host expansions. The other motivation is the study of database management cost-effectiveness improvement. The study of effectiveness includes such factors as accessibility, reliability, integrity, security, performance, expandability, and so on.

Main points vital to IQC design considerations were described one by one in some detail. The items discussed are the host/IQC logical and physical interfaces, architectural considerations, and RASIS considerations. Although special emphasis was placed on IQC, most of the main points made in this chapter are appropriate to database machines in general. An implementation study of IQC was then presented as a concrete example.

The authors feel that the initial results of the IQC implementation are encouraging toward a reasonable achievement of database independence from hosts and a significant improvement of database management cost-effectiveness. The implementation approach taken by the prototype IQC described in this chapter may be somewhat conservative. However, this prototype is believed to provide an appropriate steppingstone to more ambitious database machines for the future. Once database independence from hosts is attained, it will not be difficult to introduce more elaborate schemes or innovative technologies for further improvement of database machine cost-effectiveness. It is important to take a new step forward toward the future innovative machines rather than waiting for the advent of an innovative technology.

History shows that thousands of novel ideas have emerged but only a few of them have been actually accepted. The authors believe that overall database machine considerations that allow smooth and gradual migration from today's user environment to a new database machine environment are extremely important. It should be also added that years of assiduous effort are still needed for the development of database machines that will be widely accepted.

6.7. ACKNOWLEDGEMENT

The authors would like to thank Masayuki Hashimoto, Takuo Kitamura, and Dr. Tohru Mikami for their continuous encouragement on the work described in this paper and the members of the GDS research group of NEC C&C Systems Laboratories for various discussions on database machines.

REFERENCES

[1] Bray, O. H., and Freeman, H. A., *Data Base Computers,* Lexington Books, 1979.

[2] Hsiao, D. K., and Madnick, S. E., "Database Machine Architecture in the Context of Information Technology Evolution," *Proc. 3d Int. Conf. on Very Large Data Bases,* 1977, pp. 64–84.

[3] Su, S. Y. W., Chang, H., Copeland, G., Fisher, P., Lowenthal, E., and Schuster, S., "Database Machines and Some Issues on DBMS Standards," *Proc. AFIPS NCC,* 1980, pp. 191–208.

[4] Uemura, S., Yuba, T., Kokubu, A., Ohomote, R., and Sugawara, Y., "The Design and Implementation of a Magnetic-Bubble Database Machine," *IFIP '80, 1980,* pp. 433–438.

[5] Hakozaki, K., Makino, T., Mizuma, M., Umemura, M., and Hiyoshi, S., "A Conceptual Design of a Generalized Database Subsystem," *Proc. 3d Int. Conf. on Very Large Data Bases,* 1977, pp. 264–253.

[6] Tanaka, Y., Nozaka, Y., and Masuyama, A., "Pipeline Searching and Sorting Modules as components of a Data Flow Database Computer," *IFIP '80,* 1980, pp. 427–432. (See a more up-to-date version of the work by Tanaka in this book.)

[7] Hara, K., Goto, T., Miyazaki, T., and Takeuchi, K., "Relational Data Base Systems INQ and RIQS" (to appear in 1983).

[8] Umemura, M., and Hakozaki, K., "Buffer Management Tuned to Database Access Behavior," *Journal of Information Processing,* Vol. 4, No. 3 (1981), pp. 142–146.

[9] Makino, T., Mizuma, M., Hiyoshi, S., Watanabe, M., and Hakozaki, K., "An Evaluation of a Generalized Database Subsystem," *Journal of Information Processing,* Vol. 5, No. 1, 1982, pp. 30–37.

[10] Heller, A., and Van Dam, A., "Vertical and Outboard Migration–A Progress Report," *Proc. AFIPS NCC,* 1981, pp. 69–74.

[11] Eckhouse, R., and Estabrook, J., "Operating System Enhancement through Firmware," *Proc. 10th Annual Workshop on Microprogramming,* 1977, pp. 119–128.

[12] For instance, the 74 LS/47, *The Bipolar Digital Integrated Circuits Data Book for Design Engineers, Part 1,* Texas Instruments, 1982.

[13] Knuth, D. E., *The Art of Computer Programming: Sorting and Searching,* Addison-Wesley Publishing Company, Reading, Mass., 1973, pp. 146–149.

[14] Yao, S. B., "Optimization of Query Evaluation Algorithm," *ACM Trans. Database Systems,* Vol. 4, No. 2 (1979), pp. 133–155.

[15] Hawthorn, P. B., and DeWitt, D. J., "Performance Analysis of Alternative Database Machine Architectures," *IEEE Trans. Software Engineering,* Vol. SE-8, No. 1 (1982), pp. 61–75.

[16] Sekino, A., and Kitamura, T., "Architectural Considerations of the NEC Mass Data File Subsystem," *Proc. AFIPS NCC,* 1979, pp. 557–564.

[17] Tokunaga, T., Hirai, Y., and Yamamoto, S., "Integrated Disk Cache System with File Adaptive Control," *Proc. COMPCON,* 1980, pp. 412–416.

[18] Randell, B., Lee, P. A., and Treleaven, P. C., "Reliability Issues in Computer System Design," *Computing Surveys,* Vol. 10, No. 2 (1978), pp. 123–165.

[19] Gray, J., McJones, P., Blasgen, M., Lindsay, B., Lorie, R., Price, T., Putzolu, F., and Traiger, I., "The Recovery Manager of the System R Database Manager," *Computing Surveys,* Vol. 13, No. 2 (1981), pp. 223–242.

[20] Hashimoto, M., Goto, T., Takeuchi, K., Mabuchi, S., and Doi, T., "Database Management System; INQ (Information Query)," *NEC R&D,* No. 58, 1980, pp. 33–41.

APPENDIX 6.1.   EXECUTION-TIME EVALUATION OF INDEX
(B-TREE INDEX) SEARCH OPERATION

	Code	Frequency	Instruction	Microcode	Comment
BS:	read NE → r1	1	$2T$	T	Page header is read
	read EL → r2	1	$2T$	T	NE = # of entries
	r1 → r3	1	T	(t)	EL = entry length
	shift r3	av. 7	T	(t)	
	if r3 = 0	av. 7	T	t	
	then count down	av. 7	T	–	
	r3 = "01"	1	T	t	NE/2
	count down	av. 6	T	t	
	if count = 0	av. 6	T	–	
	else shift r3	av. 6	$2T$	t	
	r3 → r4	1	T	t	
BI:	r4/2 → r4	$\log_2 N + 1$	T	t	
	if r4 = 0 go to ED	$\log_2 N + 1$	$2T$	–	
	read line (r3)	$\log_2 N + 1$	$2T$	T	
	read entry	$\log_2 N + 1$	$2T$	T	
	compare key	$\log_2 N + 1$	$2T$	T	
	if key = entry	$\log_2 N + 1$	$2T$	t	Binary search
	then r3 + r4 → r3	$\log_2 N + 1$	T	t	
	else r3 – r4 → r3	$\log_2 N + 1$	T	t	
	if r3 ≠ r1	$\log_2 N + 1$	T	t	
	then r3 = r1	1	T	t	
	go to BI	$\log_2 N + 1$	$2T$	–	
ED:	return	1	$2T$	t	

$$14T(\log_2 N + 1) + 56T \qquad (3T + 4t)(\log_2 N + 1) + (3T + 23t)$$

7

A Data-stream Database Machine with Large Capacity

Yuzuru Tanaka

7.0. ABSTRACT

Our machine consists of two major components: the encoder/decoder, and the kernel database machine. Variable-length values in databases are encoded by one-to-one functions to fixed-length codes. Attributes used for comparison are encoded by one of the same functions. The encoding functions need not order-preserving. The encoded databases are stored in the kernel database machine, which efficiently processes fixed-length data. Coded data in the retrieved results are decoded to their values. Both the encoding and decoding processes are performed by the encoder/decoder. The kernel database machine consists of three subsystems and functional interconnection networks among them. They realize the high performance of the machine.

Files are segmented in our machine. The directory of segments is represented by a binary trie, which also handles the overflow of segments. Each segment is considered as an object with certain object description. Database processing is performed by controlling the object flow to and from the storage and processing modules. The control of the flow is facilitated by a data-flow architecture. When a segment flows through a processing module, intended operations are carried out on the segment. The processing of segments is overlapped with the transfer of segments.

In Section 7.2 we state the basic considerations that have led us to the present architecture. In Section 7.3 we explain the abstract architecture of our machine. In Section 7.4 we present the architecture of processing and storage modules, while in Section 7.5 we show the architecture of each sub-system. In Section 7.6 we show the performance improvement of the kernel database machine by the multiplicity of the subsystems.

7.1. INTRODUCTION

Studies of database machines yielded various proposals in the 1970s. According to Bray and Freeman [1], these proposals may be classified into five categories: A *single-processor-indirect-search* (SPIS) machine is a conventional computer that is used as a backend machine to off-load various functions of a database management system software from the host computer [2, 3, 4]. Some of the backends utilized not only software but also firmware [5, 6]. The new challenge stemmed from the incompatibility between conventional computer hardware and the functional requirements of database management, resulting in a *single-processor-direct-search* (SPDS) machine architecture where an associative-search (or content-addressing) mechanism is introduced into the secondary storage devices of the backend [7, 8, 9]. A *multiple-processor-direct-search* (MPDS) machine introduces a high degree of parallelism in the associative-search (or content-addressing) mechanisms to the secondary storage [10]. With the advent of solid-state rotating memories such as charged-coupled and magnetic bubble memory devices, it becomes easier to attach associative-search or content-addressing mechanisms to the rotating loops of the memory storage. Consequently, considerable research activities have focused on MPDS architecture [11, 12].

Since the capacity of solid-state devices is much smaller than that of moving-head disks, MPDS machines are confronted with the problem of storage capacity. To solve this problem, solid-state rotating memories are used as staging buffers of the moving-head disks of the MPDS machines. This improvement has resulted in a *multiple-processor-indirect-search* (MPIS) machine [13]. Recent price reduction of dynamic RAM enables the use of RAM in lieu of solid-state rotating memories as staging buffers (14). The combination of content addressing of indices on solid-state rotating memories and content addressing of data on moving-head disks entails the first total system design of a *multiple-processor-combined search* (MPCS) machine with detail considerations [15].

As the relational model of databases has established itself among the more traditional models, the join operation attracts the attention of database machine researchers. The join operation incurs heavy processing, which greatly increases the response time and diminishes the throughput performance of a conventional computer. The join operation requires cross reference of two relations. Since the SPDS architecture has no facilities for cross reference, it cannot execute join operations without collaboration with its host computer. In the MPDS and MPIS architectures, each relation is basically stored in one track of the disk storage and processed by a cell dedicated to this track. The cross reference of two relations causes heavy data transfers from one cell processor to the other, which seriously diminishes the performance. As a solution, an interconnection network is placed between a set of cell processors and a set of disk tracks. A network (e.g., cross-bar switches) may also be placed among solid-state rotating devices and moving-head disks. DIRECT is a machine of these types that provides the improvement [16].

Recent research on highly concurrent VLSI architectures has encouraged the replacement of software join with hardware join. Most of the approaches in this direction use some kind of the sort-merge algorithm for join operation. Various VLSI modules are proposed to speed up the execution of join. Among them are the systolic arrays for join [17], the DBC's join processor [18], and the search-and-sort engine [19]. Specialization of database machines on the relational model is important also in a practical sense, since there are relational software systems. However, it is also necessary to develop a relational database machine with the following capabilities:

1. To accommodate variable-length tuples.
2. To join two relations with up to 10^6 tuples each in $O(n)$ time, where n is the number of tuples of the larger relation.
3. To execute a join where the join attribute is may take a value of more than 100 characters.

This chapter presents the basic design of a relational database machine with these three capabilities.

In addition to capabilities, we focus on our choice of storage technology. Instead of utilizing the solid-state rotating memories as our database store, we employ moving-head disks, since our machine is designed for very large relational databases. We therefore impose the condition that the machine use moving-head disk units as its database store and that the disks cooperate closely with the subsystems of the machine. As a basic design, we will not address issues that may enhance the machine such as segmentation of relations, look-ahead access of tuples and their prestaging, and improvements of disk units and disk controllers.

We will consider our machine architecture in terms of two major components: (1) the encoder/decoder, and (2) the kernel database machine.

7.2. ARCHITECTURAL CONSIDERATIONS

Database machines must have high performance and large capacity. Basic features of our machine will be explained from these two viewpoints.

7.2.1. High Performance

Our ways to achieve performance are to provide a highly parallel and functionally distributed architecture and to preprocess the database for encoding and transposition.

Two database machine architectures, one with an encoded database and one without encoding, are shown in Figure 7.1. Each variable-length value in a database is transformed to a fixed-length code. When a query Q is issued against a database Δ, the encoder transforms each variable-length value in Q to its code and issues the encoded query $e(Q)$ against the encoded database $e(\Delta)$. The kernel database machine that processes the encoded database executes $e(Q)$ against $e(\Delta)$. The decoder transforms the result $e(Q)(e(\Delta))$ to $d(e(Q)(e(\Delta)))$. The two functions e and d are appropriately defined so that $d(e(Q)(e(\Delta)))$ are equal to $Q(\Delta)$ for any Q and Δ.

Since the kernel database machine processes fixed-length codes, its high performance hardware is much easier to implement than that of database machines that must process variable-length values. Besides, the kernel database machine needs far less capacity, since it stores the encoded database $e(\Delta)$ instead of Δ.

The encoding of databases is not common, however, for the following reasons. Consider the processing of a join, $R[A > B]S$, in an encoded database. Both the A-attribute of the relation R and the B-attribute of the relation S must be encoded by the same one-to-one function f, such that f preserves the order defined in the merged domain of A-attribute and B-attribute:

$$a > b \quad \text{if and only if} \quad f(a) > f(b)$$

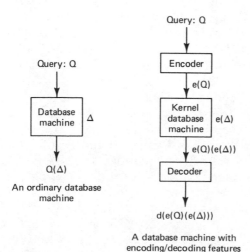

An ordinary database machine

A database machine with encoding/decoding features

Figure 7.1. Two Equivalent Database Machine Architectures: (a) An Ordinary Database Machine, (b) A Database Machine with Encoding/Decoding Features

This is referred to as an order-preserving condition. It is practically impossible to construct an order-preserving encoding function whose domain is not known a priori, since update of the database may add a new value to either one of the attribute domains. Besides, the encoding introduces new overheads in update execution. We remove the condition by further considerations on the characteristics of database processing; we also overcome the overhead by utilizing a global pipeline architecture. These will be explained in later sections.

Further performance improvement is achieved by providing transposed relations—i.e., inverted files of the encoded database $e(\Delta)$. A transposed relation of a relation R with respect to its attribute A is a table with two columns and a method with fast access to its first column values. The first column represents the values of the A attribute, the second the tuple identifier of R. Each row of the table therefore consists of a pair of an A-attribute value and a tuple identifier whose tuple has the attribute value. The provision of such files decreases the number of tuples to be processed. It also decreases the secondary memory accesses if relations are appropriately segmented in secondary memory devices. The overheads can be resolved by the concurrent processing of relations and their inverted files.

Highly parallel and functionally distributed architecture will be realized by the extensive use of VLSI technologies. They enable us to design not only high-performance microprocessors that are tailored for database processing but also nonprogrammable high-speed functional modules. Each functional module should be designed so as to embody a high-volume primitive operation that is commonly used in database processing. Examples are sort-and-batch search operations. *Batch search* denotes batch processing of many search processes with different search keys on the same table. Database processing using such functional modules requires frequent transfers of large amounts of data among various processing and storage modules. This distinguishes database processing from other fields of computation. If data are sequentially transferred, the required transfer time becomes a serious concern. High-speed functional modules require that data to be processed are sent to them ahead of time and ready for their fast processing. If the amount of data is large enough to increase the transfer time, then overlapping of processing with transfer (i.e., the effective use of the transfer time for processing) is highly desirable. Modules with overlapping capability reduce hardware complexity without any degradation of total performance. Processing that is overlapped with sequential data transfer is called *data-stream processing*. Each functional module for database processing is desired to embody data-stream processing facilities.

Early database machines such as RAP [10] are more or less based on the on-the-fly search of a rotating memory. This may be considered as a kind of data-stream processing applied to the sequential search for a single key. Data-stream processing of a join operation was proposed by the author in

1980 [19], where a join operation is decomposed into a number of sort-and-batch search operations, and two functional modules are proposed for their data-stream processing. These modules are called a *sort engine* (SOE) and a *search engine* (SEE). Our machine architecture proposed in this chapter uses these two modules as its basic components.

7.2.2. Large Capacity

Database machines with large capacity inevitably use moving-head disks as their secondary storage. Segmentation is necessary to divide each data set into accessing and processing units. High-speed processing of segmented files needs look-ahead accesses of segments and their prestaging in buffer storage. Segments are processed during their flow through various processing modules. Some architecture is necessary for controlling the (1) access to look-ahead segments, (2) prestaging of segments, and (3) flow of segments through various modules. The control of a segment does not need any information about each of its contents but a description about which relation it represents and where it is stored. Each segment can be treated as a single object with some descriptions. Therefore, the control of segments is performed by an object-oriented architecture.

The diversity of disk access times makes it difficult to schedule the control of segments prior to the execution. Besides, highly concurrent operations among seek, read, and processing are necessary for performance enhancement. These need a data-flow control architecture. In our database machine, files are segmented, and each segment is treated as an object. A data-flow mechanism controls the moves of objects to and from various processing and storing modules.

7.2.3. Data Types of the Attributes

The value domains of database attributes are classified into five data types:

1. Arithmetic numbers.
2. Identification numbers.
3. Chronological values.
4. Short character strings.
5. Long character strings.

Arithmetic numbers denote ordinary numbers with the four rules of arithmetic. Their type includes integers, fixed-point numbers, and floating-point numbers. *Identification numbers* look like arithmetic numbers, but their arithmetic operations are insignificant. *Chronological values* denote such triples as month-day-year or hour:minute:second. Examples are March-28-1982 and 11:00:00. Their arithmetic operations, such as 60 days after

TABLE 7.1. FIVE TYPES OF DATABASE ATTRIBUTES

	Order	Sort	θ-Selection	θ-Join, θ-restriction	+, -, ×, ÷
Arithmetic number	√	√	√	√	√
Identification number	√	√	√		
Chronological value	√	√	√	√	√*
Short character string	√	√	√		
Long character string					

*Limitation or restriction.

March-28-1982, have significant meanings. Types 4 and 5 are character-string types. Attributes of the short-character-string type may appear in queries as join attributes or restriction attributes, while those of the long-character-string type may appear as selection attributes but neither as join attributes nor as restriction attributes. For example, the abstract attribute of a bibliographic database is classified as the long-character-string type because it seldom appears as a join or restriction attribute.

Table 7.1 shows these types and their characteristic features. This table will be used to show that the requirement of order-preserving one-to-one functions in encoding databases is unnecessary. A checkmark indicates that it is possible for the type to have the feature. The first column indicates whether some order can be defined. The second column shows whether this order can be used to sort the output list of retrieved results. The third and fourth columns concern relational operations relating to the order of values. Selections, restrictions, and joins with comparison operators other than equality are referred to as θ-selections, θ-restrictions, and θ-joins, respectively. The third column shows whether θ-selections might be applied, while the fourth shows whether either θ-restrictions, or θ-joins might be applied. The last column indicates whether the four rules of arithmetic are defined. In practical situations, it is hard to imagine either θ-restrictions or θ-joins being applied to such types as the identification number, the short character string, and the long character string.

7.2.4. Database Processing with an Encoded Database

Since chronological values can be easily converted to arithmetic numbers, encoding is necessary only for identification numbers, short character strings, and long character strings. These types are referred to as *code types*. Two attributes A and B are said to be domain-related if the comparison of A and B is a result of either a restriction or a join. We assume that attributes are known to have their subtypes. Each subtype is included by one of the five types. Domain-related attributes are assumed to have the same subtype. These assumptions can be easily justified by some modification of database design processes. For example, attributes "employee" and "employer" may be declared to have the "name" subtype, which is a subtype of the short-character-string type.

The values of each subtype are encoded by a single one-to-one function so that equirestrictions and equijoins may be correctly computed by the encoding/decoding architecture. The order of values is referred to by such relational operations as sorted output, θ-selections, θ-restrictions, and θ-joins. In the encoding/decoding architecture, sorting of output lists can be performed after the decoding of the retrieved results. For the execution of a θ-selection, $R[A > `a`]$ for example, the encoder first finds a set of A-values v_1, v_2, ..., v_n that are greater than 'a' and sends a stream $S(A)$—i.e., $e(v_1)$, $e(v_2)$, ..., $e(v_n)$—to the kernel database machine that processes encoded databases. During this transfer $S(A)$ is sorted in the order of its codes. The kernel database machine receives a sorted stream $S(A)\uparrow$ and executes a join $R[A = A](S(A)\uparrow)$. This join can be regarded as a batch search operation. Neither a sorted output nor a θ-selection needs order-preserving encoding functions. Furthermore, neither a θ-restriction nor a θ-join requires sorted codes. Therefore, encoding functions used in the encoding/decoding architecture require no order-preserving properties.

In the encoding/decoding architecture, statistical calculations should be executed by the kernel database machine. Otherwise, a bulky intermediate result will have to be decoded for further processing of the same query. This seriously lowers the performance. Now, we have to examine whether statistical calculations can be executed by the kernel database machine. Since arithmetic operations are not defined for attributes of code types, neither the summation nor the average of such attribute values is defined. The counting of different values can be executed using an encoded database. Remaining statistical operations are the maximum-value search and the minimum-value search. These seem to have no significance for the values of code types. Therefore, statistical calculations can be executed by the kernel database machine.

7.3. ABSTRACT ARCHITECTURE

7.3.1. Encoder/Decoder

Instead of having an encoder and a decoder independently, we merge them into a single subsystem (Figure 7.2). This reduces the overheads in update operations.

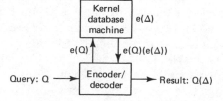

Figure 7.2. A Modified Encoder/Decoder Architecture of Database Machines

(a)   Subtype definition:
      Subtype
      _____

            Name = short_character_string;
            Place = short_character_string;
      Attribute
      _____

            Student = Name;
            Age = integer;
            Home_Town = Place;
            City = Place;
            Prefecture = Place;

(b)   Original relations:

R	Student	Age	Home Town
	Suzuki	26	Kyoto
	Tanaka	23	Sapporo
	Fukuda	24	Tokyo

S	City	Prefecture
	Tokyo	Tokyo
	Osaka	Osaka
	Sapporo	Hokkaido
	Kyoto	Kyoto

(c)   Encoding/decoding tables:

Name	Use Count	Code
Fukuda	$((R, Student), 1)$	0
Suzuki	$((R, Student), 1)$	2
Tanaka	$((R, Student), 1)$	1

Place	Use Count	Code
Hokkaido	$((S, Prefecture), 1)$	3
Kyoto	$((R, Home\_Town), 1)((S, City), 1)((S, Prefecture), 1)$	2
Osaka	$((S, City), 1)((S, Prefecture), 1)$	0
Sapporo	$((R, Home\_Town), 1)((S, City), 1)$	1
Tokyo	$((R, Home\_Town), 1)((S, City), 1)((S, Prefecture), 1)$	4

(d)   Encoded relations:

R	Student	Age	Home Town
	2	26	2
	1	23	1
	0	24	4

S	City	Prefecture
	4	4
	0	0
	1	3
	2	2

Figure 7.3. Encoding of a Database

For each subtype to be encoded, the encoder/decoder has a file as shown in Figure 7.3(c). The use-count field indicates how many places the original value appears in each attribute of each relation. For each subtype, a hash function $h: \Sigma^* \to \{0, 1\}^l$ is used to search the file for specified value. The segmentation of each file is dynamically managed by the extendible hashing technology proposed in [20]. Assume that a segment $S(b_0 b_1 \dots b_{k-1})$ stores all the values whose hash values have binary digits $b_0 b_1 \dots b_{k-1}$ as their first k bits. If an overflow occurs in $S(b_0 b_1 \dots b_{k-1})$, it is split into $S(b_0 b_1 \ldots b_{k-1} 0)$ and $S(b_0 b_1 \ldots b_{k-1} 1)$, and the records stored in $S(b_0 b_1 \ldots b_{k-1})$ are distributed to these two segments according to their hash values. The length l is chosen large enough for the overflow handling. A directory for the segment management is represented by a trie as in Figure 7.4.

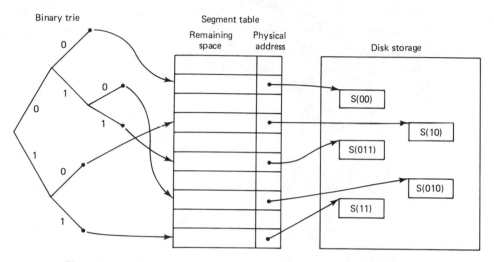

Figure 7.4. A Directory of Segments and Its Representation by a Binary Trie

In each segment, values are not necessarily arranged in sorted order. Each segment is partitioned into two portions (Figure 7.5). An entry portion has a set of hash values stored in this segment. The last l_1 bits of each hash value are used as its address in the entry portion. Conflicts are resolved by chaining synonyms. Each hash value has a pointer to a list storing records of synonymous values. A record portion stores such a list for each hash value.

The search for a specified value is performed as follows. This value is first hashed by h and the trie of the directory is searched for the hash value to obtain the segment that possibly includes this value. This segment is read out from the secondary memory. Its entry portion is searched for the hash value to get a pointer to the list that possibly includes the sought value. The list is sequentially searched for the sought value.

Instead of having an encoding table, we use hash values for the encoding. Each code consists of an l-bit hash value and an l_2-bit extension code (Figure 7.6). Extension codes uniquely identify the synonyms that have a common hash value. Only the extension code is stored for each value in the record portion of a segment.

As mentioned in Section 7.2.4, θ-selections need the encoder/decoder to find a set of codes whose original values are, for example, greater than a given value. If the hash function is arbitrarily chosen, such processing needs

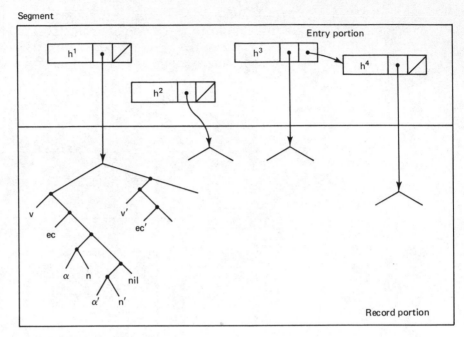

h: Hash value
v: Original value
ec: Extension code
α: Attribute code
n: Use count of v in α

Figure 7.5. An Access Structure in a Segment

the full search of a whole encoding file. To avoid this, we design each hash function h as a concatenation of two hash functions $h_0 : \Sigma^* \to \{0, 1\}^{l_0}$ and $h_1 : \Sigma^* \to \{0, 1\}^{l-l_0}$ and construct h_0 to satisfy the condition that

$$\text{if } a > b \qquad \text{then } h_0(a) > h_0(b)$$

This improvement changes the structure of a directory as shown in Figure 7.7. The function h_0 may be given as a range table. The total number of trie nodes at each level is necessarily less than or equal to the total number of

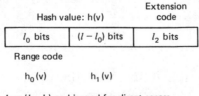

$l_1 = (l - l_0)$ and is used for direct access
         of h(v) in the entry portion

Figure 7.6. The Structure of Codes

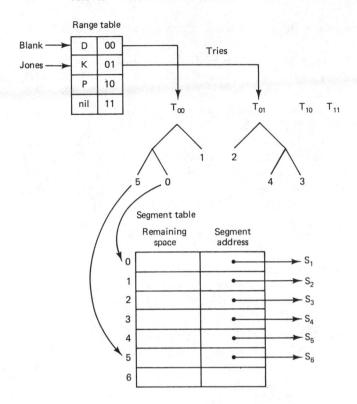

Range table

Blank →

Jones →

D	00
K	01
P	10
nil	11

Tries

T_{00} T_{01} T_{10} T_{11}

1   2

5   0   4   3

Segment table

	Remaining space	Segment address	
0		•	→ S_1
1		•	→ S_2
2		•	→ S_3
3		•	→ S_4
4		•	→ S_5
5		•	→ S_6
6			

h_0(Blake) = 00, h_1(Blake) = 10110 (for example)

Blake ϵ S_2, h(Blake) = 0010110

h_0(Jones) = 01, h_1(Jones) = 11001 (for example)

Jones ϵ S_4, h(Jones) = 0111001

Figure 7.7. A Directory of Segments and Its Representation by a Range Table and Tries

segments for this subtype. The decoding of a code c is performed as follows. The first l_0 bits of c are used to find the root of a trie. Then the next $(l - l_0)$ bits are used to traverse the trie and to find a segment. The entry portion of the segment is searched for the entire l bits of c. This part of a code is referred to as a *hash part*. The last l_1 bits of the hash part directly address a cell that stores the hash part of c. This cell points a desired list that includes c. The extension code part of c is used to search this list for the original value corresponding to c.

7.3.2. Kernel Database Machine

The kernel database machine consists of three subsystems: (1) the tuple selection (TS) subsystem, (2) the tuple construction (TC) subsystem, and (3) the aggregate operation (AO) subsystem. They are interconnected as shown in Figure 7.8, where double-stemmed arrows denote data transfer through sorters.

TS executes the selection of tuples qualified by some condition. Its output is a stream of tuple identifiers or tuple-identifier pairs. TC translates a tuple identifier to a tuple with specified attributes and their values. AO removes duplicates from a stream of tuples. It also executes group-by operations and computes, for each group, statistical calculations.

Let $R(A_1, A_2, \ldots, A_n)$ denote a relation over an attribute set $\{A_1, A_2, \ldots, A_n\}$. Since we can assign a unique number to special attribute $@R$ that represents the tuple identifier of each tuple. We regard R as $R(@R, A_1, A_2, \ldots, A_n)$. For each attribute A of a relation R, TS has the projection of R to $\{@R, A\}$ with a fast access method for each value of A. This is denoted by $R[\underline{A}, @R]$, where the underscore denotes the provision of fast access methods. TC has $R[@R, A_1, A_2, \ldots, A_n]$ for each R. The underscored attributes are referred to as *index attributes*. In our machine, each R can have no more than one index attribute.

The characteristics of this abstract architecture lie in the interconnection networks. They are functional networks with buffer storage. A label number i of each sorter indicates that the word length of the sorter is i times as long as the code length. Sorting is performed by way of data-stream processing. Sort engines are used to implement such sorters. We denote the sorting of a stream S by $S\uparrow$. Each stream is assumed to have a special attri-

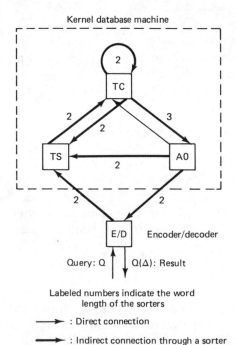

Kernel database machine

Labeled numbers indicate the word
length of the sorters

⟶ : Direct connection

⟹ : Indirect connection through a sorter

Figure 7.8. An Abstract Architecture of Our Database Machine

bute that indicates for each record the number of preceding records in this stream. This attribute is denoted by @. The projection of S without the removal of duplicates is denoted by $S[[X]]$.

The kernel database machine executes relational algebraic expressions as follows. The underscored subexpression is preprocessed and provided as a file.

1. Selection of $R(A, B, C)$: $R[A = \text{'}a\text{'}][B, C]$
   1. Encoder/Decoder: output $e(a)$ to TS,
   2. TS   : $S_1 = (R[\underline{A}, @R][A = e(a)])[@R]$; output it to TC,
   3. TC   : $S_2 = (R[@R = @R](S_1\uparrow))[[B, C]]$; output it to AO,
   4. AO   : remove duplicates from $S_2\uparrow$; output the result to Encoder/Decoder.

The third step uses a join; it is not a heavy operation, however, since $@R$ is the index of R and S_1 is sorted with respect to $@R$. Such a join is referred to as a *linear join*. A linear join can be executed as a batch search operation. The removal of duplicates in the fourth step is also easy to execute, since S_2 is already sorted.

2. Restriction of $R(A, B, C)$: $R[A = B][A, C]$
   1. TC   : $S_1 = R[A = B][[A, C]]$; (full search) output it to AO,
   2. AO   : remove duplicates from $S_1\uparrow$; output the result to Encoder/Decoder.

3. Join of $R(A, B, C)$ and $S(D, E)$: $((R[A = \text{'}a\text{'}])[C = D]S)[B, C, E]$
   1. TS   : $S_1 = (R[\underline{A}, @R][A = e(a)])[@R]$; output it to TC,
   2. TC   : $S_2 = (R[\underline{@R}, C][@R = @R](S_1\uparrow))[C, @R]$; output it to TS,
   3. TS   : $S_3 = (S[\underline{D}, @S][D = C](S_2\uparrow))[@R, @S]$; output it to TC,
   4. TC   : $S_4 = (R[@R, B, C][@R = @R](S_3\uparrow))[@S, B, C]$; output $S_5 = S_4[@, B, C]$ to AO; output $S_6 = S_4[@S, @]$ to TC,
   5. TC   : $S_7 = (S[\underline{@S}, E][@S = @S](S_6\uparrow))[@, E]$; output it to AO,
   6. AO   : $S_8 = ((S_5)[@ = @](S_7\uparrow))[[B, C, E]]$; remove duplicates from S_8; output the result to Encoder/Decoder.

7.4. BASIC FUNCTIONAL COMPONENTS

7.4.1. Binary Trie Engine

Modified extendible hashing, described in Section 7.3.1 needs the processing of a binary trie. The processing of a binary trie T with its height less than $l + 1$ consists of three kinds of primitive operations:

1. Search (T, h). Search the trie T for a segment address along a path specified by a sequence of binary digits h in $\{0, 1\}^l$.
2. Split (T, h, S_1, S_2). Split a segment along a path specified by h into two segments S_1 and S_2, which are entry addresses of segment tables.
3. Merge $(b_0 b_1 \ldots b_k, S)$. Merge two segments $S(b_0 b_1 \ldots b_k 0)$ and $S(b_0 b_1 \ldots b_k 1)$ to a single segment and set its entry address to S.

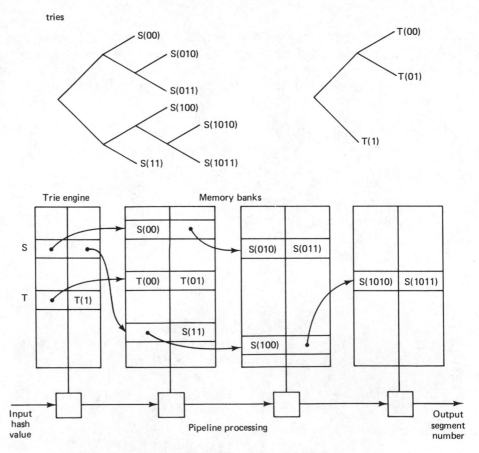

Figure 7.9. Trie Search by a Trie Engine

Tries are stored in a trie engine as shown in Figure 7.9. Transactions of the three kinds of operations are processed in pipeline. Each level of a trie engine has a dedicated memory unit and a dedicated logic circuit. The concurrent operations of these levels perform pipeline processing.

7.4.2. Search Engine (SEE)

A search engine is a data-stream processing module for batch search operations. It searches a table of keywords that is sorted in nondecreasing order for each input key and outputs the least table address whose keyword is greater than or equal to the input key. If the keywords have their own records and they are stored in RAM memory in the same order, then the address obtained as a search output can be used to access its corresponding record. For a stream of search keys, it works as a pipeline converter that changes each key to its corresponding table address. If an input key is found in the table, a hit flag is set to one and it is output together with a table address (Figure 7.10).

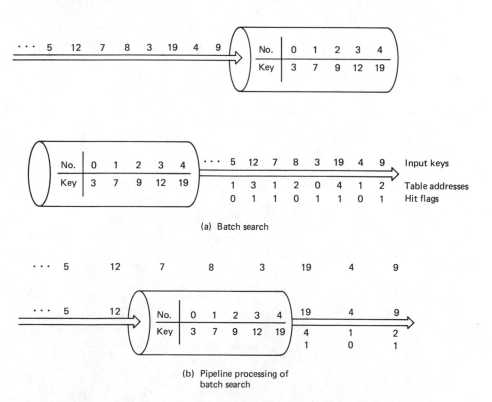

Figure 7.10. Functions of a Search Engine: (a) Batch Search, (b) Pipeline Processing of Batch Search

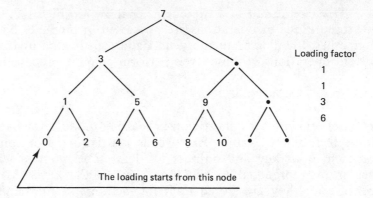

Figure 7.11. A Half-Loaded Left-Sided Binary Trie

In an SEE, a search table is represented by a binary trie called a left-sided binary trie. Sorted keywords are stored in the nodes of this trie in an order such as shown by the labels 0, 1, . . . , 14 in Figure 7.11. An SEE has a hardware configuration as shown in Figure 7.12. It has a dedicated logic circuit and a dedicated memory bank for each level of the trie. Figure 7.13 shows a single key search in a left-sided binary trie. If the selections of left and right branches are represented respectively by 0 and 1, then the concatenation of such binary digits from left to right always becomes the intra-level address of the next node to be visited. Besides, this concatenation finally becomes the table address to be obtained. An SEE concurrently searches as many keys as its levels by pipeline processing.

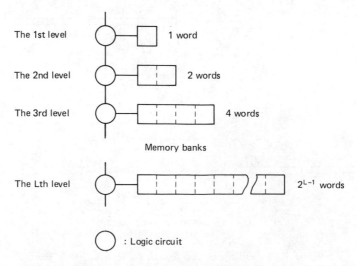

Figure 7.12. The Hardware Configurations of a Search Engine and a Sort Engine

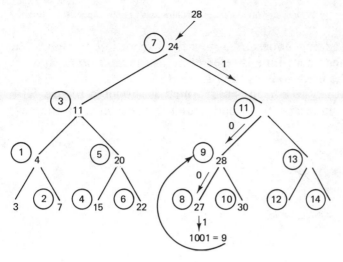

Figure 7.13. Trie Traversing in a Search Engine

7.4.3. Sort Engine (SOE)

An SOE can start to output a sorted stream of keys as soon as it receives the last key of an unsorted stream. Its sorting is based on the heap-sort algorithm. A *heap* is a binary trie in which each path from its root to a leaf has their node values in the sorted order. An SOE has a hardware configuration similar to that of an SEE. It has a dedicated logic circuit and a dedicated memory bank for each level of a heap. An SOE with l levels can sort $2^l - 1$ keys.

An SOE constructs a heap during its input of a stream. Memory cells of an SOE initially have the maximum value that is not used as an input value. Assume that a heap has already grown as shown in Figure 7.14(a). A heap

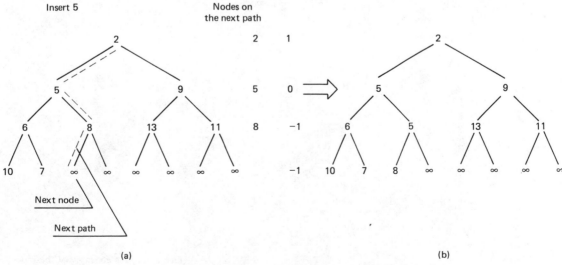

Figure 7.14. Insertion of the Next Key into the Next Path

grows from a root by adding nodes of a new level from left to right. The node to be added to a heap next time is referred to as the *next node*, and the path from the root to the next node as the *next path*.

The input of a next key to a heap is performed as shown in Figure 7.14. First, each level circuit simultaneously reads out the node value on the next

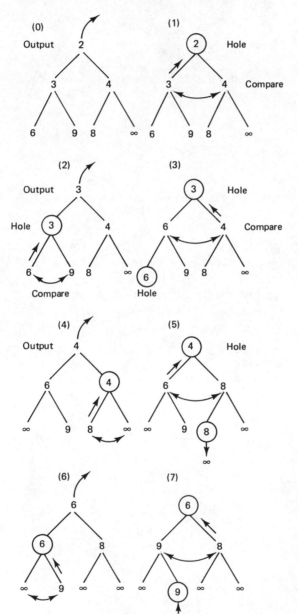

Figure 7.15. An Example of the Pipelined Heap Output Processes

path. The next key is inserted to the proper place of this list. Then each level circuit simultaneously writes each element of this list on the next path. This operation does not destroy the property of heaps.

The output of a heap is performed as shown in Figure 7.15. First, its root value is output. This generates a hole at its root. When a hole is generated at some level, the next level circuit begins to compare the values of its left son and right son and sends the smaller value to the upper-level circuit. The old hole is filled with this value and a new hole is generated at the lower level. The root always outputs its value when its hole is filled. Therefore, holes appear at every two levels. They propagate from the top level to the bottom level. Holes at the bottom level are filled with the unused maximum. When a root is first filled with the unused maximum, the SOE finishes its output. At that time, it has been automatically reinitialized.

7.4.4. Associative Disk Controller and Disk Cache

High performance needs not only the speed-up of database processing but also the high-speed access of data in secondary storage devices. Since the use of moving-head disks is inevitable for large-capacity database machines, highly concurrent operations of disk units and some feasible improvement of both the disk units and their controllers must be considered.

The disk cache is a solution to improve the concurrency of disk units. It overlaps seek, segment access, and segment transfer operations of different disk units. Figure 7.16 shows two types of disk caches. Type (a) is a buffer attached to a disk controller. It improves the concurrency among banks of disk units; however, disk units controlled by the same controller cannot operate concurrently. A disk unit may fail to transfer the accessed segment if the controller is busy receiving data from another unit. It needs one more revolution to access this segment again. Type (b) does not have such problems.

For further improvement, it is necessary to improve seek time, latency time, and transfer rate of disk units. For the first two, a double actuator disk unit seems to be a reasonable solution. For the last one, direct parallel read

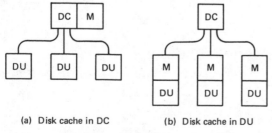

(a) Disk cache in DC   (b) Disk cache in DU

DC: Disk controller   DU: Disk unit
M: Disk cache memory

Figure 7.16. Two Types of Disk Cache Memory

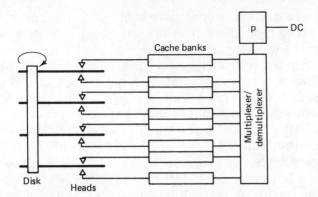

Figure 7.17. A Disk Unit with a Cache Bank for Each Head

of multiple tracks on the same cylinder might be introduced instead of multiplexing them. The direct connection of each head to the dedicated disk cache will further improve performance (Figure 7.17). These memory banks are connected to a dedicated processor through a multiplexer/demultiplexer. The processor manages the information about which track is resident in which cache page. The whole configuration in Figure 7.17 constitutes a single disk unit. A disk controller may be improved to have some associative search functions. Two types of disk controllers are necessary for our machine. Disk controllers for variable-length records are used in the encoder/decoder, while those for fixed-length records are used in TS and TC.

7.5. SUBSYSTEM ARCHITECTURE

7.5.1. Encoder/Decoder

The encoder/decoder consists of a directory processor and several file processors (Figure 7.18). Its functions are as follows;

A. Encoding:
  1. Encoding the values of code type attributes.
  2. Assigning a code to a new value and inserting it into the encoding/decoding table.
B. Decoding:
  3. Decoding codes into their original values.
  4. Deleting a code and its corresponding value from the encoding/decoding table.

Inputs for the encoding are a transaction ID, a command code, an attribute code, and an original value. A transaction ID is an identifier for each processing. A command code indicates either search or insertion. An attribute

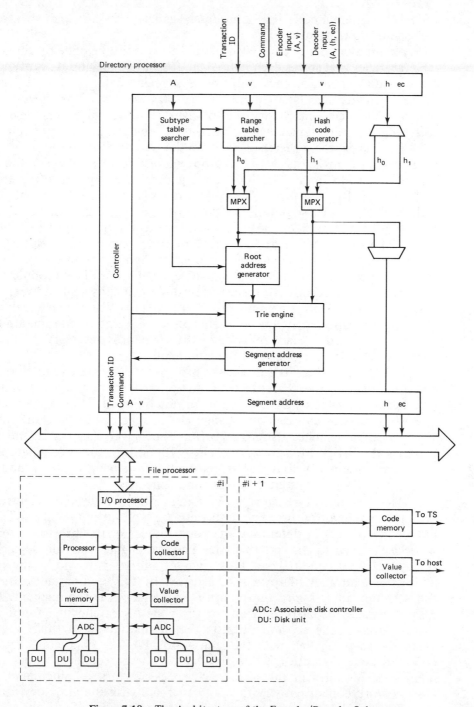

Figure 7.18. The Architecture of the Encoder/Decoder Subsystem

code is an internal code that is uniquely assigned to each pair of a relation and one of its attributes.

An input attribute code is converted to its subtype code by the subtype table searcher that stores each pair of an attribute code and its subtype code. An encoding table for each subtype is segmented into a lot of segments. These segments are classified into range classes so that the range of values stored in each class may not overlap with the ranges of others. Segments in each range class are dynamically managed by a binary trie, as shown in Figure 7.4. The range table searcher receives the subtype code and searches the range table of this subtype for an input value v. It outputs $h_0(v)$, the first l_0 bits of the code for v. The hash code generator computes $h_1(v)$, the next $l - l_0$ bits of the code for v. The root address generator receives the subtype code and $h_0(v)$. These determine the root address of the trie for the range class that includes v. This root address is sent to the trie engine together with $h_1(v)$. The bit sequence of $h_1(v)$ is used to traverse a trie specified by the root address. The trie engine finds a proper segment along this path. Its physical address is given by the segment address generator. This module stores a table whose row consists of a segment number, its physical address, and the size of the remaining free space in this segment. When a new value of an attribute is registered in the encoding table, the size of the remaining free space is examined to see if splitting of the segment is necessary. If it is necessary, the corresponding node of the trie is split.

For the encoding, the directory processor sends the transaction ID, the search command, the attribute code, the original value, the segment address, and the hashed value to the file processor determined by the segment address. The file processor accesses this segment. It is read out to the work memory. The processor searches its entry portion for a given hash value and further searches the list pointed to by the entry found for a given original value. Its extension code is read out and stored in the code memory with the transaction ID. This is read out later by the code collector.

The decoding of a hash value h of an attribute A with an extension code ec is performed as follows. The hash value h is split into h_0 and h_1. The attribute code A and h_0 determine the root address of the trie to be searched, while h_1 is used to traverse this trie. The trie engine finds the segment that stores the input code (h, ec). This segment address is found by the segment address generator. A file processor selected by this segment address receives the segment address and the code (h, ec). It accesses the segment. Its processor searches its entry portion for the code h, searches the found list for the extension code ec, and outputs the original value of this code to the value memory together with the transaction ID. The code collector gathers codes in code memories, while the value collector collects values in value memories. Modules in the directory processor work in pipeline. File processors work concurrently with each other and with the directory processor.

Since look-ahead accesses of segments cannot be effectively applied in

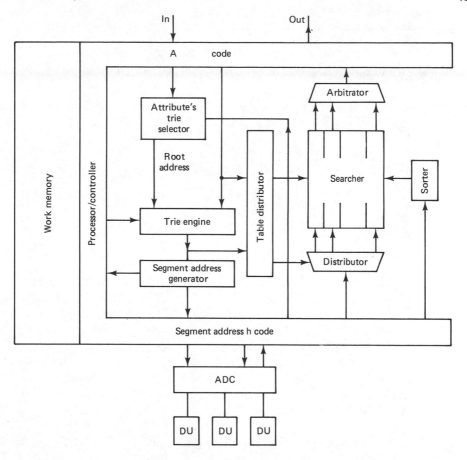

Figure 7.19. The Architecture of a Tuple Selector

the encoder/decoder, its throughput performance is bound by the multiplicity of disk units. Its throughput performance is not comparable to that of the kernel database machine that is explained later; however, this performance gap is justified by the following considerations. Its throughput need not exceed the I/O transfer rate of the whole system. Since the database processing may deal with several huge tables to output only a small table, the kernel database machine is desired to work as fast as possible. Therefore, there may be a performance gap between two systems. If the queries and the retrieved outputs are received from or sent to the printers or TSS terminals that are connected to an existing host computer system or an existing computer network, the I/O transfer rate of the database machine system cannot exceed 1 to 10 Mbyte/sec. If each tuple is assumed to have 200 characters, this corresponds to the throughput of 5000–50,000 tuples/sec. If disk units are improved as explained in Section 7.4.4, the encoder/decoder architecture in Figure 7.19 with a sufficient number of disk units and file processors is able to achieve the throughput performance corresponding to such an I/O transfer rate.

7.5.2. Tuple Selector

The tuple selector (TS) has a hardware architecture as shown in Figure 7.20 and performs the following functions:

1. Selection: $\overline{R[\underline{A}, @R]}[A = c][@R]$
2. Linear join: $\overline{(R_1[\underline{A}, @R_1][A = B]R_2[\underline{B}, @R_2])}[@R_1, @R_2]$
3. Linear join: $\overline{(R[\underline{A}, @R][A = B](S(B, @)\uparrow))}[@R, @]$
4. Insert: $\overline{R[\underline{A}, @R]} + S(B, @R)\uparrow$
5. Delete: $\overline{R[\underline{A}, @R]} - S(B, @R)\uparrow$
6. Generate: $\overline{S(A, @)\uparrow}$

    1. For a selection, A and c are used to determine the segment that includes the tuples of $R[\underline{A}, @R][A = c]$. The associative disk controller receives the segment address and the code c, accesses the desired segment, searches those tuples whose A value is c, and sends the tuple identifier codes of these tuples to the processor. The processor outputs them.

    2. For a linear join of the first type in which two relations are stored in TS, the segment address generator receives the attribute code A and B and generates a stream of paired segment numbers. One is from the segments of $R_1[\underline{A}, @R_1]$, the other from the segments of $R_2[\underline{B}, @R_2]$. Each pair of segments is such that they may possibly have common codes as their index values. The associative disk controller receives each pair of segment numbers and accesses these two segments one after another. A segment of $R_1[\underline{A}, @R_1]$ is sent to the sorter and sorted with respect to A. The sorted segment is stored as a search table in one of the free searchers. Then the fellow $R_2[\underline{B}, @R_2]$ segment is sent to this searcher. The searcher outputs pairs of tuple identifiers $(R_1[\underline{A}, @R_1][A = B]R_2[\underline{B}, @R_2])[@R_1, @R_2]$.

    The searcher performs the following operations. First, it is loaded with a search table $\{(K_i, R_i)|0 \leqslant i \leqslant n\}$. Then it receives a stream $(k_0, r_0), (k_1, r_1), \ldots, (k_m, r_m)$ and, for each element (k_j, r_j), it outputs $(R_l, r_j), (R_{l+1}, r_j), \ldots, (R_{l+l'}, r_j)$, where l is the minimum address that satisfies $k_j \leqslant K_l$ and $l + l'$ is the maximum address that satisfies $K_{l+l'} \leqslant k_j$. Such a searcher can be constructed with two SEEs and a module called an expander. Each SEE is loaded with a search table $\{K_i\}$. Their record $\{R_i\}$ is stored in the expander. For an input search key k_j, two SEEs respectively output the minimum address l and the maximum address $l + l'$. The latter function of an SEE has not been mentioned in this chapter, but it is easily added to an SEE [18]. A triple of $(l, l + l', r_j)$ is sent to the input queue of the expander. The expander takes

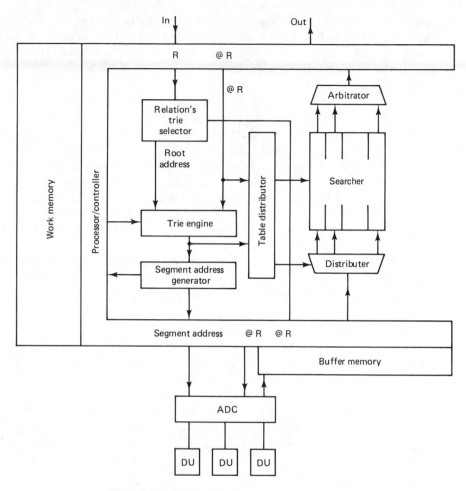

Figure 7.20. The Architecture of a Tuple Constructor

the first triple from its queue and reads out the records stored from the address l to $l + l'$ of the table $\{R_i\}$.

3. A linear join of the second type joins a relation stored in TS and an input stream that is stored with respect to its index attribute. It is performed almost in the same way as function 2. The processor receives an input stream and an input attribute code. The attribute code determines the root address of the trie. Each code in the input stream determines the path of the directory trie. The trie engine converts each code to the segment number. The table distributor stores each substream whose codes are converted to the same segment number in one of the free searchers. The different segment numbers are sent to the segment address generator, where they are converted to segment addresses. The associative disk controller receives a stream of

segment addresses and sequentially accesses them. A segment that is ready to transfer is sent to the corresponding searcher to obtain a subset of $(R[\underline{A}, @R]$ $[A = B](S(B, @)\uparrow))[@R, @]$. When all the segments whose addresses are sent from the segment address generator are sent to the searchers, the tuple selector completes its processing.

4, 5. The insert and delete operations are performed as follows. The attribute code A determines the root address of the trie. The input stream $S(B, @R)\uparrow$ is sent to the trie engine and, for each code, a segment that possibly stores this code is found. Since $S(B, @R)\uparrow$ is sorted, the output stream of the trie engine is separated into substreams, each of which consists of a single segment number. For each substream, its corresponding substream of $S(B, @R)\uparrow$ and its segment address are sent to the associative disk controller, which adds or deletes tuples of this substream to and from the specified segment. The overflow and the underflow of the segments are reported to the processor, which updates the trie.

6. The generation of a file needs the construction of a new trie and a new segment address table. New segments are selected among free segments managed by the associative disk controller.

7.5.3. Tuple Constructor

The tuple constructor (TC) has the hardware architecture shown in Figure 7.20 and performs the following functions;

1. Linear join: $(R[\underline{@R}, A_1, \ldots, A_n][@R = @R](S(@R, B_1, \ldots, B_m)\uparrow))$
$[A_1, \ldots, A_n, B_1, \ldots, B_m]$
2. Insert: $R + S\uparrow$
3. Delete: $R - S\uparrow$
4. Generate: $+S\uparrow$

The linear join is executed in the same way as a second-type linear join is executed by TS, except that it does not need the expander. Since each segment has no duplicates of tuple identifiers, each searcher of this system can be constructed with a single SEE. Other functions are also performed in the same way as by TS.

7.5.4. Aggregate Operator

The aggregate operator (AO) has a set of sorters, each of which can sort a set of codes (Figure 7.21). These sorters can be concatenated in parallel to multiply the word length of the sorting to an arbitrary length. The functions of the AO are as follows:

1. Tuple construction: (for example)
$$S[@, A] \uparrow, S[@, B] \uparrow, S[@, C] \uparrow$$
$$\downarrow$$
$$S[[A, B, C]],$$

2. Duplicates removal: $S[[A_1, A_2, \ldots, A_n]]$
$$\downarrow$$
$$S[A_1, A_2, \ldots, A_n]$$

3. Group-by operation: $S[A, (B, C)/A]$;
   B, C are grouped by A attribute

4. Set operation: $S[A, \text{average } (B/A)]$;
   for each A value, the average of B values grouped by this A value is calculated

   1. Tuple construction is easily performed by the processor using its buffer memory.

   2. For the removal of duplicates, $S[[X]]$ are sorted by a sorter with sufficient word length. After the sorting, the duplicates removal is an easy task. If there are not enough sorters to sort $S[[X]]$, the set of attributes X is divided into $X_1, X_2, \ldots, X_m$. First, $S[[X]][X_1, @]$ is sorted and its output stream $S[[X]][X_1, @] \uparrow$ is sequentially numbered from 0 so that the number is incremented by one for each change of the X_1 value. This number is considered as a new attribute $@_1$ of the sorted stream. Then, for the result stream S_1, $S_1[[@_1, X_2, @S]]$ is sorted. Its output tuples are numbered in the same way. Tuples with the same $(@_{i-1}, X_i)$ value are numbered with the same number. Finally, $S_{m-1}[[@_{m-1}, X_m, @S]]$ is sorted. Tuples of the same $(@_{m-1}, X_m)$ value are identical tuples and are represented by one of them. Its tuple value is found using its $@$. A set of tuples thus obtained is equal to $S[X]$.

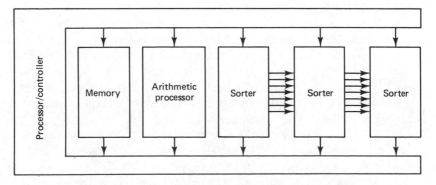

Figure 7.21.   Architecture of an Aggregate Operator

3. Group-by operations are easily performed by sorting the input streams.

4. The arithmetic processor performs an arbitrary set operation for each substream separated by a group-by operation.

7.6. A MULTIPLICITY OF SUBSYSTEMS

7.6.1. Sorting Distributor Network

The abstract architecture shown in Figure 7.8 extensively uses interconnections of subsystems through a sorter. Each subsystem described in Section 7.5 extensively utilizes pipeline processing; however, a multiplicity of such subsystems is necessary for further performance improvement. The network must perform two functions—distribution and sorting. It must deliver each tuple in a source processor to an appropriate destination processor. It is assumed that the destination of a tuple is easily calculated from the value of its specified attribute. For example, the first several bits of each tuple identifier determine the destination in the transfer of $R[\underline{A}, @R][@R]$ from TS subsystem to TC subsystem. The network must gather the tuples sent to each destination processor and sort them.

Figure 7.22 shows several network architectures to perform distribution and sorting. Network (a) has a bottleneck. Network (b) causes collisions at the entrance of each sorter. Network (c) is the most complicated and expensive; however, we use it to replace a single sorter when a multiplicity of subsystems is used. Its cost is offset by the fact that it effectively performs the heaviest operations of the total system. This type of network is called a sorting distributor (SD) network.

A sorting distributor network with n source ports and m destination ports consists of $n \times m$ sorters and a similar number of mergers. Each source port is connected to a distribution bus to which m sorters are connected. Each of these m sorters is connected to one of the output ports through some number of mergers. Each source processor delivers each tuple of a source file to an appropriate sorter connected to its distribution bus. When every source processor storing a part of the file to be transferred finishes its distribution of tuples to sorters, every destination processor takes out a sorted stream from the sorters in its column. Mergers in each column merge n sorted streams into a single sorted stream.

An SD network works also as a buffer. It needs a large capacity, though we will show later that capacity enlargement does not need a proportional number of sort engines, but only ordinary MOS memories. Since the length of a stream sent from each source processor is bounded by the size of seg-

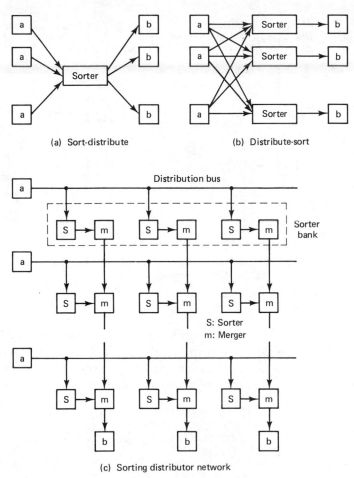

(a) Sort-distribute   (b) Distribute-sort

(c) Sorting distributor network

Figure 7.22. Interconnection Networks for Sorting and Distribution: (a) Sort-Distribute, (b) Distribute Sort, (c) Sorting Distributor

ments, the total capacity of sorters enclosed by dotted lines in Figure 7.22(c) can be designed as a constant. Such a bank of sorters is referred to as a *sorter bank*.

Assume that an output port of a processor *a* is connected to an input port of another processor *b* through a sorter. An SD network can easily multiply the input and the output processor of this configuration. If the original configuration has multiple sorters between two processors, its multiplicity has multiple planes of SD networks (Figure 7.23). Using SD networks, each of the TS, TC, and AO subsystems in Figure 7.8 can easily be improved to have an arbitrary number of copies.

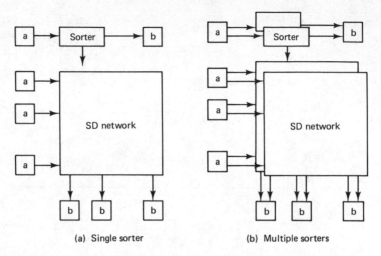

(a) Single sorter   (b) Multiple sorters

Figure 7.23. A Multiplicity of Processors Connected Through Sorters: (a) A Single Sorter, (b) Multiple Sorters

7.6.2. Sorter Bank

Capacity extension of a sort engine needs only ordinary MOS memories. Its hardware configuration is shown in Figure 7.24, while its operations are illustrated by Figure 7.25. In the example, every sort engine is assumed to have three levels. It can sort seven items. The first seven items of an input stream

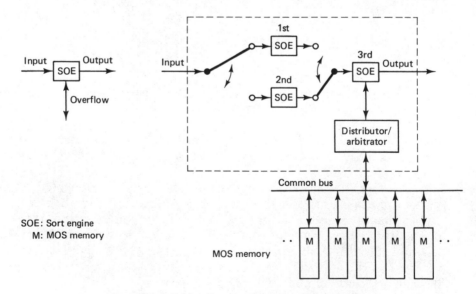

Figure 7.24. Capacity Extension of a Sorter

Input stream:

4 1 5 3 4 7 6 9 3 2 1 8 0 4 5 7 3 6 2 9 0
←   → ←   → ←   →

The first 7 values are stored in the third engine in nondecreasing order.

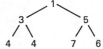

The next 7 values are sorted in nonincreasing order by the first engine, and the output stream is input to the third engine, where its next path is fixed to the leftmost path.

The overflow values are sequentially stacked in the first MOS memory unit.

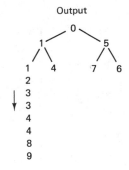

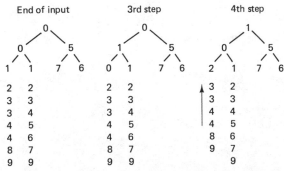

Figure 7.25. Sorting Operations of the Sorter in Figure 7.24

are directly stored in the third engine in nondecreasing order. The next seven are sorted in nonincreasing order by the first engine, and the output stream is input to the third engine, where its next path is fixed to the leftmost path. The overflow items are sequentially stacked in the first MOS memory unit. The third seven items are also sorted in nonincreasing order and input to the

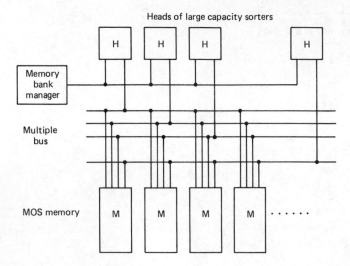

Heads of large capacity sorters

Figure 7.26. Configuration of a Sorter Bank

third engine. At this time, its next path is fixed to the second leftmost path. The overflow items are stacked in the second MOS memory unit. The output of a sorted list is performed like that of a single sort engine.

The module enclosed by dotted lines in Figure 7.24 is called a *head* of a large capacity sorter. Heads of many large sorters may share banks of MOS memory. Figure 7.26 shows such a configuration. The memory bank manager manages the allocation of memory banks to each head. This is an architecture of a sorter bank.

7.7. CONCLUDING REMARKS

We have described the basic design of our database machine, which is based on

1. The encoding of databases.
2. The segmentation of files.
3. The data-stream processing of segments.
4. The data-flow control of segment flows.

These principles were derived from our studies for a high-performance database machine with large capacity on the premise that the use of moving-head disk units as the database storage is inevitable.

Our machine consists of two subsystems:

1. The encoder/decoder.
2. The kernel database machine.

The former encodes variable-length values in a database to fixed-length codes. The encoding functions should be one-to-one but need not be order-preserving. Encoded databases are processed by the kernel database machine, which consists of three subsystems and functional interconnection networks among them. The tuple selection subsystem stores an inverted file for each attribute of an encoded relation, while the tuple construction subsystem processes encoded relations. The aggregate operation subsystem is dedicated to the calculation of aggregate functions and the removal of duplicates.

Files are segmented in our machine. Binary tries are used to manage segments and to handle their overflow. The processing of segments is performed during their flows through various modules. Their flows are controlled by a data-flow architecture that regards each segment as a single object. Each subsystem of the kernel database machine has various functional modules, whose design is based on the idea of data-stream processing. For the implementation of these functional modules, several VLSI architectures have been considered: a trie engine, a search engine, and a sort engine. The latter two have already been implemented with discrete logic circuits. Prototypes of an SEE and an SOE have 12 levels and 16-bit word length. A prototype SEE can store a search table with 4095 keywords within 4 ms, and it can search input keys at the rate of 10^6 keys/sec. A prototype SOE can sort 4095 keys within 16 ms. Each uses relatively slow memory chips with 450 ns access time. Their VLSI implementation including their memory parts will make them work ten times as fast as their prototypes. Each subsystem architecture in the kernel database machine can be replicated to an arbitrary number by replacing each interconnecting sorter with a sorting distributor network. This network is constructed from sort engines and MOS memory devices.

We have completed the overall design of our machine. The design of its functional modules is nearly complete, and some of the modules are being prototyped. However, its subsystem architectures need further consideration and simulation before being designed in detail.

REFERENCES

[1] Bray, O. H., and Freeman, H. A., *Data Base Computers,* Lexington Books, 1979.

[2] Canady, R. H., Harrison, R. D., Ivie, E. L., Ryder, J. L., and Wehr, L. A., "A Back-end Computer for Data Base Management," *CACM,* Vol. 17, No. 10 (1974), pp. 575–582.

[3] Marill, T., and Stern, D., "The Datacomputer–A Network Data Utility," *Proc. AFIPS,* Vol. 44 (1975), pp. 389–395.

[4] Hakozaki, K., Makino, T., Mizuma, M., Umemura, M., and Hiyoshi, S., "A Conceptual Design of a Generalized Database Subsystem," *Proc. 3d VLDB,* 1977, pp. 246–253.

[5] Epstein, R., et al., "The IDM 500—Communication Issues with Backend Processors," *COMPCON*, 1981, pp. 112–114.

[6] Sekino, A., Takeuchi, K., Makino, T., Hakozaki, K., Doi, T., and Goto, T., "Design Considerations for an Information Query Computer," in this book.

[7] Coulouris, G. F., Evans, J. M., and Mitchell, R. W., "Towards Content-Addressing in Data Bases," *Computer Journal*, Vol. 15, No. 2 (1972), pp. 95–98.

[8] Leilich, H.-O., Stiege, G., and Zeidler, H. C., "A Search Processor for Data Base Management," *Proc. 4th International Conference on Very Large Data Bases*, West Berlin, 1978, pp. 280–287.

[9] Babb, E., "Implementing a Relational Database by Means of Specialized Hardware," *ACM Trans. Database Systems*, Vol. 4, No. 1 (1979), pp. 1–29.

[10] Ozkarahan, E. A., Schuster, S. A., and Smith, K. C., "RAP—An Associative Processor for Data Base Management," *Proc. AFIPS*, Vol. 44 (1975), pp. 379–387.

[11] Chang, H., "On Bubble Memories and Relational Data Base," *Proc. 4th International Conference on Very Large Data Bases*, West Berlin, 1978, pp. 207–229.

[12] Uemura, S., Yuba, T., Kokubu, A., Ohomote, R., and Sugawara, Y., "The Design and Implementation of a Magnetic-Bubble Database Machine," *Proc. IFIP '80*, 1980, pp. 433–438.

[13] Schuster, S. A., Nguyen, H. B., Ozkarahan, E. A., and Smith, K. C., "RAP.2—An Associative Processor for Databases and Its Applications," *IEEE Trans. Computers*, Vol. C-28, No. 6 (1979), pp. 446–458.

[14] Oflazer, K., et al., "RAP.3—A Multi-Microprocessor Cell Architecture for the RAP Database Machine," *Proc. Int'l Workshop on High Level Language Computer Architecture*, 1980, pp. 108–119.

[15] Banerjee, J., Hsiao, D. K., and Baum, R. I., "Concepts and Capabilities of a Database Computer," *ACM Trans. Database Systems*, Vol. 3, No. 4 (1978), pp. 347–384.

[16] Dewitt, D. J., "DIRECT—A Multiprocessor Organization for Supporting Relational Database Management Systems," *IEEE Trans. Computers*, Vol. C-28, No. 6 (1979), pp. 395–406.

[17] Kung, H. T., and Lehman, P. L., "Systolic (VLSI) Arrays for Relational Database Operations," *Proc. ACM-SIGMOD Conference*, 1980, pp. 105–116.

[18] Menon, M. J., and Hsiao, D. K., "Design and Analysis of Join Operations of Database Machines," in this book.

[19] Tanaka, Y., Nozaka, Y., and Masuyama, A., "Pipeline Searching and Sorting Modules as Components of a Data Flow Data Base Computer," *Proc. IFIP '80*, 1980, pp. 427–432.

[20] Fagin, R., Nievergelt, J., Pippenger, N., and Strong, H. R., "Extendible Hashing—A Fast Access Method for Dynamic Files," *ACM Trans. Database Systems*, Vol. 4, No. 3 (1979), pp. 315–344.

8

Design and Analysis of Join Operations of Database Machines

M. J. Menon and David K. Hsiao

8.0. ABSTRACT

In this paper we propose a new and extendable organization of processors and memories for hardware realization of relational join operations. The basic organization is intended for the natural join operation. However, this organization is particularly suitable for LSI and VLSI implementation and for extension to support m-way join and inequality join operations.

Algorithmic analysis of the time complexity of the natural join operation shows that it is linear in the cardinalities of the source, target, and result relations, which is optimal. Queueing analysis of the join operation is also used to arrive at closed-form equations for various design parameters, such as the sizes and speeds of the memories associated with the processors. It is seen that in order to perform joins at a rate commensurate with the output rate of relational tuples, the memories associated with the processors in the hardware must satisfy certain constraints of speed and size. The various constraints and their order of importance are clearly indicated in the paper.

We also show how to select an optimum chip design for the join operation, where the design is considered optimal if it gives the best performance for a certain fixed cost. Both LSI and VLSI technologies are considered in the selection of an optimum chip design. These methods may be employed by database machine designers to arrive at the optimal values for (1) the number of processors on a chip, and (2) the sizes of the memories to be placed on a chip.

We then describe the extensions of the join organization to perform inequality joins and *m*-way joins. We also include a favorable comparison of this organization with hardware joins proposed for some other database machines.

8.1 INTRODUCTION TO THE HARDWARE ORGANIZATION

In order to support the relational model of data [1], the hardware join operations have been required in database machines [2–8]. In this chapter we will first propose a new organization of processors and memories for hardware realization of the relational natural join operation. We will then single out certain features of the proposed design for discussion. Algorithmic analysis of the join operation is made, indicating that the time complexity of the operation is linear in terms of the input and result relations. Queueing analysis is also used to arrive at closed-form equations for various parameters such as the sizes and speeds of the memories associated with the processors. We also present a design algorithm that allows the database machine designers to obtain an optimal chip for the hardware join operation, where a chip is considered optimal if it provides the best speed of join operation for a certain fixed cost. Both the present-day LSI technology and near-term VLSI technology are considered for the realization of the optimal chips.

Owing to the simplicity and extensibility of the organization, additional processors and memories can be incorporated into the hardware at a later time and more chips can be interconnected when the need arises.

We will then show that the same hardware organization may be used for inequality join and *m*-way join operations. Finally, we will provide a comparative study of the join hardware with those proposed elsewhere.

8.1.1. The Hardware Organization

The join operations hardware is configured with many identical processors and local memories, as shown in Figure 8.1. It consists of n processors, numbered 1 through n, where processor i is connected to processor $(i-1)$ and processor $(i+1)$ for all i, $2 \leqslant i \leqslant (n-1)$, and processor 1 is connected to processors 2 and n, and processor n is connected to processors 1 and $(n-1)$. Each of these connections is a direct processor-to-processor link. The sequence of processors $1, 2, \ldots, n$ is called the *broadcast sequence*. A controller is directly connected to all the processors, each of which is associated with four memories, referred to as the A-memory, B-memory, C-memory, and associative memory, respectively. The *A-memories* are used to store the

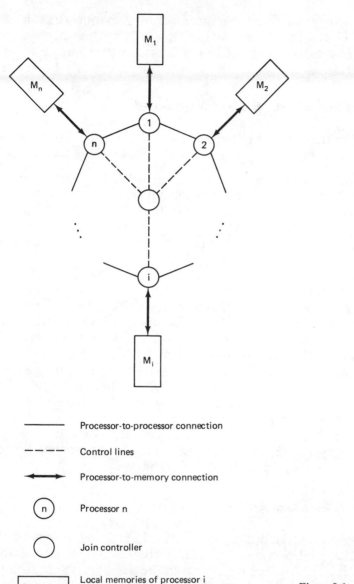

Processor-to-processor connection

Control lines

Processor-to-memory connection

n Processor n

Join controller

M_i Local memories of processor i consisting of A-memory, B-memory C-memory and associative memory

Figure 8.1. Interconnection of Processors in the Join Operations Hardware

source records (i.e., source relational tuples). The *B-memories* are used as buffer memories in order to overcome the speed disparity between the rate at which records are being output by the database store and the rate at which records are being processed by the join operations hardware. The *C-memory* will be used to store the results of the join operations. The small *associative memory* (am) is primarily used to speed up the join operation.

Both the ams and the B-memories are made of random-access memories, while the A- and C-memories are larger, slower memories made of, for example, charge-coupled devices (CCDs). Because ams are made of conventional RAMs, instead of true associative arrays, they are relatively inexpensive.

8.1.2. The Basic Join Operation Involving Four Memories

In order to make this chapter self-contained, we develop definitions and notations on join operations in the context of this hardware organization.

Definitions. Two relations (e.g., files) called the *source relation* and the *target relation* are involved in a join operation. Tuples in these relations are called *source records* and *target records,* respectively. A join operation is always performed between an attribute that belongs to the source relation and one that belongs to the target relation. We call these the *source attribute* and the *target attribute,* respectively. Furthermore, a join operation requires that the domain of values of the source attribute be the same as the domain of values of the target attribute.

The join operation is performed as follows. Each record in the source relation is examined and the value of the source attribute is determined. All records in the target relation that have the same value for the target attribute are now selected. If the user or user program is given attribute-value pairs from the selected target records, then the resulting operation is an *implicit join.* However, if the user or user program is given attribute-value pairs from both the source record used to make the selection and the target records selected, then the resulting operation is a *natural join.* From now on, we shall refer to source attribute values and target attribute values (which participate in the join) as *join values.* In this chapter, we first present our basic hardware organization for the natural join operation.

8.1.3. Phases of the Basic Join Operation

The join proceeds in seven distinct phases. In the *source input phase* the records in the source relation are first read into the B-memories of all the n processors. That is, if there are C_s records in the source relation, each processor will receive C_s/n records at the end of this phase. Each processor begins to execute the following algorithm the moment the first source record is placed in its memory. It reads the source records, one at a time, and extracts the value of the source attribute. With the source attribute value, the processor consults the local associative memory (am) for a match. Each entry in local am contains a source attribute value. If such an entry is not found, a new entry is made in am for this source attribute value. This is the *A-block calculation phase.*

The processor now hashes the join value into a block of its A-memory. The record is then stored in this block of the A-memory, if space is available in the block; otherwise it is stored in an overflow area. A few locations in each processor's A-memory are reserved to store overflow records. Each record in the overflow area contains a pointer to the next record in the overflow area that hashed to the same block. An overflow pointer in each block points to the first overflow record in the overflow area that hashed to this block. This is the *source storage phase.*

At the end of these phases of the join operation, all the source records have been placed in appropriate blocks of the A-memories, depending on their source attribute values.

Next, the records in the target relation are read into the B-memories during the *target input phase.* Each processor performs the following algorithm the moment the first target record is placed in its B-memory. It reads the target records one at a time and probes the am for a match. If a match is found, it hashes the join value of the record to a block of the A-memory. All records in this block of the A-memory (including overflows) are read and the join is performed on all relevant records. Thus, we have the *A-block calculation* and *join phases.* The target record in the B-memory is now propagated to all the other processors via the broadcast sequence. When a processor receives a broadcasted record, it treats the record like any other target record received directly from the database store by way of the B-memory. The record is discarded after it has propagated through all the n processors. This is the *target propagation phase.* We note that these last three phases may overlap considerably.

8.2. AN ALGORITHMIC ANALYSIS OF THE BASIC JOIN OPERATION

The following notations are introduced to simplify the ensuing discussion:

C_s = cardinality of the source relation

C_t = cardinality of the target relation

C_r = cardinality of the result relation

Z_a = average time to access and read (write) a record from (into) the the A-memory

Z_{bs} = time taken to read (write) next record from (into) the B-memory

Z_{am} = time taken to probe an am

N = number of blocks in the A-memory

e = efficiency of the hashing function [e.g., $e = 1$, if the hashing scheme is perfect and there are no collisions]

n = number of processors in the join operation hardware

a = fraction of target records that participate in the join operation

u = average time to output a result record

We will analyze each phase of the basic join operation, in turn.

8.2.1. Phases of Source Input and A-Block Calculation

In these phases, the following operations are performed by a processor on each source record in its B-memory. The record is read from the B-memory and its join value is stored in the am (if not already there). The join value is then hashed to a block of the A-memory and the record is stored in that block of the A-memory. Thus, the processor spends $(Z_{bs} + Z_{am} + Z_a)$ time units in serving a single record. Since each processor has C_s/n records, the total time taken for these phases is

$$(Z_{bs} + Z_{am} + Z_a)\frac{C_s}{n}$$

8.2.2. Phases of Target Input and Target Propagation

Each processor receives C_t/n target records directly from the database store and $C_t(n-1)/n$ records from the other processors. Each of these records is read by the processor from its B-memory, and then the join value of the record is checked against the list of join values in the ams. This takes the following amount of time:

$$C_t(Z_{bs} + Z_{am})$$

We could include here the time taken to route records from one processor to the next. However, we make the assumption that such routing of records is accomplished by way of a direct memory access (DMA) device, so that routing is overlapped with record processing. We also assume that the B-memories are of dual port so that a record may be placed in a B-memory by a DMA device while another record may be taken out by a processor. If we do not make the above assumptions, then an additional term, proportional to $C_t(n-1)/n$, must be included in the expression for the execution time. Nevertheless, this additional term will not affect the complexity of the execution time. The assumptions are made in order to simplify the computation of the time complexity; in no way do they affect the final result.

8.2.3. Phases of A-Block Calculation and Join

Those target records that may participate in the join operation (as indicated by the ams) are hashed to blocks of the A-memory, and result records are created and output.

Let us assume that each processor generates C_r/n of the result records. If the hashing scheme used were perfect (i.e., collision free), then the number of accesses to the A-memory should exactly be equal to the number of records generated, i.e., C_r/n, since each access of the A-memory will retrieve a record that will participate in the join operation and produce a result record. This is because the use of the am has eliminated any consideration of those target records that will not produce result records. Thus, this operation will take the following time:

$$\left(\frac{C_r}{n}\right) Z_a + \left(\frac{C_r}{n}\right) u$$

However, if the hashing scheme used were imperfect with efficiency e, then this operation would take the following time:

$$\left(\frac{Z a C_r}{ne}\right) + \left(\frac{C_r}{n}\right) u$$

8.2.4. Time Complexity of the Basic Join Operation

The total time for the entire basic join operation is, therefore,

$$\frac{C_s(Z_{bs} + Z_{am} + Z_a)}{n} + C_t(Z_{bs} + Z_{am}) + \frac{Z_a Cr}{ne} + \left(\frac{C_r}{n}\right) u$$

—that is,

$$O\left(\frac{C_s}{n} + C_t + \frac{C_r}{n}\right)$$

We see that the join time is linear in terms of the cardinality of the source, target, and result relations. No join algorithm can do better than this—for the following reasons: Since we need to read in all the source and target records, the input process has to be linear in the cardinality of the source and target relations. Also, each record in the result relation must be created and output, and this creation and output process must be linear in the cardinality of the result relation. Thus, the entire process of join has to be linear in the cardinalities of the source, target, and result relations.

The second observation we make is that if the target relation, C_t, is very small relative to C_s/n and C_r/n, we may drop this term to obtain the time complexity as

$$O\left(\frac{C_s}{n} + \frac{C_r}{n}\right)$$

In other words, we always choose the smaller of the two relations as the target relation. Another reason for dropping the middle term containing C_t is that C_t is multiplied by Z_{bs} and Z_{am}, the access times of the B-memory and the associative memory, both of which are fast memories (for example, made of static RAMs). On the other hand, the term containing C_s and the term containing C_r are both multiplied by Z_a, the access time of the much slower A-memory. From the above complexity, we observe that if we use n processors, the basic join algorithm will perform n times faster than a single processor, and this is the best that can be expected.

The above results are obtained assuming that the A-memory is large enough to hold C_s/n records. This is a valid assumption, since the A-memory is made of relatively cheap memory [for example, charge-coupled devices (CCDs) or dynamic RAMs]. This is why the time to access a record from A-memory, Z_a, can be assumed to be independent of the cardinality of the source relation, C_s. Such an assumption can be made only if the expected number of records being hashed to a block can be shown to be less than the block size, R. From Appendix 8.1, the expected number of records being hashed to a block is $C_s/(nN)$. From the following section, we learn $N = C_s^{max}/(nR)$, where C_s^{max} is the cardinality of the largest possible source relation. Thus, the expected number of records being hashed to a block is $RC_s/C_s^{max} \leqslant R$. Thus, the assumption that Z_a is independent of C_s is reasonable.

8.3. DESIGN ANALYSIS OF THE BASIC JOIN OPERATION

In this section we analyze the basic join operation in order to arrive at reasonable estimates for the sizes and speeds of the various memories. We will make no attempt to estimate the size of the C-memory associated with each processor; we merely state that it must be large enough to hold the results from any join operation. Reasonable estimates for the sizes and speeds of the A- and B-memories are, however, obtained. The analysis of the A- and B-memory sizes is made under the assumption that no associative memories (i.e., ams) are used to speed up the join. Thus, the result can be used as the lower bound of the speed of the processor and memory organization for the basic join operation.

8.3.1. Analysis of the A-Memory Size

Each processor's A-memory consists of a primary area and an overflow area. The primary area consists of N blocks, each of size R (see Figure 8.2). Thus, $N \times R = C_s^{max}/n$, where C_s^{max} is the cardinality of the largest possible source relation. If more than R records are assigned to a block, the excess records are stored in the separate overflow area common to all blocks. For each block with overflow records there is, in the overflow area, a chain of overflow records with address pointers. The overflow area must be large enough to hold the worst-case overflow, which will occur when all C_s^{max}/n source records hash to the same block. In this case, the overflow area must be large enough to hold $C_s^{max}/n - R$ records and as many address pointers. Ignoring the size of address pointers with respect to the size of records, the A-memory must be large enough to hold $(N \times R + C_s^{max}/n - R) = C_s^{max}/n + R(N-1)$ records.

8.3.2. Results on the A-Memory Size

In Figure 8.2 we also tabulate the size of an A-memory for various values of n (the number of processors) and N (the number of blocks in the A-memory) for the largest possible source relation.

From the tabulation, we observe that the size of the A-memory is reduced when a large number of processors and a small number of blocks are utilized. The minimum A-memory size should, therefore, occur when the

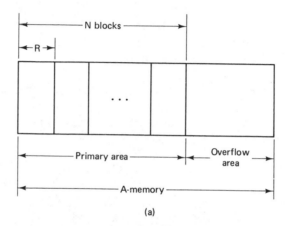

(a)

Sizes of an A-memory for various values of n
(number of processors) and N (number of blocks)

C_s^{max} : Cardinality of the largest source relation = 100,000 records

R   : Number of records per block = 10

n＼N	1	2	5	10	20	50
200						4,000
500					10,000	
1,000				20,000		
2,000			40,000			
5,000		100,000				
10,000	200,000					

(b)

Figure 8.2. Analysis of the A-memory Size

number of processors is very large and the number of blocks very small. Although it is true that increasing the number of processors will cause a decrease in the size of the A-memory attached to a processor, the total size of all the A-memories remains large because we now have more processors, each with its own A-memory. Also, increasing the number of processors will increase the cost of the join operation unit in terms of processor cost. Similarly, although decreasing the number of blocks causes a decrease in A-memory size, it also leads to an increase in B-memory size, as will be shown in the next section. Hence, it is not enough to consider the A-memory in isolation; rather, an integrated study of the A-memory, the B-memory and the number of processors is necessary. Such a study is made in a later section.

8.3.3. Analysis of the B-Memory Size

We now analyze the size of the B-memory attached to a processor. That is, we are estimating the number of records in the queue of a single processor waiting to be processed by that processor, since the B-memory serves as a buffer.

In Figure 8.3 we present the model for our analysis. Two factors contribute to the rate of record arrivals at the B-memory: (1) the arrival of records directly from the database store, and (2) the arrival of records from the previous processor in the broadcast sequence. In Appendix 8.1 we show that the queue of records waiting to be processed by a processor is a $G/G/1$ queue. The average queue length of a $G/G/1$ queue can be calculated only approximately. We choose to utilize the heavy-traffic approximation [9] and the diffusion approximation [10]. Expressions for the average size of B-memory and for the size of B-memory in order to be 95% certain of no overflows in terms of these approximations are given in Appendix 8.2.

8.3.4. Interpretation of the Results on Memory Size

We are now able to use the expressions derived in the previous sections and in Appendices 8.1 and 8.2 to arrive at the sizes of the B-memories in terms of actual numbers. We want to handle the worst possible cases. This will occur when the source relation is very large and when all the source records are selected for the basic join operation. Accordingly, we let

C_s = the cardinality of the source set = 100,000 records

P = the fraction of source-set records selected for the join operation = 100%

r = the interarrival time of records at maximum read-out rate = 50 μs. This is arrived at in the following manner. An average record is 500 bytes. For the database store, we consider the Ampex Parallel Transfer disk [11], which stores 20,000 bytes per track and can

q: Fraction of records being broadcasted by a processor
D: Average arrival rate of records from the database store
A: Average service rate of records

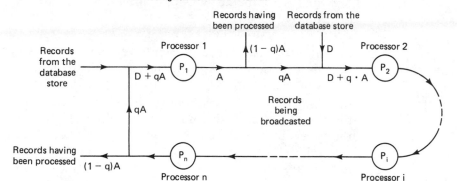

The G/G/1 Queue of Records in B-Memory

$\overline{S}_B$: Average size of the B-memory by heavy traffic approximation
$S_B\,95$: Size of the B-memory in order to be 95% certain of no overflow

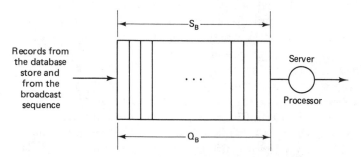

$\overline{Q}_B$: Average size of the B-memory by diffusion approximation
$Q_B\,95$: Size of the B-memory in order to be 95% certain of no overflow

Figure 8.3. Analysis of the B-Memory Size

read out of nine tracks in parallel. Assuming a disk rotation speed of 3600 rpm, we obtain the time to read one record as 50 μs.

y = the time taken to join two records = 50 μs.

R = the number of records per block of the A-memory = 10. [The average CCD segment size is 5 kbytes, and a record is approximately 500 bytes.]

n = the number of processors chosen from the set of 16, 32, and 48

N = the number of blocks chosen from the set of 10^4, 10^5, and 10^6

a = the fraction of target records that participate in the join operation chosen from the set of .2, .5, and 1

z_{as} = the time to read a record (500 bytes) from a given block of the A-memory once the block is found. [In other words, the block access time is not included. Once again, assuming that the A-memory is made of CCDs, z_{as} is chosen from the set of 5 μs, 10μs, 15 μs, 20μs, 50 μs, and 100 μs.]

z_{bs} = the time to fetch a record from the B-memory. [We note that the B-memory is not block-oriented (e.g., made of RAMs). We choose z_{bs} from the set of 10^{-9}, 10^{-8}, 10^{-7}, 10^{-6}, 10^{-5}, and 10^{-4} sec.]

z_{ar} = the time to access a given block in which the record resides and the time to read the record from the block. [For a CCD memory, the time taken to access an arbitrary block is about 100μs. However, clever arrangements of the CCD memory organization can reduce this time to about 10μs. Furthermore, the read-out time is as suggested for z_{as}. Thus, we choose z_{ar} from 15 μs to about 200 μs.]

8.3.5. Results on the B-Memory Size

Now we present the results for the size of the B-memory attached to a processor. A typical set of results for the case when the time to access a block and read a (random) record from A-memory is 55 μs and the time to read the next record (sequentially) from A-memory is 10 μs is presented in Table 8.1 and in Figure 8.4. In Figure 8.4 we plot the variation of the B-memory size as a function of the speed of the B-memory for various values of n (the number of processors) and N (the number of blocks in the A-memory). As expected, the faster the B-memory, the smaller it needs to be. For example, in Table 8.1 and Figure 8.4, when there are 32 processors each of which has an A-memory of 10,000 blocks, the B-memory has to be large enough to hold fifteen records if its record read-out time is 10^{-6} sec. On the other hand, referring to Table 8.1, if a faster B-memory with a read-out rate of one record every 10^{-7} sec is employed, then the B-memory need only be large enough to hold eight records.

One important feature of all the curves in Figure 8.4 is that at faster speed they all become parallel to the x axis—that is, the axis of B-memory speed. This means, of course, that increasing the B-memory speed (or decreasing the record read-out time) beyond a certain point will have no effect on the size of the B-memory. Thus, it is clearly not worthwhile to increase the speed of the B-memory beyond a certain point. Figure 8.4 suggests that decreasing the read-out time below 10^{-7} sec is not worthwhile, since it has a negligible impact on the B-memory size. On the other hand, all the curves in Figure 8.4 eventually become parallel to the y axis—that is, the axis of B-memory size. This means that if the time to read a record from the B-memory is 10^{-5} sec or more, the size of B-memory has to be arbitrarily large, which also means that the join operation hardware is not able to serve

TABLE 8.1. THE EFFECT OF B-MEMORY RECORD READ-OUT TIME ON
B-MEMORY SIZE UNDER VARIOUS PROCESSOR-MEMORY CONFIGURATIONS

For a (percentage of target records participating in the join operation) = 100%, Z_{as} (A-memory record read-out time) = 10 μs, and Z_{ar} (A-memory block access time) = 55 μs.

No. of blocks of an A-memory, N	No. of processors, n	Time in seconds to read out a record from a B-memory, Z_{bs}	Average size of a B-memory in records, $\bar{S}_B$	95% certain no overflow, $S_B 95$	Average size of a B-memory in records, $\bar{Q}_B$	95% certain no overflow, $Q_B 95$
10,000	32	10^{-9}	1.402	7.672	0.917	6.848
10,000	32	10^{-8}	1.408	7.706	0.922	6.878
10,000	32	10^{-7}	1.475	8.071	0.986	7.247
10,000	32	10^{-6}	2.897	15.855	2.382	15.074
10,000	48	10^{-9}	0.618	3.381	0.221	2.541
10,000	48	10^{-8}	0.620	3.390	0.222	2.551
10,000	48	10^{-7}	0.637	3.486	0.236	2.652
10,000	48	10^{-6}	0.905	4.950	0.466	4.163
100,000	16	10^{-9}	1.169	6.395	0.644	5.244
100,000	16	10^{-8}	1.171	6.407	0.646	5.256
100,000	16	10^{-7}	1.192	6.521	0.665	5.373
100,000	16	10^{-6}	1.463	8.007	0.925	6.894
100,000	32	10^{-9}	0.579	3.169	0.175	2.201
100,000	32	10^{-8}	0.580	3.174	0.175	2.207
100,000	32	10^{-7}	0.589	3.225	0.183	2.261
100,000	32	10^{-6}	0.708	3.873	0.278	2.944
100,000	48	10^{-9}	0.386	2.110	0.060	1.191
100,000	48	10^{-8}	0.386	2.113	0.061	1.194
100,000	48	10^{-7}	0.392	2.146	0.064	1.229
100,000	48	10^{-6}	0.468	2.560	0.110	1.672

the records in the B-memory fast enough because the read-out rate of the B-memory is too slow. In conclusion, we would require that *the time (i.e., Z_{bs}) to fetch a record from the B-memory is between 10^{-6} and 10^{-8} sec.*

In Figure 8.5 we plot the B-memory size as a function of the number of blocks in the A-memory for various values of n (the number of processors) and Z_{bs} (the record read-out time of the B-memory). As we increase the number of blocks in the A-memory, the need for a large B-memory decreases. We observe that the figure has twelve curves. The interesting point to note is that the curves corresponding to 16 processors are to the extreme right and the curves corresponding to 48 processors are to the extreme left. Thus, with only 16 processors, the B-memory size approaches infinity unless there are 20,000 blocks in the A-memory. That is, the join operation will not be fast enough to serve the records in the B-memory. With 32 processors, the B-memory size approaches infinity unless there are 5000 or more blocks. With 48 processors, the B-memory size approaches infinity only if there are fewer than 1000 blocks. Thus, if we want to decrease the number of blocks

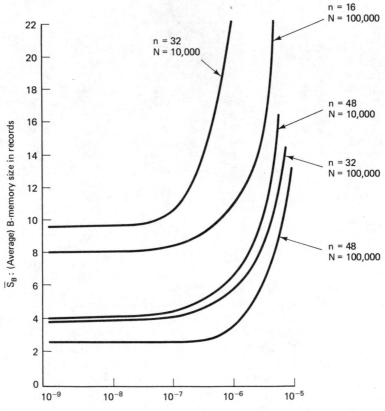

a (Percentage of target records participating
    the join operation) = 100%

Z_{ar} (Time to access an A-memory block and
    read out the first record from the
    A-memory block) = 55 μ

Z_{as} (Time to read out next record from the
    A-memory) = 10 μ

n : Number of processors
N: Number of blocks in A-memory

Z_{bs}: record read-out time of the B-memory (i.e., the
        B-memory speed) in seconds

Figure 8.4. The B-Memory Size as a Function of Processors and A-Memory
Blocks

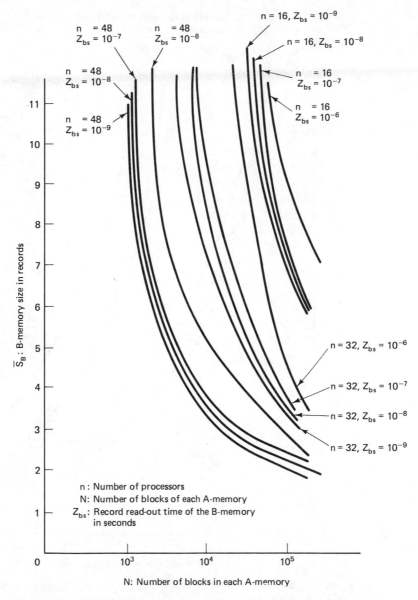

Figure 8.5. The B-Memory Size as a Function of Processors and B-Memory Speed

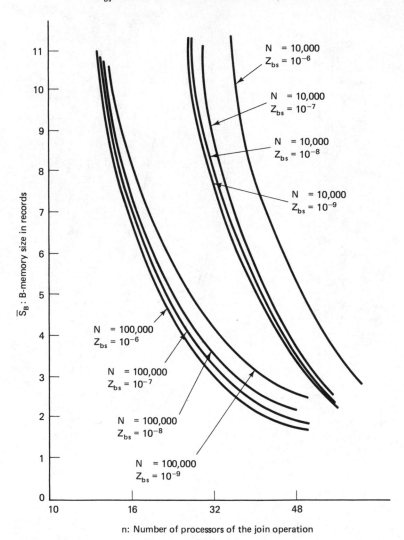

N: Number of blocks in each A-memory
Z_{bs}: Record-read-out time of the B-memory in seconds

Figure 8.6. B-Memory Size as a Function of A-Memory Blocks and B-Memory Speed

in the A-memory, we must increase the number of processors correspondingly. For example, if we allowed only 500 blocks in the A-memory of a processor, we would need 100 or more processors in the join organization. Thus, there is a memory-processor tradeoff.

In Figure 8.6 we plot the B-memory size as a function of the number of processors for various values of N (the number of blocks in the A-memory) and Z_{bs} (the record read-out time of the B-memory). As expected, the required size of the B-memory diminishes as the number of processors being utilized increases. We note that the figure has eight curves, and that the four curves corresponding to the case where the number of blocks in the A-memory is 10,000 are to the right and the four curves corresponding to the case where the number of blocks in the A-memory is 100,000 are to the left. Thus, if the number of blocks in the A-memory is fixed at 10,000, there must be 16 or more processors. Similarly, if the number of blocks in the A-memory is fixed at 100,000, then there may be four or more processors. Once again, we notice the inverse dependence between the number of processors and the number of blocks for the A-memory.

In summary, Figures 8.4, 8.5, and 8.6 are all drawn using the data shown in Table 8.1. This table calculates the size of the B-memory for various values of n (the number of processors), N (the number of blocks in each A-memory), and Z_{bs} (the record read-out time of the B-memory). $\bar{S}_B$ and $\bar{Q}_B$ represent the average size of the B-memory as calculated by the two different approximations (see Appendices 8.3 and 8.4). $S_B 95$ and $Q_B 95$ represent the size of the B-memory (as calculated by the same two approximations) in order to be 95% certain that no overflows will occur. We note that there is very good correspondence between the results of the two approximations.

8.3.6. B-Memory Size as Influenced by the A-Memory Block Access Time

Up to this point, all our observations about the B-memory size have embodied the assumption of certain characteristics of the A-memory (e.g., the time to access a block and then read a record is 55 μs and the time to read the next record is 10μs). We now wish to investigate how the size of the B-memory will be affected if we change the characteristics of the A-memory. In order to do this, we calculate the B-memory size for various combinations of the A-memory speed characteristics. The results are interesting: We discover that the key parameter with respect to the A-memory (i.e., the one that decides the size of B-memory) is neither of the two (speed) characteristics themselves, but rather their *difference*.

More formally, if Z_{as} is the time to read the next record from an A-memory block after the block is found, Z_{ar} is the time to access a block of the A-memory and then read a record from the block, and $\bar{S}_B$ is the average size of the B-memory, then $\bar{S}_B$ is dependent on $(Z_{ar} - Z_{as})$. We see from our definitions of Z_{ar} and Z_{as} that $(Z_{ar} - Z_{as})$ is really the time required to access a block of the A-memory—i.e., the *block-access time*.

The first observation we make as a result of our studies is that an A-memory with block-access time greater than 45 μs is not fast enough for our purposes, since the B-memory size will approach infinity. Thus, for example, an A-memory with $Z_{ar} = 60$ μs and $Z_{as} = 10$ μs is not good enough for our purposes, because the block-access time, as the difference, is 50 μs. However, consider a set of slower times, where an A-memory with Z_{ar} being 100 μs and Z_{as} being 60 μs is nevertheless good enough for our purposes, since the block-access time is only 40 μs. In fact, the results of the B-memory sizes obtained for this particular combination of the A-memory speed characteristics are tabulated in Table 8.2.

TABLE 8.2. THE EFFECT OF B-MEMORY RECORD READ-OUT TIME ON B-MEMORY SIZE UNDER CERTAIN A-MEMORY BLOCK-ACCESS TIMES

Let the following characteristics be fixed:

$a = 100\%$ (the fraction of target records participating the join operation)
$Z_{ar} = 100$ μs (the block-access and record read-out time of the A-memory)
$Z_{as} = 60$ μs (next record read-out time of the A-memory)

We note that block-access time of the A-memory is 40 μs (i.e., $Z_{ar} - Z_{as} = 100 - 60$).

No. of blocks of an A-memory, N	No. of processors, n	Time in seconds to read out a record from a B-memory, Z_{bs}	Average size of a B-memory in records, $\bar{S}_B$	95% certain no overflow, $S_B 95$	Average size of a B-memory in records, $\bar{Q}_B$	95% certain no overflow, $Q_B 95$
100,000	16	10^{-9}	0.918	5.025	0.413	3.830
100,000	16	10^{-8}	0.919	5.030	0.414	3.836
100,000	16	10^{-7}	0.930	5.088	0.424	3.897
100,000	16	10^{-6}	1.056	5.777	0.540	4.619
100,000	32	10^{-9}	0.393	2.153	0.052	1.095
100,000	32	10^{-8}	0.394	2.155	0.052	1.097
100,000	32	10^{-7}	0.397	2.171	0.054	1.115
100,000	32	10^{-6}	0.431	2.357	0.073	1.323
100,000	48	10^{-9}	0.254	1.390	0.009	0.429
100,000	48	10^{-8}	0.254	1.391	0.009	0.430
100,000	48	10^{-7}	0.256	1.400	0.009	0.439
100,000	48	10^{-6}	0.275	1.502	0.014	0.545

In Figure 8.7 (this figure and Figure 8.8 are drawn from data in Table 8.3) we plot the B-memory size versus the record read-out time of the A-memory. We note that these curves have fairly small slopes, indicating that a change in the record read-out time of the A-memory has only a small impact

$Z_{ar} - Z_{as}$ (Block access time of the
A-memory) = 45 μ
N (Number of A-memory
blocks) = 100,000
Z_{bs} (Record-read-out time of the
B-memory in seconds) = 10^{-6} μ

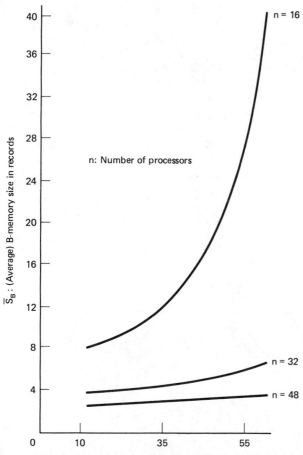

n: Number of processors

$\overline{S}_B$: (Average) B-memory size in records

Z_{as} : Time in μseconds to read-out the next record from the A-memory

Figure 8.7.   B-Memory Size as a Function of A-Memory Read-Out Time

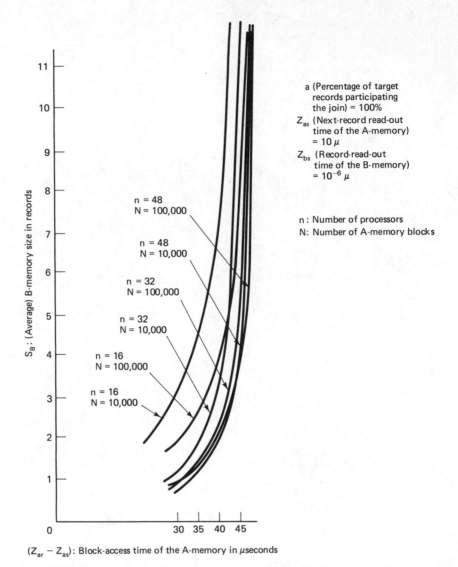

Figure 8.8. B-Memory Size as a Function of A-Memory Block-Access Time

on the B-memory size. In Figure 8.8 we plot the B-memory size versus the block-access time of the A-memory. The very large slopes of these curves indicate the very high correlation between the block-access time of the A-memory and the size of the B-memory. These curves also indicate to us that the block-access time may not exceed 45 μs.

TABLE 8.3. JOIN ORGANIZATIONS UNDER ACCEPTABLE BLOCK-ACCESS TIMES

Block-access time of the A-memory, $(Z_{ar} - Z_{as})$	No. of blocks of an A-memory, N	No. of processors, n	Time in seconds to read out a record from a B-memory, Z_{bs}	Average size of a B-memory in records, $\bar{s}_B$	95% certain no overflow, $s_B 95$	Average size of a B-memory in records, $\bar{Q}_B$	95% certain no overflow, $Q_B 95$
	10,000	16	10^{-9}	1.534	8.395	1.002	7.334
	10,000	16	10^{-8}	1.537	8.413	1.005	7.353
	10,000	16	10^{-7}	1.571	8.595	1.037	7.538
	10,000	16	10^{-6}	2.026	11.085	1.482	10.058
	10,000	32	10^{-9}	0.462	2.527	0.093	1.515
	10,000	32	10^{-8}	0.462	2.529	0.093	1.517
	10,000	32	10^{-7}	0.467	2.554	0.096	1.544
	10,000	32	10^{-6}	0.519	2.843	0.132	1.860
	10,000	48	10^{-9}	0.279	1.525	0.015	0.569
40 μs,	10,000	48	10^{-8}	0.279	1.527	0.015	0.571
where	10,000	48	10^{-7}	0.281	1.538	0.016	0.583
	10,000	48	10^{-6}	0.306	1.674	0.024	0.726
$Z_{as} = 10 \ \mu$s	100,000	16	10^{-9}	0.653	3.573	0.179	2.235
and	100,000	16	10^{-8}	0.653	3.575	0.180	2.238
	100,000	16	10^{-7}	0.657	3.598	0.183	2.264
$Z_{ar} = 50 \ \mu$s	100,000	16	10^{-6}	0.704	3.854	0.222	2.553
	100,000	32	10^{-9}	0.344	1.883	0.028	0.787
	100,000	32	10^{-8}	0.344	1.884	0.028	0.788
	100,000	32	10^{-7}	0.346	1.894	0.029	0.800
	100,000	32	10^{-6}	0.368	2.012	0.039	0.935
	100,000	48	10^{-9}	0.234	1.280	0.005	0.320
	100,000	48	10^{-8}	0.234	1.281	0.005	0.321
	100,000	48	10^{-7}	0.235	1.288	0.005	0.327
	100,000	48	10^{-6}	0.249	1.363	0.008	0.403

TABLE 8.3. *(Continued)* JOIN ORGANIZATIONS UNDER ACCEPTABLE BLOCK ACCESS TIMES

Block-access time of the A-memory, $(Z_{ar} - Z_{as})$	No. of blocks of an A-memory, N	No. of processors, n	Time in seconds to read out a record from a B-memory, Z_{bs}	Average size of a B-memory in records, $\bar{S}_B$	95% certain no overflow, $S_B 95$	Average size of a B-memory in records, $\bar{Q}_B$	95% certain no overflow, $Q_B 95$
	100,000	16	10^{-9}	1.753	9.590	1.207	8.507
	100,000	16	10^{-8}	1.758	9.618	1.212	8.535
45 μs	100,000	16	10^{-7}	1.810	9.907	1.264	8.827
where	100,000	16	10^{-6}	2.629	14.385	2.069	13.340
	100,000	32	10^{-9}	0.680	3.720	0.255	2.785
$Z_{as} = 35$ μs	100,000	32	10^{-8}	0.681	3.727	0.256	2.793
and	100,000	32	10^{-7}	0.695	3.802	0.267	2.871
$Z_{ar} = 80$ μs	100,000	32	10^{-6}	0.879	4.811	0.427	3.918
	100,000	48	10^{-9}	0.426	2.331	0.083	1.428
	100,000	48	10^{-8}	0.427	2.335	0.084	1.432
	100,000	48	10^{-7}	0.434	2.377	0.088	1.476
	100,000	48	10^{-6}	0.534	2.924	0.156	2.057
	100,000	16	10^{-9}	3.110	17.019	2.548	15.993
	100,000	16	10^{-8}	3.127	17.112	2.565	16.087
	100,000	16	10^{-7}	3.310	18.112	2.746	17.090
45 μs,	100,000	16	10^{-6}	8.357	45.732	7.780	44.744
where	100,000	32	10^{-9}	0.801	4.383	0.358	3.478
$Z_{as} = 55$ μs	100,000	32	10^{-8}	0.803	4.394	0.360	3.489
and	100,000	32	10^{-7}	0.823	4.503	0.377	3.601
$Z_{ar} = 100$ μs	100,000	32	10^{-6}	1.109	6.070	0.638	5.209
	100,000	48	10^{-9}	0.468	2.563	0.110	1.676
	100,000	48	10^{-8}	0.469	2.568	0.111	1.681
	100,000	48	10^{-7}	0.479	2.620	0.117	1.737
	100,000	48	10^{-6}	0.608	3.326	0.212	2.481

TABLE 8.3. *(Continued)* JOIN ORGANIZATIONS UNDER ACCEPTABLE BLOCK ACCESS TIMES

35 μs, where $Z_{as} = 10$ μs and $Z_{ar} = 45$ μs

10,000	16	10^{-9}	0.777	4.253	0.290	3.025
10,000	16	10^{-8}	0.778	4.256	0.291	3.029
10,000	16	10^{-7}	0.783	4.287	0.296	3.063
10,000	16	10^{-6}	0.848	4.639	0.353	3.444
10,000	32	10^{-9}	0.329	1.801	0.021	0.683
10,000	32	10^{-8}	0.329	1.802	0.021	0.684
10,000	32	10^{-7}	0.330	1.808	0.022	0.692
10,000	32	10^{-6}	0.344	1.883	0.028	0.783
10,000	32	10^{-5}	1.401	7.668	0.916	6.839
10,000	48	10^{-9}	0.214	1.171	0.002	0.208
10,000	48	10^{-8}	0.214	1.171	0.002	0.208
10,000	48	10^{-7}	0.215	1.174	0.002	0.211
10,000	48	10^{-6}	0.221	1.211	0.003	0.248
10,000	48	10^{-5}	0.618	3.380	0.220	2.540
100,000	16	10^{-9}	0.516	2.822	0.071	1.300
100,000	16	10^{-8}	0.516	2.823	0.071	1.301
100,000	16	10^{-7}	0.517	2.831	0.072	1.313
100,000	16	10^{-6}	0.533	2.916	0.084	1.432
100,000	16	10^{-5}	1.168	6.394	0.644	5.243
100,000	32	10^{-9}	0.284	1.556	0.007	0.381
100,000	32	10^{-8}	0.284	1.556	0.007	0.381
100,000	32	10^{-7}	0.285	1.559	0.007	0.385
100,000	32	10^{-6}	0.291	1.593	0.009	0.433
100,000	32	10^{-5}	0.579	3.168	0.175	2.201
100,000	48	10^{-9}	0.196	1.075	0.001	0.121
100,000	48	10^{-8}	0.197	1.075	0.001	0.122
100,000	48	10^{-7}	0.197	1.077	0.001	0.124
100,000	48	10^{-6}	0.201	1.097	0.001	0.144
100,000	48	10^{-5}	0.386	2.110	0.060	1.190

8.3.7. Preferred Characteristics

In summary, we prefer an A-memory with a slow record read-out time and a fast block-access time to one with a fast record read-out time and a slow block-access time. Intuitively, the reason may be explained as follows. During the second phase of the join operation, each target record is hashed to a block of the A-memory. The service time for that record includes an access of that block followed by a read-out of records in that block. The number of records in a block can be reduced as much as we want by the use of more processors in the organization and more blocks in the A-memories. Thus, the dominating factor in the service time of a target record becomes the block-access time. A slow block-access time will cause a large service time, and hence the B-memory as the buffer will soon overflow. This is the reason for the observed phenomenon.

We have seen, in the previous paragraphs, four different ways to reduce the size of the B-memory of a processor:

1. Increase the number of processors of the organization.
2. Increase the number of blocks in the A-memory.
3. Decrease the record read-out time of the B-memory.
4. Decrease the block-access time of the A-memory.

Even though each of these recommendations will decrease the size of the B-memory of a processor, the overall cost of the hardware may still increase.

Next we present an integrated study of the A-memory, the B-memory, and the number of processors in order to arrive at the optimum combination of processors and memories to be placed on a single silicon chip.

8.4. DESIGN OF AN OPTIMAL CHIP FOR THE JOIN OPERATION

Our interest in join operations using parallel processors is motivated by two factors:

1. The decreasing cost of logic (i.e., cheaper processors).
2. The increasing level of integration on a chip (i.e., VLSI).

Thus, our design of the parallel join operations would not be complete without a discussion of how the hardware used to perform the join may actually be implemented using large-scale integration technology. In previous sections we have developed equations that can be used to calculate how many processors, how much A-memories, and how much B-memory must be used in order to achieve a certain join speed. In this section we will estimate the "optimal" combination of processors and memories that may be placed on a chip, where a particular combination is considered optimal if it provides the best performance for a certain fixed cost. A chip that contains this optimal combination of processors and memories will be called an *optimal chip.*

We will consider the problem of finding an optimal chip for two different time frames. First, we will design a chip that would be optimal given the present state of the art of large-scale integration technology. Next, we will design an optimal chip for the year 1992, basing our calculations on the projected increases in the level of integration (number of transistors and amount of memory that can be placed on a chip with acceptable yield) by that year. We do the latter only because we believe that the optimal chip for 1992 will not be a simple extension of the one for 1982 but will be radically different. Beyond 1992, however, radical changes in the design of the optimal chip are unlikely. The reasons will become clear as our material develops in the following sections.

When such an optimal chip has been designed, the hardware may then use a single chip to attain a certain join speed, or it may use two interconnected chips to attain approximately twice that speed, or it may use three interconnected chips to attain approximately thrice that speed, and so on. Owing to the simplicity and hardware extensibility of our interconnection scheme among processors (Figure 8.1), the optimal chips may also be easily interconnected in the desired fashion to obtain the desired speed.

In Figure 8.9 we show an optimal chip and also the interconnection scheme among such chips. Each chip is connected to two others, and all the chips are connected together in a circular fashion. Each chip consists of a number of processor-memory (PM) pairs. The number of PM pairs to be placed on a chip, and the amount and type (RAM, CCD, etc.) of memory that is attached to each processor in a PM pair, will be calculated below. An important point to note about the optimal chip is that it needs only three pins; thus it is not pin-limited. In other words, the number of processor-memory pairs that can be placed on a chip is not limited by the number of pins but only by the level of integration.

8.4.1. Designing an Optimal Chip for Today

We note first that the present state of the art allows for the fabrication of 70,000 transistors on a single chip [12]. Thus, 70K bits of random-access memory (RAM) can be placed on a single chip. Next, we are interested in knowing how many charge-coupled devices (CCDs) can be placed on a chip, since the A-memories of the join operation are made of block-oriented memories such as CCDs. The maximum density available for a CCD chip today is 256K bits. Thus, we may roughly equate 1 bit of the CCD memory to $70/256$ ($\simeq 0.25$) of a transistor. This rough equivalence allows us to discuss either transistors or CCDs in terms of units per chip.

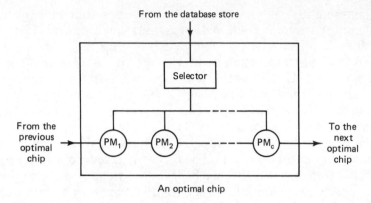

PM: Processor-memory pair
c: Number of PM pairs in an optimal chip

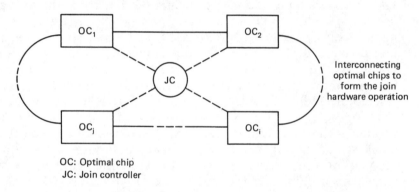

OC: Optimal chip
JC: Join controller

Figure 8.9. Description and Interconnection of Optimal Chips

Finally, we need to estimate the number of transistors needed to realize the basic join operation. It is estimated [12] that about 40,000 transistors are required to make a general-purpose processor. However, the processors we propose to use in the join operation are very simple ones and they are special-purpose rather than general-purpose processors. In fact, these processors need only compare two records on the basis of certain attribute values and, if the values in the two records are equal, concatenate the two records. In addition, the processors are required to calculate a simple hash function. Our estimate of the number of transistors for the join operation is based on a similar estimate made for a trie machine for search problems [13]. Each processor of the join operation is estimated to require at most 5000 transistors.

We assume, as before, that the maximum possible size of the source relation is 100,000 records, each of size 500 bytes. In order to store these many source records, at least 4×10^8 bits of A-memory (say, made of CCDs) are required. Even if as many as 1000 processors are employed in the hardware, we find that each will need 4×10^5 bits [i.e., $(4 \times 10^8)/10^3$] of the CCD memory. Present-day levels of integration will not allow us to put this amount of memory along with a processor on a chip. Thus, our first design decision regarding an optimal chip is that the A-memory will not be integrated into the chip containing the processors but will be on separate chips.

The B-memory (made of RAM), on the other hand, may certainly be integrated into a chip along with processors, since it is usually of very small size (i.e., a few kilobytes). In Table 8.4 we show various combinations of processors and B-memory sizes that can be placed on a chip using present-day levels of integration. These calculations are made using the estimate that 70K transistors can be put on a chip and that one processor in the join operation requires 5K transistors. For example, we may choose to integrate a single processor and 65K of the B-memory, or we may choose to put two processors, each with 30K of the B-memory, together on a chip, and so on. We will label these allowable combinations of processors and B-memory sizes as type I, type II, . . . , type VII. Our purpose is to determine which of these seven chip types would be optimal for use.

The first point to be noted is that the use of more processors and memories on a chip decreases the need for transferring records across chip boundaries, from one chip to another. Since transfers that are local to a chip are an order of magnitude faster and consume less power than record transfers across chip boundaries [12], chip type VII is the best. It also has the greatest number (i.e., 7) of processors and memories on a single chip.

Let us now take a different approach to the choice of an optimal chip type. Since, ultimately, many optimal chips will be interconnected as in Figure 8.9 to form a join operation, we would like to compare the performance obtained by connecting together a large number of chips of type I with that obtained by connecting together a large number of chips of type II, and so on. For illustrative purposes, let us consider that that join operation is built using 200 chips and that it must be able to serve records at the rate of at least one every 50 μs (which is the maximum read-out rate of a parallel

TABLE 8.4

Chip type	Number of processors per chip	Amount of B-memory per chip (Kbits)	Amount of B-memory per processor (Kbits)
I	1	65	65
II	2	60	30
III	3	55	18 · 33
IV	4	50	12 · 5
V	5	45	9
VI	6	40	6 · 67
VII	7	35	7

TABLE 8.5

Chip combination type	Number of blocks per A-memory	Size of A-memory per processor (Mbits)	Total size of the A-memory (Mbits)	Record-service time (μs)
I	1,065	44.6	8,920	49.71
II	550	23.0	9,200	49.56
III	381	15.91	9,546	49.38
IV	298	12.42	9,936	49.20
V	250	10.04	10,040	49.01
VI	220	9.133	10,960	49.8
VII	199	8.246	11,544	49.6

transfer disk as calculated earlier. Consider that the chip with one processor and 65K of the B-memory (type-I chip) is used to construct the join operation hardware. Then, it may be shown by use of the equation derived in Appendix 8.3 (for S_B95, the size of B-memory) that the A-memory (constructed on different chips) attached to each processor must contain at least 1,065 blocks. In other words, the use of fewer than 1,065 blocks of the A-memory will require the size of the B-memory (buffer) attached to a processor to be greater than 65K bits, thus making use of the type-I chip infeasible. Knowing the number of blocks in each A-memory allows us to calculate (using the equation derived previously in an earlier section) the size of each A-memory. It may be easily shown that the A-memory attached to a processor must be at least of size 44.6 Mbits, and that the total size of the A-memory required is 8,920 Mbits. Finally, the equation for $\bar{x}$ or E(service time), derived in Appendix 8.2, may be used to show that the record-service time is 49.71 μs. This explains the first row in Table 8.6. Similar calculations are made for each of the other six chip types and the results for all these chip types is presented in Table 8.6.

TABLE 8.6

Chip combination type	Number of blocks per A-memory	Size of A-memory per processor (Mbits)	Total size of the A-memory (Mbits)	Record-service time (μs)
I	1,400	58.	11,600	48.6
II	700	29.	11,600	48.6
III	467	19.33	11,600	48.6
IV	350	14.5	11,600	48.6
V	280	11.6	11,600	48.6
VI	233	9.67	11,600	48.6
VII	200	8.29	11,600	48.6

We reiterate that the results in Table 8.6 are made assuming that 200 chips are used to construct the join operation. We wish to compare the join operation created with 200 chips of type I (in terms of speed and cost) with the join operations created with 200 chips of type II, and so on. Our first observation is that 200 chips of type I will cost the same as 200 chips of type II, or type III, or any of the other types, because each of the chips are of similar complexity (since they all accommodate 70,000 transistors). We note, however, that the type-I chip has the lowest total A-memory requirement and also the slowest record-service time. The type-VII chip, on the other hand, has the largest A-memory requirement and also the fastest record-service time. In order to compare the different chip types, we need to either make the A-memory requirement uniform and compare the different service times, or make the service time uniform and compare the A-memory requirement. We choose to do the former in keeping with our definition of optimal as one giving the best performance for a fixed cost.

The normalized results are shown in Table 8.7. It is noticed that making the total A-memory requirement uniform across all chip types has caused all service times to be also uniform across chip types. Thus, all chip types are equally attractive since they have the same cost and record-service time. However, even though the service times per record are the same for all chip types, a join operation which uses more processors will have to service fewer records. Thus, the total join time (= number records serviced X time taken to service a record) is minimized, if more processors are employed in the hardware. Hence, we will prefer the chip type with the largest number of processors in it, and this is the type-VII chip. Furthermore, the use of type-VII chips will minimize record transfers across chip boundaries, thus contributing to a decrease in join time.

We conclude that *the optimal chip type is the one with 7 processors and 35K of B-memory (5K per processor) on a chip. At least 200 such chips will have to be interconnected in order to provide a service rate of one every 50 μs.* Use of more than 200 chips in the hardware would mean that the service rate would increase to more than one every 50 μs. Such use of many optimal chips is made possible by the hardware extensibility of our design and the simplicity of our interconnection scheme.

8.4.2. Designing an Optimal Chip for 1992

Using the figures provided in [12], we estimate that, by the year 1992, between 10 and 12 million transistors can be put on a chip. Let us assume, for the purposes of this calculation, that 11 million transistors can be put on a chip in 1992. This means that large amounts of A-memories (made of, for example, CCDs) can now be integrated into a chip along with a processor. This makes the optimal chip of 1992 radically different from the optimal chip of today, which does not incorporate any A-memory. We now need to find out what combinations of processors and (both A- and B-) memories should be placed on a chip. Obviously, many combinations are feasible. Our purpose will be to choose a combination that is optimal in that it gives the best performance for a certain fixed cost (where, by performance, we mean the total time to do a join operation).

As before, the optimal chip is designed so that a large number of them (say, 200) may be interconnected to perform the join operation, which should be able to service records at the rate of at least one every 50 μs. An examination of the equation for $\bar{x}$ or E(service time) derived in Appendix 8.2 shows us that the service time depends upon the product nN, where n is the number of processors in the hardware and N is the number of blocks in an A-memory. If we choose the maximum size of the source set ($C_s^{\max}$) to be 100,000 records, the record size to be 500 bytes, the number (R) of records in a block to be 10, the B-memory record read-out time to be 10^{-8} sec, the A-memory block-access time to be 30 μs, and the A-memory record read-out time to be 5 μs, we see that nN must be 2.52×10^4 for the desired record-service time of 50 μs. Now, we recall that the total size of A-memory is approximately

$$ n \left(\frac{C_s^{\max}}{n} + NR \right) \simeq C_s^{\max} + nNR \quad \text{records} $$

We see that the size of the A-memory depends only on the product nN (whereas $C_s^{\max}$ and R are constants), which is fixed at 2.52×10^4 in order to obtain a record-service time of 50 μs. Thus, the total size of the A-memories is also fixed, whatever combination of processors and memories goes on a chip, and is given by ($10^5 + 2.52 \times 10^4 \times 10$) records. This means that each chip will contain 7.04 Mbits of A-memory. Since 1 bit of A-memory is equivalent to 0.25 transistor, each chip will utilize 1.76 million (out of 11 million) transistors for the A-memory. The remaining 9.24 million transistors on a chip must be divided up between processors and the B-memory.

In Table 8.7 we show the combinations of processors and B-memory that add up to 9.24 million transistors. We need to decide first, for each combination shown, whether it is acceptable or not. That is, for the given A-memory size (fixed earlier) and the given number of processors, is the buffer size (i.e., the B-memory size) large enough to handle an arrival rate of one record every 50 μs? If the B-memory is large enough, the combination is acceptable; otherwise, it is unacceptable. The equation derived in Appendix 8.3 is used to check each of the listed combinations for acceptability. All combinations of Table 8.7 with 1021 or fewer processors are found to be acceptable.

We now conclude that the combination with the largest number of processors on a chip is the optimal one. The reasons are similar to those used earlier. First, the total cost of 200 chips of any combination type is the same,

TABLE 8.7. VARIOUS COMBINATIONS OF PROCESSORS AND MEMORIES THAT MAY BE PLACED ON A SINGLE CHIP IN 1992

Number of processors	Total size of B-memory (Kbits)	Amount of B-memory per processor (Kbits)	
1	9235	9235.00	
31	9085	293.06	
61	8935	146.48	
91	8785	96.54	
121	8635	71.36	
151	8485	56.19	
181	8335	46.05	
211	8185	38.79	
241	8035	33.34	
271	7885	29.10	
301	7735	25.70	
331	7585	22.92	
361	7435	20.60	
391	7285	18.63	
421	7135	16.95	
451	6985	15.49	
481	6835	14.21	
511	6685	13.08	
541	6535	12.08	
571	6385	11.18	
601	6235	10.37	*Acceptable:* the B-memory is sufficiently large to handle the intended rate of record arrival and to serve the given amount of A-memory
631	6085	9.64	
661	5935	8.98	
691	5785	8.37	
721	5635	7.82	
751	5485	7.30	
781	5335	6.83	
811	5185	6.39	
841	5035	5.99	
871	4885	5.61	
901	4735	5.26	
931	4585	4.92	
961	4435	4.61	
991	4285	4.32	
1021	4135	4.05	
1051	3985	3.79	
1081	3835	3.55	
1111	3685	3.32	
1141	3535	3.10	
1171	3385	2.89	
1201	3235	2.69	
1231	3085	2.51	
1261	2935	2.33	
1291	2785	2.16	
1321	2635	1.99	
1351	2485	1.84	
1381	2335	1.69	
1411	2185	1.55	
1441	2035	1.41	
1471	1885	1.28	
1501	1735	1.16	
1531	1585	1.04	*Unacceptable:* the B-memory is too small to serve as a buffer
1561	1435	0.92	
1591	1285	0.81	

since each chip combination is of the same complexity (in terms of number of transistors). Second, although the service times per record are the same for all chip types, a join operation that uses more processors will service fewer records. Thus, if more processors are used in the operation, the total join time is minimized. Moreover, with the largest number of processors on a chip, record transfers across chip boundaries will be minimized, thus contributing to a decrease in join time.

We conclude that the *optimal chip type is the one with 1,021 processors, 7.04 M bits of A-memories (3.93 K bits per processor) and 4,135 K bits of B-memories (4.05 K bits per processor) on a chip. At least 200 such chips will have to be interconnected in order to provide a service rate of one every 50 µsecs.* Use of fewer than 200 such chips for the join operation will result in a service rate lower than one record every 50 µsecs. Similarly, use of more than 200 such chips for the join operation will result in a service rate higher than one record every 50 µsecs.

8.5. INEQUALITY AND m-WAY JOIN OPERATIONS

We now describe how the basic join operation may be easily extended to handle inequality joins and m-way joins.

8.5.1. Requirements for and Phases of the Inequality Join

Like the natural join, an inequality join is an operation that involves two relations, the source relation and the target relation, and two attributes, the source attribute of the source relation and the target attribute of the target relation. Furthermore, the values of the source and target attributes must be drawn from the same domain.

There are four possible types of inequality joins, depending upon which of the four inequality operators $(<, \leqslant, >, \geqslant)$ is involved in the join. Let us denote an inequality join between relations A and B as A "op" B, where op is one of the four inequality operators. Furthermore, let us call the set of records produced as a result of the join operation the *result relation*. Then, each record in the result relation C of the inequality join A op B is a concatenation of two records r_1 and r_2, where r_1 is a record in the source relation A, r_2 is a record in the target relation B, and op holds between the source attribute value in r_1 and the target attribute value in r_2. In Figure 8.10 we show an example of a greater-than join.

In order to handle inequality joins, the hashing function HASH in use must satisfy the following criterion. *Given two attribute values x and y such that $x < y$, we require that $HASH(x) \leqslant HASH(y)$.* Such a hashing function can easily be found. For example, suppose we are hashing salaries, p, to blocks of the A-memory. Let the A-memory have N blocks. We then want

A: The source relation of the following
   five records:

⟨⟨Name, HSIAO⟩, ⟨Salary, 2000⟩⟩
⟨⟨Name, JAI⟩, ⟨Salary, 1000⟩⟩
⟨⟨Name, KERR⟩, ⟨Salary, 2000⟩⟩
⟨⟨Name, JOHN⟩, ⟨Salary, 5000⟩⟩
⟨⟨Name, JACOB⟩, ⟨Salary, 3000⟩⟩

B: The target relation of the following
   three records:

⟨⟨Benefit, 2000⟩, ⟨Dept, TOY⟩⟩
⟨⟨Benefit, 3000⟩, ⟨Dept, SALES⟩⟩
⟨⟨Benefit, 4000⟩, ⟨Dept, FINANCE⟩⟩

Let the source attribute be Salary and the target attribute be Benefit. Then the result relation where Salary of *A* is greater than Benefit of *B* consists of the following four records:

⟨⟨Name, JOHN⟩, ⟨Salary, 5000⟩, ⟨Benefit, 2000⟩, ⟨Dept, TOY⟩⟩
⟨⟨Name, JOHN⟩, ⟨Salary, 5000⟩, ⟨Benefit, 3000⟩, ⟨Dept, SALES⟩⟩
⟨⟨Name, JOHN⟩, ⟨Salary, 5000⟩, ⟨Benefit, 4000⟩, ⟨Dept, FINANCE⟩⟩
⟨⟨Name, JACOB⟩, ⟨Salary, 3000⟩, ⟨Benefit, 2000⟩, ⟨Dept, TOY⟩⟩

Figure 8.10.   An Example of a Greater-Than Join

the hashing function to return a block number between 1 and N. Furthermore, let the highest possible salary be MAXSAL. Then, a hashing function that satisfies our requirements would be

$$\text{HASH}(p) = \left\lceil \frac{p}{\text{MAXSAL}} \right\rceil N$$

Let us now describe the method used to do inequality joins. As in the case of natural join, the operation proceeds in phases. In early phases, the source records are read into the B-memories and then hashed and stored in the blocks of the A-memories. Next, the target records are read into the B-memories. Each processor now does the following for each target record in its B-memory. It reads the record from the B-memory and hashes the target attribute values of the record to a block (say, i) of the A-memory. Now, the processor accesses and searches records in every block from the first to the ith (in the case of a less-than or less-than-or-equal-to join) or from the ith to the Nth (in the case of a greater-than or greater-than-or-equal-to join). The source attribute values of these records are now examined in order to determine if they will participate in the join. The join is performed between the target record and all the qualified source records, and the concatenated records are placed in the C-memory. We note that we do *not* make use of associative memories for the inequality join.

In summary, we note that the essential difference between the method for natural joins and the method for inequality joins occurs in the later phases. For a natural join, each target attribute value will be hashed to a block of the A-memory and all source records in that block and that block alone will be examined for possible participation in the join operation. For a less-than or less-than-or-equal-to (greater-than or greater-than-or-equal-to) join, each target attribute value will be hashed to a block of the A-memory and all source records in that block and in all other blocks with lower (higher) block numbers will be examined for possible participation in the join operation. Consequently, an inequality join is a slower operation than a natural join.

8.5.2. Operations of the m-Way Join

Up to now we have considered only the manner in which two relations are joined. However, we may be required first to join two relations and then to join the result relation with another relation. We call this operation a *3-way join*. Similarly, the m-way join of $A_1, A_2, \ldots, A_m$ requires that the relations A_1 and A_2 be first joined to produce an intermediate result relation, say B_1. The relation B_1 must now be joined with A_3 to produce another intermediate result relation B_2. This process continues until B_{m-2} is joined with A_m to produce the final result relation B_{m-1}. In Figure 8.11 we show an example of a 3-way join of three relations: the NAME relation, the EMP relation, and the DEPT relation. The NAME and EMP relations are first joined using Emp# as both the source and target attributes. The resulting relation is now joined with the relation DEPT using Dept# as both the source and target attributes. We see that a 3-way join requires two joins to be performed and two source and target attributes to be specified. Similarly, an m-way join requires $(m-1)$ joins to be performed and requires the specification of $(m-1)$ source and target attributes. Let us refer to these source and target attributes as $SA_1, SA_2, \ldots, SA_{m-1}$ and $TA_1, TA_2, \ldots, TA_{m-1}$, respectively. In the paragraphs that follow, we shall describe the m-way join operation.

Let the result relation of an m-way join of $A_1, A_2, \ldots, A_m$ be represented as $A_1 \times A_2 \times A_2 \times \cdots \times A_m$. First, the relation A_1 is read and stored in the A-memories. Next, the relation A_2 is read in the B-memories and the intermediate relation $A_1 \times A_2$ is formed and stored in the C-

The NAME relation consists of the following two records:	The EMP relation consists of the following three records:	The DEPT relation consists of the following three records:
⟨⟨Name, HSIAO⟩, ⟨Emp#, 1⟩⟩	⟨⟨Emp#, 1⟩, ⟨Dept#, 2⟩⟩	⟨⟨Dept#, 2⟩, ⟨No. of Employees, 20⟩⟩
⟨⟨Name, JAI⟩, ⟨Emp#, 2⟩⟩	⟨⟨Emp#, 2⟩, ⟨Dept#, 3⟩⟩	⟨⟨Dept#, 3⟩, ⟨No. of Employees, 25⟩⟩
	⟨⟨Emp#, 3⟩, ⟨Dept#, 4⟩⟩	⟨⟨Dept#, 4⟩, ⟨No. of Employees, 19⟩⟩

(1) Join NAME and EMP; use Emp# as source and target attributes.
(2) Join the result relation of (1) and DEPT; use Dept# as source and target attributes.

The result relation of (2) is as follows:

⟨⟨Name, HSIAO⟩, ⟨Dept#, 2⟩, ⟨No. of Employees, 20⟩⟩
⟨⟨Name, JAI⟩, ⟨Dept#, 3⟩, ⟨No. of Employees, 25⟩⟩

Figure 8.11. An Example of a 3-Way Join of NAME, EMP, and DEPT

memories. Next, the relation A_3 is read in the B-memories and the intermediate relation $A_1 \times A_2 \times A_3$ is formed and stored in the A-memories. The process continues in this way, with the intermediate relations being stored alternately in the A- and C-memories. The intermediate set $A_1 \times A_2 \times \cdots \times A_i$ will be stored in the C-memories if i is even and in the A-memories if i is odd. The final result relation $A_1 \times A_2 \times \cdots \times A_m$ will be formed and stored in the C-memories if i is even and in the A-memories if i is odd.

In order to derive some time measures, let us make the assumption that each of the record relations $A_1, A_2, \ldots, A_m$ is clustered and stored in a separate content-addressable cylinder of a disk with tracks-in-parallel-read-out capability. Then each relation can be read in one disk revolution. Let us now estimate the number of revolutions needed to perform the m-way join and produce the relation $A_1 \times A_2 \times \cdots \times A_m$. In the first revolution, the relation A_1 is read in and stored in the A-memories. In the second revolution, the relation A_2 is read in, joined with A_1, and the result relation $A_1 \times A_2$ is stored in the C-memories. In an earlier section we indicated how to adjust the B-memory (buffer memory) sizes in order to ensure that joins are performed at the disk transfer rate. Thus, each additional disk revolution will cause an additional relation A_i to be read in and an additional intermediate result relation $A_1 \times A_2 \times \cdots \times A_i$ to be formed and stored in either the A- or the C-memories, depending on whether i is odd or even. Finally, at the end of m revolutions, the result relation $A_1 \times A_2 \times \cdots \times A_m$ would have been created. Thus, an m-way join will take m revolutions of the database store. In general, if we assume that each relation requires c revolutions of the database store to read it out, the join operation takes mc revolutions. That is, the join operation is performed as fast as the participating relations are being read out. To put it another way, perfect pipelining can be achieved between the database store and the join hardware during the execution of the m-way join operation. Of course, such perfect pipelining will be achieved only if the A- and C-memories are large enough to hold all the source records and also to hold each intermediate relation created during the join operation. Otherwise, multiple passes over some of the relations are required. These relations will have to be retrieved from the database store more than once.

8.6. COMPARISON WITH OTHER METHODS

In this section we survey some other available join methods and compare them with our own. The bases for comparison are (1) whether the methods can support natural, implicit, inequality, and m-way joins; (2) the time complexity of the basic join, where the time complexity is given in terms of the cardinalities of the source, target, and result relations and also in terms of the number of revolutions of the secondary storage device needed to affect the join; and (3) whether join processing may be overlapped with the input of the source and target relations. We begin with a brief description of each of the various methods. The comparison between them is summarized in Table 8.8.

The machine known as the *content-addressable file store* (CAFS) [13] supports only the implicit join operation and not the natural join. The method uses a single-bit wide random-access store in order to aid the join operation, which proceeds essentially as follows. First, each source attribute value is read and a bit in the random-access store is marked. The address of the bit to be marked is determined either by hashing the source value to an address or by using a precompiled coupling index [13]. The target records are now read. Each target attribute value will cause a bit in the random-access store to be examined. As before, the address of the bit to be examined is determined either by hashing the target value to an address or by using a precompiled coupling index. If the examined bit has been marked, then this target record (from which the target value was derived) will participate in the join and is output. Notice that the process involves one scan of the source relation, one scan of the target relation, and the creation of the result relation. Hence, the complexity of the join is

$$O(C_s + C_t + C_r)$$

In an implicit join operation, $C_r \leqslant C_t$ and hence $O(C_s + C_t + C_r)$ approaches $O(C_s + C_t)$.

There are problems with the hashing scheme and the precompiled coupling index scheme. If the method of precompiled indices is used, then we must know beforehand which relations will have to be joined. Additionally, extra space is required to store the coupling indices and extra time to update these indices during an update. On the other hand, if a hashing scheme is used, there is always the possibility of errors in the result relation; i.e., wrong target records may be chosen for the result.* The errors are caused by the collisions due to hashing. In our method we use hashing only to locate blocks and not for identifying records. We also do not discard the source records having the join values that are necessary for the natural join. Thus, our method can compare a target record with the source records on the basis of their join values, and so no error is possible in the result relation.

It seems very likely that the CAFS method can overlap I/O with join processing, since the join algorithm is such that it may begin with the arrival of the first source record. However, in order to support *m*-way joins with I/O overlap, the method will need to use an additional random-access bit store. Also, if the method of hashing is used, the number of errors in the result relation will go up when *m*-way joins are performed. That is, a 3-way join

---

*A scheme for avoiding errors has been suggested, but it is too complex to be implemented in CAFS [13].

TABLE 8.8. COMPARISON CHART OF VARIOUS JOIN METHODS

Database machines	Implicit join	Natural join	Time complexity in terms of relation cardinalities	Time complexity in numbers of secondary store revolutions (typical)	m-Way joins without rotational delays	Inequality joins	Overlapped I/O	Possibility of errors	Use of unit different from storage	No. of processors in additional unit
CAFS	√	×	$O(C_s + C_t + C_r)$	2	A.H.	A.C.	A.H.	√	√	1
CASSM	√	×	$O(C_s + C_t + C_r)$	>2	A.C.	A.C.	N.A.	×	×	N.A.
RAP	√	×	$O(C_s C_t)$	15–60	A.C.	√	N.A.	×	×	N.A.
SHAW	√	√	$O(C_s + C_t + C_r)$	20–40	A.H.	×	×	×	√	1
DIALOG	√	√	$O(C_s + C_t + C_r)$	100	A.H.	√	×	×	√	1
DIRECT	√	√	$O(C_s C_t + C_r)$	?	A.C.	√	×	×	√	1 or more (MIMD)
DBC	√	√	$O(C_s + C_t + C_r)$	2	√	√	√	×	√	1 or more (SIMD)

√ = yes
× = no
N.A. = not applicable

A.H. = additional hardware needed
A.C. = additional change in the algorithm
? = unknown or hard to estimate

C_s = cardinality of source relation
C_t = cardinality of target relation
C_r = cardinality of result relation

will result in more errors than a 2-way join, a 4-way join will result in more errors than a 3-way join, and so on. If the hashing function used has the special property suggested in this paper, then inequality joins may be supported.

The method used in the *context-addressed segmented sequential memory* (CASSM) for doing joins [4] is very similar to the one above. Thus, most of the comments we made above about CAFS will be relevant to CASSM. There are two main differences, however. First, CASSM uses a physical random-access bit store for each track of the secondary storage, and so the implementation of one virtual random-access bit store, addressable by all cells (a cell is a track of a disk and its associated logic), requires the address of a bit to be passed from one cell to the next until it arrives at the appropriate cell. This may require additional rotational delay, so that more revolutions of the secondary store may be needed for join processing than for reading the source and target relations. Second, while CAFS uses a separate unit for doing joins that is removed from the secondary storage device itself, CASSM does the join directly on the tracks of the disk that constitute the secondary store. Thus, comments regarding whether the join operation can be overlapped with I/O are not relevant, since no separate unit is used to do the join. This also implies that the intermediate relations created during the execution of the *m*-way join must be stored in the secondary storage itself.

The *relational associative processor* (RAP) [5] also supports only an implicit join operation. The source relation is stored in x cells, where a cell consists of some circulating memory and associated logic. Similarly, the target relation is stored in y cells. The circulating memories have the start-stop feature, so that the time for one rotation of the circulating memory may depend upon how much processing is required by the logic on the records in the circulating memories. The entire operation is controlled by the RAP controller and proceeds as follows. The first cell containing the source values of the source relation is read and buffered at the RAP controller, which consists of z blocks. Then, a block of source values is loaded into the cells containing the target relation, and these cells are initiated for processing. This block loading of source values is repeated until all the buffered source values are processed; then the next cell of source values is buffered at the RAP controller, and the above operations are repeated until all cells containing source values are processed.

Since the source records are stored in x cells, each cell has C_s/x records. Similarly, each target-relation cell has C_t/y target records. Since the buffer has z blocks, each block can hold C_s/xz source values. Thus, C_s/xy source values are processed in a batch. Each of the C_t/y target records in a target-relation cell has to be compared against these C_s/xz source values, and this takes $(C_t/y) \cdot (C_s/xz)$ time, if each cell logic has one processor; or $(1/n)(C_t/y)(C_s/xz)$ time, if each cell logic has n processors. This is the time to process a single block. Since xz blocks have to be processed in all, the total join time is

$$O\left(\frac{C_s C_t}{ny}\right)$$

Thus, the time complexity of join in RAP is of order $O(C_s C_t)$.

In terms of number of revolutions, the join operation takes xz revolutions, where x is typically about 15 or 20, and z is typically between one and three. However, the number of revolutions is not a good time complexity measure for the RAP join method, since the revolution time of the circulating memory, as already pointed out, is variable.

RAP is capable of doing inequality joins. However, in order to be able to do m-way joins, it must create and store temporary relations in the circulating memories.

Up to this point we have discussed machines that can do only implicit joins. The remaining machines that we discuss can do both implicit and natural joins.

The relational machine of Shaw [8] is configured as a hierarchy of associative storage devices. At the top of this hierarchy is the primary associative memory (PAM), which is a fast content-addressable memory containing between 10K and 1M bytes. The secondary associative memory (SAM) is where the database is stored and may consist of parallel head-per-track disks as in the CASSM and older RAP designs, or modified moving-head disks as in the DBC design [2]. The source and target relations are retrieved from SAM and placed in PAM, where the actual join takes place. Since the PAM is quite small, the source and target relations are brought to the PAM in pages, and this requires many accesses to the source and target relations on the SAM (i.e., many revolutions of the secondary storage devices). In [8] it is shown that the join operation in the PAM is of complexity

$$O(3C_s + C_r)$$

The factor C_t is not part of the time complexity because the author did not include the time taken to input the target relation into the PAM. In keeping with our policy of including the input time in complexity calculations, the time complexity is of order

$$O(3C_s + C_r + C_t)$$

Thus, the complexity is of the same order of magnitude as the complexity of our method, even though costlier hardware such as PAM (made of, for example, STARAN) has been utilized to achieve it.

In terms of number of secondary storage revolutions, it is shown in [8] that at least

$$\left(\frac{C_s}{P} + \frac{C_t}{P}\right)(1 + w)$$

revolutions will be needed to complete the join, where P is the size of the PAM in terms of number of records and w is a "waste factor," typically a small fraction. Typically, C_s/P and C_t/P range from 10 to 20. Thus, a typical figure for the number of secondary storage revolutions needed to complete the join is in the range from 20 to 40.

A detailed look at the join algorithm proposed in [8] reveals that the source and target relations have to be present, in their entirety, before the actual join may begin. Thus, it is not possible to overlap the join processing with I/O of the source and target relations. Also, m-way joins cannot be done without incurring waits, unless a second PAM is used. Finally, the method cannot be utilized to do inequality joins.

Let us now consider the join method used in a machine called DIALOG [6]. The source relation is initially stored in a buffer B_1. The source values from the source relation are extracted and stored in an associative sequential memory. Target records are read out from the secondary store and pass through an associative processor, which decides if the target records will participate in the join (by comparing the target attribute values with the source attribute values values stored in the associative sequential memory). Target records that will participate in the join are allowed to pass through and be stored in a buffer B_2. The join processor then joins target records in B_2 with source records in B_1 (using a buffer B_3 to decide which records in B_1 should be joined with a particular record in B_2) and outputs them. It is easily seen that the join is of complexity

$$O(C_s + C_t + C_r)$$

Clearly, buffer B_1 must be large enough to hold the entire source relation. If not, multiple passes over the source and target sets will be necessary and this may entail up to

$$\frac{C_s}{\text{size of } B_1} \times \text{(number of revolutions to retrieve target relation)}$$

revolutions of the secondary store for completion of the join operation. Thus, the choice is between a very large (and expensive) random-access buffer and a very large number of revolutions to do the join (typically 100).

The method can be used to do inequality joins. However, in order to do m-way joins without incurring waits, it is necessary to have an additional buffer (which will operate like B_1) and an additional associative sequential memory to hold source values.

We now consider the join operation of DIRECT [7]. The join operation is performed using a set of query processors and a set of CCD page frames. In this system the query processors and CCD page frames are connected to each other using a cross-bar switch, so that all processors can access all page frames.

Let us assume that the target relation resides in y pages and that n processors are used for the join operation. Each processor will join y/n pages of the target relation with the entire source relation. Thus, each processor joins C_t/n target records with C_s source records and produces approximately C_r/n result records. Thus, the join operation has complexity

$$O\left(\frac{C_t C_s}{n} + \frac{C_r}{n}\right)$$

The nice thing about the method is that n processors can do the join n times faster than a single processor can, hence, the operation is very efficient. Its drawback is that the time complexity is of the order of the product (not sum) of the source and target relation cardinalities.

The DIRECT method is the only one, besides our own, that addresses the issue of using more than one processor to speed up the join. That is, these are the only two methods that employ parallel join algorithms for doing natural joins. We feel that the study of multiple processor algorithms is important, owing to the falling cost of processing logic. However, the DIRECT method utilizes a complicated and expensive interconnection scheme (cross-bar switch) for processors and memories, which precludes easy extension and integration.

An important point to note is that the secondary store associated with DIRECT does not have content-addressability. Thus, the source and target relations have to be retrieved, in their entirety, into the CCD page frames, and the selection of the parts of these relations that will participate in the join has to be done after the retrieval from secondary store. Hence, join operation cannot be overlapped with I/O, since join can begin only after the selection.

This method can be utilized to do inequality joins and m-way joins. However, the temporary relations created during the execution of an m-way join operation may be created on half-pages, which must be "compressed" [14] to full pages before the next step may be executed in an m-way join operation. This page-compression operation, which is made necessary by the page-fragmentation problem, will slow down the m-way join operation.

Having considered each of the other methods in turn, it is now time to review our join method. First, it is of complexity

$$O\left(\frac{C_s}{n} + C_t + \frac{C_r}{n}\right)$$

where n is the number of processors. This complexity is as good as, or better than, that of any other known join method. Ours and DIRECT are the only methods that use multiple processors for doing natural joins. Unlike DIRECT, however, the interconnection scheme among the processors in our method is very simple, regular, and extensible. This is an important consideration for VLSI implementation of the join operation.

Our method is capable of doing inequality joins and m-way joins and of overlapping I/O with join processing. It is the only method that can accomplish an *m*-way natural join typically in *m* revolutions.

In Table 8.8 we summarize our discussion in the form of a comparison chart. Each method is characterized on the basis of the absence or presence of various capabilities (I/O overlap, inequality join, *m*-way join, and so on). They are also compared on the basis of time complexity in terms of relation cardinalities and in terms of number of secondary store revolutions. We refer to ours as the *DBC method,* since it is proposed for a database machine known as DBC [2].

8.7. CONCLUSIONS

This chapter reports the design and analysis of the join operations for a database machine known as the DBC. It is shown that the time complexity of the basic join is linear in the cardinalities of the source, target, and result relations. We postulate that no join algorithm can have better time complexity than this one.

The paper also provides a thorough queueing analysis of the join operation as a specialized component of DBC. The join operation consists of a number of interconnected processors, each associated with three sets of memories. The queueing analysis shows that if the operation is to perform joins at a rate commensurate with the output rate of records (i.e., relational tuples) from the database store, then these memories must satisfy certain constraints with respect to speed and size. In this respect, some constraints are more crucial than others. The chapter clearly indicates the order of importance of the various constraints.

The chapter also indicates how to select an optimum chip design for the join operation, where the design is considered optimal if it gives the best performance for a certain fixed cost. The method is one that may be employed by database machine designers in order to arrive at the optimal values for (1) the number of processors on a chip, and (2) the sizes of the memories to be placed on a chip.

Finally, the chapter describes the extensions of the join operation to perform relational inequality joins and *m*-way joins. It concludes with a favorable comparison of our join method with the join schemes proposed on some other database machines.

8.8. ACKNOWLEDGEMENTS

The research for this project was supported by the Office of Naval Research under Contract N00014-75-C-0573 and conducted in the Laboratory for Database Systems Research. Initially the Laboratory was funded jointly by Digital Equipment Corporation, Office of Naval Research, and Ohio State University and then moved to the Naval Postgraduate School.

REFERENCES

[1] Codd, E. F., "A Relational Model of Data for Large Shared Data Banks," *CACM,* Vol. 13, No. 6 (June 1970).

[2] Banerjee, J., Hsiao, D. K., and Kannan, K., "DBC—A Database Computer for Very Large Databases," *IEEE Trans. Computers,* Vol. C-28, No. 6 (June 1979).

[3] Babb, E., "Implementing a Relational Database by Means of Specialized Hardware," *ACM Trans. Database Systems,* Vol. 4, No. 1 (March 1979), pp. 1–29.

[4] Copeland, C. P., Lipovski, G. J., and Su, S. Y. W., "The Architecture of CASSM: A Cellular System for Non-Numeric Processing," *Proceedings of the First Annual Symposium on Computer Architecture,* December 1973, pp. 121–128.

[5] Oflazer, K., and Ozkarahan, E. A., "RAP.3—A Multi-Microprocessor Cell Architecture for the RAP Database Machine," *Proceedings of the International Workshop on High-Level Language Computer Architecture,* May 1980, Fort Lauderdale, Fl.

[6] Wah, B. W., and Yao, B. S., "DIALOG—A Distributed Processor Organization for Database Machine," *Proceedings of the National Computer Conference,* 1980, pp. 243–253.

[7] DeWitt, D. J., "DIRECT—A Multiprocessor Organization for Supporting Relational Database Management Systems," *Proceedings of the Fifth Annual Symposium on Computer Architecture,* April 1978, pp. 182–189.

[8] Shaw, D., "A Relational Database Machine Architecture," *Proceedings of the Fifth Annual Workshop on Computer Architecture for Non-numeric Processing,* Pacific Grove, Calif., March 11–19, 1980.

[9] Kleinrock, L., *Queueing Systems I and II,* John Wiley & Sons, New York, 1975.

[10] Gaver, D. P., "Diffusion Approximations and Models for Certain Congestion Problems," *J. Appl. Probab.,* Vol. 5 (1968), pp. 607–623.

[11] Ampex Corp., *PTD—930x Parallel Transfer Drive,* Product Description 3308829-01, October 1978.

[12] Patterson, D. A., and Sequin, C. H., "Design Consideration for Single-Chip Computers of the Future," *IEEE Trans. Computers,* Vol. C-29, No. 2 (February 1980), pp. 108–109.

[13] Bentley, J. L., and Kung, H. T., "Two Papers on a Tree-Structured Parallel Computer," Technical Report, CMU-CS-79-142, Dept. of Computer Science, Carnegie-Mellon University, August 1979.

[14] DeWitt, D. J., "Query Execution in DIRECT," *Proceedings of the ACM-SIGMOD 1979 International Conference of Management of Data,* May 1979, pp. 13–22.

[15] Denning, P. J., and Buzen, J. P., "The Operational Analysis of Queueing Network Models," *Computing Surveys,* Vol. 10, No. 3 (September 1978), pp. 225–261.

[16] Sevcik, K. C., Levy, A. I., Tripathi, S. K., and Zahorjan, J. L., "Improving Approximations of Aggregated Queueing Network Subsystems," *Computer Performance,* K. M. Chandy and M. Reiser, eds., Elsevier North-Holland Inc., New York, 1977, pp. 1–22.

APPENDIX 8.1. INTERARRIVAL-TIME AND SERVICE-TIME
DISTRIBUTIONS IN THE SINGLE-PROCESSOR CASE

We repeat the definitions of the various parameters that will be needed in our derivations:

N = number of blocks in the A-memory

C_s = cardinality of the source relation

C_t = cardinality of the target relation

v = number of distinct values of the join attribute

y = time taken by a processor to join two records

Z_{ar} = time taken to access a given block and to read (write) a record from (to) the block of the A-memory

Z_{as} = time taken to read (write) next record from (to) the A-memory

Z_{bs} = time taken to read (write) next record from (to) the B-memory

p = the probability that a source or target record is selected from the database store for the join

r = interarrival time of records at maximum read-out rate of the database store—i.e., parallel read-out disks

R = number of records that will fit in a block

$P(b)$ = the probability that a block will contain b records. For the uniprocessor case, assuming that we have an equal probability of assigning a record to any of the available blocks, the number of records b assigned to a bucket will be distributed binomially as

$$P(b) = \left(\frac{pC_s}{b}\right)\left(\frac{1}{N}\right)^b \left(1 - \frac{1}{N}\right)^{(pC_s - b)}$$

We are interested in cases where both pC_s and N are large and where the average number of records assigned to a block pC_s/N is nearly equal to the block size R. The binomial distribution is then very close to the Poisson distribution with parameter pC_s/N. Thus,

$$P(b) = \frac{e^{-pC_s/N}\left(\dfrac{pC_s}{N}\right)^b}{b!}$$

$$E(b) = \frac{pC_s}{N}, \qquad E(b^2) = \frac{2pC_s}{N}$$

$P(b, j, k)$ = the probability that a block of b records will contain exactly j records with a particular join value k. In this case, since the b records are selected from among a set of pC_s records having v distinct values for the join attribute,

$$P(b, j, k) = \frac{\left(\dfrac{pC_s}{v}\right)\left[\dfrac{(v-1)pC_s}{v}\right]}{\left(\dfrac{pC_s}{b}\right)}$$

The assumption made, of course, is that there are likely to be as many records having one particular join value as there are records having another join value.

We are now ready to analyze the interarrival and service distributions.

A8.1.1. Interarrival-Time Distribution

The records of the target relation arrive directly at the B-memory from the database store after selection. Each of the C_t target records has a probability p of being selected for the join and hence of being read into the B-memory. Thus, the probability that i records out of C_t will be selected is binomially distributed as

$$P_2(i) = \binom{C_t}{i}p^i(1-p)^{C_t-i} \cong \frac{e^{-pC_t}(pC_t)^i}{i!} \qquad \text{(for large } C_t)$$

The time taken to read C_t target records and select i of them is rC_t. Thus, the probability of i arrivals in a time interval of rC_t is

$$P_i(rC_t) = P_2(i)$$

Finally, the probability of i arrivals in time t is

$$P_i(t) = \frac{e^{-pt/r}\left(\dfrac{pt}{r}\right)^i}{i!}$$

Since the arrival process is Poisson, the interarrival time is exponentially distributed. The interarrival time, the mean, and the variance are given as follows:

$$\frac{1}{r}\,e^{-pt/r}, \qquad \frac{r}{p}, \qquad \frac{r^2}{p^2}$$

A8.1.2. Service-Time Distribution

The service time consists of the time to read a target record from the B-memory, hash its join value to a block in the A-memory, read all records in that block and all overflow records of that block, and join the record with all source records in the block overflow area having that join value. In our calculations we will ignore the hashing time. Also, the time to read all records in a block is taken as (1) the time to access the block and to read all the records of that block, and (2) the time to access overflow blocks and read their overflow records. The actual service time will depend on the architectural details of the processors and memories. Thus, if a direct memory access (DMA) is used to read records from the A-memory and write them to the C-memory, then the time to read records from the A-memory and write them to the C-memory need not be included in the service time. Conversely, if no DMAs are used, then these two times must be added to the service time. In our model we include only the time to read records from the A-memory and not the time to store records to the C-memory. Thus, the service time is

$$\begin{cases} Z_{bs} + Z_{ar} + (b-1)Z_{as} + jy & \text{(for } b \leqslant R) \\ Z_{bs} + Z_{ar} + (b-R)Z_{ar} + (R-1)Z_{as} + jy & \text{(for } b > R) \end{cases}$$

where b is the number of records in a block and j is the number of records in the block with the join value.

We now calculate E(service time) or $\bar{x}$, E(service time^2) or $\bar{x}^2$, and σ^2(service time).

$$E(\text{service time}) = \sum_{b=0}^{R} \sum_{j} (Z_{bs} + Z_{ar} - Z_{as} + bZ_{as} + jy)P(b)P(b, j, k)$$

$$+ \sum_{b=R+1}^{\infty} \sum_{j} (Z_{bs} + Z_{ar} - Z_{as} + bZ_{ar}$$

$$+ R(Z_{as} - Z_{ar}) + jy)P(b)P(b, j, k)$$

$$\sum_{j} jP(b, j, k) = \sum_{j} j \frac{\binom{pC_s}{v}{j} \left[\dfrac{(v-1)pC_s}{v} \atop b-j \right]}{\binom{pC_s}{b}} = \frac{b}{v}$$

Let $\overset{\infty}{\underset{b=s}{\Sigma}} P(b)$ be represented by the notation $Q(s)$. Then

$$\sum_{b=R+1}^{\infty} bP(b) = \frac{pC_s Q(R)}{N} \quad \text{and} \quad \sum_{b=R+1}^{\infty} b^2 P(b) = \frac{p^2 C_s^2 Q(R)}{N^2}$$

So

$$E(\text{service time}) = Z_{bs} + Z_{ar} - Z_{as} + \frac{ypC_s}{vN} + \frac{Z_{as}pC_s[1 - Q(R+1)]}{N}$$

$$+ \frac{Z_{ar}pC_sQ(R)}{N} + R(Z_{as} - Z_{ar})Q(R)$$

$$E(\text{service time}^2) = \sum_{b=0}^{R} \sum_{j} (Z_{bs} + Z_{ar} - Z_{as} + bZ_{as} + jy)^2 P(b)P(b, j, k)$$

$$+ \sum_{b=R+1}^{\infty} \sum_{j} [Z_{bs} + Z_{ar} - Z_{as} + bZ_{ar}$$

$$+ R(Z_{as} - Z_{ar}) + jy]^2 P(b)P(b, j, k)$$

Since

$$\sum_{j} jP(b, j, k) = \frac{b}{v}$$

and

$$\sum_{j} j^2[P(b, j, k)] = \sum_{j} j^2 \frac{\left(\dfrac{pC_s}{v}\right)\left[\dfrac{(v-1)pC_s}{v}\right]}{\left(\dfrac{pC_s}{b}\right)}$$

$$= \frac{b}{v^2(pC_s - 1)} [PC_s(b + p - 1) - bp],$$

We simplify the above equation as follows.

$$E(\text{service time}^2) = Z_{bs}^2 + \frac{2y^2(pC_s - v)p^2C_s^2}{v^2(pC_s - 1)N^2} + \frac{y^2p^2C_s^2(v-1)}{v^2(pC_s - 1)N}$$

$$+ (Z_{ar} - Z_{as})^2 + 2(Z_{ar} - Z_{as})Z_{bs}$$

$$+ \frac{2(Z_{ar} - Z_{as})ypC_s}{vN} + 2(Z_{ar} - Z_{as})(Z_{as} - Z_{ar})RQ(R+1)$$

$$+ \frac{2yZ_{bs}pC_s}{vN}$$

$$+ \frac{Z_{as}^2 P^2 C_s^2 [2 - Q(R)]}{N^2} + \frac{2 Z_{as} Z_{bs} p C_s [1 - Q(R)]}{N}$$

$$+ \frac{2(Z_{ar} - Z_{as}) Z_{as} p C_s [1 - Q(R)]}{N}$$

$$+ \frac{2(Z_{ar} - Z_{as}) Z_{ar} p C_s Q(R)}{N} + \frac{2 y Z_{as} p^2 C_s^2 [2 - Q(R)]}{v N^2}$$

$$+ \frac{Z_{ar}^2 p^2 C_s^2 Q(R)}{N^2}$$

$$+ \frac{2 Z_{bs} Z_{ar} p C_s Q(R)}{N} + R^2 (Z_{as} - Z_{ar})^2 Q(R + 1)$$

$$+ \frac{2 y R (Z_{as} - Z_{ar}) p C_s Q(R)}{N}$$

$$+ 2 Z_{bs} R (Z_{as} - Z_{ar}) Q(R + 1)$$

$$+ \frac{2 Z_{ar} R (Z_{as} - Z_{ar}) p C_s Q(R)}{N} + \frac{2 Z_{ar} y p^2 C_s^2 Q(R)}{v N^2}$$

Finally:

σ^2 (service time)

$= E(\text{service time}^2) - [E(\text{service time})]^2$

$$= \frac{2 y^2 (p C_s - v) p^2 C_s^2}{v^2 (p C_s - 1) N^2} + \frac{y^2 p^2 C_s^2 (v - 1)}{v^2 (p C_s - 1) N} + R^2 (Z_{as} - Z_{ar})^2 [Q(R + 1) - Q^2(R + 1)]$$

$$+ \frac{Z_{as}^2 p^2 C_s^2 [1 + Q(R) - Q^2(R)]}{N^2} + \frac{2 y Z_{as} p^2 C_s^2}{v N^2} + \frac{Z_{ar}^2 p^2 C_s^2 [Q(R) - Q^2(R)]}{N^2}$$

$$+ \frac{2 y R p C_s (Z_{as} - Z_{ar}) P(R)}{v N} + \frac{2 Z_{ar} Z_{as} R p C_s [Q(R) + Q(R + 1) - 2 Q(R) Q(R + 1)]}{N}$$

$$- \frac{2 Z_{ar}^2 R p C_s Q(R) [1 - Q(R + 1)]}{N} - \frac{2 Z_{as} Z_{ar} p^2 C_s^2 [Q(R) - Q^2(R)]}{N^2}$$

$$- \frac{2 Z_{as}^2 p C_s R Q(R + 1) [1 - Q(R)]}{N} - \frac{y^2 p^2 C_s^2}{v^2 N^2}$$

APPENDIX 8.2. INTERARRIVAL-TIME AND SERVICE-TIME DISTRIBUTIONS IN THE MULTIPROCESSOR CASE

A8.2.1. Service-Time Distribution

The calculations here are similar to those in Appendix 8.1. In fact, the final results for E(service time), E(service time^2), and σ^2(service time) may be obtained from the results for these same quantities derived in Appendix 8.1, with the replacement of all occurrences of N by the product nN (since there are now n processors, each of which stores $1/n$ of the source records).

A8.2.2. Interarrival-Time Distribution

Figure 8.3 shows the model used to derive the first and second moments of the interarrival distribution. As the figure clearly shows, two factors contribute to the arrival rate of target records to the B-memory of a particular processor: (1) the arrival rate of records directly from the database store, and (2) the arrival rate of records from the previous processor in the broadcast sequence. Note that a target record will be discarded by a processor if (1) the local associative memory indicates that it cannot participate in the join, or (2) the record has already propagated through all the processors. In this study we will ignore the presence of associative memories.

     1. E(interarrival time). In Figure A8.1, D is the expected rate of record arrivals from the database store and A is the expected rate at which records are processed and output by a processor (this is different from the service rate). By the principle of flow balance [15], the net arrival rate of target records to a processor must be equal to the net rate at which target records are being output from the processor at equilibrium. Thus

$$D + q \cdot A = A \quad \text{or} \quad A = \frac{D}{1 - q}$$

and so

$$E\ \begin{matrix} \text{net arrival rate of target} \\ \text{records to a processor} \end{matrix} = E\ \begin{matrix} \text{rate at which records are} \\ \text{output from a processor} \end{matrix}$$

$$= E(A)$$

$$= \frac{1}{1 - q} \cdot E(D)$$

For the uniprocessor case, we had calculated $E(D) = p/r$. Here, $E(D) = p/nr$, since the output from the database store is now routed to n different

D: E(arrival rate from the database store)
A: E(net arrival rate) = E(net departure rate)
q: Fraction of records not discarded by a processor

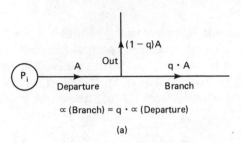

$\propto (\text{Branch}) = q \cdot \propto (\text{Departure})$

(a)

δ: Utilization factor of service facility

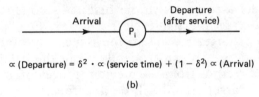

$\propto (\text{Departure}) = \delta^2 \cdot \propto (\text{service time}) + (1 - \delta^2) \propto (\text{Arrival})$

(b)

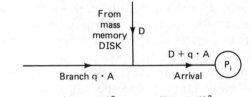

$\propto (\text{Arrival}) = \left(\dfrac{E(\text{Arrival})}{E(\text{Disk})}\right)^2 \propto (\text{Disk}) \left(\dfrac{E(\text{Arrival})}{E(\text{Branch})}\right)^2 \propto (\text{Branch})$

(c)   **Figure A8.1**

processors. Thus

$$E(\text{net arrival rate}) = \frac{1}{1-q} \cdot \frac{p}{nr}$$

and

$$E(\text{interarrival time}) = \frac{(1-q) \cdot nr}{p}$$

2. σ^2(interarrival time). In order to approximate the second moment of the interarrival time, we use the approximations of Sevcik et al. [16]. To simplify the ensuing discussion, we define

$$\alpha(x) = \frac{\sigma^2(x)}{[E(x)]^2} - 1$$

for any random variable x. Furthermore, we define four random variables designating time intervals as follows: Arrival designating the time between two consecutive arrivals, Disk designating the time between two consecutive arrivals from the database store, Departure designating the time between two consecutive record departures (after service), and Branch designating the time between the processing of two consecutive records that are not discarded. Now, from Figure A8.1(a),

$$\alpha(\text{Branch}) = q \cdot \alpha(\text{Departure}) \tag{1}$$

From Figure A8.1(b),

$$\alpha(\text{Departure}) = \delta^2 \alpha(\text{service time}) + (1 - \delta^2)\alpha(\text{Arrival}) \tag{2}$$

where

$$\delta = \lambda\bar{x}, \qquad \lambda = E(\text{arrival rate}), \qquad \bar{x} = E(\text{service time})$$

Finally, from Figure A8.1(c),

$$\alpha(\text{Arrival}) = (1 - q^2)\alpha(\text{Disk}) + q^2\alpha(\text{Branch})$$

But

$$\alpha(\text{Disk}) = \frac{\sigma^2(\text{Disk})}{[E(\text{Disk})]^2} - 1 = 0$$

So

$$\alpha(\text{Arrival}) = q^2\alpha(\text{Branch}) \tag{3}$$

Solving equations (1), (2), and (3) simultaneously, we have

$$\alpha(\text{Arrival}) = \frac{q^3\delta^2\alpha(\text{service time})}{1 - q^3(1 - \delta^2)}$$

So

$$\sigma^2(\text{Arrival}) = \frac{(1 - q)^2 n^2 r^2}{p^2}\left[\frac{q^3\delta^2\alpha(\text{service time})}{1 - q^3(1 - \delta^2)} + 1\right]$$

where q, the fraction of records not discarded by a processor, is the only quantity to be evaluated. We conclude this appendix with a calculation of q.

As we know, a record is discarded by a processor if the amsic indicates that it will not participate in the join (let us assume that a fraction a of those records participate in the join) or if it has been broadcasted to all processors.

thus

$$q = \frac{a \cdot E(\text{arrival rate from disk}) + \dfrac{n-2}{n-1} \cdot E(\text{arrival rate from previous processor})}{E(\text{arrival rate from disk}) + E(\text{arrival rate from previous processor})}$$

$$= \frac{\dfrac{ap}{nr} + \dfrac{(n-2)qp}{(n-1)(1-q)nr}}{\dfrac{p}{nr} + \dfrac{qp}{(1-q)nr}} = \frac{a}{1 + a - \dfrac{n-2}{n-1}}$$

Without the use of the am, $a = 1$. Hence

$$q = \frac{n-1}{n}$$

APPENDIX 8.3. THE HEAVY–TRAFFIC APPROXIMATION

We are interested in determining how large th B-memory should be in order to be 95% certain that it will not overflow (similar calculations can be made for 99% certainty or 99.9% certainty). Let us designate this B-memory size as $S_B 95$. $S_B 95$ may be calculated by determining the first and second moments of the queue length and then using Chebychev's inequality [9]. The heavy-traffic approximation to the G/G/1 queue tells us that the average queue length $\bar{S}_B$ is given by

$$\bar{S}_B = \frac{\lambda^2 (\sigma^2_{\text{arrival}} + \sigma^2_{\text{service}})}{2(1-\delta)}$$

where $\delta = \lambda \bar{x}$
$\lambda = E(\text{arrival rate})$
$\bar{x} = E(\text{service time})$
$\sigma^2_{\text{arrival}} = $ second moment of interarrival time
$\sigma^2_{\text{service}} = $ second moment of service time

All the above quantities have been calculated in Appendix 8.2, hence $\bar{S}_B$, the average queue length, can be obtained.

The heavy-traffic approximation gives the second moment of the queue length as $(\bar{S}_B)^2$. An application of Chebychev's inequality gives us

$$S_B 95 = \bar{S}_B \left(1 + \sqrt{\frac{1}{0.05}} \right) = 5.4721 \bar{S}_B$$

APPENDIX 8.4. THE DIFFUSION APPROXIMATION

As in Appendix 8.3, we now use the diffusion approximation [10] to determine $Q_B 95$. The probability of finding q elements in the queue is given by

$$P(q) = (1 - \hat{\delta})\hat{\delta}^q$$

where $\hat{\delta} = e^s$

$$s = \frac{-2(1 - \delta)}{\dfrac{\sigma^2_{service}}{\bar{x}^2} + \dfrac{\sigma^2_{arrival}\delta}{[E(\text{interarrival time})]^2}}$$

$\delta = \lambda\bar{x}$
$\lambda = E(\text{arrival rate})$
$\bar{x} = E(\text{service time})$
$\sigma^2_{service} = $ second moment of service time
$\sigma^2_{arrival} = $ second moment of interarrival time

1. Calculating the first moment:

$$E(q) = \sum_{q=0}^{\infty} q(1 - \hat{\delta})\hat{\delta}^q = (1 - \hat{\delta})\frac{\hat{\delta}}{(1 - \hat{\delta})^2} = \frac{\hat{\delta}}{1 - \hat{\delta}}$$

Thus

$$\bar{Q}_B = \text{mean queue length} = \frac{\hat{\delta}}{1 - \hat{\delta}}$$

2. Calculating the second moment:

$$E(q^2) = \sum_{q=0}^{\infty} q^2(1 - \hat{\delta})\hat{\delta}^q = \frac{2\hat{\delta}}{(1 - \hat{\delta})^2} - \frac{\hat{\delta}}{1 - \hat{\delta}}$$

Thus

$$E(q^2) = \bar{Q}_B \left(\frac{1 + \hat{\delta}}{1 - \hat{\delta}}\right)$$

and

$$\sigma^2(q) = E(q^2) - [E(q)]^2 = \bar{Q}_B \left(\frac{1}{1 - \hat{\delta}}\right)$$

3. Calculating $Q_B 95$: Using Chebychev's inequality, we have

$$Q_B 95 = \bar{Q}_B + \sqrt{\frac{\bar{Q}_B}{.05(1 - \hat{\delta})}}$$

9

Architecture and Operation of a Large, Full-Text Information-Retrieval System

Lee A. Hollaar, Kent F. Smith, Wing Hong Chow, Perry A. Emrath, and Roger L. Haskin

9.0. ABSTRACT

Retrieval of information from an unformatted text database differs substantially from formatted database operations, as characterized by one of the various models (such as relational). Text databases often are considerably larger, generally are not updated or altered by the unprivileged user, and, because of the lack of uniform organization and style, require a more complex search expression for satisfactory retrieval.

While a number of text-retrieval systems are currently available, their costs for searching (more than $100 for a complex search requiring a number of queries) limit the number of users. Their relatively slow response times (some searches can take minutes) often means that professional searchers are employed, rather than the ultimate users of the information, who best know how to access the material. However, the use of specialized backend processors and indexing and processing techniques optimized for text retrieval can produce a system whose cost to use is comparable to that of a conventional timesharing system, with response times satisfactory for interactive query formulation and refinement, accessing a database of tens of billions of characters.

The special characteristics of full text-retrieval systems are discussed. and a number of representative applications are mentioned. One in particular, a very large retrieval utility for the searching of patents, is presented in detail. The problems associated with processing such an application using conventional digital computers are then covered, and a system with special hardware enhancements introduced. These enhancements include backend processors for the parallel searching of the database using processors attached to each disk drive and hardware for manipulating a special index structure. Finally, the hardware configuration anticipated for the patent database is discussed.

9.1. INTRODUCTION

One of the early promises of computer technology was an automated reference library, where the user could retrieve all pertinent information on a subject quickly and at negligible cost. As yet this promise has not been fulfilled, although an intensified interest in database systems, and a realization by users of the importance of low-cost, rapid access to the information in a large database, seems to be providing the push necessary for success. Most recent work has concentrated on formatted databases, generally those following the relational model [1].

9.1.1. Text Information-Retrieval Systems

While there are many applications to which formatted databases are well suited, particularly those with well-structured data (such as the classic applications of employment records and inventories), there are a number of important applications whose data are less structured and cannot be efficiently handled using a conventional formatted database system. Of primary importance in this category are text information-retrieval systems. These vary in size from a single user's collection of documents, accessed through a conventional filing system and the search commands of an editor, to large information utilities with multiple databases and billions of characters. Large commercial systems include System Development Corporation's ORBIT, containing over fifty different databases; a similar system offered by Lockheed Information Systems (DIALOG); WESTLAW, a legal retrieval system from West Publishing; and LEXIS, another legal system from Mead Data Central (NEXIS, also from Mead, is a twin to LEXIS providing nonlegal databases). Within the federal government, systems include MEDLINE from the National Library of Medicine, JURIS at the Department of Justice, and a number of systems in the defense and intelligence agencies.

Differences from other database systems.   Besides their lack of formatting, text information-retrieval systems differ in many respects from formatted databases. They are often orders of magnitude larger than formatted databases, because their information cannot be as readily encoded as, say, information regarding a parts inventory. Furthermore, all the richness of the written language increases the amount of information stored representing a single concept. While a five-million-byte formatted database would be considered reasonably large, it would only hold one volume of the National Computer Conference proceedings, something that certainly does not require automated searching to find a particular item. Indeed, this chapter itself contains over 100,000 characters and is larger than the demonstration databases provided with some formatted retrieval systems.

The second major difference is in the operations permitted a nonprivileged system user. In a formatted retrieval system, the user is allowed to alter or update the database, in addition to accessing its information. A person using an inventory management system must be able to update the status of a particular part whenever one is added or removed from inventory, in addition to simply seeing how many are available. With most text-retrieval systems, the user is allowed only to access the information, with any updating being done by the system management. The system may allow special, personal files, logically associated with a particular document, to be either searched or updated by a user, but access to the main database is limited to searching or reading. This is analogous to a reference library, where the user can read the material but must not alter or destroy it.

Because of this different nature of access and since many formatted databases contain numeric information, the interfaces to the systems are quite different. For a text-retrieval system, the result of a query is to bring the applicable portion of the database to the users' terminal screens for viewing. A more sophisticated system may also include an interface to a word processing system, so that relevant citations from the database can be included in a new work. While formatted retrieval systems also provide for the display of their results directly on the users' terminals, in many cases the results are instead incorporated into a printed report or used as the basis of a numeric calculation. For example, if the average cost of a part in inventory were desired, the formatted retrieval system commonly would provide the necessary functions to find that cost and display it, rather than displaying the information about all parts in inventory. Furthermore, many formatted database operations are not the result of a direct interface with the user but are generated by, and their results returned to, an application program, such as a computer-aided design system.

But the major difference between most formatted database systems and text-retrieval systems is in the form and power of their query languages. While relational systems have powerful commands to combine, or join, two or more relations, their search criteria are often limited to exact matches or inequalities on specific fields, sometimes combined with Boolean operators. In contrast, the query language for text retrieval contains a much richer set of pattern-matching operations, in addition to the exact matching of particular terms and combining of match results using Boolean operators. Operators specifying that two or more terms must appear in a particular *context* or within a given *proximity,* or indicate that the characters in a given location should be ignored (*don't care characters*), are generally included. Figure 9.1 illustrates a typical collection of text-retrieval operations, which may be combined in any reasonable fashion to form a complex query [2].

Even such rich query language may be insufficient for retrieval with both high *precision* (the ratio of the number of relevant documents retrieved to the total number of documents retrieved) and high *recall* (the ratio of

A	Finds any document that contains the word A.
@A	Directly substitutes the previously defined value of A in the expression (macro).
A OR B	Finds any document that contains either the word A or the word B.
A AND B	Finds any document that contains both the word A and the word B anywhere in the document.
A AND NOT B	Finds any document that contains the word A but not the word B.
A AND B IN SENT	Finds any document that contains both word A and word B in the same sentence (specified context).
A B	Finds any document that contains the word A immediately followed by the word B (finds a contiguous word phrase).
A . . . B	Finds any document that contains the word A followed (either immediately or after an arbitrary number of words) by the word B.
A .n. B	Finds any document that contains the word A followed by the word B within n words (directed proximity).
<A,B>n	Finds any document that contains the words A and B within n words of each other (undirected proximity).
(A,B,C,D)%n	Finds any document that contains at least n of the different words A, B, C, or D. Note that if $n = 1$, this operation is an OR, while if n equals the number of different words specified, it is an AND (threshold OR).
A??B	Matches the character string A, followed by two arbitrary characters, followed by the string B (fixed-length don't care).
A*B	Matches the character string A, followed by an arbitrary number of characters (possibly none), followed by the string B. Note that *A matches A with any prefix, while A* matches A with any suffix (variable-length don't care).

Figure 9.1.   Typical Text-Retrieval Operations

relevant documents retrieved to the number of relevant documents in the database). This is because full text contains widely varying context lengths, differences in author style, inconsistent spellings ("color" and "colour"), words with many different meanings ("will," "retort"), acronyms, and other anomalies that complicate retrieval. Rather than specify a single query to locate the desired information, as is common with formatted database systems, a series of queries are often used. The result of one query is used to refine the form of the next query, further subsetting the database until all the desired information remains, with the minimal extraneous material.

9.1.2. Classes of Text-Retrieval Systems

Text-retrieval systems can be divided into three major classes. A *selective-dissemination-of-information* (SDI) system takes documents being added to the database and routes them, according to complex and predefined queries, to users who might be interested in their topic or content. For example, an SDI system for documents on information retrieval may route documents relating to database machines, but not relational databases, to a particular user.

Systems of the next class, *retrospective retrieval systems*, allow the user to retrieve information already stored in the database, rather than routing new information to them. Many SDI systems also include a subsystem of this class. The system can be either *bibliographic*, containing indices and abstracts for retrieval but not the actual document (similar to *Computing Reviews* or *Dissertation Abstracts*), or *full text*, containing the entire document and allowing searching for information not contained in an index or the abstract. The large systems mentioned previously belong to this class.

The final class of systems, *hybrid systems,* combine formatted databases and text retrieval, using a common query language. This allows formatted index or header information for rapidly subsetting the database, using, for example, relational operations, while permitting extensive searching of the unformatted fields.

For retrospective systems, there are three major subclassifications, depending on the amount of data stored and the source of the data: information utilities, electronic file cabinets, and looseleaf services.

Information utilities. Large, centralized information utilities, such as LEXIS/NEXIS, DIALOG, and JURIS, currently play the major role in information retrieval in both government and private industry. These are the best-known examples of retrospective information retrieval systems and are generally what comes to mind when text retrieval is mentioned. The existing utilities continue adding to their collections as more material becomes available (at low cost, since most of the information can be captured during its computerized photocomposition), and new utilities are being established.

Publishers will enter the field as a natural outgrowth of their publishing activities and to prevent their products from becoming obsolete. Within the government, the Patent Office is currently studying the use of automation in their activities, with a retrieval system for prior patents playing a key role.

Most current systems run on very large, conventional computers, generally of the IBM System/360–370 architecture. Because of these large utilities' size and importance, they are prime potential users of specialized text database machines.

Electronic filing cabinets.   The second class of information-retrieval system, now starting to appear, is a considerably smaller version of the utilities, able to retrieve from a database well under a billion characters using similar commands. It is generally a portion of an office automation system or word processing system, acting as an intelligent file server to hold memorandums and reports. The user is able to search for a document based on its contents or any keywords specified by its creator. An indexing scheme may be used to improve its efficiency.

Looseleaf services.   The final class of information-retrieval system, which shows promise for the future, combines many of the attributes of the other two systems. Small and inexpensive like the electronic file cabinet, its database will be on particular subjects and will be created and maintained by a supplier, rather than its user. It corresponds directly to the looseleaf services on particular subjects (such as tax from Commerce Clearing House or Prentice-Hall) currently available, where the user buys an initial collection and pays a yearly fee to have periodic updates supplied. The replacement of the current system of updating individual pages in a binder with an automated search system not only assures timely and accurate information (often updates are not filed immediately when received and at least some will be filed incorrectly), but also eliminates a labor-intensive, and hence progressively more expensive, operation.

Much like the large utilities, the probable supplier of such a system to an end user will be an existing publisher, who already has access to both the information and the market. In fact, it is reasonable to assume that the supplier of the service will also operate a utility searching the same information. This would handle customers whose needs are not sufficient to justify their own system but who occasionally need to perform a special search. It would also serve as a back-up to the in-house systems, allowing the latest information to be accessed or storing detailed information that is not cost-effective to distribute to all users.

An excellent medium for such a distributed looseleaf service appears to be based on the laser video disk. Since data can be duplicated on the disk using a stamping process from a master, reproduction costs can be much lower than for magnetic media. The disk is easy to ship and requires no special treatment, further lowering the distribution costs. Finally, the actual storage medium is sent, rather than something (like a tape) that must be loaded onto the storage device; this eliminates the need for an additional peripheral device.

A number of problems, however, are associated with video disk technology. Surprisingly, the major difficulty that most people see in video disks—that they can be written only once, complicating the updating of information—has little effect for text storage and retrieval, where data are only added and searched, not manipulated. However, the seek times are several orders of magnitude higher than for magnetic disks, since the read mechanism has considerably more mass. This means that seeks must be eliminated as much as possible. The amount of data that the video disk can store can be overwhelming, especially since there is only a single read station so that it cannot be accessed in parallel. This high *access granularity* means that high parallelism is not available for searching unless many units store the same information (reducing or eliminating its cost-per-bit advantage over magnetic disks). Exhaustive searching also is precluded, since the time to search an entire video disk would be excessive for most applications.

9.1.3. An Example Application

An example of a large retrospective information-retrieval utility is one that might be employed by the United States Patent and Trademark Office to search the "prior art" (patents already granted, pending applications, journal articles, and other generally available material) to determine whether the subject of a new patent application really reflects a new invention. This search is performed both by potential applicants, to assure that they are not inadvertently preparing an unacceptable application, and by the Patent Office examiners. This searching dramatically affects two major objectives of the Patent Office: improved quality and reduced pendency [3]. Quality dictates that a thorough search be made of all available information to assure that the invention is, in fact, novel and the statutory requirements have been meet. This is vital to assure that a patent's claims do not overlap with an existing patent and it can withstand challenges. If patents are routinely overturned in court decisions, the validity of the entire patent system becomes questionable.

The need for exhaustive searching affects the second objective of the Patent Office, the minimization of pendency (the time between application for and rejection or issuance of a patent). Although some time is unavoidably consumed in assuring that the application is in the proper form and that all other requirements for issuing a patent have been met, much of the pendency results from the examiners' need to perform a complete search. Currently the Patent Office utilizes a systematically organized manual filing system for prior patents, with some specialized search systems employed in selected areas (such as a computer-based microform retrieval system for some computer patents).

Even with a well-organized manual filing scheme and examiners familiar with the patents in their areas, this searching is a time-consuming, labor-intensive activity that, because of the special technical knowledge required, cannot be delegated by the examiner to clerical personnel. Searching the prior art for even a simple patent application can take hours and for a complex application in a rapidly changing area (such as electronics or computers) may take many days. On the average, an examiner will search about 2000 separate documents for a given application [3].

Estimated size and performance.   Since the inception of the patent system in the United States, over four million patents have been issued. Currently about 58,000 patents are issued every year, based on about 105,000 applications. Since 1970 these have been processed using a computerized typesetting system, with the data being available for an information-retrieval system. Currently the Patent Office is exploring means to convert patents issued prior to 1970 to a machine-readable form [3]. Although the size of a patent varies widely (from a couple of pages to 469 pages, plus 495 pages of figures, for the patent on the IBM System/360), on the average a patent contains about 35,000 characters, exclusive of figures. To aid in manual retrieval they are divided into 300 main groupings, or classes, and 108,000 subclasses, with a patent often being placed in more than one subclass. The Patent Office search file also contains about 20 million other documents, such as foreign patents, journals, and textbooks.

Although a database containing all issued patents would take over 140 billion characters, it would contain a large amount of unimportant data (such as patents on buggy whips). A reasonable subset would be all patents since about 1950, which would contain about 65 billion characters.

Rather than try to estimate the number of queries based on some expected performance of the 900 patent examiners, it is reasonable to base the calculation on the number of applications received each year. It is reasonable to assume that the examiner will be able to find the necessary information using about a dozen queries, the initial ones grossly subsetting the database to a particular subclass of invention and the final ones refining the search to improve precision (recall must be total to satisfy the quality objective). This is in keeping with a study of user statistics for the MEDLINE retrieval system, which indicated that the average session involved 7.7 queries [4]. It is also reasonable to assume that for each search by an examiner there have been two searches by potential applicants, one resulting in a filed application and the other in the abandonment of the application. This gives approximately 3.75 million queries per year.

Since there are about 250 working days a year, or about 2000 prime-time working hours and 1000 nonprime hours, and if it is assumed that the number of queries issued in prime time is about five times those in nonprime time, the average prime-time query arrival rate will be 1500 per hour, or one every 2.4 seconds.

Difficulties with conventional software approaches. While it might seem that a conventional digital computer could simply search the database, perhaps batching the requests of a number of examiners, this is not the case. For complex search expressions, a high-end digital computer can search at the rate of about 100,000 characters per second [5]. Even if the search were performed ten times faster, it would take over 18 hours to search the 65-billion-character database. In fact, at current processing speeds, it would take about five hours just to search the 2 billion bytes added to the database each year.

Most existing information-retrieval systems do not exhaustively search their entire databases, but instead use inverted files or some other indexing technique. To find a document that contains particular terms, one simply forms the intersection of the lists of all documents that contain the terms. However, it has been pointed out that there are a number of difficulties in using inverted files [6]. Extra storage must be used to store the inverted file's lists of pointers. This can increase the required on-line storage by as much as 300%, a high and perhaps impossible price to pay for a database that is already extremely large. Furthermore, this may only shift the processing load from searching to the merging of lists of pointers [7], especially for a large database with long lists of pointers.

9.2. A HARDWARE-ENHANCED INFORMATION-RETRIEVAL SYSTEM

Because of the difficulties inherent in using a conventional digital computer to implement a very large text information-retrieval system, such as that for the Patent Office, special-purpose hardware may be necessary to enhance the system to achieve the desired cost and performance. While it may be possible to implement a text-retrieval system on a single, specialized piece of equipment, it is more reasonable to subdivide the tasks and implement each on a processor best suited for the task.

Figure 9.2 shows the configuration of a hardware-enhanced text information-retrieval system [8]. It consists of four major sections: the host processor, the resource scheduling processor, index file processing, and text searching.

9.2.1. Host Processor Operations

Many operations can be performed efficiently on the conventional host processor, rather than using special processors. These include operations that are very complex but are not used often, such as system initialization, or that

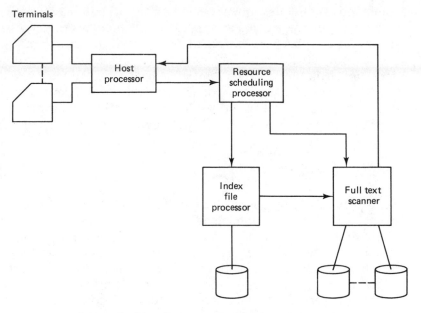

Terminals

Figure 9.2. A Hardware-Enhanced Text-Retrieval Computer System

can change in response to new or unanticipated system requirements. Because of the cost of developing specialized processors, these functions are best left on the host processor or an attached conventional computer.

In the proposed system the tasks of the host processor include terminal control, output formatting, accounting, and utility routines. The host processor may also run a word processing system, so the results of a query can be combined with other information to create a new document. There may be multiple host processors in the system, each accessing the database through the resource scheduling processor. This is particularly true when the text-retrieval system is being used as an adjunct to a word processing system, such as in a law office. Documents can be retrieved from the database and stored and processed locally on a user's personal or shared word processor.

9.2.2. Backend Processors

As opposed to the frontend functions, the operations of the index processing and text scanning systems remain similar for a variety of retrieval systems. Their performance is also highly dependent on the size of the database, with large databases requiring extraordinary processing rates. For these reasons they are prime candidates for implementation as special-purpose systems, backending the host processor.

The resource scheduling processor, which is probably a high-speed mini-computer, receives requests from a host processor and translates them into commands and request queues based on the scheduling algorithm determined to be best for the particular application. It prepares the necessary command strings for each backend processor and starts it in operation. When the operation is completed, the resource scheduling processor is interrupted and a new operation is initiated. It also initiates diagnostic sequences to determine potential system problems and collects statistics to aid the system management. In many respects the resource scheduling routines behave like the I/O supervisor of an operating system, scheduling device operations on a channel.

9.3. THE TEXT SEARCHER

Text-retrieval systems are well suited for parallel searching of the database by specialized processors connected to each disk drive, head, or group of drives, as appropriate for the desired performance. These processors must have low cost when compared to the disk drives, yet they must be fast enough to match the transfer rate of the disk drives. As shown in Figure 9.3, the basic structure of this backend search system consists of a disk memory system and controller, a term comparator, a query resolver, and some overall controller for the backend system.

The most difficult engineering problem to solve when building a pattern matcher is designing special hardware systems for the term comparator, since it must be able to find terms (strings of tokens representing characters or character types) at a speed equal to the character delivery rate of the disk memory system. The query resolver, which processes the results of the term comparator, indicating which term has been found, determines whether the terms occur in the correct proximity or match the required Boolean expression. Its processing requirements are substantially less than the term comparator's and can be implemented using a high-speed microprocessor, perhaps with hardware augmentation [9]. The search controller function can be performed by either the query resolver or another microprocessor, while the disk controller must only drive the positioner for the disk heads.

Although this search processing system can be attached to the disk

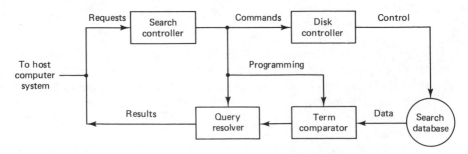

Figure 9.3. The Backend Search System

drive system at a number of points, there are a number of advantages to attaching it directly to the output of the disk drive. For the term comparator discussed below, no buffer memory is required. Furthermore, data are transferred only a short distance from the drive, so no elaborate cabling is required. Finally, if a searcher is connected to each disk drive, a high degree of parallelism results. In fact, the amount of data each searcher must handle, and hence its processing time, is independent of the database size, since each increase in the database size results in an increase in the number of searchers.

However, the direct connection of the searcher to the disk drive without the use of a buffer memory imposes some severe requirements on the term comparator. First, if a mismatch is detected, no mechanism is available to backtrack and try another alternative (as in the case of trying to find "ISSIP" in "MISSISSIPPI" and detecting a failure when trying to match the "P" of the pattern against the third "S"). This means that the term comparator must be aware of every pattern start and begin tracking a new start even though it is currently tracking a previous start. Additionally, the term comparator must be able to process a character before the next character arrives from the disk. As will be seen below, a special form of finite-state machine can easily handle both these requirements.

Since there is no buffer memory, a problem occurs whenever a data error from the disk is detected. Normal error-correction techniques consist of calculating the location and extent of the bits in error and altering them in a buffer memory before indicating the completion of the operation to the user. Since there is no buffer memory, error correction is impossible. However, this is really not a problem, since the incidence of data errors is very low for current disk technology. The rate of recoverable errors is better than one error in 10^{10} bits or, for continuous reading, every 2.67 hours. Assuming a reasonable balance between seeking and reading, a recoverable error will occur about every 8 hours. Better than 99% of these errors can be recovered from by rereading the data (sometimes with an increase in amplifier gain or a slight change in head position). This may require one or more additional disk revolutions to complete the search, but the effect on search performance will be insignificant. In most cases, an error that cannot be corrected by rereading will occur about once a year per drive, and these can easily be processed by error correction and software searching on the host system. In fact, the chance of an unrecoverable data error is substantially less than the chance of an error during the positioning of the read heads (which occurs about every 10^6 seeks, or 16.67 hours).

Three different classes of approaches to the implementation of the term comparator have been proposed: parallel comparators, cellular comparators, and finite-state machines (see the tutorial by Hollaar [2]). While the finite-state recognizer approach to term comparison has substantial advantages over other approaches (such as ease in handling don't cares, configuring by loading a table rather than some interconnection network, and the ability to handle an arbitrary number of terms of arbitrary length, subject only to the size of the state-table memory [2]), its efficient implementation is difficult to achieve. However, a new class of finite-state automaton has been proposed [9–11] based on the nondeterministic finite-state automaton (NFSA) [12] concept of allowing the machine to be in more than one state at a given time, but without the NFSA's dynamic scheduling or replicated state tables.

9.3.1. The Partitioned Finite-State Automaton

This new FSA associates a single token (either a specific character or a class of characters such as numerics or delimiters) with a state. If the current input character matches the token, a transition is made to the state specified by the next state field in the current state, while an unsuccessful match causes the current state to be terminated without transferring to a successor state. Since a state specifies only a single token, if a pattern indicates that more than one token is acceptable as the next input character, transitions to multiple next states, one per token of interest, must occur.

For example, consider a pattern consisting of "DOG" and "DOT". Matching starts with a state specifying the token "D", and, if successful, a transition is taken to a state that specifies the token "O". When in the state representing the token "O", if a successful match occurs, a transition must be made to two different states, one representing a "G" and the other a "T"; this transitioning to multiple states is called *forking*. After the fork occurs, at least one of the states will result in an unsuccessful match, resulting in the termination of that state with no successor specified, since the input character cannot be both a "G" and a "T". The partitioned FSA differs from a conventional GSA by branching to multiple states if the *next* position in the pattern can match a number of alternatives, while the FSA has a branch from the current state for each alternative, only one of which is taken.

Unlike a classical nondeterministic FSA, where complete copies of the state table are created whenever a transition to multiple states occurs, with this new class of FSA only a specific subset of the original state table is needed for each successor in a fork operation. In the example above, one portion of the FSA might have a state table containing "D", "O", and "G", while another might have only "T". Since the state table of a conventional FSA is partitioned between one or more portions of the new FSA, it is called a *partitioned finite-state automaton,* or PFSA.

9.3.2. A PFSA Implementation

The implementation of a suitable partitioned FSA is quite simple, but not as obvious as that of a conventional FSA or NFSA. Since, for any pattern, a partitioned state table can be generated requiring only one token to be matched in any state, the sequencing logic is considerably simpler than for a conventional FSA. The major implementation difficulty is how to support the requirement that the PFSA can be in more than one state at a given time.

The basic structure of the PFSA implementation is illustrated in Figure 9.4 and consists of two major components. The first is the match controller, which acts as an interface between the PFSA and the other system components, such as the query resolver and the memory system. It takes serial characters, such as the bit stream from a disk drive or a string of bytes from a memory, performs any operations necessary to determine the start of data, and transfers complete characters a byte at a time to the character matchers (labeled as CM_x in the figure). It also takes hit reports, consisting of state addresses and CM numbers, from the character matchers, correlates them with the character address in memory, and reports them to the user (generally the query resolver). The match controller also contains logic common to all the character matchers, such as timing generators and logic to load the state tables.

The character-matcher ring.   The second major component shown in Figure 9.4 is the character matcher, or CM. This unit actually performs the comparisons and the sequencing through the states. The PFSA implementation consists of a number of identical CMs, based on the number of mutually incompatible classes of states—basically the maximum number of states that can be active at any time. (State compatibility will be discussed later.) Each character matcher is connected to the match controller over a common bus and to its neighbor CMs to form a ring. This connection is used when a CM must fork to multiple successor states.

Since a CM is capable of being in only one state at a given time (and matching only single token), it must activate other character matchers whenever a fork to multiple states is desired. It does this by sending a forking vector, consisting of the desired starting state address, to one or both of its

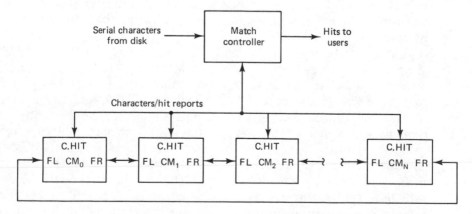

Figure 9.4. Basic Structure of the PFSA Implementation

neighbors in the ring, causing the next state of the receiving CM to be the specified address. Surprisingly, no dynamic scheduling of the character matchers is required. The process of partitioning the state table among the character matchers assures that when a fork operation is made to a particular character matcher, it is not doing any other operation (other than looping in a dummy, idle state).

The ring structure offers benefits for VLSI implementation of the PFSA, with little penalty. Each CM requires only a limited number of connections: the bus connection to the match controller and the lines to its two neighbors. Unlike a more general interconnection scheme, such as one that allows any CM to fork to any other, the number of connections required by the ring scheme for each character matcher remains the same for any number of CMs. Furthermore, if a number of character matchers are combined in the same VLSI package, the number of pins remains the same, allowing easy growth as integrated circuits of increased density become available. Although forks can be made only to the two neighbors in the ring, an extensive number of simulations based on randomly selected terms indicated that, in almost all cases, the number of CMs required in the ring configuration was identical to that required when any CM could fork to any other without any network constraints [9].

Character-matcher implementation. A block diagram showing the major components of the character matcher and their interconnections is given in Figure 9.5. The transition-table and fork-table memories are addressed by register A, which holds the last address placed on the address bus. The start-up table memory is addressed by the current input character broadcast to all character matchers from the match controller, so if N-bit characters are used, the start-up table contains 2^N words. For the present discussion, the only use of the start-up table will be to define the type of the current input character (into classes such as alphabetic, numeric, and delimiter); the TYPE field is an encoded value that indicates the type of the current input character, with a value of 0 indicating that the type is not one of interest.

Most of the logic of the character matcher is centered in the character-comparator section, labeled CHAR COMP in Figure 9.5. It has as inputs the current input character and the type of the current character from the start-up table through the type decoder/register (TDR), and the next token of interest and four control bits (H, L, T, and C) from the transition table. The T bit indicates that a type comparison should be made; the type from start-up table is tested against the bit mask contained in the TOKEN field of transition table, and if the type corresponds to one of the bits set in the mask, a successful comparison results. If the T bit is not set, the current input character is compared against the character specified in TOKEN, and a successful comparison occurs if they are identical. The C bit indicates that

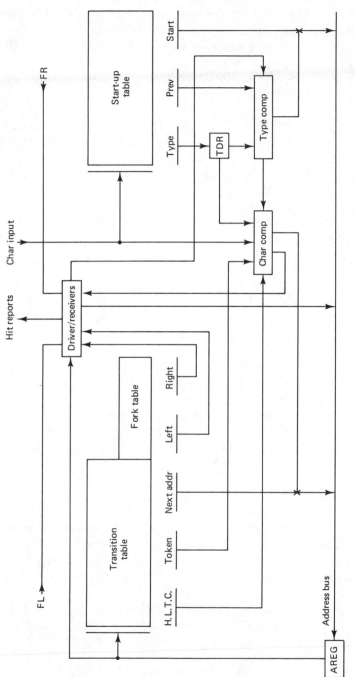

Figure 9.5. The Character Matcher

the case of the input character should be ignored when it is compared against TOKEN; it will not be considered in the following examples.

A successful comparison causes the NEXT ADDR field from transition table to be gated onto the address bus (unless fork or start-up transitions, to be discussed later, occur, in which case they have priority). If the L control bit is set, NEXT ADDR is gated to the bus regardless of the result of the comparison. If no address is gated onto the address bus, as would be the case on an unsuccessful comparison with the L bit reset, a default address of zero is transferred into the A register, causing the next state to be the default or *idle* state.

If a successful comparison occurs and the H control bit was set, indicating that a *terminal state* has been reached and a term of the pattern has been detected, a *hit* is reported to the match controller. This is done by enabling the line drivers for the HIT bus, gating the current state address from the A register on the result bus and sending a special signal to the match controller indicating the particular CM that found the term. This information allows the match controller to identify the term matched.

A successful comparison also allows the gating of a fork vector to the CM's left or right neighbor, using the FR or FL line drivers. This forking is controlled by fields from the fork-table memory, each of which contains a control bit indicating if a fork can occur and the address to be sent to the neighbor CM. The fork table is actually a portion of the transition table, but since most states do not specify a fork (experiments indicate that only about 10% do so [9]) and states can be assigned any address, all states that specify forks are collected into a contiguous block of memory. The remaining portion of the fork table, corresponding to states that do not fork, does not need to be implemented, reducing the space requirements on the integrated circuit. If these unimplemented states are addressed, they respond with a dummy word specifying no forking is to occur.

When a fork vector is received by a character matcher, two actions occur. First, the address in the fork vector is placed on the address bus to be loaded into the A register. Second, a control signal is passed to the type comparator and to the character comparator, preventing them from gating any addresses onto the bus. This means that forking has priority over any other type of transition. State-table partitioning assures that a fork operation cannot improperly override a match or start-up transition.

Special start-up operations. Although the discussion above details how the PFSA implementation normally operates, it does not indicate how the operation is begun. While the starting of a normal FSA or NFSA presents little difficulty, consisting simply of placing the FSA in some initial state that has transitions from it for any possible initial character of a term, the same is not true for the PFSA implementation. Its states represent single tokens of interest, so it is not possible to designate a single starting state with transitions out for each initial character.

While it is possible to assign a number of CMs the responsibility of looking for starting sequences, possibly forking to their neighbors immediately after their particular starting character has been found, it is efficient to include special start-up logic in each CM. In Figure 9.5 the start-up table used to supply the type of the current input character to the character comparator is also used to initiate these special transitions. For each possible input character a start address can be designated that will force the character matcher into the proper state to recognize the rest of the term that starts with that input character. To reduce memory requirements, the starting states are limited to the first quarter of the transition table. While this limits each CM to 32 different starting states, fewer starting states than 32 occur in practice.

Just like forking, this transition has priority over normal transitions (but has a lower priority than a fork from a neighboring character matcher). In fact, this memory behaves like a special character matcher looking for one or more initial characters and forking to an appropriate address when one is found.

In many instances, immediately after a start-up transition an unsuccessful match often occurs. If the start-up sequence were based on something more complex than just a single character, most start-up transitions would be eliminated, reducing the total number of character matchers required in a system. The PFSA implementation bases its start-up determination on not only the current input character but the type of the previous input character. This is done by saving the last character's type in the TDR register and then comparing it against a bit mask specified in the PREV field of the start-up table with the type comparator. If a successful test-under-mask results, and if there is not an incoming fork operation indicated, the type comparator causes the starting address designated for the current input character to be gated onto the address bus and inhibits the gating of the normal next address by the character comparator. If no start-up is desired for an input character, a mask of all zeros will assure failure of the test-under-mask operation.

9.3.3. State-Table Partitioning

It is clear that, for the PFSA to function properly, the state table representing the pattern specified by the user must be properly partitioned among the character matchers. Although the detailed algorithms for such a partitioning are beyond the scope of this paper, a brief discussion of the basic principles of the partitioning methods and their performance will be presented. Detailed descriptions of the state partitioning techniques are available elsewhere [9].

Two conceivable problems in the PFSA implementation could make it only an intellectual curiosity, much like the conventional nondeterministic FSA or the straightforward FSA implementation techniques: (1) that the state-table partitioning procedure necessary to its operation could not be done in real time; (2) that an impractically large number of character matchers be required for normal-sized queries. An analysis of the performance of the state-table partitioning algorithms, which follows, provides answers to both problems.

Basic principles.   The primary task of state partitioning is to assure that no two states assigned to the same character matcher can be occupied at the same time. If this can be assured for a particular pair of states, they are called *compatible* and can be assigned to the same character matcher. This means that when a normal transition occurs during the continuing matching of a term through a sequence of states, no other transition that can force the character matcher into another state, such as a fork from its neighbor or a start-up sequence, can occur. In general, the only time a fork or start-up transition can properly occur is when an unsuccessful comparison has occurred, causing the next transition to the idle state, or when the character matcher is already in the idle state. An exception is when a start-up or fork transition is used to terminate a sequence of states or a loop when some special condition exists, such as the detection of a word delimiter (an alphabetic type followed by a character like a space or punctuation mark).

The basic principles of state-table partitioning are straightforward. The first consideration is to make sure that, when a sequence of states is being followed, a start-up transition cannot incorrectly interrupt the sequence. This requires ensuring that no two-character start-up sequence (a character of a specific type followed by a specific character) can occur in any sequence of states in the character matcher. For example, if one sequence handled by a particular CM is the string "#COMPUTER#" (where "#" indicates any word delimiter), the strings "BALLOON" and "#UTAH" would be compatible, while the string "UTAH" would not. The word "#UTAH" is clearly compatible with "#COMPUTER", since the reception of a word delimiter "#" would terminate the searching for "#COMPUTER" before the initial "U" arrived. The same is true for receiving the "B" at the start of "BALLOON", since it is not a valid character in "#COMPUTER". However, the initial "U" in "UTAH" is contained in the sequence "#COMPUTER" and is therefore incompatible with it and must be assigned to a separate CM.

The second major area of state incompatibility is with forking. First, the same arguments given for start-up transitions hold for fork transitions into a character matcher: the state entered must have a distinct entry sequence from any normal state in the character matcher. It is also clear that if two states have the same predecessor state, they are incompatible, since one must result in a fork operation to another character matcher.

Performance.   If done in its most obvious manner, state-table partitioning involves checking each state against all other states to see if they are compatible. While this may seem like a simple task, it requires extensive computing for all but a handful of states—of the order of N^2 operations if there are N states. Since a reasonable application may have well over 1000 states, it is clear that exhaustive pairwise checking for compatibility is undesirable. A number of heuristics can be applied, however, to allow state-table partitioning to be done using fewer compatibility tests.

First, in practical applications of the PFSA, there will be a fixed number of character matchers in the configuration, sufficient to handle all but exceptional queries. Therefore we need to find, not an assignment of states that requires the *minimum* number of character matchers, but any assignment that can fit in the available number of character matchers. Once an assignment has been found that fits the configuration, all further computation of state compatibility is unnecessary.

Second, the state table can be broken down into small portions that are processed independently, taking an N^2 process and making it into m different n^2 processes, where $N = mn$ and $n \ll N$. This provides a speed-up by a factor of m and reduces the partitioning algorithm's memory requirements, since only that portion of the state table used by each smaller process need be in storage at a given time. The most convenient means of dividing the state table into blocks is by the initial labels (previous type and initial character) of each term, although the blocks will not all be the same size and some terms must be placed in more than one block. Care must be taken to assure that all states incompatible with a given state are assigned to at least one block with that state [9].

Finally, a futility heuristic, called *tail removal,* can be used. In most cases, if two states in different terms are compatible, all subsequent states in both terms are also compatible, so no further checking is necessary. However, the futility heuristic stops as soon as it determines that there are no more incompatibilities, in effect removing the final portions of the pattern terms, or tails, from detailed consideration. The exception occurs when fork, loop, or start-up transitions occur in the two terms.

While it is difficult to calculate other than an upper bound on the number of computations required, a number of experiments were performed using terms chosen at random to determine the performance of each heuristic. Figure 9.6 indicates the number of compatibility tests or comparisons required for state tables of varying numbers of terms. The average number of characters per term is 7.69. Curve 1 indicates the number of tests that must be performed if each pair of states must be compared; it goes off the scale at 20 terms. Curve 2 is the result of breaking the large N^2 process into a

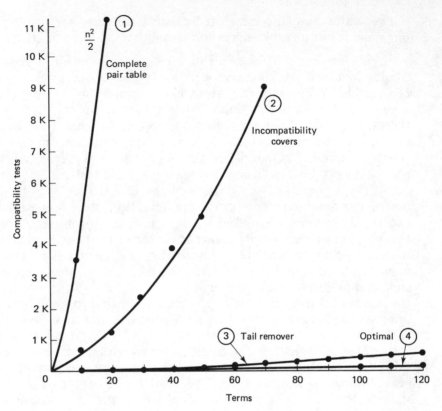

Figure 9.6. The Compatibility Tests

number of smaller n^2 processes as discussed previously. Although it shows a substantial improvement over curve 1, it is still not suitable for real-time state-table partitioning. Curve 3 is the result of using both maximal incompatibles and tail removal. Although it is beginning to show the increasing slope of the other curves, even at 120 terms its magnitude and slope are reasonable. In fact, it is very close to curve 4, the average number of incompatible state pairs in the table and the minimum number of compatibility tests required.

Using the algorithms, partitioning can be performed on a PDP-11/40 with a 1.75-microsecond cycle time at the rate of about a millisecond per state, so that the state table for a 120-term query, containing about 1000 states, can be done in about a second. Faster machines or ones with wider word lengths (since much of the work consists of extended-precision Boolean operations) yield correspondingly better performance. It is clear that the first potential problem with the PFSA approach, that of not being able to partition the state tables in real-time, does not exist.

9.3.4. Operational Characteristics

The second potential problem concerns the number of character matchers required for a system. If a large number of CMs are required, such as one or more per term, little benefit would result from using the PFSA instead of one of the other schemes previously discussed. The example presented above gives some cause for hope, since only three character matchers were necessary to handle seven terms, each character matcher requiring only a few states. In the discussion that follows, the number of character matchers required and their memory sizes will be evaluated for queries with considerably more terms, and three example configurations will be presented.

Hardware requirements.   In much the same way as we determined the performance of the partitioning algorithms by applying them to sets of random terms and measuring the results, we can estimate the number of character matchers required. Patterns containing from 10 to 120 words were selected at random from the list of words in the Brown Corpus, a one-million-word collection of representative samples of English text, and a version of the partitioning algorithm was used that determined best-fit (minimal number of CMs) rather than first-fit. The results of these trials are illustrated in Figure 9.7.

The figure shows the results for twenty different trial groups for each

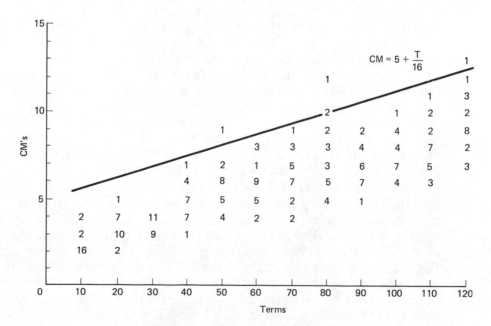

Figure 9.7. Trial Groups for Query Sizes

query size. The numbers indicate the number of trial groups for a given size that required a particular number of character matchers; for example, for the trials with 10-term queries, sixteen groups required only 2 CMs, two required 3 CMs, and two required 4 CMs. It can be seen that, with only a few exceptions (such as at 80 terms), the number of CMs required is bounded by the equation

$$\text{CMs required} = 5 + \frac{\text{terms}}{16}$$

This means that the number of character matchers necessary for most queries starts out small (about five or six) for queries with few terms and increases linearly as the number of terms increases. Additional trials have shown that this equation appears to hold for at least 160 terms, with no reason to believe that it will not hold for more. Limitations imposed by the processor used (a small PDP-11), primarily memory capacity to hold the state tables and compatibility vectors, prevented exhaustive testing beyond that indicated in Figure 9.7. Similar tests run for unlimited interconnection, rather than being able to fork only to the two neighbor CMs in a ring, indicated no meaningful reduction in the required number of character matchers, an indication that forks with more than three types do not often occur in practice.

What happens if the number of character matchers in a configuration is not sufficient to handle the number of terms in a query, such as for the one 80-term query in the figure that requires 12 CMs, rather than the 10 predicted by the equation? This will cause a premature failure of the first-fit partitioning algorithm, because a maximal incompatible will have more entries than there are available character matchers. On a failure, special techniques can be used to divide the query into two or more subqueries, which can then be separately processed and their results combined. This early indication of insufficient resources prevents the problems inherent in dynamically scheduled techniques, such as the conventional NFSA, where a failure due to lack of resources can occur during the middle of a match operation when another unit is required and all are already active.

Using the number of character matchers and the number of states necessary for various query sizes estimated above, it is possible to determine the memory requirements for a character matcher. Since each character matcher handles approximately 16 terms, and each term contains an average of 7.69 characters, about 128 words are required for the start-up table each CM. Forks exist for about 4% of the states in a CM, so a fork table with 16 words should be more than sufficient. The start-up table requires a word for each character in the input alphabet, so for 6-bit characters, 64 words are required, and for 8-bit characters, 256 words. The number of bits in each word is a function of the number of different types permitted and the number of bits necessary to address the transistion and fork tables of the CM and, for

Configuration	Start-Up Table	Transition Table	Fork Table	Total Size
6-bit characters, 3 character types	64 × 10 640 bits	128 × 17 2176 bits	16 × 16 256 bits	3072 bits
6-bit characters 6 character types	64 × 14 896 bits	128 × 17 2176 bits	16 × 16 256 bits	3328 bits
7-bit characters 7 character types	128 × 15 1920 bits	128 × 18 2304 bits	16 × 16 256 bits	4480 bits
8-bit characters 7 character types	256 × 15 3840 bits	128 × 19 2432 bits	16 × 16 256 bits	6528 bits

Figure 9.8. Memory Requirements for a Variety of CM Configurations

forking, its neighbors. Figure 9.8 illustrates the memory requirements for a variety of CM configurations.

9.3.5. VLSI Implementation of the PFSA

The character matcher has been fabricated as an integrated circuit, using a silicon gate N-channel metal-oxide-semiconductor (NMOS) process. The circuit uses 6-micron feature-size design rules, to allow the easy fabrication of test circuits using the University of Utah's Hedco Microelectronics Laboratory. During the final fabrication process the masks are shrunk to 83% of the original size, which reduces the circuit feature size to 5-micron rules. There are seven layers in this NMOS fabrication process. Figure 9.9 gives a description of each layer and the symbols used for the layers in this chapter.

Layer	Description	Outline	Fill
1	diffusion	solid	none
2	ion implant	dash-dot	none
3	buried contact	solid	left-hatch
4	polysilicon	solid	right-hatch
5	contact	solid	cross
6	metal	dash	none
7	pyro overlay	dot	none

Figure 9.9. Layers Used in the NMOS Fabrication Process

A floorplan of the circuit composed of these elements is shown in Figure 9.10. Some connections have been removed for clarity. The smaller blocks at the edge of the circuit are inputs, whereas the larger blocks can be either inputs or outputs. As a rough estimate, the chip dimension is about 320 mils on a side (with 6-micron rules) and the power consumption is about 600 mW. The use of the 5-micron shrink reduces the chip dimension

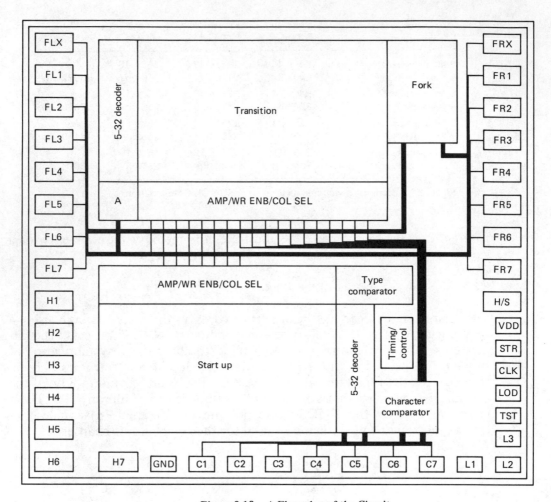

Figure 9.10. A Floorplan of the Circuit

to about 265 mils on a side, improving yield while reducing the power consumption. This particular implementation is intended to run at a 1.2-MHz clock rate to match the character rate of an SMD-style disk drive. A further shrink will reduce the chip dimensions to approximately 200 by 200 mils, allowing it to operate at the higher character rate of the new generation of disk drives.

Memory Implementation. Since the majority of the active area of the circuit is occupied by memories, it is obviously the most critical component of the implementation. While a dynamic RAM has the advantages over a static RAM of being more compact (one gate per memory bit) and having lower power consumption, it requires more complex circuitry for refreshing the memories' complicated internal timing. For the memory size needed for the character-matcher circuit (about 4.5 Kbits) a static RAM will be more appropriate owing to its simplicity in design and fabrication.

The schematic diagram of a static RAM bit and its composite layout is shown in Figure 9.11. The RAM bit has six transistors; the load transistors are thin and long to minimize power consumption. The use of small load transistors in the RAM will result in a slightly slower writing speed, but it

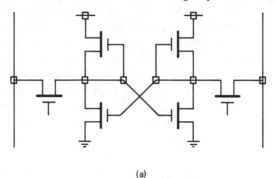

(a)

(b)

Figure 9.11. A Static RAM Layout

will not affect the speed for reading. In the character-matcher circuit, most operations require reading from the memory and the writing time is comparatively insignificant, so the slower writing speed has little effect on the total speed of the circuit.

For the same reason, the idea of using lightly doped polysilicon resistors to replace the load transistors is being considered for future versions of the circuit. The resistance of lightly doped polysilicon is of the order of 10 Mohm (the actual resistance depends on the length, cross-sectional area, and the doping level), and resistors can be fabricated on a square of minimum-feature-size polysilicon. As shown in Figure 9.10, the memories occupy about half of the chip area and consume about half of the total power as well. The replacement of the depletion load transistors by poly load resistors can provide significant improvements in power consumption and circuit area (hence in yield and speed). The poly load resistor technique requires one extra mask in the fabrication process.

In the NMOS process there are two and one half layers for connections. They are metal, diffusion, and poly, but diffusion and poly cannot cross each other or a transistor will be formed. Metal is the best layer for connections, since it has the lowest resistivity and the lowest capacitance. Polysilicon has a similar capacitance but the highest resistance, while diffusion has the highest capacitance and a resistance similar to that of polysilicon. Usually the power supply and the ground connections are metal, since the lowest resistance is needed for the high current density at these lines. However, this forces the use of diffusion as the signal lines in the memory cells. There are two problems when diffusion is used: (1) the high capacitance of the diffusion, which slows down the circuit speed considerably, and (2) the series resistance of these long diffusion connections.

The series-resistance problem can be illustrated by examining the start-up table. There are 128 words in this memory, with each bit of the memory word organized as 4 columns of 32 rows, each row 90 microns long. A signal line with minimum-width runs across these 32 rows of memory cells would have about 10 Kohm of resistance. If a current of only 0.1 mA is flowing in this line, the potential difference between the line's two ends will be about one volt, which is the threshold voltage of an enhancement device. In other words, some transistors will not be able to transfer a "low" signal to the amplifier at the other end of the memory unit.

The series-resistance problem can be solved by using the method of dynamic output. The signal lines are precharged before each writing or reading of the memories, so there is no steady current in them. Thus, these lines are only capacitors and there is no series resistance to worry about, but lower speed is still a problem when diffusion is used for the signal lines. In the present circuit, the RAM cells use dynamic output and the signal lines are metal for better speed, since the metal has the lowest capacitance and resistance. The tradeoff is that the power lines have to be diffusion, which means that some nodes in the memory cells cannot reach the full power-supply voltage, since the series-resistance problem has been transferred to the cells.

    Random Logic Portions.   In addition to the three random-access memories and the pin drivers and receivers, there are four areas of random logic in the VLSI implementation. As shown in Figure 9.10, these are the A register, the type comparator, the character comparator, and the timing and control generator. The A register is simply an array of D-type flip-flops, constructed from two inverters and pass transistors to provide the appropriate loading and feedback, with additional circuitry to reset them to zero (the idle state) at the start of a search.

    The type comparator is also a very simple circuit, consisting of three sections. The first is a decoder, which converts the encoded type field (three bits, indicating seven different types plus an untyped specification) into outputs corresponding to each of the seven types. This is sent to the character comparator and stored in a 7-bit register, similar in design to the A register. Finally, the seven outputs of the register ANDed with the corresponding previous type bits from the start-up table memory, and the results of these ANDs ORed together. This gives the test-under-mask operation needed to gate the start address from the start-up table to the address bus whenever one of the specified previous types matches the type of the last character.

    The character comparator has two major sections: one for type comparison, identical to the one discussed above, and one for exact character matching. The exact matcher consists of seven exclusive-or gates, with their outputs feeding a NOR. An additional transistor is included for the second most significant bit, allowing it to be ignored if the C bit of the transition table memory is set. This makes the comparison insensitive to case for ASCII alphabetic characters. A selector controlled by the T bit from the transition table determines which of the two sections' outputs will be used for the comparison, while additional random logic controlled by the H and L bits drives the hit output or forces a match transition for a loop state.

    The final section of random logic is the timing and control logic for the circuit. It takes the external timing signals (a fast clock, corresponding to the bit clock of the disk, and a character strobe) and generates the internal signals needed for correct circuit operation. Of particular importance are the precharge signals for the memories. It also controls the loading of the state table when a special control signal is given, changing the meaning of the character-input bus to a memory address and the hit-report bus to the data to be loaded. Another mode allows the data stored in the memories to be read. By using common memory diagnostics to assure that the memories function correctly and special state tables and inputs, it is possible to verify completely the correct operation of each CM.

9.3.6. The Query Resolver

Implementation of the query resolver is influenced more heavily by the characteristics of the database and the query language than is that of the term comparator. The latter simply looks for patterns at disk transfer speeds, while the query resolver is activated whenever a term is found (highly dependent on the database characteristics) and processes it according to the form of the query language. For example, if the query language only allows the specification of a number of terms all of which must occur in documents of interest, a very simple bit-vector scheme can be employed, while directed proximity operations can be handled by a simple FSA.

One form of query resolver, optimized for handling information specified by Boolean operations and contexts, uses a tree-structure marking technique [9]. A possible tree organization is shown in Figure 9.12. The terminal nodes in the tree correspond to terms of interest. A mapping translates the hit report from the CMs into the address of the appropriate terminal nodes. The other nodes of the tree correspond to Boolean operations and contexts. The basic operation of the algorithm is simple. Whenever a term is found, the terminal nodes corresponding to it are checked to see if the term has already been found, as indicated by the flag bits being set. If it has already been found, no further action is taken. Otherwise, the

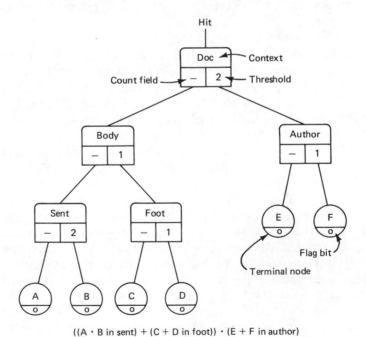

$$((A \cdot B \text{ in sent}) + (C + D \text{ in foot})) \cdot (E + F \text{ in author})$$

Figure 9.12. A Query Resolver

flag bit is set and the count field of the next higher node in the tree is incremented. When the count field equals the threshold value specified in the node, the next higher node is marked. When the root node has been marked, the query has been satisfied. It is easy to see that if the threshold of a node is 1, the operation performed is an OR, while if it is equal to the number of nodes below the node, it is an AND. Other values allow for threshold-OR operations.

Whenever the end of a context of interest occurs, the portions of the tree corresponding to that context are reset to their initial values. This requires the rapid clearing of the flag and count fields, since the next hit may occur in only a few characters. This can be done by using a special memory that has a master reset signal or by allocating a number of flag fields. In the latter case an indicator tells which particular field is currently being used. A background task clears the flag fields not currently in use.

The implementation of proximity operations along with context operations complicates the structure of the query-resolver tree and its processing. When a term involved in a proximity operation is found, a word-counter value must be stored, and when another term in the proximity relation is found, this stored word counter is compared to the current counter value, and the node is marked if the value meets the proximity specification. An alternative approach is to implement a tree-marking method for context operations and an FSA for proximity, combining their results to find if the query is satisfied. The choice of the algorithms used depends on the particular application.

For most databases and query languages, the query resolver can be implemented using a standard microprocessor, such as the National 16000-series or Digital Equipment J-11 (a PDP-11/70 class processor in a single package), or a bit-sliced microprocessor, such as the AMD 2900-series. The former results in a simpler design, since a wide-word microstore is not necessary, but the latter can operate at higher hit rates. In either case, since the query resolver is not active during disk seek times or when text is not being scanned, it can also be used to control the positioning mechanism of the disk, disk header verification, and loading of state tables into the character matchers, assuming the roles of the search and disk controllers.

9.4. INDEX STRUCTURES AND PROCESSING

While the use of backend search processors may seem to eliminate the need for an index or inverted file as in software-implemented systems, in fact for a very large, interactive system indexing in some form may be necessary. A major difficulty with text scanning is that search bandwidth requirements are very high for databases of any practical size. The bandwidth of the search system is essentially that of the disk. Current disk transfer rates are of the order of 1 Mbyte/sec, meaning that it would take about 5 minutes to read all the data on a 300-Mbyte disk, even ignoring any seeks necessary.

The problem is that while disk transfer rates have increased, capacities have increased at a greater rate. Regardless of the technology, the minimum time to transfer the complete contents of a disk drive has been of the order of minutes. Unless parallelism is achieved within the disk drive itself, say by enabling multiple read heads with a separate scanning processor for each one (and this may be difficult or impossible to do, particularly for the newer disk drives using self-servicing tracks), it appears that such systems will never achieve the response times necessary for interactive systems. The limiting factor is determined solely by the storage device. If the ratio of its capacity (in bits) to its transfer rate (bandwidth in bits/sec) is much greater than 10, the device will be ineffective for interactive full-text scanning systems. This ratio is simply the amount of time it takes to read the entire storage device, in seconds. This characteristic of storage devices is its *access granularity*.

Current moving-arm magnetic disk technology has an access granularity in the range of 100 to 300. Over the past decade this ratio has slowly been increasing, and so this problem is severe and is being aggravated by disk-technology trends. Unfortunately, other storage-device technologies that provide adequate capacity and acceptable cost per bit have even greater capacity-to-bandwidth ratios. New devices, such as video disks, that have enormous capacities are not suitable for full-text scanning systems because of this problem. To achieve satisfactory performance, some form of indexing to limit the extent of the search is necessary.

9.4.1. Previous Indexing Systems

Most indexing schemes do not have pointers to every word in the database. To include all the pointers would give an index file considerably greater than the actual database [6]. Some words occur too frequently to be of use in retrieval and are excluded from the index (although proper index processing can make these *stop lists* transparent to the user). The index size can be further reduced, perhaps to less than the database size, by indexing to a particular context, where a pointer indicates only that a term occurs in the context, and not its actual position.

The main advantage of context indexing is that reasonable response time can be achieved using general-purpose hardware, even for large databases. Typically, queries consist of a Boolean expression of search terms to be found in a specified context, such as title, author, or document. If the database has a suitable context structure, index searching may be used to process all queries without requiring access to the full-text, until the displaying of final results. Other advantages of using indexing are the ability to query the index as a special form of database and to construct the index in such a way as to serve also as a thesaurus.

The problems with using indexing exclusively for large full-text retrieval systems are the resulting size of the index and the complexity of constructing and modifying it. The time to construct such an index for a large database is many hours of machine time, for the process is essentially that of sorting all the tokens in the database, a very large list, without removing duplicates. Furthermore, queries that specify a context higher than that used to produce the index require special processing, while lower contexts cannot be directly handled. This latter problem means that proximity operations cannot be supported unless the context is an individual word.

Hybrid Systems.   A system that combines text scanning with context indexing generally benefits from the advantages of each search technique while alleviating many of their problems. Because text scanning is possible, the database can be inverted to an intermediate or high level, such as a section or document. This results in a much smaller index than when a low inversion level is used, hence storage cost will be lower. In addition, the time required to construct the index will be less, because duplicate postings can be removed as the sorting is being done. In such a hybrid system the index search is performed first, and the result eliminates most of the database from further consideration. In the average case, the text scanner will have to access only a small fraction of each storage device, greatly reducing the required text-scanning bandwidth of the system. The advantage of a hybrid system is that a greater performance-to-cost ratio can be obtained relative to a system that uses just context indexing or just full-text scanning.

The problem with designing a hybrid index-scan system is that system performance not only depends on the speeds of the system components and the database size, but also depends strongly on the database inversion level. An ancillary problem is that index size (and hence storage cost) is determined by the inversion level of the database.

If a given hardware/software system is assumed, then how does the inversion level affect system performance? Raising the inversion level (to larger contexts) will result in a smaller index. The average postings list will be shorter, hence the average time to perform index searching will decrease. However, as the inversion level is raised, contexts that must be scanned are larger and so the average scan time per query will increase.

The problem with using context indexing in a hybrid system is selecting the inversion level in order to optimize performance. If the database is given, then the inversion level can be selected and a system designed so that optimum performance is achieved. However, this system may not perform well when applied to a different database unless the new database has similar context-structure characteristics. When changing the database, it may be necessary to change the inversion level. For example, a new database may have documents ten times larger than those for which the system was originally designed. Indexing the larger documents or switching to paragraph-level inversion upsets the balance of merge processing against full-text scanning. This results in poor performance and a need to change component processing capacities.

Additionally there is the problem that context structures within a database vary widely in size, often by more than an order of magnitude. In some instances system design may be restricted by other factors, so the only reasonable inversion level is one in which the indexed items do vary in size as dictated by the context structure of the database. In such cases the average system performance may be acceptable, but the response of a significant number of queries may be inordinately long, owing to the variability of the inversion level. For example, if the index search for a query hits many of the extraordinarily large indexed items, the effective inversion level is shifted upward for this query, and the system will be operating at a point far from that for which it was designed. A much greater than expected amount of text scanning would be done, causing poor response for this query and hindering query throughput.

9.4.2. The Page-Indexing Method

Page indexing is a hybrid scheme that combines indexing and scanning while attempting to eliminate the dependence of performance on the context structure of the database [13]. The two key points of the page-indexing scheme are that (1) the text of the database is broken up into fixed-length pages, essentially regardless of context boundaries, and (2) each page defines the start of an indexed item that is somewhat larger than that page. In other words, the indexed items overlap such that some of the text is indexed twice. Figure 9.13 shows a page-indexed database, with P the size of each page in bytes and L the amount of overlap between indexed items. Note that, since A occurs in both page 36 and the overlap from page 2, both pages are included in the index entry for A.

Another important point of the page-indexing technique is that context names are stored with the text and indexed as tokens. Hence, the set of context names is supplied with the database and can be arbitrarily large. Furthermore, the contexts need not be structured, but any desired structure may be used without restrictions. In Figure 9.13, entries for the context "doc" show that it exists in both pages 12 and 25.

In order to implement the page-indexing scheme, the text of the database is broken up into equal-length pages. Each page is given a unique page number, which may or may not be directly related to the physical storage address where the page is stored. The mapping from page numbers to physical addresses is unimportant and is often trivial. The page size is essentially the only soft parameter to be selected by the system designer. Selecting a good page size involves a tradeoff between storage overhead costs and text scanning bandwidth costs.

Database:

```
Page 12:    doc[     author[ K ]
Page  2:            para[    B
Page 36:    A ]  |            para[    C
Page 25:          |    E ]    ]    doc[    A
Page 29:    B    |            ]
```

←—L—→

←——————————— P ———————————→

Page Index:

```
        A - 2,25,36
   author - 12
        B - 2,25,29
        C - 36
      doc - 12,25
    doc$ - 2,12,25,36; 25,29;
        E - 25
        K - 12
     para - 2,36
   para$ - 25,36;
```

Figure 9.13. Organization of a Page-Indexed Database

As mentioned, increasing the page size will reduce the size of the index for a given database. When using practical constraints of today's technology, doubling the page size generally reduces the size of the index by about 12% to 25%. Similarly, the number of resultant postings, or page hits, after doing the index searching for a typical query will be reduced by a like amount. Pages that are twice as large result in a hit list that is about 80% as large with between 50% and 75% more text scanning for a typical query.

The size of a page is restricted by characteristics of the storage device and by comparison with L, the amount of overlap between indexed pages. The choice of L is also a soft parameter, but it will be seen that this should be determined by the context characteristics of the database and needs of the user community. As long as P remains large compared to L, then L has very little effect on index size or scanning requirements. In addition, it makes no sense to allow P to be a fraction of the physical record size of the storage device, such as a sector of a disk track. At the other extreme, the maximum size of a page is limited by the amount of time it takes to read and scan the page. For a system design utilizing conventional moving-arm magnetic disk storage technology, it seems reasonable to think of pages as ranging from one sector to no more than a few cylinders, or about 1K to 1M bytes.

The physical structure of a page can be quite simple, consisting of two parts: a header or control section and an unformatted block of text. The header is used for storing pointers to other pages and possibly other state information used by the retrieval or updating systems. This can aid in the implementation of powerful browsing capabilities and the ability to edit a database, by connecting all the pages of a database into a doubly linked list.

In this case, pointers to the next and previous pages (among other things) would be stored in each page header. Other uses for the header will surface when the storage of context structures is discussed.

The structure of the page header can be fairly complicated, depending on implementation details. However, even if the average header stores 10 pointers and each pointer averages 12 bytes, the amount of space required for the headers is quite small compared to the remaining space, which is devoted to storing the database proper—even when using small pages. If storage costs are a critical factor, it may be that minimum page sizes are dictated by the size of the page header rather than device characteristics or the value of the parameter L. As the page size increases, the average number of pointers required in each header, and therefore the absolute size of the header, decreases.

Contexts.   Each context in a database can be given a name. The left context delimiter will be the name of the context followed by a "[", and the right context delimiter a "]" followed by the context name. Left and right context delimiters all having the same name can be nested like parentheses independently of context delimiters having other names. When the context structure forms a hierarchy, the name on the right delimiter can be deleted; an unnamed "]" matches the last unmatched "[" seen, regardless of its name. For example, a document might look like:

doc[title[. . .] author[. . .] abstract[. . .] body[. . .]]

or

doc[title[. . .] publisher[. . .] date[. . .]
chap[. . .] chap[. . .] chap[. . .] . . .]

·   In the event that the contexts are not strictly hierarchical, a code can follow the closing context delimiter to indicate the particular context to which it applies.

Context specifications for a query can be implemented in a similar way. For example, "[alpha and beta] document" would mean to find any context named "document" that contains both "alpha" and "beta". Context specifications can also be nested within search expressions to form meaningful queries, such as "[[Smith] author and [alpha and beta] sentence] document".

The text of a database is divided into pages and stored without regard to the positions of context delimiters. The only requirement is that (physical) page boundaries don't fall within a token. If a context requires more than one page, then pointers to the start of the context are placed in the page headers. To create the page index, each page defines an indexed item that includes all the text in that page plus some text (up to some limit L) from the next logical page. The purpose of overlapping the indexed items is to ensure that any search query that defines a pattern that has bounded length less than or equal to L will not miss any occurrences that happen to cross page boundaries. Examples of such bounded patterns are phrases, proximity searches, and small contexts such as sentences or lines. All context names are indexed just like all the other tokens.

A special case arises when a context crosses an indexed page boundary. In this case, query terms may occur in different indexed pages, and a normal index search for contexts with this name may miss some such contexts. In order to make it possible to accurately search for large page-spanning contexts, a special entry is made in the index, consisting of the context name followed by a "$". This entry is in addition to the normally generated entry for the context name treated as a token. The postings lists for $ types also take on a special structure and meaning. These lists actually contain multiple sublists. Each sublist contains the numbers of all the pages that contain segments of the same context. Note that every sublist of a $ type contains at least two page numbers. To facilitate merging, each sublist is sorted by placing the smallest page number of a sublist at the beginning of the sublist and other page numbers in increasing order after the first. Sublists are then arranged in the increasing order of the first pages numbers of the sublists. A special merging algorithm must be invoked whenever a $ type is involved.

This is illustrated in Figure 9.13, where the pages are listed in the order in which the database text should appear. That is, the text in page 2 immediately follows the text in page 12 and is part of the "doc" that starts in page 12. When significant, a "|" is used within a page to indicate the end of the previous indexed item. Because A appears before the | in page 36, A is also posted to page 2. Similarly, B is posted to page 25. A ";" is used to separate the sublists of a $ type in the index.

Generally, in a context-indexed database, the information stored in a posting indicates in which context the token appears (document or paragraph). This information is essentially repeated in the full text of the database for accessing purposes. In the page-indexed scheme, practically no context information is stored in the postings. Since it is assumed that every query involves a context or proximity specification, every query will require access to the full text in order to obtain this context information. Solving queries that involve contexts that are small and never span page boundaries is very straightforward. Whether these be sentences or documents, every page in the result list of the index search must be fetched and scanned in order to determine whether or not any context in those pages actually satisfies the query. If the search context specifies any contexts that are large enough to span pages, then a $ type can be found in the index and an additional database-searching algorithm must be invoked. This approach can be justified by the fact that many, if not most, queries specify contexts or patterns that are known to be small. A context index at such a level generates a very large index, while use of a higher-level index would necessitate the scanning anyway.

To completely process a query, two search algorithms are applied. One locates contexts that are wholly contained within a page, while the other finds contexts that span page boundaries. The former will be called the *page search,* the latter the *spanning search.* If a query has no context specification, then it must represent a bounded pattern, or else the query makes no sense. In this case only the page-search algorithm is used and the pattern is bounded by L. The page-search algorithm forms a Boolean expression tree by ANDing the context name, if any, with the search expression, performs the index search, and finally scans each page resulting from the index search. The scanner handles any proximity specifications as well as the context specification. The spanning search algorithm is more involved, requiring an initial step that AND merges the $ type for the specified context name with each term in the search expression. The special merge processor is used to do this because of the structure of the $ postings list. Each term is taken separately in order to generate a new list for that term. The list for a term is actually merged with each sublist from the $ list. However, the output list is formed as follows: if the term has no pages in common with the sublist, then nothing is put out; if the term has some number of pages in common with the sublist, then the first (lowest) page number in the sublist is put out. Note that the output list must be in order because of the way sublists of a $ type are sorted. Because each sublist of a $ type represents some context having that name, the new term lists now effectively identify *contexts* that may contain those terms. These new term lists are then merged according to the search expression in the query. Finally, scanning must be done to verify that contexts actually match the query. It is no problem getting from the page that is lowest to the page that contains the start of the context because of the pointers stored in the page headers, although in most cases the lowest-numbered page will be the start of the context.

Clarification of the searching algorithms is best provided by examples. Figure 9.14 illustrates a simple database with only three pages, a query against it, and the resulting processing. For the page search, page 2 is scanned up to the end of the indexed item (L bytes into page 3) but not into the "section" that runs past this point. For the spanning search, the index search doesn't tell which "section" is a possible hit—the one that runs into page 1 or the one that begins in page 1 and runs off the end. In this case the scan should start in page 1 but then return and follow the pointer to page 2 and begin another scan there. The "section" that starts in page 2 and ends in page 1 will be found to match the query.

Figure 9.15 shows how it is possible to evaluate subexpressions of a query that have context specifications and then use these results to evaluate a composite query. The subexpressions need not all be entered at one time but can be entered as refinements to an original simple query. Saved results from each subexpression of the query can then be used to evaluate the composite query. If the entire query is entered at one time, it might be more

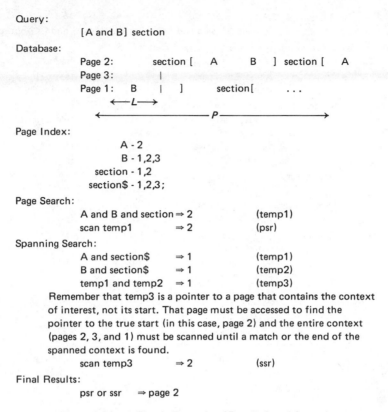

Query:

       [A and B] section

Database:

Page 2:	section [	A	B	]	section [	A	
Page 3:		|					
Page 1:	B	|	]		section[	...	

     ←—L—→

    ←————————————— P —————————————→

Page Index:

       A - 2
       B - 1,2,3
   section - 1,2
   section$ - 1,2,3;

Page Search:

   A and B and section ⇒ 2   (temp1)
   scan temp1   ⇒ 2   (psr)

Spanning Search:

   A and section$ ⇒ 1   (temp1)
   B and section$ ⇒ 1   (temp2)
   temp1 and temp2 ⇒ 1   (temp3)

Remember that temp3 is a pointer to a page that contains the context of interest, not its start. That page must be accessed to find the pointer to the true start (in this case, page 2) and the entire context (pages 2, 3, and 1) must be scanned until a match or the end of the spanned context is found.

   scan temp3   ⇒ 2   (ssr)

Final Results:

   psr or ssr   ⇒ page 2

Figure 9.14. A Simple Example of Page-Indexed Operation

efficient to evaluate it by removing all the context specifications except the outermost, doing the index search (merging), and then applying all the context specifications during scanning.

9.4.3. Specialized Index Processors

While the index operations just described can easily be performed on a conventional digital computer, it has been shown [7] that the ratio of actual data handling instructions to overhead instructions (data alignment, loop and flow control) is low, providing either slow response time or requiring a powerful processor. This is especially true for pure context indexing schemes, where the lists of pointers can be extremely long.

    Even for hybrid schemes, such as page indexing, the processing of a single query involving a thesaurus or explode operation that generates a large number of terms can require extensive processing. For example, assuming that each list contains about 5000 terms (as would be expected for useful query terms for a database with about one to two million documents), and

Query:

    [[A and B] para and [(C or D) and E] para and [K] author] doc

Database and page index same as in Figure 9.13

Page Search for   [A and B] para:

    A and B and para   ⇒ 2   (temp1)
    scan temp1   ⇒ 2   (psr1)

Spanning Search for   [A and B] para:

    A and para$ ⇒ 25   (temp1)
    B and para$ ⇒ 25   (temp2)
    temp1 and temp2   ⇒ 25   (temp3)
    scan temp3   ⇒ empty   (ssr1)

Results for   [A and B] para:

    psr1 or ssr1   ⇒ 2   (res1)

Page Search for   [(C or D) and E] para:

    (C or D) and E and para ⇒ empty   (psr2)

Spanning Search for   [(C or D) and E] para:

    C and para$ ⇒ 25   (temp1)
    D and para$ ⇒ empty   (temp2)
    E and para$ ⇒ 25   (temp3)
    (temp1 or temp2) and temp3 ⇒ 25   (temp4)
    scan temp4   ⇒ 36   (ssr2)

Results for   [(C or D) and E] para:

    psr2 or ssr2   ⇒ 36   (res2)

Page Search for   [K] author:

    K and author   ⇒ 12   (temp1)
    scan temp1   ⇒ 12   (psr3)

Spanning Search for   [K] author:

    K and author$ ⇒ empty   (ssr3)

Results for   [K] author:

    psr3 or ssr3   ⇒ 12   (res3)

Page Search for complete query:

    res1 and res2 and res3 and doc ⇒ empty   (psr)

Spanning Search for complete query:

    res1 and doc$ ⇒ 2   (temp1)
    res2 and doc$ ⇒ 2   (temp2)
    res3 and doc$ ⇒ 2   (temp3)
    temp1 and temp2 and temp3 ⇒ 2   (temp4)
    scan temp4   ⇒ 12   (ssr)

Final Results

    ssr or psr   ⇒ page 12

Figure 9.15. A More Complex Example of Page-Indexing Processing

the query ultimately specifies 100 terms, with each list entry containing 32 bits. This means that the input to the merge process contains 16 million bits of information. Assuming a reasonable transfer-to-seek ratio for a disk drive, it would take almost a minute to read the data from a disk drive. This would certainly not provide the interactive response time necessary for ideal system operation.

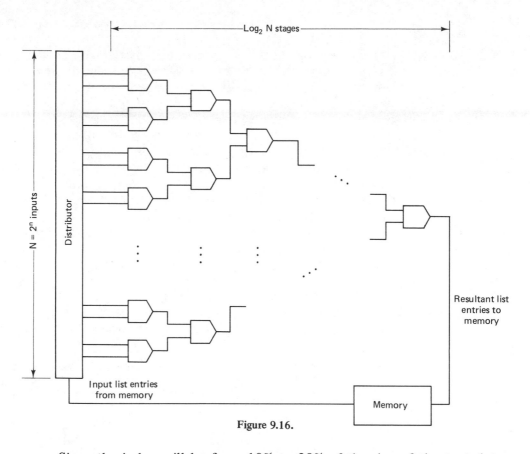

Figure 9.16.

Since the index will be from 10% to 20% of the size of the text database, it will probably be stored on multiple disk drives. This allows parallel transfers from the disks to the index processor, possibly reducing the read time to a reasonable value. However, once the data are in the processor's memory, they still must be combined to form the final result. It has been shown that the effective bandwidth (number of bits from the list completely processed in a given time) for a conventional processor is under 10% of the available memory bandwidth for the processor [7]. This means that if the memory has a raw bandwidth of 32 MHz (16 bits every 500 ns), it would take about six seconds to process the 100-term query, considering both the transferring of data from the disk and processing in memory, but ignoring any system overhead for I/O scheduling and other support activities. This is marginally satisfactory for an interactive system.

Rather than use a conventional digital computer, with its accompanying inefficiencies, a processor customized for list merging can be constructed. This can either be implemented using a bit-sliced microprocessor, with its data paths and parallelism optimized for the problem, or a totally custom processor [7]. In the latter case, a number of simple bit-serial processors are connected together to form a binary tree, as shown in Figure 9.16, with each element of the tree programmed to perform a particular Boolean merge operation (AND, OR, AND NOT, or PASS, which logically removes an element from the tree). Given available integrated circuit technology, it should be possible to process the 100-term query in just over a second, using a network containing 127 merge elements.

Often a query will specify only a few terms, while infrequently a large number (100 or more) of terms will be specified. Since the size of the merge tree is fixed at installation, what size should it be to give good performance? If the tree is much larger than necessary for most queries, hardware remains idle and the cost of processing a query is higher, while if the tree is smaller than the number of terms in the query, multiple passes through the tree must be made, with the additional overhead of storing and later reading intermediate results. Although the particular size selected for best operation depends on a number of characteristics of the particular retrieval system (such as query arrival rate, query complexity, and list size), there is an alternative organization for the merge-processing system that gives uniform response times for a variety of loadings and query complexities.

Figure 9.17 shows a two-level list-merging network, with each level

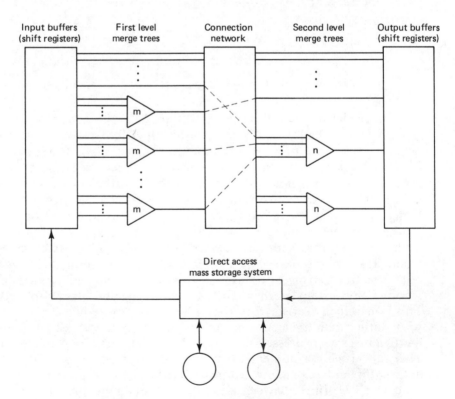

Figure 9.17. A Two-Level List-Merging Network

consisting of a number of merge trees of uniform size, and an interconnection network between the two levels. For simple queries, the results can be formed in the first level and routed directly to the output buffers, while complex queries can be processed by a larger tree produced by a second-level tree taking its inputs from one or first-level trees and the input buffers. When a user's query arrives, it is scheduled as soon as the required number of trees is available, with small queries being processed almost immediately. Since multiple processors are available for processing queries, the response time of the system remains relatively uniform as long as the number of queries to be processed matches the number of processors available [14].

While these specialized merge processors were initially designed for a system using conventional context (rather than page) indexing, the modifications necessary for the special operations required by page indexing are quite straightforward, in many cases simply requiring the proper programming of the merge tree.

9.5. REQUIREMENTS FOR THE EXAMPLE SYSTEM

Going back to the example of the Patent Office search system, with its 65-billion-character database and query arrival rate of one every 2.4 seconds, a possible configuration can be developed. Assuming currently available 300-Mbyte disk technology, it will take about 220 drives to hold the text database. The use of a 300-Mbyte drive gives a good tradeoff between total system cost and parallelism in searching. While the total system cost (including the host processor and terminals) would decrease very slightly if the capacity of the disk drives were doubled to 600 Mbytes (perhaps less than a 10% change), there would be about a 50% increase in response time. Preliminary simulations indicate that the response time based on a random distribution of data of interest across the system would be about 1.5 seconds for an index efficiency of 0.1% (the index system eliminates 99.9% of the database before searching) and 10 seconds for an index efficiency of 1%.

Based on normal distributions of words (Zipf's law), the approximately 1.8 million patents in the database will have about 900 to 1500 types, or indexed terms, per patent (a database containing state statutes has about 1000 types for each page the length of the average patent). If each posting takes 4 bytes, the index will take somewhere from 5 to 10 gigabytes, about 10% to 15% the size of the text database. This will require another 30 disk drives, so the total system will take about 250 disk drives.

Again assuming a reasonable ratio between reading and seeking, the expected aggregate bandwidth of the 30 disks would be 12 million bits per second, or 375,000 postings per second. For a normal query with four or fewer terms, as would be the case much of the time [4] under 10,000 postings need to be processed. If the postings processor performance is limited by the disk transfer rate, as would be the case for the tree-based system discussed previously, only a small fraction of a second would be required to handle the index processing. Even if an explode or thesaurus operation generates a large number of terms, the response time would be reasonable, since 250 terms of 10,000 entries each can be processed in under seven seconds using a sufficiently large tree structure operating at disk transfer speeds. The use of precomputed posting lists for common thesaurus terms or phrases can substantially improve this performance, and a marginal increase in cost.

An additional means of reducing the index processing time, which is available for the Patent Office application and many others, is to view the database not as a single collection of documents but as logical clusters of documents. For example, one cluster may contain all patents related to electricity while another may have all those related to chemical compounds. Some documents might be members of more than one cluster, such as a patent on a new method of electrolysis belonging to both the electrical and chemical clusters. Since most examiners' searches would be within their specialty, only index entries for a term in their particular interest's cluster would need to be processed. If they wished to access the entire database, the lists from all clusters would need to be ORed together to produce the final search list. The determination of whether clustering is appropriate and how the clusters are constructed is a highly system-dependent problem, affecting not only storage requirements (since a document can be in more than one cluster, additional pointers must be stored) but response time (which is improved for operations within a cluster but degraded for those involving multiple clusters).

If the index reduces the number of tracks that must be searched to about 0.3% of the total database size (which is still 195 million characters), statistically only one search per drive is necessary [9] so an elaborate parallel read-out is not necessary for the disk drive. Furthermore, the time necessary to perform the average search will be less than the expected query arrival rate, 2.4 seconds. The use of special list-merging processors to handle the index processing should also yield a response time comparable to the query rate, so that in most cases users will receive the results of their queries in less than 10 seconds. Based on current disk costs and maintenance expenses, the average cost for a query will be under a dollar, or about $10 for each patent search.

9.6. SUMMARY

The structure and implementation of a hardware-enhanced text information-retrieval system has been discussed. Text information retrieval differs substantially from formatted databases: the databases are much larger, the query language more powerful, and the basic user operation is searching, with any updating being done by the system management.

A potential application for a large information-retrieval utility, the automation of the Patent Office's search file of prior patents, was discussed. It is clear from the size of the database that conventional digital computers cannot provide satisfactory performance at a reasonable cost.

Two specialized backend processing systems were proposed: a search system attached to each disk of the database, based on a new finite-state machine implementation capable of processing characters directly as they come off the disk, and an index-processing system, using an improved form of indexing. The resulting system provides excellent response times (less than 10 seconds) and low costs (about 50 cents per query).

REFERENCES

[1] Codd, E. F., "A Relational Model of Data for Large Shared Data Banks," *Comm. ACM,* Vol. 13, No. 6 (June 1970), pp. 337–387.

[2] Hollaar, L. A., "Text Retrieval Computers," *Computer,* Vol. 12, No. 3 (March 1979), pp. 40–50.

[3] United States Patent and Trademark Office, *P.L. 96–517, Section 9, Automation Plan,* 1981.

[4] Milner, J. M., "An Analysis of Rotational Storage Access Scheduling in a Multi-programmed Information Retrieval System," Ph.D. dissertation.

[5] Roberts, D. C., "A Specialized Computer Architecture for Text Retrieval," *Workshop on Computer Arch. for Non-Numeric Processing,* August 1978, pp. 51–59.

[6] Bird, R. M., Newsbaum, J. B., and Trefftzs, J. L., "Text File Inversion: An Evaluation," *Workshop on Computer Arch. for Non-Numeric Processing,* August 1978, pp. 42–50.

[7] Hollaar, L. A., "Specialized Merge Processor Networks for Combining Sorted Lists," *ACM Trans. Database Systems,* Vol. 3, No. 3 (September 1978), pp. 272–284.

[8] Hollaar, L. A., and Stellhorn, W. H., "A Specialized Architecture for Textual Information Retrieval," *Proc. AFIPS Natl. Comptr. Conf.,* June 1977, pp. 697–702.

[9] Haskin, R. L., "Hardware for Searching Very Large Text Databases," Ph.D. dissertation, University of Illinois, August 1980.

[10] Haskin, R. L., and Hollaar, L. A., "Operational Characteristics of a Hardware-based Pattern Matcher," *ACM Trans. Database Systems,* Vol. 8, No. 1 (March 1983).

[11] Haskin, R. L., "Hardware for Searching Very Large Text Databases," *Workshop on Computer Arch. for Non-Numeric Processing,* March 1980, pp. 49–56.

[12] Hopcroft, J. E., and Ullman, J. D. *Introduction to Automata Theory, Languages, and Computation,* Addison-Wesley Publishing Company, Reading, Mass., 1979.

[13] Emrath, P. A., "Page Indexing for Text Information Retrieval Systems," Ph.D. dissertation in progress, Department of Computer Science, University of Illinois at Urbana-Champaign.

[14] Huang, H-M., "On the Design and Scheduling of an Index Processing System for Very Large Databases," Ph.D. dissertation, University of Illinois, August 1980.

10

The Implementation of a Multibackend Database System (MDBS): Part I—An Exercise in Database Software Engineering

David K. Hsiao, Douglas S. Kerr, Ali Orooji, Zhong-Zhi Shi, and Paula R. Strawser

10.0. ABSTRACT

This exercise represents a rigorous application of modern software engineering techniques to the implementation of a new database system. Our purpose is to test the adequacy of the software engineering methodologies used. We also attempt to modify existing methodologies and propose new ones to tailor them for effective software engineering of database systems. They include an evolutionary implementation strategy; methodologies for team organization, cross communication, and uniform documentation; and techniques for program design, specification, modularization, coding, and testing. Our effort is not limited to the production of a prototype database system but is aimed broadly toward a methodology for database software engineering.

10.1. INTRODUCTION

10.1.1. Why Do We Have an Exercise?

Having designed and analyzed the architecture of a new database management system in [1] and [2], we wanted to prototype the system. To do so properly, we wanted to apply well-known software engineering techniques to the effort. Such techniques have not been widely applied to database system implementations, although they have been applied to the development of application programs and the writing of compilers and operating systems.

10.1.2. What Is the Exercise?

This exercise includes the selection and use of software engineering techniques and methodologies for the entire implementation effort of the database system. We first address the issues of selecting software tools, hardware systems, and operating system supports. We then emphasize the organization and management of the implementors and the control of the quality of their work. To facilitate this control of quality, we include the issues of identifying the role of the individual implementors in the team effort, partitioning the implementation effort in terms of phases and versions, facilitating the communication among and education of the implementors, enforcing the specification, documentation, and testing standards of the system modules, and, finally, providing the means for migrating from one phase of implementation to another. These and other issues are addressed in this chapter.

10.1.3. What Benefits Do We Expect?

As researchers in the design and analysis of database system architectures, we had no prior experience in the application of modern software engineering techniques to database system implementations. In other words, we did not know how to prototype database systems with modern software engineering methodologies. By doing this exercise, we hope to find the proper methodology for the software engineering of database systems. We also have plans to use the prototype system for benchmarking database applications and their effects on system performance. Obviously, a properly prototyped system will provide us with a good testbed to conduct more accurate benchmarking.

10.1.4. What Results Do We Have to Date?

The main tangible finding is that most of the known software engineering techniques may be used with some improvements in prototyping the database system, regardless of the novelty of its system architecture. These techniques include an evolutionary implementation strategy, a modified chief-programmer team organization, the use of structured walkthroughs, a uniform documentation standard, the use of a top-down design strategy combined with the use of data and service abstractions, a formal program specification language, a standard for module decomposition, structured coding, and, finally, a "black-box" testing approach.

Several intangibles affect the morale of the implementors and the quality of the software. For example, the use of structured walkthroughs not only facilitates communication among the members of the same team, but also guarantees dialog across the teams, which in turn tends to increase the morale of everyone involved in the implementation effort. Second, the fact that known software engineering techniques such as structured walkthroughs and a formal program specification language are being used for the first time by the team members tends to increase their enthusiasm and to heighten their awareness of the importance of software quality control. Finally, by reassigning the roles of the implementors in the chief-programmer team at appropriate milestones, we are able to assess the strong and weak points of the individuals involved. Such an assessment would not be possible with fixed assignments.

This chapter relates our experience in the application of well-known software engineering techniques to the prototyping of database systems. We also try to assess the usefulness of the techniques to database software engineering. The particular system we have chosen for prototyping, known as the multibackend database system (MDBS), is not the focus of our discussion. For our purposes we could have chosen a different system. However, the design and analysis of MDBS were well documented and known to the implementors, thus minimizing the lead time for selecting a system for prototyping. Further, we had an added reason to prototype MDBS, because in subsequent research efforts we intend to use MDBS as a testbed for benchmarking database applications and their impact on system performance.

10.1.5. What Is the Database System Being Prototyped?

Although the purpose of this chapter is to describe the database software engineering experience rather than the particular database system architecture being implemented, a brief introduction to that system is necessary to understand some of the software engineering issues discussed later. Full details on the design and analysis can be found in [1] and [2]. The implementation effort is described in more detail in Chapter 11 of this book.

10.1.5.1. The organization and design issues of MDBS. The basic motivation of MDBS is to develop an architecture that spreads the work of the database system among multiple backends, each of which executes the *same* system software. In order to simplify the control of these multiple

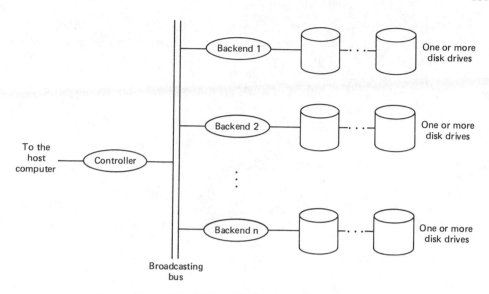

Figure 10.1.   The MDBS Hardware Organization

backends, i.e., PDP11/44s and their disks, the control function is centralized in a controller computer, the VAX11/780. The resulting hardware organization is shown in Figure 10.1.

It is a major aim of this design to allow capacity growth by the use of additional disk drives and performance improvement by the use of additional backends. With this aim it is important that the software be properly developed. Any sloppy implementation and error in the software in one backend will be replicated in all the other backends, since all the backends have identical system software. It is also important that the software in the controller be free from any sloppy implementation and error, since a malfunction in the controller may cause improper control of the backends.

10.1.5.2. The basic characteristics of MDBS.   Parallel processing of the database itself, simultaneous processing of the information about the database, and concurrent processing of the user requests are the basic characteristics of MDBS. First, similar records are grouped into logical *clusters*. Then the records in a cluster are distributed across the backends. When a request for a particular group of records is received, MDBS transforms the request into an equivalent request for clusters. Since requested clusters are distributed across the backends, the particular group of records can now be accessed and processed by the backends in parallel.

In order to identify the location of the clusters readily, information about the clusters is kept in a *directory*. Thus the processing of a database request consists of two steps: *directory management* determines those clusters that have records relevant to the request and *record processing* retrieves and processes relevant records. The computations within the directory management step are performed simultaneously by the backends. Similarly, the computations within the record-processing step are also performed in parallel across the backends.

Since it is a multiuser system, many users may issue requests to MDBS. Requests of the same user, as well as requests of different users, are processed by the backends concurrently. Consequently, MDBS is a multiple-request-and-multiple-data-stream system.

10.1.6. The Organization of the Chapter

Section 10.2 describes in more detail the rationale for implementing an MDBS prototype. In Section 10.3 we first describe the several approaches that may be taken in the actual implementation strategy. Then we describe the implementation strategy and versions we have chosen to employ.

In Section 10.4 we describe several management techniques that may be used and then discuss those that we have chosen. In Section 10.5 we describe how we are applying particular software engineering techniques to the different stages of the database system implementation. In Section 10.6 we summarize the results of our experience thus far.

10.2. WHY IMPLEMENT MDBS?

As stated earlier, we have chosen to implement a prototype MDBS in order to conduct benchmarking of database applications and to determine their impact on system performance. We also want to validate the design and analysis of MDBS. We now describe these goals more precisely.

10.2.1. Validation of Simulation and Analytic Results

The first reason for building a prototype system is to validate the simulation and analytic results on system performance obtained earlier in the course of our design studies. The main goal is to measure the extensibility of the system; i.e., how does it perform as more backends are added? In particular, is the performance gain proportional to the number of backends? If this proportionality holds for a number of backends, how many backends can be added before performance improvement becomes impossible? The simulation and queuing models used to develop the design predict improved performance with an increase in the number of backends for the same amount of data. They also predict constant performance with an increase in data, if the number of backends is increased. Will these predictions be verified in practice?

10.2.1.1. System evaluation with program-generated databases.   The first set of experiments will use test data that are generated by a test file generation package using parameters specified by experimenters. The record formats will be determined by the experimenter. The actual data will then be generated from distributions specified by the experimenter. For example, one file may have 10,000 records, each with 10 fields. The value in the first field of a record may be drawn from a uniform distribution on the interval [0, 100]; the second field may be drawn from a predefined set of values, while the third field may come from a normal distribution. The number of records and their formats can be varied in the experiments.

Requests will also be constructed in a similar way. This approach is taken first because these experiments are easy to perform. However, we also intend to run experiments on actual databases borrowed from the Department of Defense's user community.

10.2.1.2. System evaluation with actual databases.   To test the system performance, we will also use data taken from actual databases. Thus the second step will be to obtain one or more actual databases. Sets of "typical" requests will then be developed on the basis of the data languages of the databases. These databases and sets of requests will be used for conducting experiments, which will provide more insight into how a multibackend system may actually perform. Furthermore, the performance data may be used to validate our simulation and analytic results. Finally, they will provide insights into the relative performance of the multibackend system vs. either a single-backend system or a conventional system.

10.2.2. Toward a Methodology for Database Applications Classification

After experimenting with several actual databases, our goal is to develop a methodology for classifying database applications. With such a methodology it should be easier to predict the performance of a new application on an existing multibackend system. Such a classification would allow much more specialized testing of the system performance.

For example, two gross application classification schemes may be used. One is to distinguish between "query-intensive" and "update-intensive" applications. In the first case most requests only seek information from the database, while in the second case most requests require addition and modification to the database. A second classification scheme involves the complexity of the queries. For example, some queries are very simple, involving few attribute values—e.g., finding the address of the employee whose employee number is 123456. Other queries are much more complex, consisting of Boolean expressions of attribute values and attribute value ranges—e.g., finding the names and addresses of all employees who live in Columbus, earn between $20,000 and $32,000 per year, and have worked for the company for at least 10 years. Still more complex queries require reference to multiple files, say, for joins and links of tuples of different relations. It seems likely that some designs will provide better performance on simple queries, while other designs will provide better performance on more complex queries. These and other classifications need to be developed.

One such classification scheme was developed in [3]. This scheme divides requests into classes: overhead-intensive, data-intensive, and multiple-file. Overhead-intensive requests tend to be short ones that require access to only a small part of the database. Data-intensive requests typically involve an aggregation operation on a large number of records. Multiple-file requests require combining information from several files, as in a relational join operation. Using this classification scheme, benchmarks were run against an INGRES system [4]. Later, an analytic model based on this classification scheme was developed and applied first to specific database system designs [5] and then to classes of systems [6].

10.2.3. Benchmarking the System Performance

A well-known method for comparing the relative performance of computer systems is to compare the average execution time of a standard instruction mix [7]. One such mix, the Gibson mix [8], was derived from the average relative usage of IBM 7090 CPU instructions in a scientific environment. Similarly, this approach has been applied to high-level programming languages. One such mix [9] was collected for the average relative usage of FORTRAN statements. Once such a mix has been developed, it can be used to estimate the performance of a new computer system by first determining the execution time of each instruction type and then computing the weighted average execution time for the typical mix of instructions.

This same technique may be generalized and applied to the performance of database systems. Corresponding to a standard CPU instruction mix would be a mix of low-level database processing statements such as the requests provided by MDBS. Corresponding to the high-level programming statement mix would be a mix of high-level query language statements provided by a language such as SQL [10]. The relative mix of MDBS requests or SQL statements would be determined by examining several typical database applications. This new mix could then be used to estimate the performance of a new database system after the execution time of each type of MDBS request or SQL statement was known.

10.3. AN EVOLUTIONARY IMPLEMENTATION STRATEGY— WHAT AND WHY?

Many different implementation strategies have been proposed. Several such strategies are suggested in [11]. For example, the *build-it-twice full-prototype* approach is recommended when the implementation team is in a new undertaking. In this case the first implementation gives insight that may make the second implementation much more satisfactory. A frequently suggested approach is the *level-by-level top-down* approach. This approach allows integration of modules to occur as they are developed. Thus, the need for a massive system integration phase is reduced.

Two refinements of the build-it-twice full-prototype approach and the level-by-level top-down approach have also been suggested [11]. The *incremental development* approach consists of developing several complete systems, with each succeeding system having increased functionality. The *advancemanship* approach consists of two components. The first is to develop some *anticipating documentation,* i.e., user documentation developed before the system is actually developed. The second, called *software scaffolding*, consists of developing some of the supporting software before developing the actual system.

The implementation strategy we have chosen takes the strong points of the above techniques with modification. We have chosen to implement five versions of MDBS, each with increasing functionality. Because we were inexperienced when we began, we have also adopted a build-it-twice approach, although we do not expect to develop more than one full system. Finally, we chose to implement some of the supporting software as our initial effort, and we chose not to develop any anticipatory user documentation. In particular, we first implemented a program to generate test data files. We also implemented a program to handle the initial loading of a database from an existing file. The early implementations of these less critical programs allowed us to gain experience with our new computers, operating systems, and programming languages before we began the implementation of the multibackend database system, MDBS.

The actual implementation strategy chosen is described next. It begins with the implementation of a very simple system.

10.3.1. Version I—A Very Simple System: Single Mini without Concurrency Control and with Simplified Directory Management

We started the implementation effort with a system that was intended to be as simple as possible. The aim was to get something running so that we could gain some experience with both the MDBS design and our new computer systems. Thus we had chosen to simplify the design as much as possible. MDBS-I, which is in the final stages of implementation, executes only a single request at a time. It runs on a single computer. There is no separate controller. Directory management is simplified by storing all directory data in the main memory. There is no concurrent execution of requests. Since the whole system runs as a single operating system process, the interface with the operating system is minimized.

10.3.2. Version II—A Simple System: Single Mini with Concurrency Control

The second version will allow concurrent execution of requests but will still be restricted to a single mini. We plan to use the services of our operating system to facilitate this concurrent processing. Thus we will use the capability of creating independent concurrent processes that communicate among themselves. These processes will execute in parallel so that MDBS-II will be able to execute requests in parallel. This version will allow us to gain experience with the problem of multiple processes and the problem of concurrency control. Details have been designed and the implementation effort has been completed; version II is running.

10.3.3. Version III—The First "Real" System: Multiple Minis with Concurrency Control

After MDBS-II is working, we will transfer the system to our real environment including a controller (i.e., VAX 11/780) and several backends (PDP 11/44s). The major changes required will be to replace communications between processes in one computer by communications between processes running on different computers. This version will allow us to see how the intercomputer communication overhead affects system performance. This system, MDBS-III, will still not be sufficient for a full MDBS, since it has a very simplified directory management subsystem. However, it will allow us to begin preliminary testing of the MDBS design.

10.3.4. Version IV—The Real System with "Good" Directory Management

This version will include a fully implemented directory management subsystem utilizing the secondary memories. It will be a complete prototype system, except for the lack of access control features. This system, MDBS-IV, will be the one on which we will try to validate the simulation studies used in the development of the original design. Detailed design is underway.

10.3.5. Version V—The Full System with All the Designed Features Included

The final version will incorporate access control in the backends and a friendly user-interface in the controller or host computer.

10.4. TEAM ORGANIZATION AND MONITORING THE DEVELOPMENT EFFORT

In the choice of software engineering techniques for the MDBS implementation effort, three issues in management strategy are specifically addressed: (1) How should the group be organized? (2) What specific techniques should be adopted to monitor the development effort? (3) What documentation standards should be adopted?

10.4.1. A Three-Level Chief-Programmer-Team Organization without Librarians

The classic chief-programmer team [12] is headed by a chief programmer who has absolute decision-making authority. Other permanent members of the team include a senior-level back-up programmer and a librarian. Additional programmers may be added as necessary. The *chief programmer* does all the design work and writes all the critical sections of code—for example, the routines for subsystem interfaces. The *back-up programmer* is an understudy for the chief programmer and participates in design and coding; he takes over if the chief programmer leaves the team. The *librarian* maintains the group's program libraries and coordinates the documentation effort.

One advantage of such a two-level organization is that, since the levels of communication between team members are minimized, development is likely to proceed at a faster pace than with a higher-level organization. Also, the system that is developed is likely to be more coherent and consistent, since it was designed primarily by one person.

The MDBS implementation group is organized as a *three-level chief-programmer team without the librarian.* The entire implementation effort is headed by a team supervisor. Separate teams are organized for each sub-project being developed; each team is composed of a chief programmer, one back-up programmer, and one or more programmers. An organization chart of the group, depicted in Figure 10.2, shows three such teams working on directory management, test file generation, and database load.

We also change the roles of team members during the implementation effort. Thus we are better able to fit each of our team members into a role that best suits his or her abilities. Although there is a danger of instability caused by too frequent role changes, this capacity to change roles is especially important to our effort, since none of the team members had worked together before the project began. Such role changes are also depicted in Figure 10.2. The team supervisor appoints members to the teams, establishes a uniform documentation standard as described in a later section, and provides overall supervision of the implementation.

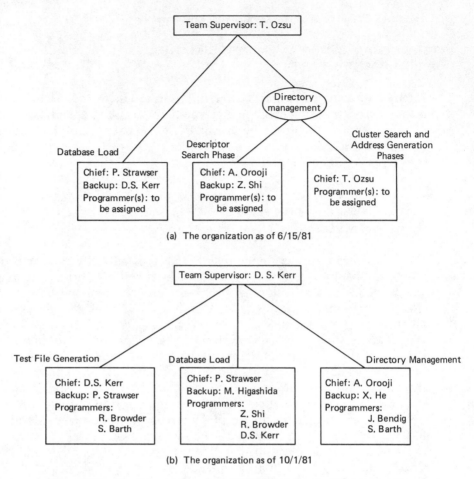

(a) The organization as of 6/15/81

(b) The organization as of 10/1/81

Figure 10.2. The Organization of the MDBS Design and Implementation Teams

10.4.2. The Structured Walkthrough

A *structured walkthrough* is a formal review of the software development effort at a given stage in its development cycle. The work is reviewed by a walkthrough committee, with the purpose of finding any errors that may be present. The purpose of a walkthrough is not to solve problems, only to identify them; neither is a walkthrough a management tool to evaluate any employee's performance.

Each member of the walkthrough committee has a well-defined role. A *coordinator* organizes and runs the meeting. The *presentor,* the originator of the work, presents his work to the group and answers questions. The *reviewers* examine the material before the walkthrough is held, and during the walkthrough they present their findings. A *scribe* records the proceedings. Each member votes on the outcome; the material may be accepted as presented, accepted with revision, or returned for revision and subsequent walkthrough.

The MDBS teams use this technique at both the design stage and the coding stage. All detailed program specifications and source code are reviewed by walkthrough committees. These committees are chosen to include members from more than one chief-programmer team. This practice contributes to a more effective walkthrough, since not all participants are involved in the development of the material being reviewed. It is also valuable in cross-training team members in areas other than those to which they are currently assigned. The status of a task can be determined by reviewing the walkthrough reports for that task. Figure 10.3. shows a sample walkthrough

---

Walkthrough Report

Coordinator: _P. STRAWSER_

Project: MDBS _DATABASE GENERATION SETS MODULE_

Coordinator's checklist:

1. Confirm with producer that material is ready and stable.

2. Issue invitations, assign responsibilities, distribute materials.

   Date _8/27_   Place _230 CA_
   Time _11:00_   Duration _30 min._

	Participant	Role	Can attend	Has material	Initials
1.	KERR	PRODUCER	✓	✓	Dik
2.	BROWDER	REVIEWER	✓	✓	RS
3.	BARTH	REVIEWER	✓	✓	✓
4.	STRAWSER	COORDINATOR	✓	✓	Pr
5.	Orooji	SCRIBE	✓	✓	
6.					

Agenda:

___ 1. All participants agree to follow the (same!) set of rules.

___ 2. New project: walkthrough of material.
       Old project: item-by-item checkoff of previous action list.

___ 3. Creation of new action list (contributions by each participant).

___ 4. Group decision.

___ 5. Deliver copy of this form to project management.

Decision: ___ Accept product as-is

       _✓_ Revise (no further walkthrough)

       ___ Revise and schedule another walkthrough
       (Participants should initial above.)

[30,3] chklist, txt

Notes: Refer to Figure 10.2(a), which shows the MDBS organization chart in effect at the time this walkthrough was held. Note that two of the three chief programmers are represented in this walkthrough committee.
       This module is a part of the test file generation programming task.

Figure 10.3.   A Sample Walkthrough Report

report. A good reference describing the structured-walkthrough technique is [13].

10.4.3. A Uniform Documentation Standard

The objectives of a uniform documentation standard [14] are:

1. To achieve precise and unambiguous communication among staff members.
2. To produce complete and accurate documentation.
3. To assist in project management.
4. To reduce dependence on individuals.

For our documentation standard, we have added a fifth objective:

5. To integrate the documentation effort into the design and development stages.

A documentation standard is developed in three steps. First, the terminology to be used must be selected. For MDBS, we adopt a set of standards for naming programs, program source files, and documentation text files. More specifically, each program will have a mnemonic name that describes its function as well as a coded name that identifies its place in the *subsystem hierarchy*. For example, the hierarchy chart in Figure 10.4 shows both the mnemonic and coded names for the procedures of the database load subsystem.

In the second step, the end products of the documentation effort are described. The organization and content of each document are planned in detail. For MDBS, two formal documents are proposed: a *systems reference manual* (SRM) and an *operating procedures manual* (OPM). The SRM will be developed around the design documentation, thus minimizing the amount of new material to be written. The design documentation is being developed in a formal system specification language (SSL), which will be described in the next section. Material for the OPM will be developed during the design of the system's user interface.

The above steps define the documentation task. The next step is to define procedures for managing the documentation effort. A *documentation coordinator* will assist the project manager to monitor the MDBS documentation process. Milestones in the documentation effort are identified to establish a schedule by which the coordinator can measure progress. The first milestone is delivery of the SSL specification to the programmer; progress of the documentation will be monitored starting at that point. A step-by-step procedure is established that charts the documentation process from the

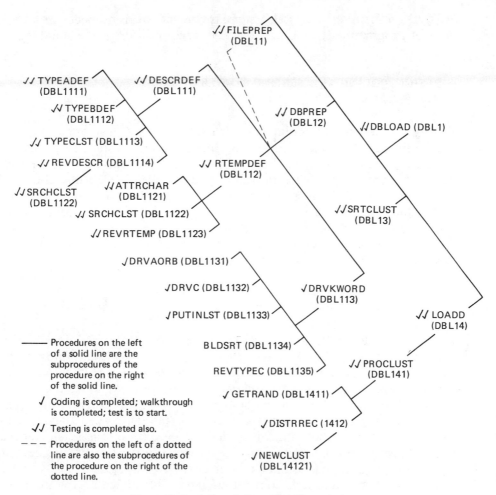

Figure 10.4. A Sample Procedure Hierarchy

first milestone to the last milestone, which is the assembly of the finished document.

Conformity to the uniform documentation standard will assist the development group to prepare complete, accurate, and timely documentation. The MDBS implementation strategy calls for multiple versions of the MDBS prototype to be developed; some of these versions will be based on previous versions. The organization of the implementation teams is based on specific tasks; as new tasks replace completed tasks, the team will be reorganized. These are two of the reasons that good documentation and a uniform documentation standard are especially important to the MDBS implementation effort. Finally, because the work on uniform documentation is required of every team member and is also standardized, there is no need for a librarian in chief-programmer teams. The team supervisor enforces the standard.

10.5. THE DESIGN, CODING AND TESTING STAGES OF THE SYSTEM VERSIONS

During the design and coding stages of the software development cycle, the detailed program specification is developed, and code in some programming language is generated from the program specification. The design strategy and methodology and the approach to coding must be carefully chosen to be complementary. A design strategy is selected first; then a design methodology with which to implement the strategy is chosen. The approach to coding follows logically from these decisions. A top-down design strategy, implemented in a formal system specification language, and a structured coding technique are used in the MDBS implementation effort.

10.5.1. A Top-Down Design Strategy and the Use of Data and Service Abstractions

A top-down design strategy is a natural choice for MDBS. The design and analysis study in [1] and [2] clearly describes the top level of design. It also suggests the possibility of functional decomposition; i.e., the entire system can be broken into discrete functional units. For example, the execution phases of a retrieval request can be broken down into directory management and record processing, as depicted in Figure 10.5. Directory management, an example of a functional unit, includes the descriptor-search, cluster-search, and address-generation phases of request execution. (For precise definitions of these terms and phases, the reader may refer to Chapter 11.)

At a lower level, the concept of data and service abstractions, which originated in the bottom-up design approach, is used. Since MDBS is being developed as a prototype system for research into performance evaluation, we anticipate that data structures and system services will be routinely modified in attempts to measure the effect of different data structures on system performance. The abstractions allow us to separate the basis system functions from the data structures and from the implementation of the services, minimizing the effect on the system when data structures or implementation services are modified.

10.5.2. A Formal Systems Specification Language (SSL)

The design methodology which the MDBS implementation group uses is a systems specification language (SSL) modeled on the process design language (PDL) described in [15]. The SSL is characterized by a number of constructs

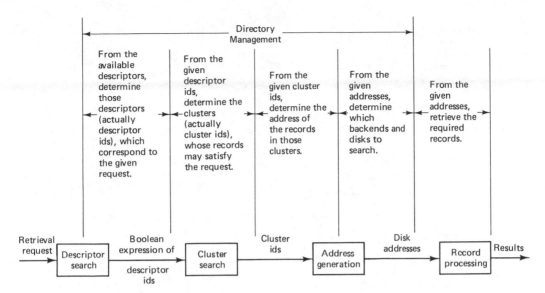

Figure 10.5. Execution Phases of a Retrieval Request

for the expression of the different levels of a system: system, subsystems, module, and procedure. A *system* is at the highest level of the hierarchy. MDBS, for example, is a system.

At the second highest level of the hierarchy we have the level of subsystem. A *subsystem* is a separate component of a system. In other words, each system may consist of several subsystems. The MDBS controller, for example, is a subsystem, as is each MDBS backend. The system, consisting of the controller and the backends, is the MDBS.

Below the level of subsystem we have the level of module. A *module* is intended for the implementation of a data or service abstraction. It consists of the procedures and data structures implementing the abstraction.

A *procedure* is at the lowest level of the hierarchy. It corresponds to the usual notion of a subroutine. Procedures are invoked to perform some work on some input data and produce some output. However, they are not allowed to retain data between invocations. A formal *outer syntax* and an informal *inner syntax* are used in a procedure. The outer syntax allows only the following three types of constructs: sequence, decision, and iteration. Below is an example of the if-then-else decision construct.

> if expression
> > then statement sequence
> > else statement sequence
> endif

The underlined words represent the formal outer syntax. The other words represent the informal inner syntax; the only requirement for this inner syn-

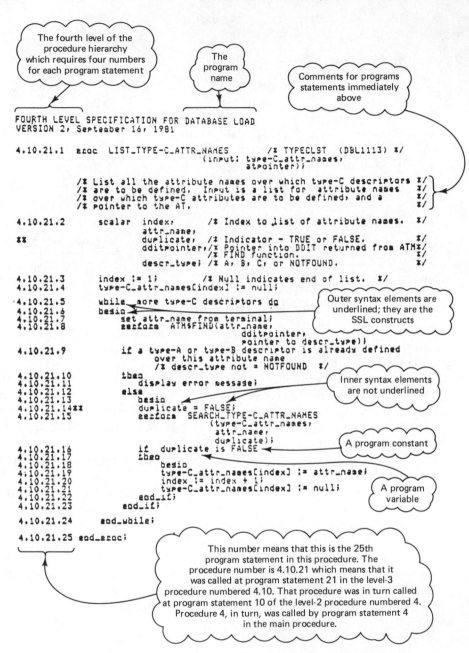

```
FOURTH LEVEL SPECIFICATION FOR DATABASE LOAD
VERSION 2, September 16, 1981

4.10.21.1    proc  LIST-TYPE-C-ATTR_NAMES            /* TYPECLST  (DBL1113) */
                              (input: type-C_attr_names,
                                      atpointer);

             /* List all the attribute names over which type-C descriptors */
             /* are to be defined.  Input is a list for  attribute names    */
             /* over which type-C attributes are to be defined, and a       */
             /* pointer to the AT.                                          */

4.10.21.2        scalar  index,       /* Index to list of attribute names.  */
                         attr_name,
                         duplicate,  /* Indicator - TRUE or FALSE.          */
                         dditpointer,/* Pointer into DDIT returned from ATM*/
                                     /* FIND function.                      */
                         descr_type; /* A, B, C, or NOTFOUND.               */

4.10.21.3        index := 1;         /* Null indicates end of list.  */
4.10.21.4        type-C_attr_names[index] := null;

4.10.21.5        while  more type-C descriptors do
4.10.21.6        begin
4.10.21.7            set attr_name from terminal;
4.10.21.8            perform  ATM$FIND(attr_name,
                                       dditpointer,
                                       pointer to descr_type));

4.10.21.9            if a type-A or type-B descriptor is already defined
                             over this attribute name
                             /* descr_type not = NOTFOUND */
4.10.21.10           then
4.10.21.11               display error message;
4.10.21.12           else
4.10.21.13               begin
4.10.21.14               duplicate = FALSE;
4.10.21.15               perform  SEARCH_TYPE-C_ATTR_NAMES
                                       (type-C_attr_names,
                                        attr_name,
                                        duplicate);

4.10.21.16               if  duplicate is FALSE
4.10.21.17               then
4.10.21.18                   begin
4.10.21.19                   type-C_attr_names[index] := attr_name;
4.10.21.20                   index := index + 1;
4.10.21.21                   type-C_attr_names[index] := null;
4.10.21.22                   end_if;
4.10.21.23               end_if;

4.10.21.24       end_while;

4.10.21.25 end_proc;
```

Figure 10.6.   An SSL Specification of a Program Procedure

tax is that it must be understood by all project members. Figure 10.6 shows a typical SSL procedure specification.

10.5.3. The Use of Jackson Charts

Our original designs were developed using only SSL. More recently, we have begun using a technique, Jackson charts, to represent the program structures. Three constructs are used in a Jackson chart:

1. *Sequence.* Figure 10.7(a) shows a sample sequence. In this example the sequence A consists of B followed by C followed by D.
2. *Iteration.* Figure 10.7(b) shows a sample iteration. In this example the iteration A consists of multiple occurrences of B.
3. *Selection.* Figure 10.7(c) shows a sample selection. In this example the selection A consists of one of B, C, or D.

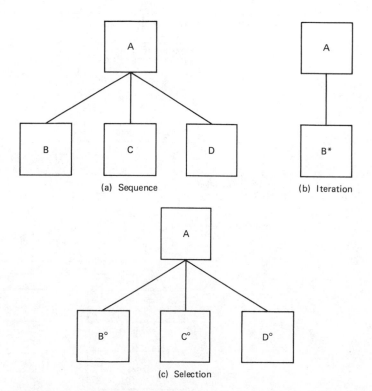

Figure 10.7.   The Constructs Used in a Jackson Chart: (a) Sequence, (b) Iteration, (c) Selection

A sample program structure and its corresponding SSL are shown in Figures 10.8 and 10.9, respectively.

Jackson charts contain fewer details than the SSL specifications and provide a two-dimensional representation of program structure. These charts, along with the SSL specification, are used to document the detailed design.

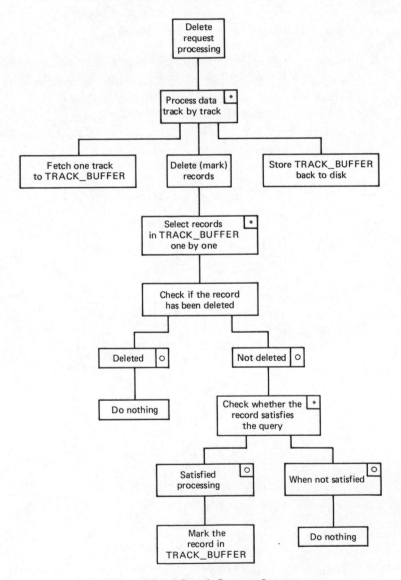

Figure 10.8.   A Sample Program Structure

```
10.1     proc DELETE_PROCESSING( input:  QUERY,ADDRESSES);
         /* This procedure is to be used for processing of DELETE requests. */

10.2         list QUERY: string;
10.3         set ADDRESSES: integer:
10.4         array TRACK_BUFFER: word;
10.5         scalar indexA,indexB: integer;
                 /*These are pointers for ADDRESSES AND TRACK_BUFFER, respectively.*/
10.6         scalar satisfied: logical;

             /* Process data track by track. */
10.7         for each address ADDRESSES(indexA) in ADDRESSES do
                 /* Fetch one track into TRACK_BUFFER. */
10.8             perform FETCH_TO_TRACK_BUFFER(indexA,TRACK_BUFFER);
                 /* Select records in TRACK_BUFFER one by one. */
10.9             for each record TRACK_BUFFER(indexB) in TRACK_BUFFER do
10.10               if the record is not marked for deletion
10.11                 then begin
                         /* Check whether the record satisfies the QUERY. */
10.12                     perform CHECK_QUERY(QUERY,TRACK_BUFFER,indexB,satisfied);
10.13                     if satisfied-'true'
                             then
                                 /* Mark the retrieved record in TRACK_BUFFER(indexB).*/
10.14                                 perform DELETE(TRACK_BUFFER,indexB);
10.15                     end if
10.16                 end begin
10.17               end if
10.18             end for  /* indexB */
                 /* Store TRACK_BUFFER back to disk. */
10.19             perform STORE_TRACK_BUFFER(indexA,TRACK_BUFFER);
10.20         end for   /* indexA */
10.21     end proc
```

Figure 10.9. The SSL Corresponding to the Sample Program Structure in Figure 10.8

10.5.4. A Measure of Modularity

As explained in Chapter 11, the entire MDBS system has been designed as a set of discrete functional units. We propose to apply the same idea of functional decomposition at the level of subsystem design. We need some way to evaluate the modularity of our decomposition. This need became apparent when we began designing the top-level scheme for MDBS subsystems. It is necessary that we develop a unified view of the overall function of the subsystems of the controller and the backends before proceeding to design the abstractions and procedures. We have added to our collection of software engineering strategies two measures of modularity, or functional decomposition.

The first of these measures is strength of cohesion [16]. *Cohesion* is defined as the relatedness of processing elements within a single component of a system—i.e., a subsystem, a module, or a procedure. The degree of relatedness determines the *level of cohesion.* Several levels of cohesion, ranked from least to most desirable, are recognized. A component is said to be *functionally cohesive,* the most desirable level of cohesion, if "every element of processing is an integral part of, and is essential to, the performance of a single function." An ad hoc measurement is that the description for a functionally cohesive component should consist of one imperative sentence containing one transitive verb and one nonplural object. We have applied this ad hoc measurement to our current design work. The designer is required to write a functional description of each program component, say an abstraction, of the design. Each description begins with a single sentence that concisely describes the function of that component. For example, the following sentence describes the function of a procedure of the MDBS controller, the Aggregate Post Operation:

> Aggregate Post Operation performs the final aggregation operation on the partial aggregate results returned from the backends.

The second measure of modularity is the degree of interconnections between components. *Coupling* is a measure of the *strength of interconnection* between components. Several categories of coupling are recognized, ranked from lowest (best case) to tightest (worst case). Two components are said to have *no direct coupling,* the lowest level of coupling (best case), if each can function without knowledge of the other. We now give an example to show how we employed these standards for component decomposition. The original design for the controller, Figure 10.10, had a function called Insert/Update Information Generator. This function was intended to perform the following operations:

1. To select a backend for record insertion when executing an insert request.
2. To generate new descriptor ids.
3. To generate new cluster ids.

In addition to performing the above operations by itself, Insert/Update Information Generator was intended to perform the following operations together with Request Composer:

1. To initiate the actions required for the insertion of the records that change cluster as a result of executing an update request.
2. To generate update requests with type-0 modifier for update requests with type-III or type-IV modifier.

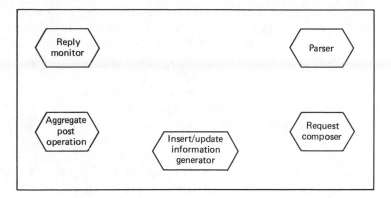

Figure 10.10. The Original Design for the MDBS Controller

This function, Insert/Update Information Generator, is not functionally cohesive and it is tightly coupled with Request Composer. Thus, we changed the original design of the controller.

10.5.5. A Practice of Structured Coding

Structured coding refers to a methodology for problem solving as well as to the particular programming constructs used in code development. The *structured-coding methodology* is a top-down approach to the application of the principle of modularity—i.e., that a program procedure should have only one function. Function in this context means the transformation of input into output. A large problem is broken down into smaller subproblems. This process is repeated until the solution for the smallest subproblem is expressed as a single procedure.

Structured code requires the procedure to be written with a small set of programming constructs: the statement sequence, the if-then-else and case for decisions, the do-while for iteration. It has been proven that any program can be written with only these constructs. Referring to Section 10.5.2, we learn that the practice of structured coding begins where the practice of the formal system specification ends.

10.5.6. A "Black-Box" Testing Approach

In the *black-box approach to testing,* test data are selected without reference to the internal structure of the program. Instead, test data are generated based on the program functions described in the requirements analysis study. In the *structural approach* to testing, by contrast, test data are selected based on some characteristics of the internal program structure, such as the number of paths through the program.

Intuitively, the black-box testing approach is applicable to testing database systems, since database users generally know more about the content of their databases than about the inner workings of the database system. Test data selected using the black-box approach will more closely resemble a realistic test of the system. Another advantage of the black-box approach is that, since no knowledge of internal program structures is required to develop the test data, it is easier to integrate into the testing phase the people who are not involved in the development phase.

One application of the black-box approach is functional testing [17]. In this application, programs are viewed as functions that map values from the program's domain of input variables into its domain of output variables. Test data are selected based on the important properties of elements in these domains. The functional testing method is particularly suited to the MDBS implementation. The requirements analysis study in [1] and [2] describes the functional components of MDBS and their input and output domains. For example, the input domain of the descriptor-search phase of request execution includes the set of retrieval requests. The output domain is the set of Boolean expressions of descriptor ids.

10.6. CONCLUSIONS

Our concluding remarks are organized into two sections. In the first section, as novices in software engineering, we discuss our general feelings about our early fears and our present excitement in pursuing the prototype work. In the second section we discuss our specific findings about the choice and use of software engineering methodologies and the evaluation of the work that has been accomplished thus far.

10.6.1. Our Year-Long Experience in the Exercise of Database Software Engineering

Although our exercise in database software engineering has not yet been completed, our experience thus far has been both rewarding and exciting. It is rewarding because we started with a minimal knowledge and experience in software engineering in general and database system engineering in particular, yet we were able to select and utilize a large number of software engineering techniques and to cover a broad spectrum of the implementation issues. We gained considerable confidence in engineering our new database system. For the first time we are sufficiently convinced that if we adhere to the software engineering techniques and methodologies adopted for the implementation of our multibackend database system, MDBS, we have a good chance to produce a properly implemented and well-understood system. It is also extremely exciting to all the authors of this chapter that the probability of developing a working prototype database system is high. Despite the complexity and novelty of the original design of MDBS, the implementors, so far, have a thorough grasp of all the implementation details. The fact that the implementation has been going on for twelve months with the equivalent of at least five man-years of effort has not diminished our interest.

At the beginning we were concerned that techniques applicable to our work could not be found. We were concerned that we might not be able to use the techniques effectively. We were also concerned that the techniques we chose might not complement each other. Such concerns no longer exist. In fact, we are sufficiently confident to say that, if we could have two full-time system programmers, then the full prototype system, i.e., version MDBS-V, could be completed by the end of the summer of 1983.

10.6.2. Our Specific Findings about the Exercise in Database Software Engineering

First, we think our choice of a multibackend database system for the exercise in database software engineering is a good one because all the implementators have a thorough knowledge of the principles and details of the MDBS design and analysis. Furthermore, the design and analysis document for MDBS is well written and easy to follow.

Second, because a number of future research efforts depend on the availability and proper engineering of the MDBS prototype, we have been highly motivated in our implementation effort.

Third, we are particularly happy with our selection of software engineering techniques in the following three areas:

1. Stages of implementation.
2. Management of people and the quality of the work.
3. The prototype of the versions of the system itself.

We now offer some concluding remarks about each of these three areas.

10.6.2.1. Multiversion software and multisystem hardware. We are particularly happy in implementing a rather complex prototype in stages. Not only are we able to evolve the software gradually from a very simple system to a full system, but we are also able to phase in our hardware in stages. For example, initially we used a PDP11/44 system as the host for both the controller and the backend portions of the simple system. In other words, a primitive version of MDBS can be implemented on a single PDP11/44 and its associated disks. Now that we have two PDP11/44s, we can use one for program development and the other for running the simple system, i.e., MDBS-I. By the time the controller portion is well developed, our VAX 11/780 will be delivered. We will then be able to create a new version requiring the controller, the VAX 11/780, and one backend, a PDP11/44. Later, the full system will use both PDP11/44s as backends under the control of the VAX11/780. At that time our concurrency control mechanism will be complete and we will have established a method to replicate the backend software on each backend. From the above it can be seen that the multi-version, multisystem strategy is both practical and timely.

10.6.2.2. The people and their work. An organization of people whose roles are assigned without any change for a period of time will not work in an implementation effort staffed mainly by novices. The reason is that we do not know each other well in terms of our aptitudes and experiences in software engineering. Consequently, we adopted a more stringent control structure than that in the chief-programmer team approach. We added a level of hierarchy to this approach so that we have a project supervisor with several small chief-programmer teams. Furthermore, we have changed, at least four times in the last year, the individuals' roles in the team organization. By now most of the team members are quite happily settled into their proper roles. We have discovered that some of them are better chief programmers, others are better back-up programmers, still others are best at other roles. We have also discovered that the role of a librarian is now taken up by every programmer—chief, back-up, or otherwise—since we impose a uniform documentation standard.

The uniform documentation standard enables us to finish a programming task without having to wait for a final wrap-up. Such delay is avoided because the documentation of the programming task is usually completed at the same time as the programming task.

The use of structured walkthroughs has helped us to identify most of the design and program code problems. Furthermore, most of the suggestions made by the reviewers in the walkthroughs have been very useful to the presenters. A presenter, of course, investigates the comments and suggestions made about his work, instead of simply modifying his work to incorporate the suggestions.

Finally, the use of a formal system specification language has been very effective. More specifically, by using the SSL:

1. Precise and unambiguous communication among the project members is achieved.
2. Complete and accurate documentations are produced.
3. Dependence on individuals is reduced.
4. Project management becomes easier.

One useful concept that we have not employed is multilevel data abstractions (having higher-level data abstractions that use lower-level data abstractions that in turn use lower-level data abstractions, and so on). We have used data abstractions only at the lower levels. The reason is probably that we are not used to the concept of multilevel data abstractions. This concept, however, leads to better and well-structured design, so it should be employed.

10.6.2.3. Database software engineering steps. In the development of system software, we have found enough good techniques to use at all levels of system design, specification, modularization, coding, and testing. This area is, perhaps, our best exercise of the software engineering techniques to database system implementation. We shall use these techniques repeatedly for the development of each successive version in the near future.

10.7. ACKNOWLEDGEMENT

This work is supported by Contract N00014-75-C-0573 from the Office of Naval Research and by an equipment grant from the External Research Program of the Digital Equipment Corporation.

REFERENCES

[1] Hsiao, D. K., and Menon, M. J., "Design and Analysis of a Multi-Backend Database System for Performance Improvement, Functionality Expansion and Capacity Growth (Part I)," Technical Report, OSU-CISRC-TR-81-7, The Ohio State University, Columbus, Ohio, July 1981.

[2] Hsiao, D. K., and Menon, M. J., "Design and Analysis of a Multi-Backend Database System for Performance Improvement, Functionality Expansion and Capacity Growth (Part II)," Technical Report, OSU-CISRC-TR-81-8, The Ohio State University, Columbus, Ohio, August 1981.

[3] Hawthorn, P. B., and Stonebraker, M., "Performance Analysis of a Relational Data Base System," *Proc. ACM-SIGMOD 1979 Int. Conference on Management of Data,* May 1979, pp. 1–12.

[4] Stonebraker, M., et al., "The Design and Implementation of INGRES," *ACM Trans. Database Systems,* Vol. 1, No. 3 (September 1976).

[5] DeWitt, D. J., "A Performance Evaluation of Database Machine Architectures," in *Proc. 7th International Conference on Very Large Data Bases,* September 1981, pp. 199–213.

[6] Hawthorn, P. B., and DeWitt, D. J., "Performance Analysis of Alternative Database Machine Architectures," *IEEE Trans. Software Engineering,* Vol. 8, No. 1 (January 1982), pp. 61–75.

[7] Howden, W. E., "Functional Program Testing," *IEEE Trans. Software Engineering,* Vol. 6, No. 2 (March 1980), pp. 162–169.

[8] Gibson, J. C., "The Gibson Mix," *IBM Technical Report,* TR00.2043, June 1970.

[9] Knuth, D. E., "An Empirical Study of FORTRAN Programs," *Software—Practice and Experience*, Vol. 1, pp. 105–133.

[10] Astrahan, M. M., et al., "System R: Relational Approach to Database Management," *ACM Trans. Database Systems*, Vol. 1, No. 3 (September 1976), pp. 189–222.

[11] Boehm, Barry W., *Software Engineering Economics*, Prentice-Hall, Englewood Cliffs, N.J., 1981.

[12] Mills, H. D., "Chief-Programmer Teams—Principles and Procedures," IBM Report FSC 71-5108, 1971.

[13] Yourdon, E., *Structured Walkthroughs*, 2d ed., Prentice-Hall, Englewood Cliffs, N.J., 1979.

[14] Gilmour, R. W., *Business Systems Handbook: Analysis, Design, and Documentation Standards*, Prentice-Hall, Englewood Cliffs, N.J.: 1979.

[15] Linger, R. C., Mills, H. D., and Witt, B. I., *Structured Programming—Theory and Practice*, Addison-Wesley Publishing Company, Reading, Mass., 1979.

[16] Yourdon, E., and Constantine, L. L., *Structured Design: Fundamentals of a Discipline of Computer Program and Systems Design*, Prentice-Hall, Englewood Cliffs, N.J., 1979.

11

The Implementation of a Multibackend Database System (MDBS): Part II—The Design of a Prototype MDBS

*Xin-Gui He, Masanobu Higashida, Douglas S. Kerr, Ali Orooji, Zhong-Zhi Shi,
Paula R. Strawser, and David K. Hsiao*

11.0. ABSTRACT

The multibackend database system, MDBS, uses one minicomputer as the master or controller and a varying number of minicomputers and their disks as slaves or backends. No special hardware is required. The backends are configured in a parallel manner. A new backend may be added by replicating the existing software on an additional minicomputer and its disks.

A prototype MDBS is being implemented in order to carry out design verification and performance evaluation studies. This chapter discusses the implementation issues and describes in detail the implementation of the controller and backend functions. The data model and the data manipulation language are discussed; the use of record clusters and the process of request execution are explained; and the functions of the controller and backends and the process structure of MDBS are described. The final sections describe in detail the implementation of the controller functions and of the backend functions.

11.1. LOGICAL DESCRIPTION OF MDBS

Four approaches to the running of a database management system have been proposed in the literature:

1. Running the database management system along with all other software on a single general-purpose computer, the *host*.
2. Running the database management system on a second general-purpose computer system, the *backend*. This is the *single-backend software* approach.
3. Developing a special-purpose database machine with specially designed hardware to perform the database management functions. This is the *database machine* or *hardware-backend* approach.
4. Running the database management system on multiple general-purpose computer systems. This is the *multibackend software* approach.

Database management systems built using the first approach have some limitations; e.g., as the database grows and the rate of requests to the database system increases, the host computer performance decreases. Database management systems built using the second approach have the same limitation; i.e., the performance of the single-backend system also decreases. Thus, overall performance of the host and backend will be degraded. The third approach may be promising, but not until its cost-effectiveness is demonstrated.

The *multibackend database system* (MDBS) adopts the fourth approach. MDBS uses off-the-shelf hardware and a novel software architecture to build an easily extensible database system. One minicomputer serves as the controller; multiple minicomputers and their disks are configured in a parallel manner to serve as backends. Each backend executes the same software. Backends may be added to the system to increase performance by replicating the existing software on additional minicomputers.

The controller and the backends are connected by a broadcast bus. The controller broadcasts each request received from the host computer to all backends at the same time. The data from each file in the database is distributed across all backends. Each backend has a number of dedicated disk drives. A backend processes only the data from its own disk drives. Because the files are distributed across the backends, a request can be executed by all backends in parallel. A queue of requests is kept at each backend. As soon as a backend finishes executing the current request, it can begin executing the next request from the queue.

In this section we describe the overall design and implementation of MDBS. In Section 11.1.1 we first discuss the data model used and summarize the data manipulation language adopted. As is described in Chapter 10, records are grouped into clusters. Thus we next discuss in Section 11.1.2 the notion of record clustering.

In Section 11.1.3 we summarize the entire process of request execution in MDBS. Finally, in Section 11.1.4 we give an overview of the MDBS implementation.

11.1.1. The Data Model and the Data Manipulation Language

In this section we develop in detail the attribute-based data model used in MDBS. We then describe the data manipulation language in which users may issue requests to MDBS. The language also encompasses the useful notion of a transaction.

11.1.1.1. Concepts and terminology.   The smallest unit of data in MDBS is a *keyword,* which is an attribute-value pair, where the attribute may represent the type, quality, or characteristic of the value. Information is stored in and retrieved from MDBS in terms of records. A *record* is made up of a collection of keywords and a record body. The *record body* consists of a (possibly empty) string of characters that are not used for search purposes by MDBS. For logical reasons, all the attributes in a record are required to be distinct. An example of a record without a record body is shown below:

(<FILE, Employee>, <JOB, Mgr>, <DEPT, Toy>, <SALARY, 30,000>)

The record consists of four keywords. The value of the attribute DEPT, for instance, is Toy. The first attribute-value pairs in all records of a *file* are the same. In particular, the attribute is FILE and the value is the *file name.* For example, the above record is from the Employee file. When dealing with the records of the same file, we frequently omit the first attribute-value pair, i.e., the file name.

Three Kinds of Keywords.   MDBS recognizes several kinds of keywords: simple, security, and directory. *Simple keywords* are intended for search and retrieval purposes. *Security keywords* are intended for access control Since we have not yet considered any access-control feature, no reference to security keywords will be made in this chapter. *Directory keywords* are used for forming clusters. As described in Chapter 10, records of a cluster are distributed across the backends. Within a backend, records of a cluster are stored in close proximity. We will discuss the concept of a cluster and cluster algorithms in Section 11.1.2.

Keyword Predicates.   A *keyword predicate,* or simply *predicate,* is of the form (attribute, relational operator, value). A *relational operator* can be one of $\{=, \neq, >, \geqslant, <, \leqslant\}$. A keyword K is said to *satisfy* a predicate T if the attribute of K is identical to the attribute in T and the relation specified by the relational operator of T holds between the value of K and the value in

T. For example, the keyword ⟨SALARY, 15,000⟩ satisfies the predicate (SALARY > 10,000).

Three Types of Descriptors.   A *descriptor* can be one of three types:

Type A. The descriptor is a conjunction of a less-than-or-equal-to predicate and a greater-than-or-equal-to predicate, such that the same attribute appears in both predicates. An example of a type-A descriptor is

$$((SALARY \geqslant 2000) \text{ and } (SALARY \leqslant 10,000))$$

This is written more simply as

$$(2000 \leqslant SALARY \leqslant 10,000)$$

Thus, to create a type-A descriptor, the database creator merely specifies an attribute (i.e., SALARY) and a range of values (2000 and 10,000) for that attribute. We term the value to the left of the attribute the *lower limit* and the value to the right the *upper limit*.

Type B. The descriptor is an equality predicate. An example of a type-B descriptor is

$$(POSITION = Professor)$$

Type C. The descriptor consists of only an attribute name, known as the *type-C attribute*. Let us assume that there are n different keywords $K_1, K_2, \ldots, K_n$, in the records of a database with a type-C attribute. Then this type-C descriptor is really equivalent to n type-B descriptors $B_1, B_2, \ldots, B_n$, where B_i is the equality predicate satisfied by K_i. In fact, this type-C descriptor will cause n different type-B descriptors to be formed. From now on, we shall refer to the type-B descriptors formed from a type-C descriptor as *type-C subdescriptors*. For instance, consider that DEPT is specified as a type-C attribute for a file of employee records. Furthermore, let all employees in the file belong to either the Toy department or the Sales department. Then, two type-B descriptors will be formed as follows for this file:

$$(DEPT = Toy) \quad \text{and} \quad (DEPT = Sales)$$

They are the type-C subdescriptors of DEPT.

The Rules of Providing Descriptors.   The database creator may cause clusters to be formed for a database by giving the MDBS a list of descriptors. However, certain *rules* must be observed in providing the descriptors:

1. Ranges specified in type-A descriptors for a given attribute must be mutually exclusive.
2. For every type-B descriptor of the form (attribute1 = value1), no

type-A descriptor can have the same attribute (i.e., attribute1) and a range that contains its value (i.e., value1).

3. An attribute that appears in a type-C descriptor must not also appear in type-A or a type-B descriptor defined previously.

4. Type-A descriptors are specified first; type-B descriptors next; type-C descriptors last.

The Relationship of Keywords and Descriptors.   A keyword is said to be *derived* or *derivable* from a descriptor if one of the following holds:

1. The attribute of the keyword is specified in a type-A descriptor and the value is within the range of the descriptor.

2. The attribute and value of the keyword match those specified in a type-B descriptor.

3. The attribute of the keyword is specified in a type-C descriptor.

Query Conjunctions and Queries.   A *query conjunction,* or simply *conjunction,* is a conjunction of predicates. An example of a query conjunction is

(SALARY > 25,000) and (DEPT = Toy) and (NAME = Jai)

We say that a *record satisfies a query conjunction* if the record contains keywords that satisfy every predicate in the conjunction.

A *query* is any arbitrary Boolean expression of predicates. An example of a query is

((DEPT = Toy) and (SALARY < 10,000))   or   ((DEPT = Book) and (SALARY > 50,000))

11.1.1.2. The data manipulation language (DML).   The data manipulation for MDBS is a nonprocedural language which supports four different types of requests—retrieve, insert, delete, and update. The syntax of these various requests and examples of them are presented below.

Retrieve Requests.   The syntax of a retrieve request is

RETRIEVE Query Target-List [BY Attribute] [WITH Pointer]

That is, it consists of five parts. The first part is the name of the request. The second part is a query, which identifies the portion of the database to be retrieved. The third part, the *target-list,* is a list of elements. Each element is either an attribute, e.g., SALARY, or an aggregate operator to be performed on an attribute, e.g., AVG(SALARY). We will support five aggregate operators—AVG, SUM, COUNT, MAX, MIN—in MDBS. An example of a target-list of two elements is (DEPT, AVG(SALARY)). The values of an attribute in the target-list are retrieved from all records identified by the query. If no aggregate operator is specified on the attribute in the target-list, its values in all the records identified by the query are returned directly to the user or user program. If an aggregate operator is specified on the attribute in the target-list, some computation is to be performed on all the attribute values in the records identified by the query, and a single aggregate value is returned to the user or user program.

The fourth part of the request, referred to as the *BY-clause,* is optional, as designated by the square brackets around it. The use of the By-clause is explained by means of an example. Assume that employee records are to be divided into groups on the basis of the departments for the purpose of calculating the average salary for all the employees in a department. This may be achieved by using a retrieve request with the specific target-list, (AVG(SALARY)), and the specific BY-clause, BY DEPT.

Finally, the fifth part of the request, which is an optional WITH-clause, specifies whether pointers to the retrieved records must be returned to the user or user program for later use in an update request. Some examples of retrieve requests are presented below.

Example 1

Retrieve the names of all employees who work in the Toy Department.

RETRIEVE (FILE = Employee) and (DEPT = Toy) (NAME)

Example 2

Retrieve the names and salaries of all employees making more than $5000 per year.

RETRIEVE (FILE = Employee) and (SALARY > 5000) (NAME,SALARY)

Example 3

Find the average salary of an employee.

RETRIEVE (FILE = Employee) (AVG(SALARY))

Example 4

List the average salary of all departments.

RETRIEVE (FILE = Employee) (AVG(SALARY)) BY DEPT

Insert Requests.   The syntax of an insert request is

INSERT Record

where the Record is to be inserted into the database. An example of an insert request is

INSERT (⟨FILE, Employee⟩, ⟨SALARY, 5000⟩, ⟨DEPT, Toy⟩)

Delete Requests.   The syntax of a delete request is

DELETE Query

where the Query specifies the particular records to be deleted from the database. An example of a DELETE request is

DELETE (NAME = Orooji) or (SALARY > 50,000)

Update Requests.   The syntax of an update request is

UPDATE Query Modifier

where the Query specifies the particular records to be updated from the database and the Modifier specifies the kinds of modification that need to be done on records that satisfy the query. In an update request, if a single attribute value is to be changed, then the attribute is termed the *attribute being modified*. The modifier in an update request specifies the new value to be taken by the attribute being modified. This new value is specified as a function f of the old value of either the same attribute or some other attribute (say, attribute1). More specifically, the modifier may be one of the following five types:

Type 0:   ⟨attribute = constant⟩

Type I: ⟨attribute = f(attribute)⟩

Type II: ⟨attribute = f(attribute1)⟩

Type III: ⟨attribute = f(attribute1) of Query⟩

Type IV: ⟨attribute = f(attribute1) of Pointer⟩

Let a record whose attribute is being modified be referred to as the *record being modified*. Then a type-O modifier sets the new value of the attribute being modified to a constant. A type-I modifier sets the new value of the attribute being modified to be some function of its old value in the record being modified. A type-II modifier sets the new value of the attribute being modified to be some function of some other attribute value in the record being modified. A type-III modifier sets the new value of the attribute being modified to be some function of some other attribute value in another record uniquely identified by the query in the modifier. Finally, a type-IV modifier sets the new value of the attribute being modified to be some function of some other attribute value in another record identified by conjunction of predicates.

We may also recall that a query in a user request is a Boolean expression of predicates. Thus, a given user request will require the retrieval of data that satisfy the predicates of the expression. Since clusters are formed by the definition of descriptors and both descriptors and queries utilize the common notion of predicates, the data retrieved for the request are actually one or more clusters. Clusters therefore become the ideal formation (or unit) of data for storage and retrieval and for performance optimization.

Next we describe how the clusters are formed in MDBS and how they are used. We begin with some definitions.

11.1.2. The Notion of Record Clusters

11.1.2.1. Cluster formation.   For a database, the creator of the database specifies a number of descriptors called *clustering descriptors,* or simply *descriptors.* An attribute that appears in a descriptor is called a *directory attribute.* We say that a directory attribute *belongs* to a descriptor if the attribute appears in that descriptor.

We recall that a record consists of attribute-value pairs or keywords. For purposes of clustering, only those keywords of the record that contain directory attributes are considered. Such keywords of the record are termed *directory keywords.* From the rules for forming descriptors specified earlier, it is easy to see that a directory keyword is derivable from at most one descriptor. For example, consider a database with SALARY as the only directory attribute. Furthermore, let $(0 \leqslant SALARY \leqslant 50{,}000)$ be the only descriptor D1 on SALARY specified by the database creator. Now, consider two records, one containing the directory keyword ⟨SALARY, 25,000⟩ and the other containing the directory keyword ⟨SALARY, 75,000⟩. Clearly, the former directory keyword is derivable from the descriptor D1 and the latter directory keyword is not. Hence, the latter keyword is not derivable from any descriptor in the database, and we say that the *directory keyword is derivable from no descriptor.* Since a record may have many directory keywords, each of which will be derivable from at most one descriptor, we say that the record is *derived from a set of descriptors*.

It is possible for a record to be derived from the empty set of descriptors. There are two such cases. In the first case, it may happen that a record does not contain any directory keyword. In this case, it is said that the record is derived from the empty set of descriptors. Thus, going back to the previous example with the single directory attribute, SALARY, and the single descriptor, $(0 \leqslant SALARY \leqslant 50{,}000)$, a record that contains no salary information (i.e., no keyword with the attribute SALARY) is said to be derived from the empty set of descriptors. The second case is when the record does indeed contain directory keywords, but these keywords are not derivable from existing descriptors. In the previous example, a record with the directory keyword ⟨SALARY, 75,000⟩ that is not derivable from the descriptor is therefore derived from the empty set of descriptors also.

If two records are derived from the same set of descriptors, they are likely to be retrieved together in response to a user request, since these two records have keywords that are derivable from the same set of descriptors. Thus, these two records should be stored together in the same cluster. A *cluster* is, therefore, a group of records such that every record in the cluster is derived from the same set of descriptors. We say that a record cluster is *defined* by the set of descriptors from which all records in the cluster are derived.

It is easy to see that a record belongs to one and only one cluster. The reasoning is as follows. A record consists of zero or more directory keywords. If it consists of zero directory keywords, it belongs to the cluster defined by the empty set of descriptors. If the record consists of one or more directory keywords, then it must be derived from one and only one set of descriptors, since each directory keyword is derived from at most one descriptor. This unique set of descriptors defines the unique cluster to which the record belongs. Thus, we have used the concept of descriptor sets to partition the database into equivalence classes, namely clusters.

In order to form clusters for the records in a database, the *record-to-cluster algorithm* is provided to take a record and determine its cluster. For each attribute-value pair in the record, determine if the attribute is a directory attribute. If it is not, then that attribute-value pair is not used for cluster determination. If the attribute is a directory attribute, determine the descriptor, if any, from which it is derived. We refer to this descriptor, if any, as the *corresponding descriptor* for the given attribute-value pair. The set of corresponding descriptors for all the attribute-value pairs in a record defines the cluster to which the record belongs. By using the algorithm on every record of a database at database-creation time, we may form the record clusters of the database.

11.1.2.2. Cluster determination during request execution.
Up to this point we have been describing the process of cluster formation. We will now explain how clusters are used during request execution. More specifically, we will explain how to determine the cluster to which a new record belongs and how to determine the set of clusters that must be retrieved in order to satisfy a query for retrieval, deletion, or update.

Inserting Records into Clusters.   During the process of cluster formation described above, MDBS uses the record-to-cluster algorithm repeatedly for determining the cluster of a record in the database. This same algorithm may now be used by MDBS to determine the cluster of a record for the record's insertion. In insertion, the *cluster definition table* (CDT) is used in order to determine the secondary memory address (addresses) of this cluster. CDT is a table maintained by MDBS. There is an entry in this table for every cluster. Each entry consists of a cluster number, a set of descriptor ids defining the cluster, and addresses of the records in the cluster. A sample CDT is depicted in Figure 11.1.

Retrieving, Deleting, and Updating Records from Clusters.   Let us describe how MDBS determines the set of clusters that satisfy the query in a retrieval, deletion, or update request. First we must introduce some concepts and terminology.

Cluster number	Corresponding set of descriptor ids	Address of the record in the cluster
C1	D2, D3	R1, R6, R7
C2	D1, D3, D7	R4, R8
C3	D4, D6	R2, R3

.
.
.

Notes:

1. Clusters have unique cluster numbers.

2. No two clusters have a record in common.

3. A cluster is defined by a set of descriptors.

4. The keywords of the records in a cluster are derivable from the descriptors of the set defining the cluster.

5. Two sets of descriptors defining two clusters may have descriptors in common.

Figure 11.1. A Sample of the Cluster Definition Table (CDT)

Descriptor X is defined to be *less than* descriptor Y, if the attributes in both descriptors are the same and one of the following holds.

1. Both descriptors are of type A and the upper limit of descriptor X is lower than the lower limit of descriptor Y.

2. Both descriptors are of type B and the value in descriptor X is smaller than the value in descriptor Y.

3. Descriptor X is of type A and descriptor Y is of type B and the upper limit of descriptor X is lower than the value in descriptor Y.

4. Descriptor X is of type B and descriptor Y is of type A and the value in descriptor X is smaller than the lower limit of descriptor Y.

The above definition also covers the case where either X or Y is a type-C descriptor, since type-C descriptors are stored as type-B descriptors in MDBS. An exactly parallel description for the *greater-than* relation among descriptors may also be given.

As an example, let us assume that we are given the descriptors D1 (10,000 ≤ SALARY ≤ 20,000), D2 (0 ≤ SALARY ≤ 8000), D3 (SALARY = 9000) and D4 (SALARY = 21,000). Thus, D3 is less than D1; D2 is less than D3; and D1 is less than D4.

Using the above definition of less-than and greater-than for the descriptors, we are ready to describe the algorithm for determining the corresponding set of clusters for a query in a user request. The query is assumed to be in disjunctive normal form—i.e., disjunction of conjunctions. The algorithm, known as the *query-to-cluster algorithm,* will proceed in three steps.

Since a query conjunction consists of predicates, we will determine, in the first step, a *corresponding descriptor* or a *corresponding set of descriptors for each predicate.* This is done as follows. If the predicate in a query conjunction is an equality predicate, then the corresponding descriptor is the one from which the keyword satisfying the predicate is derived. For example, if the predicate is (LOCATION = Napa), then the keyword satisfying the predicate is ⟨LOCATION, Napa⟩ and the corresponding descriptor is (LOCATION = Napa). If the predicate is either a less-than or less-than-or-equal-to predicate, it is first treated as an equality predicate and the corresponding descriptor D for that equality predicate is first determined. Then all the descriptors less than D, along with D, form the corresponding set of descriptors for the less-than or less-than-or-equal-to predicate. If the predicate is a greater-than or greater-than-or-equal-to predicate, then it is first treated as an equality predicate and the corresponding descriptor D for that equality predicate is first determined. Then all the descriptors greater than D, along with D, form the corresponding set of descriptors for the greater-than or greater-than-or-equal-to predicate. Thus we have determined a corresponding set of descriptors for a predicate.

The above procedure is repeated for every predicate in the query conjunction. Thus we will have determined a corresponding set of descriptors for every predicate in a query conjunction.

Our next step is to determine the *corresponding set of clusters for a query conjunction,* since a query consists of one or more query conjunctions. Let the query conjunction have p predicates. Let the set of descriptors corresponding to the ith predicate be S_i. Now, form all possible groups, where each group consists of one descriptor from S_i for i ranging from 1 to p. In other words, we are forming the cross-product of S_i. The reason for forming this cross-product of p sets is that a query conjunction consists of a conjunction of p predicates, each having a corresponding set S_i of descriptors. Each element in this cross-product is termed a *descriptor group,* which is, of course, a set of descriptors. Intuitively, a group defines a set of clusters whose records satisfy the query conjunction.

We now consult the cluster definition table, CDT (Figure 11.1). However, the definitions kept in the table may not be identical to the definitions of the groups. Without relating the descriptor groups to the descriptor sets kept in the table, we may not be able to determine the clusters involved. Thus, this second step includes the determination of whether there are descriptor sets in the table that contain a descriptor group. If there are such sets, then the clusters defined by the descriptor sets are indeed the clusters referred to by the descriptor group.

By repeating this procedure for every descriptor group in the cross-product, we are able to determine the corresponding set of clusters for a query conjunction. The entire second step, which is used to determine the corresponding set of clusters for a query conjunction, is then repeated for every query conjunction in the query. Thus, we have determined a corresponding set of clusters for every query conjunction in the query.

The final step of the algorithm determines the *corresponding set of clusters for the query* from the corresponding set of clusters for each query conjunction in the query. Since the query is a disjunction of conjunctions, the corresponding set can be obtained simply as the union of the sets of clusters for each query conjunction in the query.

11.1.3. The Entire Process of Request Execution

We now discuss the entire sequence of actions performed by MDBS in processing the four different types of requests. We shall discuss each type of request in turn.

11.1.3.1. Executing an insert request. The syntax of an insert request in MDBS is

INSERT Record

The controller will first parse the request and determine that it is an insert request. Next the controller will broadcast the request to all the backends. The backends will perform descriptor processing. At the end of the descriptor-search phase, the single cluster to which the record to be inserted is known to the backend(s) whose secondary memory (memories) has (have) been accommodating the cluster. The reason that more than one backend may be involved in accommodating the cluster under consideration is that the cluster, being sufficiently large, has been evenly distributed by the data placement strategy over several backends' secondary memories at the database-creation time. Consequently, MDBS must decide which backend's secondary memory is to be used for accommodating the new record. By consulting the *cluster-id-to-next-backend table* (CINBT), MDBS can select the secondary memory of a specific backend for record insertion. The CINBT is created at the database-creation time by the data placement strategy. A sample CINBT is depicted in Figure 11.2.

11.1.3.2. Executing a retrieve request. We recall that the syntax of a retrieve request in MDBS is as follows:

RETRIEVE Query Target-List [BY Attribute] [WITH Pointer]

The controller will first parse the request and determine that it is a retrieve request. Next the controller will broadcast the request to all the backends. The backends will perform descriptor processing and address generation. Upon completion, each backend has a list of secondary memory addresses of the tracks that contain the relevant records. These tracks are accessed by

Cluster number	Backend number of the next backend for inserting the record of the cluster
C1	B3
C2	B1
C3	B2
C4	B1
C5	B6
.	.
.	.
.	.

Notes:

1. The number of backends in a MDBS may be large, say, 6.

2. A cluster of many records is stored in a specific round-robin way among the backends' disk drives.

3. This table is kept up to date by MDBS as new records are inserted into the database and existing records are modified that result in changes of clusters.

Figure 11.2. The Cluster-Id-To-Next-Backend Table (CINBT)

the backend. The query in the request is used to select the records from these tracks.

First the records satisfying the query are selected. If a BY-clause is specified in the retrieve request, the selected records are grouped by the values of the attribute in the BY-clause. If no By-clause is specified in the retrieve request, all the selected records are treated as a single set. Next, for each set of selected records, the values of all attributes in the target-list are extracted from the records of the set. If no aggregate operator is specified on an attribute in the target-list, the extracted values of the set are returned to the controller. If an aggregate operator is specified on an attribute in the target-list, some computation is performed on all the attribute values in the records of the set, and the results are returned to the controller. For example, to compute the average salary, each backend computes the sum of all the salaries in its set of retrieved records. It then returns this sum and a count of the number of records in the set to the controller. The controller combines the sums and counts from all the backends to give the average salary, which is returned to the user. This completes the actions performed by a backend on each set of selected records. If a WITH-clause is specified in the retrieve request, the secondary memory addresses of all selected records must also be sent to the controller by each backend.

The controller will wait for responses from all the backends. Upon receiving all the responses (i.e., attribute values, aggregate values, or addresses) from all backends, the controller will forward these responses to the user that issued the retrieve request. This completes the execution of the retrieve request.

11.1.3.3. Executing a delete request. As we recall, the syntax of a delete request is

DELETE Query

The execution of this request in MDBS is similar to the execution of a retrieve request. The controller will first parse the request and determine that it is a delete request. Next the controller will broadcast the request to all backends. The backends will perform descriptor processing and address generation. Upon completion, each backend has a list of secondary memory addresses of tracks that contain relevant records. Records of these tracks are retrieved from the secondary memory by respective backends. The query in the delete request is used to select the records that are to be deleted. The selected records are then marked for deletion. The track space occupied by the marked records is not immediately recovered; such recovery of space will be done during database reorganization time.

After the records are marked, the marked records are written back to the same tracks by each backend. If all the records in a track are marked for deletion, the address of this track is removed from all entries in which it appears in the cluster definition table (CDT). Finally, each backend will send an acknowledgement to the controller to indicate that it has finished executing the delete request. Upon receiving the acknowledgements from all the backends, the controller will inform the user or user program that the delete request has successfully been completed.

11.1.3.4. Executing an update request. The syntax of an update request in MDBS is as follows:

UPDATE Query Modifier

We recall that the modifier in an update request specifies the new value to be taken by the attribute being modified and that it may be one of the types described below.

Type 0: $\langle$attribute = constant$\rangle$
Type I: $\langle$attribute = f(attribute)$\rangle$
Type II: $\langle$attribute = f(attribute1)$\rangle$
Type III: $\langle$attribute = f(attribute1) of Query$\rangle$
Type IV: $\langle$attribute = f(attribute1) of Pointer$\rangle$

An update request containing a modifier of types 0, I, or II is broadcast by the controller to all the backends. The backends will perform descriptor processing and address generation. Afterward, each backend has a list of secondary memory addresses of the tracks containing the relevant records. These tracks are accessed by respective backends, and the records satisfying the query are selected from these tracks. These are the records being modified.

Each of these records is changed according to the modifier in the update request. If the modifier is of type 0, the new value is provided in the modifier. If the modifier is of type I, the new value is computed as a function (specified in the modifier) of the value of the attribute. Finally, if the modifier is of type II, i.e. of the form $\langle$attribute = f(attribute1)$\rangle$, the new value is computed as a function f of the value of the attribute1 in that record.

Owing to its change in attribute values, an updated record may remain in the same cluster to which it (more precisely, the preupdated version) belonged, or it may now belong to a different cluster. In the latter case, a record is said to *change cluster*. Recall that a cluster is a group of records such that every record in the cluster is derived from the same set of descriptors. Thus, an updated record will belong to a different cluster only if the set of descriptors from which it is derived is different from the set of descriptors from which the preupdated version was derived. If the attribute being modified in an updated record is not a directory attribute, the updated record continues to be derived from the same set of descriptors, since only directory attributes affect the descriptors. Hence, the updated record does not change cluster. If the attribute being modified is a directory attribute, an updated record may change cluster. If an updated record changes cluster, the preupdated record is marked for deletion and the updated record is inserted in the appropriate cluster.

Finally, each backend will send an acknowledgement to the controller to indicate that it has finished processing the update request. When it has received acknowledgements from all backends, the controller will return a message to the user to signal successful completion of the update request. This completes the processing of an update request containing modifiers of types 0, I, or II.

Now, let us describe the execution of an update request containing a type-III or type-IV modifier. Recall that these modifiers have the form $\langle$attribute = f(attribute1) of Query$\rangle$ and $\langle$attribute = f(attribute1) of Pointer$\rangle$. Thus, in this case, another record must first be retrieved by MDBS on the basis of a user-provided query or pointer. After the record is retrieved, the controller will extract the attribute1 value v from the retrieved record. It will then compute the function f(specified in the type-III or type-IV modifier) on the value v and thus obtain a new value v'. The controller will then form a type-0 modifier of the form

$$\langle attribute = v' \rangle$$

where the attribute is the one that appeared to the left of the equality sign in the type-III or type-IV modifier. The original type-III or type-IV modifier in the update request is now replaced with this newly created type-0 modifier. In other words, MDBS converts an update request containing a type-III or type-IV modifier to an update request containing a type-0 modifier. This update request containing a type-0 modifier may now be executed in the same manner described previously.

11.1.4. An Overview of the MDBS Implementation

Having described the entire process of request execution, we now give an overview of the implementation effort to date. The implementations are described in more detail in later sections.

11.1.4.1. A top-level view of MDBS.   The MDBS is viewed in terms of controller functions and backend functions (see Figure 11.3). We now describe the functions performed in the controller and the backends, respectively. Then we will describe the process of request execution for four types of request: delete, insert, retrieve, and update.

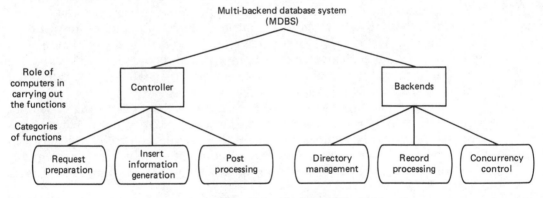

Figure 11-3. The MDBS Structure

Some essential functions, however, are not included in either of these divisions. Among these are system generation, system start-up/shutdown, and other system utilities such as database load, file generation, and database reorganization. These functions will generally be initiated in the minicomputer that serves as the MDBS controller. They are not, however, a logical part of the major functions of the controller.

11.1.4.2. Functions of the controller. The MDBS controller consists of three categories of functions: request preparation, insert information generation, and post processing (Figure 11.3). The *request-preparation functions* are those that must be performed before a request or a transaction can be broadcast to the backends. For example, each request must be parsed and checked for syntax errors before it can be broadcast to the backends. The *insert-information-generation functions* are those that must be performed during the processing of an insert request to furnish additional information required by the backends. For example, a backend should be selected for storing the record being inserted into the secondary storage of the backend. The *post-processing functions* are those that must be performed after replies are returned from the backends but before the results of a request or a transaction are forwarded to the host machine. For example, the results for a request returned by each backend should be collected. After receiving the results from each backend, the response to the request can be sent to the host machine.

We note that there are no *concurrency-control functions* in the controller. Since user requests are carried out by the backends, there is no need for concurrency control in the controller. The controller must only associate sequence numbers with the user requests.

11.1.4.3. Functions of each backend. Each backend in MDBS consists of three categories of functions: directory management, record processing, and concurrency control (Figure 11.3). The *directory-management functions* perform descriptor search, cluster search, address generation, and directory table maintenance. For example, these functions find the ids of descriptors corresponding to a set of predicates (keywords), determine the cluster id corresponding to a set of descriptors, and determine the secondary storage addresses of the records in a cluster. The *record-processing functions* perform record storage, record retrieval, record selection, and attribute value extraction of the retrieved records. For example, these functions store records into the secondary storage, retrieve records from the secondary storage, and select the records that satisfy a query from a set of records. The *concurrency-control functions* perform operations that ensure that the concurrent and interleaved execution of user requests will keep the database consistent. For example, these functions schedule a user request for execution based on the set of clusters needed by the request. In this section we do not consider concurrent and interleaved execution of user requests. We describe the concurrency-control mechanism in detail in Section 11.4.

11.1.4.4. Request execution in MDBS. We now describe briefly the sequence of actions taken by MDBS in executing insert requests and non-insert requests (delete, retrieve, and update). The sequence of actions is described in terms of flow of data and in terms of the functions categorized above. The sequence of actions taken by MDBS in executing each of the four types of request—insert, delete, retrieve, and update—is described in more detail in the later sections.

Sequence of Actions for an Insert Request. The sequence of actions for an insert request is shown in Figure 11.4. Some flow of data is common to all types of request, shown as dotted lines in the figure. We first describe these common data flows. The arrow entering Request Preparation indicates that a request or a transaction is the input to this module. The input comes from the host machine. Request Preparation sends the number of requests in a transaction to Post Processing. The number of requests in a transaction is used by Post Processing to determine whether processing of the transaction is complete. Request Preparation also sends a request (transaction) along with error messages to Post Processing if the request (transaction) has syntax errors. Post Processing collects all the results related to a request (transaction) and sends the results to the host machine. The arrow leaving Directory Man-

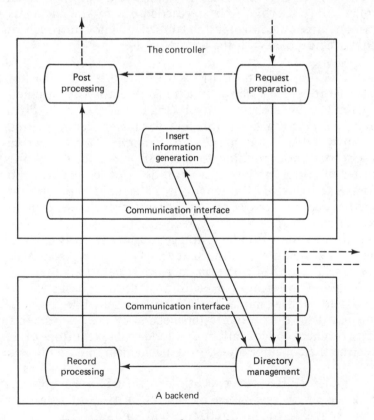

Figure 11.4. Sequence of Actions for an Insert Request

agement indicates that the descriptor ids found by a backend are sent to the other backends. The arrow entering Directory Management indicates that the descriptor ids found by the other backends are sent to this backend.

We now describe the flow of data specific to insert requests, shown as solid lines in Figure 11.4. After receiving, parsing, and formatting a request, Request Preparation sends the formatted request to Directory Management in the backends. The record part of the request consists of many keywords, and each backend performs the descriptor search for a different set of keywords in the record. Thus, Directory Management at a backend finds the ids of descriptors corresponding to the set of keywords to be processed at the backend and broadcasts the ids to the other backends. After receiving the descriptor ids sent by the other backends, Directory Management determines the cluster id, if any, of the cluster to which the record belongs. It then sends the cluster id to Insert Information Generation in the controller. Insert Information Generation determines the backend at which the record is to be inserted and broadcasts a message to Directory Management in the backends. The backends that are not to insert the record discard the record. Directory Management in the backend that is to insert the record determines the secondary storage address for inserting the record. That address and the formatted request are then passed to Record Processing. Record Processing stores the record into the secondary storage and sends a completion signal to Post Processing in the controller. Post Processing then sends a completion signal to the host machine.

Sequences of Actions for Noninsert Requests.   The sequences of actions for noninsert requests are all similar. Thus, we describe here the sequence of actions only for a retrieve request (see Figure 11.5). (We assume that the retrieve request was not caused by an update request. Details on retrieve requests caused by update requests are given in Section 11.2.)

Request Preparation, after receiving, parsing, and formatting a request, sends the formatted request to Directory Management in the backends and sends the aggregate operators, if any, in the request to Post Processing in the controller. The query part of the request consists of many predicates, and each backend performs the descriptor search for a different set of predicates in the query. Thus, Directory Management at a backend finds the ids of descriptors corresponding to the set of predicates to be processed at the backend and broadcasts the ids to the other backends. After receiving the descriptor ids sent by the other backends, Directory Management determines the cluster ids. Finally, it determined the secondary storage addresses of the records in the clusters so identified and sends the record addresses and the formatted request to Record Processing. Record Processing fetches the records from the secondary storage and selects the records that satisfy the query. It then extracts the values from the selected records. If aggregation is not needed, Record Processing sends the extracted values to Post

Processing in the controller. Post Processing collects all the results related to the request and sends the results to the host machine.

If some aggregations are to be applied, Record Processing, after selecting the records and extracting the values, applies the aggregate operations on the set of values. It then sends the results to Post Processing in the controller. The partial results from all the backends are collected in Post Processing. Post Processing performs the aggregate operations on the partial results and sends the results to the host machine.

11.1.4.5. The role of the communication interface. Let us now describe the boxes labeled Communication Interface in Figures 11.4 and 11.5. They provide the mechanism for communications between two functions in two different computers. There is a communication interface in each computer, i.e., the controller and the backends, since certain functions in each computer must communicate with certain functions in the other computers.

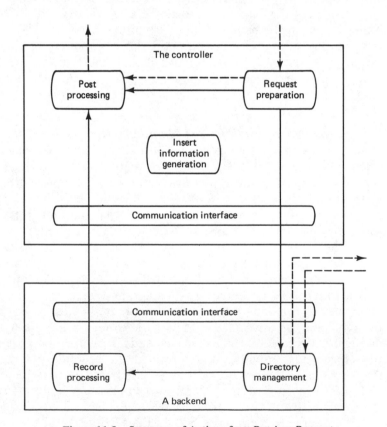

Figure 11.5. Sequence of Actions for a Retrieve Request

11.1.5. The Organization of the Rest of the Chapter

In the remainder of this chapter we describe in detail the MDBS implementation. In Section 11.2 we give a functional description of MDBS. The controller and the backends functions are described in detail in Section 11.3 and 11.4, respectively. Finally, in Section 11.5, we summarize the implementation efforts and status.

11.2. A FUNCTIONAL DESCRIPTION OF MDBS

As described in the previous chapter and depicted in Figure 11.3, MDBS is viewed in terms of controller functions and backend functions. In this section we describe the functions of the controller and backends in detail. We also describe in detail the process of request execution for four types of request: delete, insert, retrieve, and update.

11.2.1. Functions of the Controller

The MDBS controller functions are considered in three categories: request preparation, insert information generation, and post processing. (As described in Section 11.1.4, there are no concurrency-control functions in the controller.) We now describe the functions of each of the three categories. We will not discuss the system functions such as system start-up/shutdown in this section. Details on the system functions such as database load and file generation can be found in [1].

11.2.1.1. The request-preparation functions.   These are the functions that must be performed before a request or a transaction can be broadcast to the backends. The function names are Parser and Request Composer.

The Parser Function.   This function parses the requests and checks for syntax errors. Input to Parser comes from the host machine. The input is either a request or a transaction. If the input request (transaction) is parsed correctly, then the parsed request (parsed transaction) is passed to Request Composer. If the input request (transaction) contains syntax errors, Parser returns the request (transaction) along with error messages to Reply Monitor. MDBS does not execute a transaction unless all the requests in the transaction are parsed correctly; i.e., a transaction is rejected if one or more requests contain syntax errors.

For retrieve requests with aggregate operators, Parser sends the type of aggregate operators (AVG, MAX, MIN, SUM, COUNT) to Aggregate Post Operation, where the specific aggregate operations are to be performed on the partial results to be returned by the backends.

When the input to Parser is a transaction, Parser passes the number of requests in the transaction to Reply Monitor. The number of requests in a transaction is used by Reply Monitor to determine whether the processing of the transaction is complete.

The Request-Composer Function.   Before describing this function, let us review the update requests in MDBS. The syntax of an update request is

UPDATE Query Modifier

where the modifier specifies the kinds of modification that need to be done on records that satisfy the query. The modifier may be one of the following five types:

Type 0: $\langle$attribute = constant$\rangle$
Type I: $\langle$attribute = f(attribute)$\rangle$
Type II: $\langle$attribute = f(attribute1)$\rangle$
Type III: $\langle$attribute = f(attribute1) of Query$\rangle$
Type IV: $\langle$attribute = f(attribute1) of Pointer$\rangle$

We note that, in order to execute an update request containing a type-III or type-IV modifier, a record must first be retrieved by MDBS on the basis of a user-provided query or pointer. We now describe the Request Composer function.

This function transforms a parsed request into the form required for processing at the backends. Request Composer receives each parsed request (parsed transaction) from Parser. For all requests except updates with type-III or type-IV modifier, Request Composer formats the request and sends it to the backends for processing. For update requests with type-III or type-IV modifier, Request Composer first generates a retrieve request. It then saves all the information necessary to generate an update request with type-0 modifier when the value from the retrieve request is received. When the value is received from a backend, the update request with type-0 modifier will be generated and sent to the backends.

Processing an update request may cause one or more updated records to change cluster. When this occurs, the old records should be marked for deletion and the updated records should be inserted. Request Composer initiates the actions required for the insertion of the updated records that change cluster.

11.2.1.2. The insert-information-generation functions.   These functions must be performed during the processing of an insert request to furnish additional information required by the backends. The function names are Backend Selector, Cluster Id Generator, and Descriptor Id Generator.

The Backend-Selector Function.   When processing an insert request, Backend Selector determines the backend at which the record is to be inserted. The backend selection is based on the criterion that the records in each cluster should be distributed among the backends. (As described in Section 11.1, the records in each cluster are spread across the backends to allow the records in the cluster to be accessed in parallel.)

The Cluster-Id-Generator Function.   In order to save storage and time, each cluster is identified by a cluster id instead of by a set of descriptors that characterizes the cluster. Cluster Id Generator produces a new cluster id for a new cluster.

The Descriptor-Id-Generator Function.   To further save storage and time, each descriptor is also identified by a descriptor id instead of by an attribute and its attribute value (attribute-value ranges). Descriptor Id Generator produces a new descriptor id for a new descriptor.

11.2.1.3. The post-processing functions.   Before the results of a request or a transaction are forwarded to the host machine, the post-processing functions must be performed on the replies returned by the backends. The function names are Aggregate Post Operation and Reply Monitor.

The Aggregate-Post-Operation Function.   When there is an aggregate operator in a retrieve request, each backend performs the aggregate operation on those records in that backend satisfying the query. The partial aggregate results are sent to Aggregate Post Operation by the backends. Parser sends the type of aggregate operator (AVG, MAX, MIN, SUM, COUNT) to Aggregate Post Operation, where the partial results are received from the backends and are combined to give the final result of the specific aggregate operation. The results are then forwarded to Reply Monitor.

The Reply-Monitor Function.   This function collects all the results for a request or a transaction and forwards them to the host machine. As described earlier, Parser sends the number of requests in a transaction to Reply Monitor. Reply Monitor uses this number to determine whether the processing of the transaction is complete.

11.2.2. Functions of Each Backend

Each backend in MDBS consists of three categories of functions: directory management, record processing, and concurrency control (Figure 11.3). (As in Section 11.1.4, we do not consider concurrent and interleaved execution of user requests here; we describe the concurrency-control mechanism in detail in Section 11.4.) We now describe the functions of each of the first two categories—directory management and record processing.

11.2.2.1. The directory-management functions. These functions perform directory operations such as cluster determination, address generation, and directory-table maintenance. The function names are Descriptor Search, Cluster Search, and Address Generation.

The Descriptor-Search Function. This function determines the descriptor ids of the descriptors that satisfy the predicates (keywords) in a query (record). Input to Descriptor Search comes from Request Composer in the controller in the form of a formatted request. As described in detail in [2], if there are N backends processing a query (record) with X predicates (keywords), then each backend performs the descriptor search on X/N predicates (keywords) and broadcasts the descriptor ids to the other backends.

The Cluster-Search Function. This function determines either the cluster id of the cluster to which a record belongs (for an insert request) or the cluster ids of the clusters whose records satisfy a query (for a noninsert request). Input to Cluster Search are the descriptor ids found by Descriptor Search in all the backends. For insert requests, Cluster Search passes the cluster id, if any, to Backend Selector in the controller. For noninsert requests, the cluster ids are passed to Address Generation.

The Address-Generation Function. This function determines either the secondary storage address for storing a record when processing an insert request or the addresses of all the records in a set of clusters when processing a noninsert request. For insert requests, Backend Selector in the controller determines which backend is to insert the record. When a backend is selected, Address Generation in that backend determines the secondary storage address for record insertion. That address and the formatted request are then passed to Physical Data Operation.

For noninsert requests, Cluster Search passes the cluster ids to Address Generation. Address Generation finds the addresses of the records in these clusters and passes the addresses and the formatted request to Physical Data Operation.

11.2.2.2. The record-processing functions. These functions perform operations such as record selection and field extraction of the retrieved records. The function names are Physical Data Operation and Aggregate Operation.

The Physical-Data-Operation Function. Input to this function comes from Address Generation. The input is a set of secondary storage addresses and a formatted request. Physical Data Operation performs different actions, depending on the type of the request. For an insert request, Physical Data Operation stores the record being inserted into the secondary storage.

For a noninsert, i.e., delete, retrieve, or update, Physical Data Operation fetches the records from the secondary storage and selects those that satisfy the query in the request. It then performs intended operation on the basis of the type of the noninsert request. For delete requests, Physical Data Operation marks the selected records for deletion.

For retrieve requests, Physical Data Operation extracts the values from the selected records and passes them either to Aggregate Operation, if an aggregation is to be applied, or to Reply Monitor, if aggregation is not needed. For retrieve requests caused by update requests with type-III or type-IV modifier, Physical Data Operation sends the results to Request Composer in the controller. The results will be used in the controller to form update requests with type-0 modifier from the update requests with type-III or type-IV modifier.

For update requests, Physical Data Operation updates the selected records and returns those updated records that have not changed cluster to the secondary storage. If one or more records change cluster, Physical Data Operation marks the old records for deletion and sends those that have changed cluster to Request Composer in the controller. Request Composer initiates the actions required for the insertion of these records into their new clusters.

The Aggregate-Operation Function.   This function performs the partial aggregate operations in retrieve requests. Input to Aggregate Operation comes from Physical Data Operation in the form of a set of values and the aggregate operators to be applied. Aggregate Operation applies the aggregate operations on the set of values and passes the results to Aggregate Post Operation in the controller.

11.2.3. Request Execution in MDBS

We now describe in detail the sequence of actions taken by MDBS in executing each of the four types of request: insert, delete, retrieve, and update. As in Section 11.1, the sequence of actions is described in terms of flow of data and in terms of functions presented earlier.

11.2.3.1. Sequence of actions for insert requests.   The sequence of actions for an insert request is shown in Figure 11.6. As in Section 11.1, we first describe the flow of data common to all types of request, shown in Figure 11.6 as dotted lines. The arrow entering Parser indicates that a request or a transaction is the input to this function. The input comes from the host machine. Parser sends the number of requests in a transaction to Reply Monitor, which uses this number to determine whether the processing of the transaction is complete. Parser also sends a request (transaction) along with error messages to Reply Monitor if the request (transaction) has syntax errors. Reply Monitor collects all the results related to a request (transaction) and sends them to the host machine. The arrow leaving Descriptor Search in-

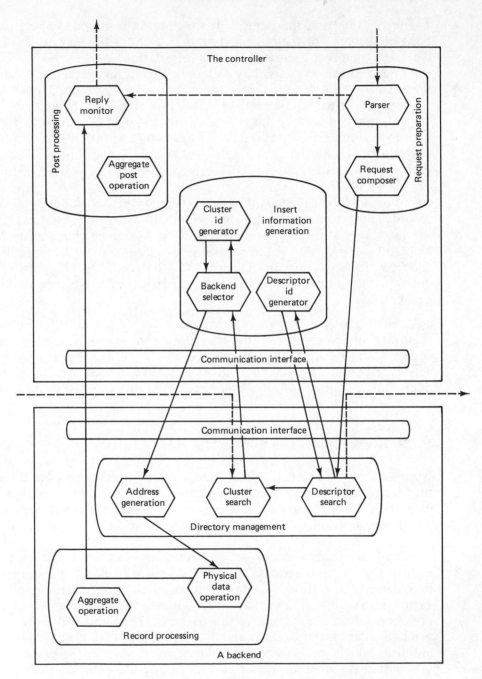

Figure 11.6. Sequence of Actions for an Insert Request

dicates that the descriptor ids found by a backend are sent to the other backends. The arrow entering Cluster Search indicates that the descriptor ids found by the other backends are sent to this backend.

We now describe the flow of data specific to insert requests, shown in Figure 11.6 as solid lines. Parser, after receiving and parsing a request, sends the parsed request to Request Composer. After transforming the parsed request into the form required for processing at the backends, Request Composer sends the formatted request to Descriptor Search in the backends. We recall that the record part of the request consists of many keywords, and each backend performs the descriptor search for a different set of keywords in the record. Thus, Descriptor Search at a backend finds the ids of descriptors corresponding to the set of keywords to be processed at the backend, broadcasts the ids to the other backends, and forwards them to Cluster Search. Cluster Search determines the cluster id, if any, of the cluster to which the record belongs. It then sends the cluster id to Backend Selector in the controller. Backend Selector determines the backend at which the record is to be inserted and broadcasts a message to Address Generation in the backends. The backends that are not to insert the record discard the record. Address Generation in the backend that is to insert the record determines the secondary storage address for storing the record. That address and the formatted request are then passed to Physical Data Operation. Physical Data Operation stores the record into the secondary storage and sends a completion signal to Reply Monitor in the controller. Reply Monitor then sends a completion signal to the host machine.

11.2.3.2. Sequence of actions for delete requests.

The sequence of actions for a delete request is shown in Figure 11.7. Parser, after receiving and parsing a request, sends the parsed request to Request Composer. After transforming the parsed request into the form required for processing at the backends, Request Composer sends the formatted request to Descriptor Search in the backends. Descriptor Search at a backend finds the ids of descriptors corresponding to the set of predicates to be processed at the backend, broadcasts them to the other backends, and forwards them to Cluster Search. Cluster Search determines the cluster ids and gives them to Address Generation. Address Generation determines the secondary storage addresses of the records in these clusters and sends the record addresses and the formatted request to Physical Data Operation. Physical Data Operation fetches the records from the secondary storage. It then selects the records that satisfy the query, marks the selected records for deletion, returns them to the secondary storage, and sends a completion signal to Reply Monitor in the controller.

11.2.3.3. Sequence of actions for retrieve requests.

The sequence of actions for a retrieve request is shown in Figure 11.8. Parser, after receiv-

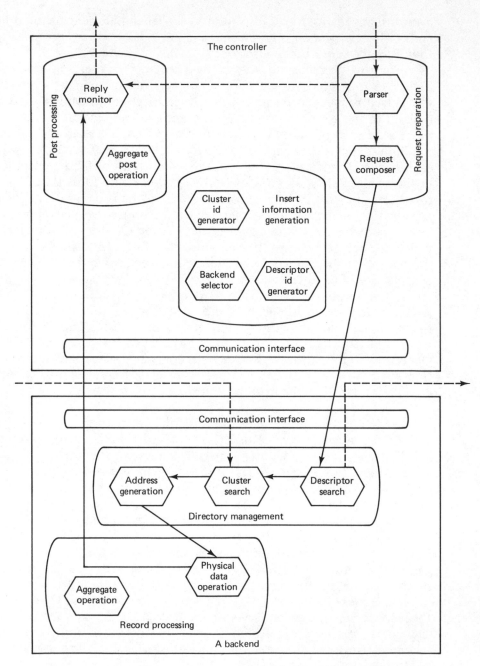

Figure 11.7. Sequence of Actions for a Delete Request

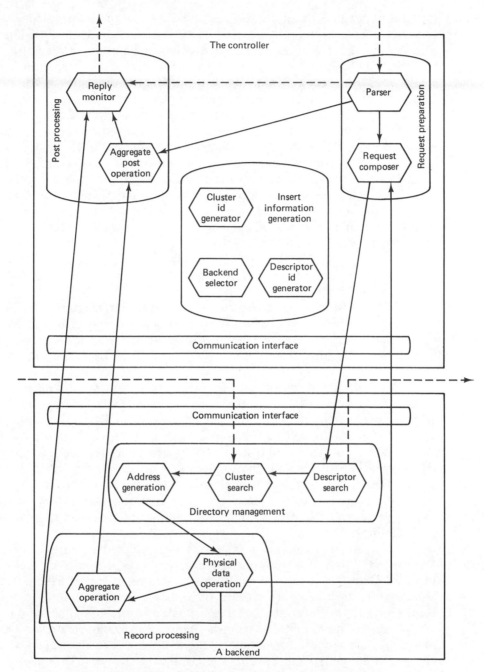

Figure 11.8. Sequence of Actions for a Retrieve Request

ing and parsing a request, sends the parsed request to Request Composer and the aggregate operators, if any, in the request to Aggregate Post Operation. The sequence of actions taken by Request Composer, Descriptor Search, Cluster Search, Address Generation, and Physical Data Operation (up to the selection of the records that satisfy the query) is the same as for the other noninsert request—i.e., delete; thus we do not repeat it here.

If the retrieve request was not caused by an update request, Physical Data Operation extracts the values from the selected records. If aggregation is not needed, Physical Data Operation sends the extracted values to Reply Monitor in the controller. If some aggregations are to be applied, Physical Data Operation passes the extracted values along with the aggregate operators to Aggregate Operation. Aggregate Operation applies the aggregate operations on the set of values and sends the results to Aggregate Post Operation in the controller. The partial aggregate results from all the backends are collected in Aggregate Post Operation, which performs the aggregate operations on the partial results. The results are then forwarded to Reply Monitor. Reply Monitor collects all the results related to the request and sends the results to the host machine.

If the retrieve request was caused by an update request, Physical Data Operation sends the results, if any, to Request Composer in the controller. (The results will be used in the controller to form an update request with type-0 modifier from the update request with type-III or type-IV modifier.)

11.2.3.4. Sequence of actions for update requests.

The sequence of actions for an update request is shown in Figure 11.9. Parser, after receiving and parsing a request, sends the parsed request to Request Composer. The sequence of actions will be different, depending on the type of modifier in the update request. We first describe the case where the modifier is not type III or type IV. In this case the sequence of actions taken by Request Composer, Descriptor Search, Cluster Search, Address Generation, and Physical Data Operation (up to the selection of the records that satisfy the query) is the same as for the other noninsert request—i.e., delete; thus we do not repeat it here.

Physical Data Operation updates the selected records. It then uses Descriptor Search to determine which updated records have changed cluster. Physical Data Operation stores those updated records that have not changed cluster into the secondary storage. It will then send a completion signal to Reply Monitor in the controller if no updated record has changed cluster.

If one or more updated records change cluster, Physical Data Operation marks the old records for deletion and sends the records that have changed cluster to Request Composer in the controller. Request Composer initiates the actions required for the insertion of these records into their new clusters. After these records are inserted, the original update request is complete.

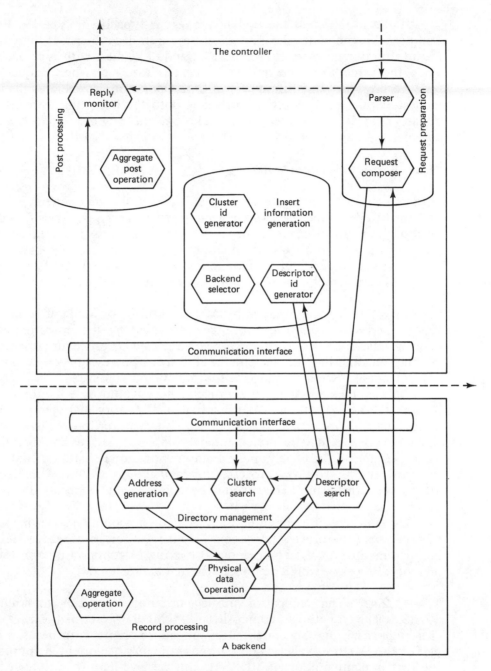

Figure 11.9. Sequence of Actions for an Update Request

If the modifier in the update request is type III or type IV, Request Composer in the controller first generates a retrieve request. It then saves all the information necessary to generate an update request with type-0 modifier when the value from the retrieve request is received. When Request Composer receives the value from Physical Data Operation, it generates the update request with type-0 modifier and sends it to the backends. After this new update request is executed to completion, the original update request is complete.

11.2.4. Process Structure of MDBS

Most operating systems provide mechanisms for allowing concurrent execution of different processes. These mechanisms include primitives for communication and synchronization among processes. Process communication and synchronization primitives of the operating system are the basic system primitives that MDBS-II utilizes for concurrent execution of multiple requests as well as concurrent control of common resources.

11.2.4.1. Two alternative process structures for implementing MDBS. Process and synchronization primitives provided by the operating systems may be characterized as either message-oriented or procedure-oriented, depending on how they implement the notion of process and synchronization [3]. We could use either approach for implementing MDBS.

Using a message-oriented approach, there would be a fixed number of processes (one process per MDBS activity). Directory management, for example, may be implemented as a process. Synchronization of directory management activities may be implemented by passing messages among processes. There would be a relatively limited amount of direct sharing of data in the memory among processes. Processes for each activity would be created when MDBS was started up. They would be deleted only when MDBS was shut down.

Using a procedure-oriented approach, there would be a varying number of processes (one process per user). Synchronization of user activities might be implemented by direct sharing and locking of common data in the main memory. Processes would be rapidly created and deleted.

11.2.4.2. The choice of message-oriented approach to implement MDBS. The functional composition of MDBS described earlier allows either approach, message-oriented or procedure-oriented, to be used for implementing MDBS. We have chosen to use the message-oriented approach for the first implementation of MDBS-II, and we give here the rationale behind our choice.

Two major problems are associated with the procedure-oriented approach [4]:

1. *Process-switch overhead.* When a process must be put to wait, a process switch is necessary in order to run another process. Process switching is costly, because the information related to the blocked process must be saved and the processor scheduler must conduct considerable work to choose the next process to run. Since the procedure-oriented approach causes more process switches than the message-oriented approach, the process-switch overhead is higher in this approach.

2. *Critical sections.* Some processes have critical sections in which holds on locks are placed. If the processor scheduler deschedules a process while it is in its critical section holding some locks over some resource, all other processes will be queued up behind the locked resource. Thus, the database system performance will be degraded.

The real-time operating system, RSX11, used in MDBS facilitates message passing. It also allows a process to receive messages from multiple processes. Because of the aforementioned two problems with the procedure-oriented approach and because of the environment provided by RSX11, we have decided to use the message-oriented approach.

11.3. AN IMPLEMENTATION OF THE CONTROLLER FUNCTIONS

11.3.1. Design and Implementation Goals for the Controller

The primary goal in designing and implementing the controller subsystem of MDBS is to alleviate the *controller-limitation problem*—i.e., to limit the amount of work that the controller must perform. The choice of a solution to the controller-limitation problem is prompted by another design and implementation goal for MDBS, that of *minimizing communication among the backends and between the backends and the controller.* Without increasing workload and excessive communication, the throughput of MDBS will continue to increase as additional backends are added.

The controller-limitation problem occurs in RDBM [5], a relational database machine, where a general-purpose minicomputer is used to control the different hardware components of the system and to preprocess user requests. Request preprocessing includes a detailed analysis of the request to determine the pages in the secondary memory to be accessed. The speed of the minicomputer is therefore a limiting factor to the throughput of RDBM. Consider a simplified example, where preprocessing a user request requires 10 seconds of CPU time at the minicomputer, regardless of the number of backends in the system. The throughput rate of RDBM is limited to six requests per minute.

Another view of the controller-limitation problem is from the perspective of response time. The total response time of the system may be viewed as the sum of controller execution time and backend execution time. Adding more backends can decrease the backend execution time, but controller execution time remains constant. So in order to minimize request execution time, we must also minimize controller execution time.

Our controller design is based on the principle that the major portion of the MDBS workload should be distributed among the backends. In adherence to this principle, the controller is conceptually simple and includes primarily those functions that cannot be performed by the multiple backends.

11.3.2. The Concept of "Traffic Unit"

Input to MDBS originates from a user working at some host computer. The host computer translates the user's instructions into the MDBS Data Manipulation Language (DML) and transmits the translated requests to MDBS. This transmission or "traffic" may take two forms: it may be a *single request* or a *transaction*. Recall that in MDBS terminology a transaction is defined to be a prespecified set of requests that the user may use repeatedly.

In order to generalize the description of input to MDBS, we introduce the concept of a *traffic unit*. A traffic unit may be a single request or a transaction. The identification of a traffic unit is important to the host, since it must return to the user all output from MDBS associated with the traffic unit. The recognition of a traffic unit as a single request or as a transaction is also important to MDBS, since transactions must be processed in a manner that preserves the *consistency* of the database. Since the traffic unit is recognized in the host, we assume that the host will associate with each traffic unit currently in the system a unique identifier, which we call the *traffic id*.

11.3.3. The Structure of the Controller

The MDBS Controller is implemented in three functional categories: Request Preparation, Insert Information Generation, and Post Processing. The Request-Preparation functions include those that must be performed before a request or transaction can be broadcast to the backends. The Insert-Information-Generation functions include those that must be performed during the processing of an insert request to furnish additional information required by the backends. The Post-Processing functions include those that must be performed after replies are returned from the backends but before results of a request or a transaction are forwarded to the host machine. These three categories of functions have been described in Section 11.2. In this section we present details of the implementations of these functions.

11.3.3.1. The request-preparation functions.   The Request-Preparation functions include the Parser and Request Composer. The Parser function parses the requests and checks for syntax errors. The Request-Composer function transforms a parsed request into the form required for processing at the backends. These functions have been described in Section 11.2.1.1. Here we emphasize the implementation.

The Parser Function.   Parser does both lexical and syntactic analyses of the MDBS DML statements. Input to Parser is in terms of a traffic unit— i.e., either a single request or a group of requests that constitute a transaction. As described in Section 11.2.1.1, the various outputs of the parser are the error messages and aggregation operators to the Post-Processing functions and correctly parsed requests to the Request-Composer function.

The lexical analyzer was built using the LEX program available with the UNIX operating system. LEX [6] is a lexical-analyzer generator that can be used to generate programs in C. The input to LEX is a specification of the tokens of the language (i.e., the tokens of the MDBS DML statements) in regular expression form, and subroutines that specify the actions to be taken upon recognition of the tokens. LEX generates a program in the C language. This program includes a representation of a deterministic finite-state automaton generated from the regular expressions of the source, an interpreter that directs the control flow, and the subroutines from the source. The lexical analyzer produced by LEX is easily interfaced with the parser generated by YACC.

The parser was built using the YACC program available with UNIX. YACC [7], "Yet Another Compiler-Compiler," was used to generate a parser that calls the LEX-generated lexical analyzer for tokens and organizes the tokens according to rules of a grammar. When a rule is recognized, some specified action is taken. The input to YACC is a specification that includes declarations of token names, the rewriting rules of the grammar, and action programs. YACC produces a C program, i.e., the parser, according to the specification. The parser operates like a finite-state automaton with a stack. The top-of-stack represents the current token. The parser also has access to the next token, called the look-ahead token. Using this simple mechanism, the parser can determine whether input DML statements are syntactically correct. For a detailed explanation of YACC, see [7].

The Request-Composer Function.   The Request Composer receives parsed requests from the Parser and transforms them into the form required for processing at the backends. Recall from Section 11.2.1.1 that update requests with type-III and type-IV modifiers require the Request Composer to generate a retrieve request and a subsequent update request with a type-0 modifier. The Request Composer also initiates the actions required for the insertion of updated records that have changed cluster. Since the implementation of the Request Composer is straightforward, it will not be described further.

11.3.3.2. The insert-information-generation functions. Insert Information Generation consists of three functions: Backend Selector, Cluster Id Generator, and Descriptor Id Generator. When processing an insert request, the Backend-Selector function determines the backend at which the record is to be inserted. The Cluster-Id-Generator function produces new cluster ids for new clusters. The Descriptor-Id-Generator function produces new descriptor ids for new descriptors. The functions are described in Section 11.2.1.2. Before we describe any implementation details, let us review the types of descriptors that are defined in MDBS.

As described in Section 11.1, records in the database are clustered on the basis of attribute values and attribute-value ranges called descriptors. There are three types of descriptors: type A, type B, and type C. A type-A descriptor defines an inclusive range of values. Each type-A descriptor is a conjunction of a less-than-or-equal-to predicate and a greater-than-or-equal-to predicate. An example of a type-A descriptor is

$$((SALARY \geqslant 2000) \text{ and } (SALARY \leqslant 10,000))$$

A type-B descriptor defines a single value. Each type-B descriptor consists of an equality predicate. An example of a type-B descriptor is

$$(POSITION = Professor)$$

A type-C descriptor designates an attribute name as a type-C attribute. As records are inserted into the database, a single-valued descriptor is created for each unique value associated with the type-C attribute. These descriptors, which are identical to type-B descriptors, are referred to as type-C subdescriptors.

Type-A, type-B, and type-C attributes and type-C subdescriptors are created at database-load time. No additional descriptors can be defined after the database is loaded. Type-C subdescriptors, however, will be created dynamically as new records are inserted into the database.

The Backend-Selector Function. In order to conform to the data placement strategy described in [2], the controller must determine the backend at which the record is to be inserted. This is the function of Backend Selector.

The information required for selecting the backend is maintained in the cluster-id-to-next-backend table (CINBT). There is an entry in the table for each cluster. Each entry contains the number of the next backend into which records are to be inserted and the remaining track capacity at that backend. The CINBT is created at database load time. CINBT is implemented as a data abstraction. The operations on this data abstraction—insert, find, and update—will be invoked by Backend Selector in accessing CINBT.

At the end of the descriptor-search phase in processing an insert request, each backend will send to Insert Information Generation the cluster id for the record to be inserted. Since the cluster-definition table (CDT) is not replicated, backends at which no records of a cluster are stored will not find a cluster id for that cluster. There is also the case where the record being inserted has caused a new type-C subdescriptor to be generated; in this case no backends will return a cluster id. When Backend Selector determines that all backends have responded, it will proceed to select the backend at which the record is to be inserted.

The Cluster-Id-Generator Function.   In order to save storage and time, each cluster is identified by a cluster id. The Cluster Id Generator generates a new cluster id when there is a new cluster. The two cases that require a new cluster id are described in the paragraph above.

The Descriptor-Id-Generator Function.   When an insert request contains a record with a type-C attribute and the value associated with that attribute does not appear in a type-C subdescriptor, a new type-C subdescriptor will be created. The assignment of descriptor ids is handled by the controller to prevent coincidental creation of different descriptor ids by the backends for the same descriptor. If two simultaneous insert requests requiring the creation of the same type-C subdescriptor were processed by the backends independently, different descriptor ids would be assigned for the same descriptor. In MDBS, descriptors must have unique ids.

Descriptor Id Generator will generate a new descriptor id when requested and will broadcast descriptor id and descriptor to all backends. Descriptor Id Generator will retain a list of all descriptors to which it has assigned descriptor ids. This list will be consulted each time a request for a new descriptor id is received in order to prevent coincidental creation of different descriptor ids for the same descriptor. The list will also be purged periodically.

11.3.3.3. The post-processing functions.   The Post-Processing functions include Aggregate Post Operation and Reply Monitor. The Aggregate-Post-Operation function performs the final aggregate operation on partial aggregate results returned from the backends. The Reply-Monitor function collects all the results for a request or transaction and forwards them to the host machine. These functions are described in Section 11.2.1.3. No further implementation details are presented here.

11.3.4. The Process Structure of the Controller

Since a message-oriented approach to concurrency control is being used, we must choose a process structure for the controller. There are several obvious choices.

First, all the functions of the controller can be combined into one process. This alternative is unattractive, because it limits the controller to one function at a time. A greater degree of concurrency can be obtained by using multiple processes and the multiprogramming facilities of the underlying operating system. A second alternative is to create a process for each of the seven functions of the controller. While this does allow a high degree of concurrency, it is unattractive because of the message-passing overhead.

A third alternative is to use a smaller number of processes to facilitate concurrency, while keeping the message-passing overhead at an acceptable level. A good candidate organization is one that parallels the categories of functions we have described above. There are three processes: the Request-Preparation process, the Insert-Information-Generation process, and the Post-Processing process. Look again at Figures 11.6, 11.7, 11.8, and 11.9. These figures show the flow of data between controller and backends functions for insert, delete, retrieve, and update requests. Requests flow from the host through the Request-Preparation process to the backends, and from the backends through the Post-Processing process to the host. In the case of insert and update requests, the Insert-Information-Generation process will be exchanging data with Directory Management in the backends. Notice that the only interprocess communication in the controller will be between the Request-Preparation and Post-Processing processes. This is the organization we adopt for the process structure of the MDBS controller.

11.4. AN IMPLEMENTATION OF BACKEND FUNCTIONS

As discussed in Section 11.3.1, a basic design goal of MDBS is to assign as much work as possible to the backends in order to alleviate the controller-limitation problem. Consequently, the backends' functions are more complex than those of the controller. They fall into three categories: Directory Management, Record Processing, and Concurrency Control.

The Directory-Management functions perform directory operations such as cluster determination, address generation, and directory-table maintenance. According to the incremental development strategy described in Chapter 10, two versions of Directory Management will be developed. A simplified Directory Management, where all directory information is stored in main memory, is described in Section 11.4.1. This simplified Directory Management will be used in the first three versions of MDBS (Versions IV and V will employ a secondary-memory-based directory management).

The Record-Processing functions perform operations such as record selection and attribute-value extraction. The design of these functions is described in detail in Section 11.4.2.

A second design goal for MDBS is that the software should support concurrent execution of requests in the backends in order to maximize system throughput. The cluster-based concurrency-control functions, described in

[8], will be implemented in Version II of MDBS. In Section 11.4.3 we present a preliminary design of the Concurrency-Control functions.

11.4.1. The Process of Primary-Memory-Based Directory Management

We now describe the detailed design and implementation of directory management in MDBS-I. This implementation stores the directory information in primary memory.

   11.4.1.1. The input: noninsert requests and insert requests. The input to directory management is a request—i.e., insert, retrieve, delete, or update. The three *noninsert request* types—retrieve, delete and update—require the same directory management, but the insert request type requires a different one. Thus we will describe directory management in terms of two categories: noninserts and inserts.

   We recall that the directory management in MDBS-I consists of three phases. In the first phase, MDBS determines the corresponding descriptors either for each predicate of a query in the case of a noninsert request or for each keyword of a record in the case of an insert request. In the second phase, MDBS determines either the corresponding set of clusters in the case of a noninsert request or the corresponding single cluster or a new cluster in the case of an insert request. In the third phase, MDBS determines either the addresses of clusters in the case of a noninsert request or a single address for inserting the record in the case of an insert request. The following tables are used in the three phases for processing either noninsert or insert requests.

   Four Directory Tables: The Descriptor-to-Descriptor-Id Table (DDIT), The Attribute Table (AT), The Cluster-Definition Table (CDT), and The Cluster-Id-to-Next-Backend Table (CINBT). These tables are an integrated part of the directory management. Logically, they are defined as follows.

   All the descriptors defined by the database creator are stored in the *descriptor-to-descriptor-id table* (DDIT). There is a descriptor id associated with each descriptor. A sample DDIT is depicted in Figure 11.10.

   There is an entry in the *attribute table* (AT) for every directory attribute. A pointer to the DDIT is stored with each directory attribute. The pointer points to the first descriptor whose attribute is identical to the corresponding directory attribute. A sample AT is depicted in Figure 11.11, together with the DDIT of Figure 11.10. By showing these two tables together, we can easily depict the pointers of AT.

   The cluster-definition table (CDT) is described in Section 11.1.2.2. A sample CDT is also depicted earlier in Figure 11.1, so we do not repeat the figure here; however, we do repeat the definition. There is an entry in this table for every cluster. Each entry consists of the cluster number, the set of

Descriptor	Descriptor ID
20 = < age = < 30	D1
40 = < age = < 65	D2
5000 = < balance = < 10000	D3
Balance = 20000	D4
30000 = < balance = < 45000	D5
Location = OSU	D6
Location = ONR	D7

Figure 11.10. The Descriptor-To-Descriptor-Id Table (DDIT)

Notes:

1. Descriptors are provided by the database creator.
2. A set of descriptors defines a cluster.
3. Clusters are system entities that are "transparent" to the user.

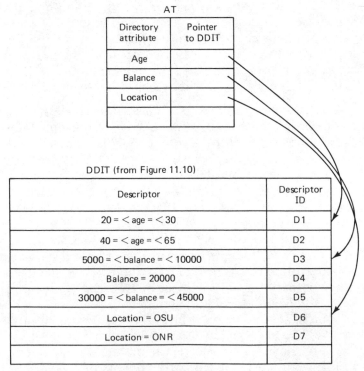

AT

Directory attribute	Pointer to DDIT
Age	
Balance	
Location	

DDIT (from Figure 11.10)

Descriptor	Descriptor ID
20 = < age = < 30	D1
40 = < age = < 65	D2
5000 = < balance = < 10000	D3
Balance = 20000	D4
30000 = < balance = < 45000	D5
Location = OSU	D6
Location = ONR	D7

Figure 11.11. The Attribute Table (AT) and its Relationship to DDIT

descriptor ids whose descriptors define the cluster, and addresses of the records in the cluster.

The cluster-id-to-next-backend table (CINBT) is also depicted earlier in Figure 11.2. A backend for record insertion is chosen on the basis of this table.

Three Phases of Processing: Descriptor Search, Cluster Search, and Address Generation.   As described earlier, directory management has three phases. In the first phase, both AT and DDIT are searched to determine the corresponding descriptors either for each predicate of a query in the case of a noninsert request or for each keyword of a record in the case of an insert request. This is the *descriptor-search phase.* In the second phase, the CDT is searched. For descriptors produced from the previous phase, either the corresponding single cluster in the case of an insert request or the corresponding set of clusters in the case of a noninsert request is determined. This is the *cluster-search phase.* By searching the same CDT, the addresses of clusters can be found in the third phase. This is the *address-generation phase.*

The Choice of a Processing Strategy for the Controller and the Backends. In previous discussions we have made no distinction whether the three phases are carried out in a single computer (i.e., either the controller or one of the backends) or in multiple computers (a controller and several backends). In [2], six different strategies for carrying out the descriptor-search phase in the multiple backends and one strategy for carrying it out in the controller are examined. There are also two strategies for carrying out the cluster-search and address-generation phases: one in the controller and the other in the backends.

If we are to achieve an ideal system in which the response time is inversely proportional to the number of backends, we need to distribute the directory-management work among the backends. By carrying out the directory management in the backends, MDBS may be alleviated from the controller-limitation problem, as suggested in [2].

We next describe those three strategies that distribute the work among the backends and utilize parallel processing by the backends. All three carry out the cluster-search phase and the address-generation phase in all the backends. By carrying out these two phases in the backends, each backend would need to generate only those secondary-memory addresses associated with that backend. On the other hand, if the addresses were to be generated by the controller, the controller would need to generate all the relevant secondary-memory addresses associated with all the backends. Thus, the former case distributes address-generation work among the backends; the latter case does not and concentrates all the work in the controller.

1. *The fully duplicated strategy.* In this strategy, AT and DDIT are fully duplicated in all the backends. However, CDT is not duplicated. Instead, only the portion of CDT that is relevant to those clusters stored in the

backend is placed in that backend. The descriptor-search work is distributed among the backends. More specifically, if there are n backends in MDBS and a query contains x predicates, each backend will perform descriptor search, by using AT and DDIT, on x/n predicates and generate x/n corresponding descriptor sets, which will, in turn, be communicated to each other. Each backend then performs, by using its portion of CDT, the cluster-search phase and the address-generation phase.

2. *The descriptors-division-within-attribute strategy.* In this strategy, AT is duplicated in all the backends. DDIT and CDT are not duplicated. If there are i descriptors on each directory attribute, each backend will maintain for each attribute i/n descriptors. Each backend performs descriptor search on all the predicates to generate part of the corresponding descriptor sets. After each backend obtains some results, they exchange their results. Then, each backend proceeds with its own cluster-search phase and address-generation phase.

3. *The fully replicated strategy.* In this strategy, as in strategy 1, AT and DDIT are duplicated in all the backends. CDT is not duplicated. However, unlike strategy 1, each backend during the descriptor-search phase will work on the entire query instead of x/n predicates of the query. The advantage of letting each backend do the descriptor search on all predicates is that exchanges of descriptors among backends are unnecessary, because each backend has all the needed descriptors. After completing the descriptor search, each backend does its cluster-search phase and address-generation phase.

According to the analyses in [2], strategy 2 has a poor average-and-worst-case performance for a typical number of attributes and typical number of descriptors per attribute; strategy 3 replicates the descriptor-search phase; strategy 1 does not have the shortcomings of the other two strategies. Consequently, we choose to design and implement strategy 1 for directory management. In addition to utilizing strategy 1 for parallel processing of the three directory-management phases for noninsert requests and the first two phases for insert requests by the backends, we choose the strategy of placing the CINBT entirely in the controller. (CINBT is then used only by the controller.) For insert requests, the controller consults this table to select a backend for record insertion. Thus, records in a cluster can be distributed across the backends in order to achieve maximum parallel processing by the backends for subsequent requests.

11.4.1.2. The use of abstractions and tables for implementation. We detail here the first implementation of the directory management of MDBS-I. As outlined in Chapter 10, this implementation does not provide concurrency control and access control. It maintains the directory information in the main memory only. In this implementation, cluster search and address generation are carried out together. Thus, in what follows, we refer to descriptor search as *phase I* and to cluster search and address generation as *phase II*. The input to phase I is either the record part of an insert request or the query part of a noninsert request, and the output is a set of descriptor ids corresponding to the descriptors derived from either the keywords of the record or the predicates of the query in the user request. Phase II makes use of these descriptor ids to come up with the corresponding cluster ids and, in turn, the set of secondary-memory addresses for I/O operations.

Two Data Abstractions for Descriptor Search.   In compliance with the design decision of treating data structures and services, which are necessary in the phase I processing, as abstractions, both AT and DDIT tables are enclosed in data abstractions. For AT, the abstraction is the *attribute-table module* (ATM), and for DDIT it is the *descriptor-to-descriptor-id-table module* (DDITM). This approach requires access to these tables via explicit calls to procedures that operate on the tables.

The Difference Between Descriptor Sets and Descriptor Groups.   We now distinguish between descriptor sets and descriptor groups by means of an example. Let us assume that MDBS has the following DDIT and CDT for the employee file:

$10{,}000 \leqslant$ SALARY $\leqslant 15{,}000$	D1		C1	{D2, D4, D8}	R1
$20{,}000 \leqslant$ SALARY $\leqslant 30{,}000$	D2		C2	{D1, D5, D7}	R3, R4
$40{,}000 \leqslant$ SALARY $\leqslant 60{,}000$	D3		C3	{D3, D4, D8}	R2, R6, R7
$20 \leqslant$ AGE $\leqslant 30$	D4		C4	{D3, D5, D7}	R5, R8
$31 \leqslant$ AGE $\leqslant 50$	D5				
$51 \leqslant$ AGE $\leqslant 70$	D6				
SEX $=$ F	D7				
SEX $=$ M	D8				

For this file the descriptor set for cluster C1, for example, is

$$\{20{,}000 \leqslant \text{SALARY} \leqslant 30{,}000, 20 \leqslant \text{AGE} \leqslant 30, \text{SEX} = \text{M}\}$$

Now, consider the following retrieval request:

RETRIEVE (FILE = Employee) and (SALARY $\geqslant$ 20,000) and (AGE $\geqslant$ 50) (NAME)

In referring to DDIT, we see that the predicates of the requests have the following derivability. The predicate (SALARY $\geqslant$ 20,000) is derivable from either the descriptor $(20{,}000 \leqslant \text{SALARY} \leqslant 30{,}000)$ or the descriptor $(40{,}000 \leqslant \text{SALARY} \leqslant 60{,}000)$; and the predicate (AGE $\leqslant$ 50) is derivable from either the descriptor $(20 \leqslant \text{AGE} \leqslant 30)$ or the descriptor $(31 \leqslant \text{AGE} \leqslant 50)$. Using their descriptor ids instead of the descriptors themselves, we learn that the query of the request is derivable from the following

(D2 or D3) and (D4 or D5)

So, for the employee file MDBS should look for clusters whose descriptor-id sets contain {D2, D4} or {D2, D5} or {D3, D4} or {D3, D5}.

To distinguish sets in CDT from those derived from the predicates, we term the aforementioned four collections of descriptor ids the *descriptor-id groups* and their corresponding descriptor collections the *descriptor groups*. For {D2, D4}, for example, the descriptor group is

$$\{20,000 \leqslant \text{SALARY} \leqslant 30,000, \ 20 \leqslant \text{AGE} \leqslant 30\}$$

Thus, descriptor sets are associated with clusters and created either at the database creation time or when there is a new cluster, whereas descriptor groups are obtained from the query part or the record part of the request and they change from request to request. For the above retrieval request, the descriptor-id set of cluster C1 contains the descriptor-id group {D2, D4}, and the descriptor-id set of cluster C4 contains the descriptor-id group {D3, D5}. Thus, the records in these clusters, i.e., {R1, R5, R8}, are retrieved, selected, and the NAME values in the selected records returned to the user.

Phase II needs descriptor-id groups to come up with cluster numbers and, in turn, addresses of the records in those clusters. Next we describe how MDBS-I generates descriptor-id groups.

The Generation of the Descriptor-Id Groups for a Request. In order to generate the descriptor-id groups readily, we introduce the encoding scheme of *location parameter*. From the query part of a noninsert request, the scheme extracts the conjunctions of the query and numbers them consecutively. Each predicate is then identified by its conjunction number followed by its relative position in that conjunction. For example, in the following query part of a noninsert request.

((DEPT = Shoe) and (SALARY > 10,000)) or ((DEPT = Toy) and (SALARY < 15,000))

the predicate (DEPT = Shoe) has the location parameter 11, since it is the first predicate of the first conjunction. Thus, for this query the predicates have their location parameters represented on the left-hand side:

11   DEPT = Shoe

12   SALARY > 10,000

21   DEPT = Toy

22   SALARY < 15,000

In the case of insert requests, the keywords of the record are treated as one conjunction, so the first number of the location parameter is always 1. Furthermore, the second number of the location parameter is not the relative predicate number but the relative keyword number, since the record to be inserted consists of keywords instead of predicates.

A Service Abstraction for Passing Descriptor-Id Groups to Cluster Search. The output of phase I, the corresponding descriptor ids, are the input to phase II. Since the format of the input to phase II depends on the cluster-search strategy on CDT employed in that phase, changes in format and strategy in one of the phases can affect the other phase. In order to make each phase immune to the changes made in the other phase, a service abstraction is placed between the two phases. This abstraction, known as *directory interface* (DIRINT), accepts the output of phase I and produces the input for phase II.

For the output of phase I, DIRINT produces a table called *request descriptor-id table* (RDIT), upon receipt of a query part or a record part of the request. Each entry of the table is an ordered pair of location parameters and descriptor ids. Thus, an entry of RDIT indicates the id of a descriptor derived from the predicate or the keyword and is uniquely identified by the location parameter in the entry. If multiple descriptors are derived from a predicate, then there are multiple entries in RDIT, one for each such descriptor. In this case, RDIT contains the descriptor ids of all the descriptors derived from the predicate. In Figure 11.12 we depict a sample of RDIT.

A Data Abstraction and Three Directory Tables for Cluster Search and Address Generation.   In phase II, MDBS-I makes use of three tables: the descriptor table, the descriptor-to-cluster map, and the extended-cluster-definition table. Each entry of the *descriptor table* (DT) contains the id of a descriptor that has been defined for a given database, the number of clusters defined for the descriptor, and a pointer to the first cluster of those defined for the descriptor.

The *descriptor-to-cluster map* (DTCM) serves the purpose of mapping descriptors to clusters. It is maintained in such a way that all the DTCM entries for a descriptor are linked together. Each DTCM entry, then, points to a cluster definition whose descriptor-id set contains the descriptor id of this descriptor.

Location parameter	Descriptor ID
11	D4
12	D6
12	D7
12	D9
⋮	
47	D2

Multi-descriptors for the same predicate

Figure 11.12. A Sample Request-Descriptor-Id Table (RDIT)

The *extended-cluster-definition table* (ECDT) contains more information about each cluster than CDT, which was discussed in Section 11.1.2.2 and depicted in Figure 11.1. Each entry consists of the cluster number of a cluster, the number of descriptors defining the cluster, a pointer to the list of descriptor ids whose descriptors define the cluster, and a pointer to the list of addresses of records belonging to this cluster.

All these tables are enclosed within a data abstraction called *cluster-definition-table module* (CDTM). A sample of the tables is depicted in Figure 11.13.

A Typical Sequence of Directory-Management Actions for an Insert Request.

When there is a request for inserting a record, the following directory management takes place in MDBS-I. An equality predicate is constructed for each keyword of the record. For example, the keyword <NAME = Kerr> becomes the predicate (NAME = Kerr). Then, for each predicate, the descriptor id of the descriptor derived from the predicate is found by using AT and DDIT. This process is repeated for every keyword of the record. All the descriptor ids are then put into RDIT via the service abstraction DIRINT.

The descriptor-id group corresponding to the record being inserted is obtained from RDIT via DIRINT. We note that there is only one descriptor-id group, because each of the equality predicates constructed from the keywords is derived from at most one descriptor. Among the descriptor ids in the descriptor-id group, the id of the descriptor that participates in defining the smallest number of clusters is chosen by using DT. Let us call this descriptor id Dm. By using DT, DTCM, and ECDT, all the clusters whose descriptor-id sets contain Dm are examined. If there is a cluster whose descriptor-id set matches the descriptor-id group, then the record being inserted belongs to the cluster identified. We note again that for an insert request, the descriptor-id set must match the descriptor-id group so that the record may be inserted in the cluster whose records are derived from the same set of descriptors.

A Typical Sequence of Directory-Management Actions for a Noninsert Request.

When there is a noninsert request, the following directory management takes place in MDBS-I. For each predicate in the query part of the request, all the descriptor ids of the descriptors derived from the predicate are found by using AT and DDIT. All the descriptor ids are put into RDIT via the service abstraction DIRINT.

Each of the descriptor-id groups corresponding to the query is obtained from RDIT via DIRINT. We note that there may be more than one descriptor-id group because each predicate of the query may be derived from more than one descriptor (see the example on page 373). Among the descriptor ids in the descriptor-id group, the id whose descriptor participates in defining the smallest number of clusters is chosen by using DT. This descriptor id is designated with Dm. By using DT, DTCM, and ECDT, all the clusters whose descriptor-id sets contain Dm are examined. The clusters whose descriptor-id

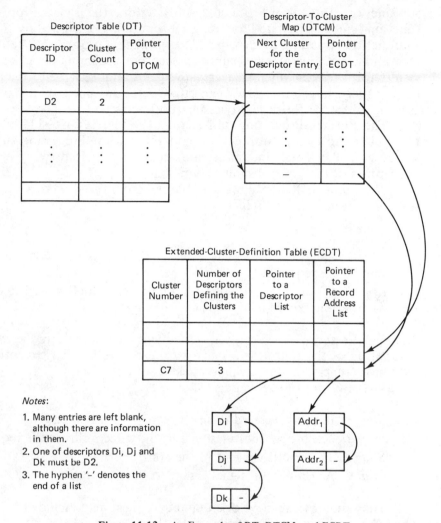

Figure 11.13. An Example of DT, DTCM, and ECDT

sets contain the descriptor-id group are therefore found. This process is repeated for each descriptor-id group. We note that for a noninsert request, the descriptor-id set does not have to be identical to the descriptor-id group as long as the set contains the group. Then, the addresses of the records in the clusters just found are obtained.

11.4.2. The Record-Processing Functions

The Record-Processing functions are Physical Data Operation and Aggregate Operation. The Physical-Data-Operation function includes a control subfunction and a subfunction for each type of request. The Retrieve-Processing subfunction, the Insert-Processing subfunction, the Delete-Processing sub-function, and the Update-Processing subfunction are invoked by the Control subfunction according to the type of request being processed. The Aggregate-Operation function includes subfunctions that accumulate partial aggregate results for a request when an aggregate operation is specified for an attribute in the query target list. The Aggregate-Operation subfunctions are invoked as required by the Retrieve-Processing subfunction.

The Retrieve-Processing subfunction, the Insert-Processing subfunction, the Delete-Processing subfunction, and the Update-Processing subfunction are described in detail in the sections that follow. Here we give a general description of the Control subfunction.

The input to Record Processing comes from the Directory-Management functions. Input data include

1. A request.
2. A set of physical (disk) addresses of the tracks that contain data relevant to the request.
3. In the case of an insert request, an indicator which is used to determine whether the record is to be placed on a new track.

The specific form of the output varies with the type of request; a general description of the output is a signal to the controller that execution of the request is completed, and giving the results of execution.

The sequence of events is as follows:

Step 1. Input is received from Directory Management.
Step 2. The proper subfunction is invoked according to the request type.
Step 3. The results are sent to the controller.
Step 4. A completion signal is sent to the controller.

The results of a retrieve or an update request may include many records. Thus, the results are buffered independently via a data abstraction, the Block_Buffer_Abstraction, which is also described below.

11.4.2.1. The block_buffer_abstraction. In MDBS, a cluster may correspond to more than one physical track of data on the disk. Therefore, for one cluster, there may be more than one physical address in the set of addresses furnished to Record Processing by Directory Management. Data are accessed from or to the disk track-by-track. So, a fixed-length buffer can be used for input data.

The amount of output data varies from request to request. This implies that, given a fixed-length output buffer, the Record-Processing functions must include logic to empty the output buffer when it is filled during execution of a request. In order to simplify the Record-Processing functions, a data abstraction is used to implement a virtual variable-length output buffer. This technique has two advantages. First, the Record-Processing functions will not need to include logic to monitor the state of the output buffer. Second, all the logic required to use the communication interface for sending results to the controller can be localized in the code of the data abstraction.

The Block_Buffer_Abstraction furnishes a data object, the Result_Buffer, and a set of operations. The operations include a function to reserve a buffer, a function to stuff data into a buffer, and a function to flush a partially filled buffer. The actual data structure used by the abstraction is a fixed-length buffer. However, the stuff operation includes logic to empty filled buffers; it appears to the user that the output buffer is as large as required.

11.4.2.2. The retrieve processing subfunction.

A retrieve request has the form:

RETRIEVE Query Target-List [BY clause] [WITH pointer]

The purpose of the Retrieve Processing is to fetch the clusters of relevant data from the disk, to select from the clusters of relevant data the records satisfying the query, and to output the results according to the target list and the optional BY and WITH clauses.

The algorithm is as follows:

Step 1. Reserve a result buffer.

Step 2. For each address in the set of track addresses furnished by Directory Management, fetch the track from the disk into the track buffer in the main memory.

Step 3. Examine the records in the track buffer one-by-one. If a record is marked for deletion, disregard it. If a record does not satisfy the query of the request, disregard it. If a record satisfies the query of the request, extract the values for the attribute names in the target-list of the request; if an aggregate operation is specified for an attribute on the target-list, invoke the appropriate aggregation subfunction with the appropriate value. Stuff results from extraction and/or aggregation into the result buffer. Repeat for each record in the track buffer.

Step 4. Repeat steps 2 and 3 until the set of track addresses is exhausted.

Step 5. Flush the result buffer.

If the optional WITH clause is included, a pointer or physical address of the record is stuffed into the result buffer for each record. The optional BY clause is used in conjunction with aggregate operator, as explained next.

11.4.2.3. The aggregation subfunctions. MDBS supports five aggregate operations on attributes in the target-list of retrieve requests. These are AVG, SUM, COUNT, MAX, and MIN. An example of a target-list is

(DEPT, AVG(SALARY))

No aggregate operator is specified for the attribute DEPT; the values of DEPT will be retrieved from all records identified by the query. The aggregate operator AVG will be applied to the values of SALARY retrieved from all records identified by the query. Thus, the average salary will be obtained.

An optional BY clause may be used with an aggregate operator. Assume that we wish to find the average salary of employees in each department. This can be achieved by using a retrieve request with the target-list (AVG(SALARY)) and the clause BY DEPT.

The aggregation subfunctions are invoked by the Retrieve-Processing function as required. For AVG, a sum of values and a count is accumulated. For SUM, a sum of values is accumulated. For COUNT, a count of values is accumulated. For MAX and MIN, the maximum and minimum elements are selected.

11.4.2.4. The insert-processing subfunction. The insert request has the form:

INSERT Record

The purpose of the Insert-Processing subfunction is to insert the record in the request into a cluster. The record may be added to a partially filled track of data or may be inserted as the first record of a newly allocated track. The input to Record Processing for an insert request includes a new-track indicator. Since only one record is being inserted into one track of one cluster, Directory Management will furnish only one track address.

The algorithm for the Insert-Processing subfunction is very simple:

Step 1. If the new-track indicator is off (meaning that the record is to be added to a track that already contains other records from the cluster), then fetch the track from the disk into the track buffer. If the new-track indicator is on, then initialize the track buffer (no data are fetched from the disk).

Step 2. Insert the record in the request into the track buffer.

Step 3. Store the track buffer on the disk.

11.4.2.5. The update-processing subfunction. The update request has the form:

UPDATE Query Modifier

The modifier in an update request specifies the new value to be taken by the attribute being modified. The modifier may be one of the types described below:

Type 0: $<$attribute = constant$>$
Type I: $<$attribute = f(attribute)$>$
Type II: $<$attribute = f(attribute1)$>$
Type III: $<$attribute = f(attribute1) of Query$>$
Type IV: $<$attribute = f(attribute1) of Pointer$>$

The Update-Processing subfunction handles requests with modifiers of type 0, I, or II. An update request with the modifier of type III or type IV is decomposed by the controller into a retrieve request followed by an update request of type 0.

The main function of the Update-Processing subfunction is to select records satisfying the query and to update the value of the attribute specified by the modifier. When a type-0 modifier is specified, the new value is the constant from the modifier. When a type-I modifier is specified, the new value is a function of the old value. When a type-II modifier is specified, the new value is a function of the value of some other attribute in the record.

If the attribute being updated is a directory attribute, the updated record may change cluster. This occurs when the updated value does not correspond to the same descriptors as the value before update. In this case, the set of descriptors that can be derived from the record is not the same as the set of descriptors that defines the current cluster. If the updated record changes cluster, then the original record is marked for deletion and the updated record is sent to the Request Composer in the controller. The Request Composer will generate an insert request for the updated record. If the updated record does not change cluster, then it is simply rewritten in the same cluster.

The algorithm is as follows:

Step 1. Reserve a result buffer.

Step 2. For each address in the set of track addresses furnished by Directory Management, fetch the track from the disk into the track buffer in the main memory.

Step 3. Examine the records in the track buffer one-by-one. If a record is marked for deletion, disregard it. If a record does not satisfy the query of the request, disregard it. If a record satisfies the query of the request, compute the new value according to the modifier and update the record in the track buffer. Check the updated record to determine whether it changes cluster. If it does, then the updated record is added to the result buffer and marked for deletion from the track buffer.

Step 4. After all the records in the track buffer have been examined, store the track buffer back to the disk.

Step 5. Repeat step 2 through step 4 until the set of track addresses is exhausted.

Step 6. Flush the result buffer and send the results to the Request Composer in the controller.

11.4.2.6. The delete-processing subfunction.   The delete request has the form:

DELETE Query

The purpose of the Delete-Processing subfunction is to delete all the records satisfying the query. Records are not physically deleted from the database; they are marked for deletion. Records will be physically deleted only when the database is reorganized.

The algorithm is as follows:

Step 1. For each address in the set of track addresses furnished by Directory Management, fetch the track from the disk into the track buffer in the main memory.

Step 2. Examine the records in the track buffer one-by-one. If a record is marked for deletion, disregard it. If a record does not satisfy the query of the request, disregard it. If a record satisfies the query of the request, set a deletion flag in the record.

Step 3. Repeat step 1 and step 2 until the set of track addresses is exhausted.

Step 4. Store the track buffer on the disk.

11.4.3. Concurrency Control

In previous sections we have omitted all consideration of the concurrent execution of requests. However, as mentioned in Section 11.1, the backends must allow concurrent execution of requests in order to assure efficient processing of the requests. We present here, first, a brief review of the concurrency-control mechanism that was described in detail in [8]; then we provide more details on the implementation.

Concurrency control is a mechanism by which we insure the consistency of the database while allowing concurrent execution of multiple requests. To insure the consistency of the data, locks are utilized. These locks are administered at the cluster level (i.e., individual clusters are locked). There are five phases of execution of a request in the presence of access control and concurrency control: (1) directory management determines the clusters needed by the request. (2) cluster-access control determines the authorized clusters, (3) concurrency control determines when all clusters needed by the request are available, (4) address generation determines the record addresses, and (5) record processing actually executes the request.

11.4.3.1. Two types of consistency.

The MDBS Concurrency-Control mechanism differs from others in the types of locks as well as in their utilization. The mechanism distinguishes the four types of requests (Update, Retrieve, Insert, and Delete) and utilizes a different lock mode for each type.

Two types of consistency must be assured. The first type is called *interconsistency*. An example of the type of problem that concerns us is two concurrent updates of a record, which might result in the loss of one of the updates. This problem must be considered in both single- and multiple-backend systems. To preserve interconsistency, nonconcurrent execution must be assured among requests that may have different results when executed simultaneously. Requests that may execute concurrently are called *compatible* requests. The compatibility of two requests depends on the mode of access; e.g., two retrieve requests are compatible, whereas two update requests are not. When considering a new request, if its mode is not compatible with that of one of the earlier requests that is executing, then the execution of the new request must be delayed. Thus the MDBS concurrency mechanism locks clusters so that only compatible requests can be using a cluster at the same time.

As just described, requests are executed at the backends in the order they are received from the controller. For performance reasons, however, it may sometimes be desirable to permute the order of execution of two requests that are not compatible. For example, suppose a sequence of three requests R1, R2, and R3 are received and R1 requires cluster C1, R2 requires clusters C1 and C2, while R3 requires cluster C2. In a single-backend system, it would be possible to permute the execution of requests R2 and R3, allowing R3 to execute concurrently with R1, since R1 and R3 require different clusters. In order to permute the order of execution of requests in a multibackend system, however, a mechanism must be found to assure that all backends execute the requests in the same order; otherwise, inconsistent results can again occur. Thus in a multibackend system it is also necessary to assure *intraconsistency;* i.e., requests that are not compatible must execute in the same order at all backends.

A general mechanism to allow the permutation of requests that are not compatible would be complex, because it would require communication among all the backends. However, a simple mechanism can be found that will handle the special case involving an insert request. The actual insertion of a new record is performed at only one backend; it is not distributed across all the backends. Therefore, if the backends are allowed to permute a noninsert request and an insert request, then the *effective* order of execution of the requests at all the backends is the order used by the backend that actually performs the insertion. In general, two requests that are not compatible are called *permutable* if they do not have to be executed in the same order at all the backends. Thus we see that an insert request and a noninsert request are permutable, and we can assure intraconsistency if we permute the execution order only of permutable requests.

The compatibility and permutability of requests can be summarized as follows:

	Delete	Insert	Update	Retrieve
Delete	C	P	N	N
Insert	P	C	P	P
Update	N	P	N	N
Retrieve	N	P	N	C

C = compatible
P = permutable
N = not permutable and not compatible

This table shows that two delete requests, or two insert requests, or two retrieve requests are compatible because they can be executed concurrently without the possibility of developing inconsistency. It also shows that an insert request can be permuted with a noninsert request—i.e., a delete, an update, or a retrieve. As explained above, this permutability of an insert request with a noninsert request is due to the fact that the actual insert occurs at only one backend. Only the delete, update, or retrieve is actually performed at all the backends. Thus the effect is the same as it would have been if all the backends had executed the requests in the order used by the backend performing the insert.

The concurrency-control mechanism described in [8] assures that requests that are not permutable or compatible are executed, without overlap, in the order received by the controller. Permutable requests can, however, be executed in any order, so long as they do not overlap at the same backend. So as to keep track of all the requests, each backend maintains a queue of requests for each cluster, in the order in which the controller received them. Thus no later request can execute before an earlier request that is not permutable has been executed. Also no permutable requests can execute concurrently, although the order of execution can be modified. On the other hand, compatible requests can execute together.

11.4.3.2. Two categories of locks. Unfortunately, allowing the permutation of requests means that a new problem may now occur—the problem of *starvation*. It may be possible to permute one request indefinitely. Thus that request will never be allowed to execute. In order to prevent starvation, we introduce two categories of locks: *to-be-used* and *being-used*. As soon as a request reaches a backend, it locks the clusters it needs in the to-be-used category. Before it can execute, it must convert the locks to the being-used category. Only requests that are locking a cluster in the to-be-used category are allowed to be permuted. Thus starvation can be prevented. Details of the conversion of a lock from to-be-used to being-used and of how this mechanism allows the permutation of requests while preventing starvation are given below. First, however, we must relate transactions to concurrency control.

11.4.3.3. The notion of transaction.

A user may wish to treat a set of requests as a *transaction*. Such a set of requests is known by the user to preserve the *consistency* of the database if executed alone on a database system running on a single computer. Users may want execution of a transaction to begin before all the requests in the transaction have been provided to MDBS. In this case, we call the transaction *incompletely specified*. Unfortunately, because all clusters required by the incompletely specified transaction cannot be determined before execution of the transaction is to begin, there is no algorithm that allows the use of incompletely specified transactions without sometimes having to *back up* one of two transactions that have been executing concurrently. Thus in MDBS we have chosen to restrict transactions to those that are *prespecified;* i.e., all the requests in a transaction must be submitted to MDBS at the same time and before execution of any of the requests in the transaction begins. Then MDBS must convert all locks to the being-used category before execution of the transaction can begin. Locks can be released as requests in the transaction finish execution.

Earlier, when we discussed compatible and permutable requests, we assumed the requests were not part of a transaction. We must now reexamine these concepts in the context of transactions. Since two compatible requests have no effect on each other, we can still allow their concurrent execution even when one is part of a transaction. On the other hand, the order of execution of two permutable requests does affect the result. Thus the whole transaction should be permuted, rather than one of its requests. Because of the complexity of permuting a whole transaction, we have chosen to permute only requests that are not part of a transaction.

11.4.3.4. Concurrency control using a message-oriented approach.

The concurrency-control mechanism described in [8] used a procedure-oriented approach. Thus there was to be a *lock table* shared by all users. In addition, transactions were *deactivated* when a needed cluster was locked by other requests and were *activated* when the needed cluster became available.

This basic mechanism must now be transformed to reflect a message-oriented approach. In this approach, as described earlier, there is a *concurrency-control process*. This process receives messages from the directory-management process (a request to be executed) and from the record-processing process (a report that a request has completed execution). When the concurrency-control process determines that a request is ready for execution, it forwards the request to record processing. The "shared lock-table" evident in the procedure-oriented approach now appears as a table internal to the concurrency-control process. This table, called the *cluster-to-traffic-unit table* (CTUT), is described below. The concept of "deactivating" a transaction is replaced by having concurrency control hold the request in a queue until it can be forwarded to record processing for execution. The algorithms for concurrency control are described below.

The Process Structure in the Backends.   Once a message-oriented approach has been selected, it is necessary to break up the functions of each backend into processes. The most obvious choice would be to have one process per function—i.e., five processes corresponding to descriptor search, cluster search, concurrency control, address generation, and record processing, respectively. (The sixth function, cluster-access control, is omitted because it is not included in our initial implementation.) However, since there is added overhead for each interprocess message, it is desirable to reduce the number of processes. One easy way to do this is to combine descriptor search and cluster search into a single directory-management process. Address generation must take place after concurrency control, since records may be added to a cluster while a request is waiting to lock the cluster. Thus, address generation cannot be included in a directory-management process. However, it could be combined with either concurrency control or record processing. For the purposes of discussing concurrency control, it is easiest to assume that address generation is not part of concurrency control. Thus the function of concurrency control is to schedule the execution of requests based on the clusters that are required as determined by directory management.

Cluster-to-Traffic-Unit Table (CTUT).   As described earlier, information about the locks held on each cluster is stored in the CTUT. This table contains a queue for each cluster. Each cluster queue contains an entry for each of the requests requiring that cluster. Each entry contains an identifier for the request (the traffic unit and the request number), the MODE of access required (delete, insert, retrieve, or update), and the CATEGORY of lock held (to-be-used or being-used). A sample CTUT with four clusters is shown in Figure 11.14. This table contains entries for five single requests and one transaction consisting of two requests.

Traffic-Unit-to-Cluster Table (TUCT).   In a procedure-oriented implementation there is a process associated with each user, and this process keeps track of how many locks are still to be acquired before a transaction can be executed. However, in a message-oriented implementation there is of course no such process for a user; thus this information must be maintained in a dif-

Clusters	Traffic Units			Comments
C1	TU1 I BU	TU2 I BU	TU3 U BU	TU1 and TU2 are compatible and are executing. The lock for TU3 has been converted to being-used, but since U and I are not compatible, TU3 must wait.
C2	TU4 I TBU	TU3 U BU		TU3 and TU4 have been permuted.
C3	TU4 I BU	TU5,R1 D BU		TU5,R1 would be permutable with TU4, except that it is part of a transaction.
C4	TU5,R2 U TBU	TU6 I BU		

C = cluster   TU = traffic unit
                               R = request within traffic unit

MODE of Request   CATEGORY of Request
   D = delete   BU = being-used
   I = insert   TBU = to-be-used
   R = retrieve
   U = update

Figure 11.14.   A Sample of a Cluster-To-Traffic-Unit Table (CTUT)

ferent way. The concurrency-control process stores this information in a *traffic-unit-to-cluster table* (TUCT), which it can then use to determine the status of any traffic unit. This table is essentially an inverse of the CTUT. It is a reference, by traffic unit, of which clusters are required for each request of the traffic unit. In addition, this table keeps track of how many requests of the transaction have not yet been sent to record processing for execution. Figure 11.15 shows the TUCT table corresponding to the CTUT shown in Figure 11.14.

The Processing of Concurrency-Control Information.   The concurrency-control process receives messages from directory management and from record processing. A message from directory management consists of a new request to be executed and a list of clusters required by that request. A message from record processing means that execution of a request has been completed. Concurrency control must send messages to record processing, notifying it to begin execution of a request.

In order to handle these messages, concurrency control must perform three basic functions. When a new traffic unit is received from directory management, an initialization must be performed, locking all the required

Traffic-Units	Requests		
TU1 (one request)	C1 BU		Executing
TU2 (one request)	C1 BU		Executing
TU3 (one request)	C1 BU	C2 TBU	Waiting for C1
TU4 (one request)	C2 BU	C3 BU	Executing
TU5 (two requests)	C3 BU	C4 TBU	Waiting for C3
TU6 (one request)	C4 BU		Waiting for C4

Compatible

Permutable

TU = Traffic-unit
C = Cluster
BU = Being-used
TBU = To-be-used

*Note that a transaction must acquire all locks before it can proceed. It can, however, release the locks as each request finishes execution.

Figure 11.15. The Traffic-Unit-To-Cluster Table (TUCT) Corresponding to the CTUT in Figure 11.14.

clusters in the to-be-used category. When concurrency control receives a message from record processing that execution of a request has been completed, then concurrency control must remove that request from the TUCT (and CTUT) and determine the clusters that were locked by that request. Finally, whenever a new request is received or an old request has completed execution, concurrency control must try to convert as many locks in the clusters required by that request to the being-used category. When all locks required by a request have been converted to being-used, the process must notify record processing to begin execution of the request.

11.5. CURRENT STATUS OF THE IMPLEMENTATION

The implementation of MDBS is progressing well. Except disk-based directory management and the concurrency control mechanism the Version IV has begun. Without concurrency control and with in-core directory management, Version IV is demonstrable. The detailed design of concurrency control and directory management is finished and coding has begun. In addition to MDBS itself, we have completed several required auxiliary programs such as a database load utility. We expect to begin testing the full features of MDBS-IV in the spring of 1983. We expect to finish Version V in the summer of 1983.

11.6. ACKNOWLEDGEMENTS

This work is supported by Contract N00014-75-C-0573 from the Office of Naval Research and by an equipment grant from the External Research Program of the Digital Equipment Corporation.

We would like to thank all those who have helped with the MDBS project. In particular, the MDBS design and analysis were developed by Jai Menon (now, Dr. Jai Menon of IBM Research Laboratory, San Jose). He also provided much help in the detailed designs. Involved with the MDBS project are several graduate students: Richard Boyne, Patti Dock, and James Kiper; and several undergraduate students: Julie Bendig, Raymond Browder, Chris Jeschke, Drew Logan, Jim Mckenna, William Mielke, and Joe Stuber. Tamer Ozsu and Steven Barth provided much help in the detailed designs and coding. Jose Alegria, Tom Bodnovich, and David Brown contributed background material that we needed in making our design decisions.

REFERENCES

[1] Kerr, D. S., et al., "The Implementation of a Multi-Backend Database System (MDBS): Part I—Software Engineering Strategies and Efforts Towards a Prototype MDBS," Technical Report, OSU-CISRC-TR-82-1, The Ohio State University, Columbus, Ohio, January 1982.

[2] Hsiao, D.K., and Menon, M. J., "Design and Analysis of a Multi-Backend Database System for Performance Improvement, Functionality Expansion and Capacity Growth (Part I)," Technical Report, OSU-CISRC-TR-81-7, The Ohio State University, Columbus, Ohio, July 1981.

[3] Lauer, H., and Needham, R., "On the Duality of Operating System Structures," in *Proc. Second International Symposium on Operating Systems,* IRIA, October 1978, reprinted in *Operating Systems Review,* Vol. 13, No. 2 (April 1979), pp. 3–19.

[4] Stonebraker, M., "Operating System Support for Database Management," *Communications of the ACM,* Vol. 24, No. 7 (July 1981), pp. 412–418.

[5] Auer, H., "RDBM—A Relational Database Machine," Technical Report No. 8005, University of Braunschweig, June 1980. (see also the article on RDBM in this volume.)

[6] Lesk, M. E., and E. Schmidt, "lex—A Lexical Analyzer Generator," *UNIX Time-Sharing System: UNIX Programmer's Manual,* Bell Telephone Laboratories, Inc., Murray Hill, N.J., 1979.

[7] Johnson, Steven C., "Yacc: Yet Another Compiler—Compiler," *UNIX Time-Sharing System: UNIX Programmer's Manual,* Bell Telephone Laboratories, Inc., Murray Hill, N.J., 1979.

[8] Hsiao, D. K., and Menon, M. J., "Design and Analysis of a Multi-Backend Database System for Performance Improvement, Functionality Expansion and Capacity Growth (Part II)," Technical Report, OSU-CISRC-TR-81-8, The Ohio State University, Columbus, Ohio, August 1981.

Index